D0207818

Translating *Clergie*

THE MIDDLE AGES SERIES

Ruth Mazo Karras, Series Editor
Edward Peters, Founding Editor

Translating *Clergie*

Status, Education, and Salvation
in Thirteenth-Century Vernacular Texts

Claire M. Waters

PENN

UNIVERSITY OF PENNSYLVANIA PRESS

PHILADELPHIA

Published by
University of Pennsylvania Press
Philadelphia, Pennsylvania 19104-4112
www.upenn.edu/pennpress

Printed in the United States of America on acid-free paper
1 3 5 7 9 10 8 6 4 2

Library of Congress Cataloging-in-Publication Data
ISBN 978-0-8122-4772-5

For Livy and Seb

Contents

Preface   ix

List of Abbreviations   xv

Introduction. Translating *Clergie* in the Thirteenth Century   1

Chapter 1. The Face and the Mirror: Teachers
and Students in Conversation   19

Chapter 2. Teaching Death: Narrative Assimilation
and the Point of Distinction   61

Chapter 3. Last Among the First: Salvation, Status,
and Reversal in *L'Évangile de Nicodème*   94

Chapter 4. Getting the Riffraff into Heaven: Jongleurs, Whores,
Peasants, and Popular Eschatology   138

Chapter 5. Queen of the Rabble, Empress of Clerks: Learning Humility
in Marian Miracles   164

Afterword   209

Notes   213

Bibliography   257

Index   277

Acknowledgments   287

Preface

This book centers on a tradition that has not always been recognized as such: medieval works in the vernacular—here, specifically the French vernacular, though the tradition itself is not limited to any one language—that not only transmit Christian teaching but reflect on its practices and participants. Didactic, homiletic, and narrative works that aim to inculcate and show the value of Christian instruction are, despite their variety, all deeply engaged with the pressing issue of what one needs to learn in the present life to be prepared for its end, and I argue here that they pursue this question by imagining, in various ways, how the scene of teaching, the interaction between teacher and student, is linked to the moment of death and the scene of judgment. In doing so they revivify and personalize medieval religious education, reminding us of the extensive informal education that lies behind the more visible institutional teaching of the later Middle Ages.

If the works considered here have not always received sustained attention, this is in part because, coming from different sides of the Channel, though all in various dialects of Old French, they have not been seen as a coherent part of the great wave of translation and cultural transmission that swept late medieval Europe. In addition, then, to arguing for their importance as texts that both practice and represent teaching in new ways, the chapters that follow present them as part of a shared culture that encompasses not only different social statuses and roles but readers of French on the Continent and in the British Isles. While not all the works considered here circulated on both sides of the Channel, as a group they are rooted in a broadly dispersed twelfth-century monastic and scholastic culture, the biblical tradition, and preaching. They also form part of the rise of French as a privileged vernacular and a kind of European lingua franca—a role well recognized in secular literature but perhaps less acknowledged for religious works.[1] Whether or not a given text circulated in both areas (and many of them did), the main genres I address here—handbooks of doctrine and theology, versified sermons, Marian

miracles and other hagiography, eschatological fabliaux, and biblical or apocryphal narratives—were clearly known to an international francophone audience in the thirteenth century. Throughout, then, I consider these works
collectively as manifesting shared concerns and interests that are not limited
to any one territorial context.

This said, the status of the French language was obviously not identical in
France and in England, and thus the afterlife and implications of these texts dif-
fer in the two contexts. French's complex role in England is conveyed by the fact
that the very name of the language under discussion is vexed: thus, the familiar
"Anglo-Norman" has increasingly been questioned on the grounds that there
quickly ceased to be anything distinctively Norman about the variety of French
used in England, though the name retains a good deal of institutional currency;
recently "the French of England" has gained ground as an alternative, with other
scholars preferring "insular French" or "Anglo-French."[2] In the present book I use
the latter terms—Anglo-French and insular French—interchangeably, finding
useful their similarity of form to "Old French" (of which English French is, of
course, a dialect) or "Continental French." Whichever name(s) one chooses to
designate the French spoken in England, the fact remains that its English context
colors our reception of this literature in ways that distinguish it from French literature produced on the Continent. Later events and controversies can easily influence our sense of insular French texts of the twelfth and thirteenth centuries:
the conflicts we know as the Hundred Years' War, the rise of Wycliffism, and the
emergence of English as an "illustrious" vernacular all, in different ways, place
these earlier works in a light not their own.

This book attempts to address its Anglo-French texts on their own terms,
as part of a transnational French tradition that includes both Continental and
insular strands, rather than as mere sources and analogues of the Middle English literature that remains at the center of medieval English literary scholarship, despite the country's multilingualism. Thus while many of these works
have echoes (or, indeed, translations) in Middle English literature, I have kept
references to these sparse, hoping that I have provided the means for interested readers to make those connections for themselves. A fuller exploration
of Continental and insular teaching texts certainly provides a truer sense of
the emergence and import of the later English tradition; the English implications, however, are not my main focus in the present book, which is why I
address them here rather than extensively in the chapters that follow. Christopher Cannon has noted that works in Middle English in the twelfth and thirteenth centuries are distinctive precisely because they do not see themselves as,

or indeed become, part of an overarching literary tradition; instead, the works that form the "grounds" of later Middle English literature are, to a considerable extent, French.[3] There was, of course, a long and substantial tradition of spiritual instruction and dialogue in Anglo-Saxon, and key early Middle English didactic or dialogic texts including the *Ancrene Wisse* date from precisely the period under discussion here, but it remains the case that the *majority* of the insular doctrinal material produced in the twelfth and thirteenth centuries was in the French rather than the English of England and that Anglo-French was "the principal medium in which the formation of the self and the politics of access to vernacular texts were thought and experienced" in this period.[4]

This is worth emphasizing, since many excellent studies of medieval English texts that address questions closely related to those explored here tend to move from Latin to Middle English with scant attention to Anglo-French works that (as the present book argues) mediate between laity and clergy in similar ways at a considerably earlier date. Thus, for example, Katherine C. Little observes in relation to the fourteenth and fifteenth centuries that "as pastoral and devotional writings were translated into English, the lines between clerical and lay discourses began to be blurred": but this blurring was already under way in some respects by the twelfth century, and is ever more strongly in evidence in the insular French works of the thirteenth.[5] To speak of "the beginnings of an extensive translation of Latin learning into the vernacular from the mid-fourteenth century onward"—that is, to consider only the translation of Latin learning into the *English* vernacular—is to erase a century and a half of crucial, "basic" translation whose transformative power has been underestimated by *clerici* both medieval and modern.[6] The overlooking of French is not a novelty: Vincent Gillespie's important essay "*Doctrina* and *Predicacio*: The Design and Function of Some Pastoral Manuals," published in 1980, emphasizes the "flexibility" and "ambiguity of . . . appeal" that we see in many works of the "distinct manual culture" that arose in England after Lateran IV, as well as their suitability to a range of teaching situations, but he too focuses his inquiry exclusively on Latin and Middle English, even as his central observations are equally applicable to the contemporary Anglo-French context.[7]

The elision of French literature written in England has in part to do, of course, with its status as an elite vernacular, spoken primarily by the nobility and upper gentry as well as in legal and administrative (clerical) contexts. Thus Katharine Breen, in her *Imagining an English Reading Public, 1150–1400*, explicitly excludes Anglo-French from consideration on the grounds that it "did not serve a reading public in the widest sense of the term."[8] This is true, but as Malcolm

Parkes long ago noted, "The literate recreations of the cultured nobility had a profound effect upon the development of a literary public. They set a secular example of literate culture that other laymen sought to emulate" and that contributed to the rise of "middle-class" literacy.[9] This "secular example" of literacy set by the nobility, it should be noted, was surely not limited to their reading of secular literature. Anglo-French texts in many ways laid the groundwork for the broad emergence of religious writing in English; Nicholas Watson has suggested that "a work's existence in the French vernacular legitimated its rendering into the English," making French a kind of stepping-stone.[10] The point is not to undermine work that emphasizes translation from Latin to Middle English, or to claim that there was no difference, for the English, between Latin-French translation and Latin-English translation, but only to point to the way such statements erase a French tradition that underlay much of the later composition and transmission in Middle English. I share, then, Ardis Butterfield's interest in exploring the "multilingual literary perspectives" that link France and England rather than privileging "our own retrospective isolation of English."[11]

Thus, in exploring thirteenth-century French texts from England, I am deliberately addressing what is often seen as "intermediate ground"—lying both between the intellectual ferment of the twelfth and fourteenth centuries and between English and Latin.[12] Anglo-French was a "middling" language, vernacular in relation to Latin but high status and of limited circulation in relation to English, and as noted above it occupies a middle place in the schematic history of English writing, in that many early works in English are translations of French translations of Latin and the wide dissemination of French texts in England precedes that of most texts in Middle English.[13] Because French eventually ceased to be one of the languages of England, the history of Anglo-French is often overshadowed—as middles tend to be—by the "ends" that surround it, Latin and English. In the context of doctrinal instruction in England, however, Anglo-French was an essential middle, one that laid the foundations not only for the later challenges to clerical dominance and monopoly well studied by scholars of fourteenth-century Middle English but indeed for developments in mass education well beyond that.

Here as elsewhere, if you look from the middle everything changes; the middle "is where things pick up speed."[14] Didactic texts in Anglo-French could circulate quite widely—most of those discussed here circulated, in whole or in part, in ten or more manuscripts—creating a substantial body of written religious teaching in the vernacular that both served as a basis for later English translations and, given these works' frequent emphasis on re-transmission, likely expanded the accessibility of religious teaching to the laity more broadly, not only those immediately able to own or hear such books. Like the thirteenth-century Latin confession manuals studied by Catherine Rider, Anglo-French works that practice and meditate on religious pedagogy can help answer the question, "where did these engaged laypeople [of the fourteenth and fifteenth centuries] come from, and when?"[15] This is a case where, in Marshall McLuhan's famous phrase, the medium truly is the message: while such works aimed to convey established teaching, their mere existence as (often versified) vernacular doctrine exemplified the drive toward greater access to religious instruction, with implications that were not fully evident until much later.

Even as this book seeks, then, primarily to consider its Anglo-French texts within their own transnational French context, rather than simply in light of later Anglocentric ones, I hope it will also help fill in some of the no-man's-land created by the peculiar status of insular French and give a truer picture of later Middle English literary history. That history has been more accommodating of secular than of religious writings in French, thanks in part to francophiles like Geoffrey Chaucer and John Gower; but as Dorothy Owen long ago noted, even an author whose bilinguality is primarily Anglo-Latin, like William Langland, can have substantial occluded debts to French texts.[16] Indeed, *Piers Plowman* X.411–65 offers a thumbnail sketch of key themes of this book: simultaneous suspicion of and reliance on higher learning; the promise offered by sinner-saints like the good thief or Mary Magdalene; the power, as well as the limits, of holy simplicity and basic instruction.[17] To take another example, works that in a fourteenth- or fifteenth-century Middle English context engage the controversial topic of vernacular religious writing, like the versified sermons of the Middle English *Mirror* or the semi-Wycliffite Cambridge Tracts, can turn out to be not radical innovations responding solely to their own time but translations of, or borrowers from, the thoroughly uncontroversial, mid-thirteenth-century *Miroir* (also known as the *Évangiles des domnées*).[18] Both works like *Handlyng Synne*, whose French source, the *Manuel des pechiez*, is well-known (though not so well-known as its Middle English offspring), and works that do not explicitly claim their French debts may take on a new appearance in light of a broader knowledge of francophone religious works of the late twelfth to early fourteenth centuries.

Reading Middle English works with an eye to their francophone predecessors, moreover, also reminds us that it was not only the elite status of French in England that enabled extensive transmission of religious teaching in the vernacular. Thirteenth-century Paris produced a vernacular Bible without sparking widespread panic, and alleged pronouncements about the dangers of lay access to Scripture have been exaggerated, possibly in part because scholars read them through the lens of later controversy.[19] It may be that another reason for the relatively unknown status of the works considered here is that they are less combative, less disruptive, less oppositional than later vernacular works (particularly, though not exclusively, those in Middle English). If we see the potential for "criticism and dissent" only in texts that explicitly and immediately deploy their learning for those purposes, however, we miss the crucial foundation provided by "basic" teaching that does not envision such ends. Nor, of course, important though they are, are criticism and dissent the only valuable things that can come out of an education.[20] In the French works considered here, vernacular religious teaching appears not simply as the site of a power struggle, despite its inherently hierarchical aspects, but as an endeavor of mutual assimilation whose transfer of learning to the unlearned had significant and unexpected consequences.

Thus while one of the aims of this study is certainly to draw further attention to the Anglo-French antecedents of much Middle English literature, my larger goal is to put in the foreground French texts, insular and Continental, that practice and thematize religious instruction. In doing so I hope to convey the ways in which medieval religious literature engaged with basic Christian teaching not only at the level of content—in the material such texts presented and reflected upon—but also at the level of form and audience: by practicing the humility and loving engagement, and exploiting the status reversals, that are fundamental to Christian belief and Christian teaching. That in doing so they by no means erase or escape from hierarchical or even coercive models does not, in my view, suggest that such models in the end must always prevail or that they should be the sole focus of scholarly attention to medieval religion; instead these works remind us that medieval teaching literature is fully part of the history of learning and pedagogy in which modern *magistri* also stand, and may even contain lessons of which we can usefully be reminded.

A note on textual conventions: All translations are mine unless otherwise specified. In transcribing from manuscripts, I have normalized u/v and i/j and added capitalization, punctuation, and word division in accordance with modern usage. For ease of reading, I have also normalized u/v and i/j when quoting from editions that retain manuscript usage. Any other emendations or changes are noted in the text.

Abbreviations

ANTS	Anglo-Norman Text Society.
BnF fr.	Bibliothèque nationale de France, fonds français.
EETS	Early English Text Society.
MP EETS	*Robert of Brunne's "Handlyng Synne," A.D. 1303, with those parts of the French treatise on which it is founded, William of Wadington's "Manuel des Pechiez."* Part I. Ed. Frederick J. Furnivall. EETS o.s. 119, 123. London: Kegan Paul, Trench, Trübner & Co. for the EETS, 1901. Reprint, Millwood, N.Y.: Kraus Reprint Co., 1973.
MP Roxburghe	*Roberd of Brunne's "Handlyng Synne" (written A.D. 1303) with the French treatise on which it is founded, "Le Manuel des Pechiez," by William of Wadington.* Ed. Frederick J. Furnivall. London: J. B. Nichols and Sons for the Roxburghe Club, 1862. Text available at http://books.google.com/books?id=wpxTA-AAAcAAJ, accessed March 17, 2015.
Pierre d'Abernon, *Lumere*	Pierre d'Abernon of Fetcham. *Lumere as lais.* Ed. Glynn Hesketh. 3 vols. ANTS 54–58. London: ANTS, 1996–2000.
PL	*Patrologia cursus completus: Series latina.* Ed. Jacques-Paul Migne. 221 vols. Paris: apud Garnier Fratres, 1844–64.
Robert of Gretham, *Miroir*	*The Middle English "Mirror": Sermons from Advent to Sexagesima; with a Parallel Text of the Anglo-Norman "Miroir."* Ed. Thomas G. Duncan and Margaret Connolly. Heidelberg: Universitätsverlag Winter, 2003.

Translating *Clergie*

Translating *Clergie* in the Thirteenth Century

"Deu, qe sanz nus nus cria,
Sanz nus ne nus rectifiera,"
Ceo dit seint Austin, le clerc parfit,
En un livre qe il escrit.

["God, who created us without us,
Will not save us without us":
So says St. Augustine, the perfect cleric,
In a book that he wrote.][1]

These lines from William of Waddington's *Manuel des pechiez* (c. 1260) encapsulate the inadvertent radicalism of the thirteenth-century effort at universal religious education. That universality is implied by, though it did not originate in, the Fourth Lateran Council's decree of yearly confession by "omnis utriusque sexus fidelis," every believer of either sex, and the preaching that was to enable that confession. The two together implied a necessarily joint instructional undertaking by the clergy and the laity. William conveys, in one brief translation, the lay learner's responsibility to work toward his or her own salvation, the teacher's essential participation in that project, and the transformative effects of the transfer of doctrine into the vernacular. While they inherit a great deal from institutional and communal educational contexts—the universities, the cathedral schools, the pulpit—Old French and Anglo-French texts that convey and rework Christian doctrine also allow us a glimpse of the

informal and interpersonal networks that animated "basic" religious education in the thirteenth century and shaped imaginative representations of that
education.

This education had unforeseen consequences, since the inherent complexity of Christian doctrine and the importance of status reversal in the Christian
religion meant that even the most introductory teaching inevitably touched on
crucially important and often volatile theological issues.[2] The works I explore
here, often depicted as offering harmless, rote teaching of the basics of the
faith, are not sufficiently recognized as part of the much larger transfer of various forms of knowledge into the vernacular in this period; while less obviously
ambitious or scholarly than some other texts, they opened the door, by way of
"basic" teaching, to much more advanced learning and inquiry on the part of
the laity.[3] They did so, I argue, by linking the responsiveness and mutual assimilation central to Christian belief and emblematized in the Incarnation with
the scene of teaching itself. Even as lay Christians were instructed in and reminded of the radical reversals and paradoxes that constitute their faith, they
were positioned, through the dialogues and scenes of instruction that pervade
teaching texts, to see themselves in a transitional, potentially transformative
light: as learners engaged, cooperatively, in the project of their own education
rather than as passive recipients of preformulated teachings.

Thirteenth-century doctrinal texts, that is, are less focused on the disciplining of the laity (in our post-Foucauldian sense) than on the teaching of
the laity—or, to put it another way, they are focused on the disciplining of the
laity in the sense of making them *discipuli*, students, learners; though, as I will
discuss below, Foucault himself, in his later work, offers useful ways to think
about that shift.[4] The interactivity and exchange of informal medieval religious teaching deserve more of our attention, and more credit, than they have
usually received, and we can begin to see their workings in a passage like the
one from William of Waddington quoted above. Translating Augustine's declaration, "Qui ergo fecit te sine te, non te justificat sine te," William, like
many another medieval translator, reshapes and enriches Augustine's teaching
as much as he depends on it: the elegant parallels of Augustine's Latin prose
are intensified by the compression and rhyme of the French verse couplet.[5]
Like other poetic works of the period, doctrinal verse "not only transmits
what we can reasonably call 'knowledge,' but also, though its own reflective
and self-reflective procedures, shapes that knowledge and determines how it is
received."[6] William reinforces the instructional element of the passage by giving the source of his quotation in a scholarly way, but also accommodates

those readers who might be less familiar with the great Father of the Church by giving him a brief identification—"seint Austin, le clerc parfit"—that casts him as, in effect, the *ne plus ultra* of clerical knowledge. In so doing, William depicts the ideal to which he himself, as a clerical teacher, aspires, one that melds theological complexity with effective teaching.

Most strikingly, what William adopts from Augustine is God's requirement of human help in saving humankind: God can begin the work, but without human effort that work will not be completed; or, as his contemporary Pierre d'Abernon puts it, "seint Pol dit en ceste manere / Ke nus sumes a Deu aidere" (St. Paul says that in this way we are God's helpers).[7] William's lines appear in a discussion of the four things needed for effective confession: faith in the remission of sins; humility; the will to escape the Devil and to attain salvation (where this couplet appears); and good intention toward God. Since valid confession and religious instruction are the twin engines that drive the pastoral writing of the thirteenth century, the Augustinian couplet thus has implications for the relationship between teacher, learner, and doctrine more generally. If it is true that God will correct no one without that person's own effort and will, it is all the more true that the clergy cannot save the faithful without the faithful's own efforts. And the "te" of Augustine's Latin—the preacher's address to a listener—becomes the inclusive "nus" of William's written teaching. Teacher and learner are collaborators in this project, equally dependent on one another's goodwill and spiritual labor to succeed in the aim of salvation, and their relationship has shifted from that implicitly conveyed by Augustine: where his "qui . . . te . . ." formulation elides the clerical speaker himself, William's "nus" puts the teacher and the student on common ground.[8]

That crucial reframing, by which the longstanding image of master and disciple engaged in an instructional conversation about religion comes to include a lay participant in the role of the disciple, is, I argue, particularly characteristic of the thirteenth century; and while it is echoed in various contexts, from anchoritism to the rise of the fraternal orders, the versions I consider here seem to have been the particular concern of the secular clergy broadly understood, from household chaplains to Augustinian canons to parish priests—though there are contributions from monks, hermits, and secular poets.[9] These pastoral efforts did not emerge from a vacuum, of course, and the twelfth-century (and earlier) roots of the broadening and vernacularization of religious teaching are important precedents addressed throughout this study. Caroline Walker Bynum's work on the regular canons has shown the growing "emphasis on the obligation to love and serve one's neighbor," including through preaching, that is evident in many of the texts considered here, and we see increasing interest in the instruction of the laity in other contexts as well. Groups like the eleventh-century Patarene heretics or the Waldensians of the late twelfth and early thirteenth centuries exemplify the desire for greater lay contact with and access to religious knowledge; from the pastoral side, anthologies for priests or biblical glosses that emphasize preaching above contemplation show the growing attention to the tools of instruction.[10] The effort to transfer interactive teaching into text, and to preserve some of the teacher's presence in written form, also has echoes of the "charismatic" culture of the cathedral schools as discussed by Stephen Jaeger, a culture that shaped many of the figures whose ideas in turn influenced the preachers and teachers of the later twelfth and thirteenth centuries.[11]

Similarly, the twelfth-century texts discussed below, such as Honorius Augustodunensis's *Elucidarium* and *Speculum ecclesiae* and Maurice de Sully's vernacular homilies (the first sermon cycle disseminated in the French vernacular), the writings of Peter Abelard, and some French versions of biblical and apocryphal texts, serve as an important reminder that the designation "post–Lateran IV," while accurate for many of the works I consider, should not be taken to imply that the great council originated the interest in basic instruction and pastoral care. It was, rather, a crystallization of a process already well underway.[12] And while texts written and manuscripts copied in the thirteenth century are my primary focus, there is no hard line at either 1200 or 1300; thirteenth-century manuscripts continue to transmit earlier texts, and many early fourteenth-century manuscripts and works showcase precisely the kinds of foundational religious instruction I emphasize here.

As this suggests, it would be misleading to draw too sharp a temporal—or geographical—boundary. Both northern France and England produced extensive synodal statutes encouraging clerical and lay education, the earliest being those of Eudes de Sully (c. 1204).[13] If England was especially active in producing vernacular works on penitence and Christian instruction early in the thirteenth century, the concerns those works address are equally alive on the Continent; in some cases, the French versus Anglo-French origin of a work remains uncertain, and many works—like their authors—crossed the Channel freely.[14] Aden Kumler has recently explored this traffic, examining luxury manuscripts of religious instruction that reflect the "communication, exchange, and the movement of people and ideas across the shifting territorial bounds that divided England and northern France."[15] There are biblical paraphrases from both the British Isles and the Continent beginning in the mid-twelfth century; doctrinal compilations, especially in Anglo-French, beginning in the early thirteenth; and a rich trove of imaginative texts from throughout the thirteenth century, particularly though not exclusively from the Continent, that convey how such teaching might be worked out in contexts beyond the strictly instructional. And the outpouring of religious teaching in the vernacular on both sides of the Channel was, of course, only one part of a broader *translatio studii*—scientific, theological, geographical, philosophical, medical, and so forth—from Latin into the other languages of Europe. Both the emphases and the manuscript contexts of religious works remind us that they, and their readers, were participating in a cultural shift toward greater lay literacy and learnedness.[16]

In studying early vernacular didactic works, primarily in Anglo-French, as well as other texts from both England and the Continent that disseminate religious teaching through homily and narrative, I explore how the teaching imperative of the thirteenth century was imagined and received, what models it made available to readers, and what mechanisms it offered that over time, mutatis mutandis, could give rise to far different and more widespread uses of the material it made available than the original translators imagined. French texts of the thirteenth century offered audiences able to read or hear them a new way of imagining themselves as religious subjects. Rather than shaping their audiences primarily as readers, these texts imagine and address them as students, as *discipuli*, in a model sometimes explicitly and more often implicitly tied to the monastic and scholastic modes in which their teachers had been trained, but one that became available, as these texts were copied, recopied, and retranslated, to an ever-wider audience. A better understanding of the attempts made, in thirteenth-century France and England, to convey Christian learning "from the schools to the parishes" requires a sense of how active lay learners might have shaped clerical teaching—an influence implicitly visible both in the prologues to didactic works and in imaginative works designed for widespread reception. The "we," the direct address of the preacher, and the dialogue form that governs or contributes to many of these texts all encourage their audiences to place themselves in the role of the interlocutor, engaged in a joint project of inquiry with the teacher who stands before them.

Teaching and Death

The increased focus on the lay learner as an active contributor to the process of learning can be seen in the way the didactic and imaginative texts studied here return to and, in many cases, organize themselves around two key moments of face-to-face encounter. The first of these, already alluded to, is the moment of teaching. Both manuscript illuminations and the explicitly dialogic form of some key didactic works make it clear that the authors of these works were imagining a scene of teaching, often in imitation of influential models like Gregory the Great's *Dialogues* or Honorius Augustodunensis's *Elucidarium*. Even in works where that teaching scene is not made explicit, the addresses to the reader, accounts of the author's intentions or process, and discussions of translation—as well as the shift from Latin prose to (in most cases) French verse, making doctrine visible and accessible in a new way by putting it in a new form—make it clear how closely these clerical writers were engaging with their lay audiences.[17]

This is partly, of course, because at the other key face-to-face moment, the moment of death, the clerical teacher becomes crucially responsible for the student's eternal fate, whether salvation or damnation: as the thirteenth-century *Dialogue du père et du fils* puts it (citing Ezekiel 34:10, "Ego ipse requiram gregem meum"), priests' flocks will be required of them at the Last Judgment.[18] The twelfth-century bishop Étienne de Fougères, in his *Livre de manières*, a work of estates satire, makes the link to teaching even clearer. Concluding his discussion of bishops, he writes,

> Quan l'en l'apele sire et mestre,
> Ne s'en glorit, ainceis deit estre
> en grant porpens qui les deit pestre
> et mener a gloire celestre.
>
> Quant il vendrunt au jugement
> ou arami n'iert seirement,
> ne demandé amendement,
> ne treve pris n'esloignement,
>
> molt ert gueri et clerc et prestre
> qui o les bons sera a destre,
> et molt pora cil mari estre
> qui tornera soz la senestre.

Jhesu qui ses graces devise
si con li plest en meinte guise,
nos face saus et sanz devise
toz cels qu'avon en conmandise.[19]

[When people call him lord and master,
he should not glory in this, but rather should be
greatly aware that he must feed them
and lead them to heavenly glory.

When they come to the Judgment
where no oath can be called upon,
no improvement asked for,
no truce or delay taken,

that clerk or priest will be well off
who is on the right with the just,
and he will be greatly cast down
who must turn to the left.

May Jesus, who distributes his grace
in many ways, as it pleases him,
save without hesitation both us
and all those we have in our care.]

Teaching is intimately and fundamentally linked to the death and judgment of both teacher and student; the moment of instruction looks forward, across time, to the moment of death, with its remorseless emphasis on eternal status. The omnipresence of death and judgment as the context for all moral teaching highlights the status implications already present in the relationship between teacher and student, and makes death itself a setting for instruction in both pastoral and imaginative works; I explore the implications of their conjunction throughout this book.[20]

A further face-to-face moment, that of confession, lies between teaching and death and crucially influences both. While the focus on the self that confession requires is important here, its punitive and disciplinary aspects have—as Katherine Little has argued for a later period—been overstressed as *the* defining element of medieval religious practice. Like Little, I am interested in the "language (of instruction) through which we might approach medieval self-formation and the kinds of selves this language made possible," though unlike her I look for it primarily in instructional texts rather than in its strictly confessional context.[21] As a result, my focus is less on *individual* self-formation than on the interactions that enable and reflect that process of formation: in short, on the teaching and dialogue that offered both laity and clergy new ways to position themselves in relation to their own salvation.[22]

The experience of dialogic teaching is inherently a particular one, but in this period the concept of death was also taking on increased particularity, via the concepts of Purgatory and of the individual judgment that takes place upon a person's death.[23] The numerous otherworld journeys and visions of the afterlife produced and recounted in this period, as well as fabliaux and Marian miracles that depict individuals' deaths, show an intense desire to understand in more detail this moment of transfer and transformation. The means of doing so often involve, quite literally, putting a face on the experience of death—whether by means of otherworld visions where the traveler returns to tell his tale, or (sometimes within those tales) by the appearance of saints as guides or examples, or even through an actual face-to-face meeting with God. Scholarly accounts of medieval views on death often emphasize "sin and fear" (in Jean Delumeau's memorable phrase), and efforts to terrify the faithful are certainly widely available even before the fourteenth to sixteenth centuries, Delumeau's main focus.[24] But it is easy to overemphasize terror, which was, after all, a means rather than an end; the true aim, that of meeting death and the individual judgment on the best possible terms, admitted of more hopeful, curious, affectionate, even cheerful depictions than the hellfire and brimstone that have colonized the modern imagination.

My aim in this book, then, is twofold. I hope to convey, first, the extent to which thirteenth-century vernacular *doctrina*—in its original, dynamic sense of "teaching" rather than its modern, static sense of "what is taught"—involved an effort on the part of teacher and learner to face up both to one another and to their common fate as mortal sinners.[25] Concomitantly, I aim to bring modern readers more fully face-to-face with the variety and liveliness of texts that respond to the teaching imperative of the thirteenth century, with a particular eye to these texts' account of the relation between teacher and student. In medieval handbooks, often written or copied (or both) for specific patrons and incorporating detailed addresses to imaginatively individualized readers, we may begin to see the outlines of the personal encounters that shaped medieval teaching as deeply as did the institutional forms that structured it; though we can never, of course, recover such encounters, we can see their traces in the texts that put student and teacher face-to-face. And in narrative works that depict individuals living out the implications of what they have been taught, testing and sometimes even passing on that instruction, we can equally see particular receptions and reworkings of doctrine that, as I will argue, very often emphasize the inherent, but unstable, status disparity of teaching.

Clergie and the Laity

That status disparity continues to influence our reading: these texts' reflection on their own project of education, and on the collaborative as well as competitive relationship between authors and audiences, teachers and students, highlights the temptation to think in binaries like lay/clerical or elite/popular. The universality of death, however, and the pervasively available tropes of saving humility and holy simplicity tend to undermine such binaries. Death helps, paradoxically, to vivify the process of instruction just as instruction helps at the point of death; and both require a transition to a state of greater understanding and a chance to challenge received ideas about status. In the theological realm the *mediocriter boni* or "moderately good"—those not quite ready for Paradise but not deserving of eternal damnation—created the need for the in-between realm of Purgatory; in the context of pastoral care, the *mediocriter litterati*, the moderately learned (a category that could include both clerics and laypeople), gave rise to a new literary genre, the popularizing vernacular handbook.[26] For a medieval reader, *mediocriter litteratus* referred to someone with inadequate Latin; I adapt it here to refer to the "middling" category of vernacular literacy. More precisely, I look not at literacy in either the modern or the medieval sense but rather at the murky area of lay *learnedness*, and I read basic religious instruction as a more significant mode of learning than it is generally considered to be.

What Eamon Duffy characterizes, that is—looking back from the fifteenth-century English context—as "the original modest aims of the thirteenth-century Church," namely, "to equip the laity with basic prayers, the means of examining their consciences, and the bare essentials of belief," are not as modest or bare as they might initially appear; indeed, the instruction provided to the laity in the thirteenth century seems quite similar to what Duffy finds in the fifteenth.[27] While the knowledge *required* of the medieval laity in a formal sense may have been limited, their opportunities to know more were considerable.[28] "[T]he level of education of the mass of medieval people" is a tricky and elusive subject, especially given the variety contained in that mass, but such figures as St. Godric, traditionally believed to be of peasant background, or Peter Valdes, the merchant converted (according to legend) by a jongleur, or the implied audiences of thirteenth-century Parisian preachers remind us that the educational evidence that survives in manuscripts is only the echo of a far broader, livelier, more individualized and more interactive process of learning.[29] That process and the characterizations of both teachers and learners that it used and created are the focus of this book.

The term that marks the supposed divide between teachers and learners, and that most nearly approximates the concept of "learnedness" in Old French, is *clergie*. The word seems to have no actual Latin source; the equivalent term in Latin, meaning "learning, scholarship," is *clericatus*.[30] *Clergie* seems, rather, to be formed from the noun *clerc*, the designation for someone having knowledge or learning. While the term might well designate a "cleric" in the modern sense, its other meaning of "clerk" or "learned person" is one with increasingly porous boundaries from the twelfth century onward.[31] This is perhaps especially evident in relation to the knightly class, but it is clear that merchants too had access to various forms of instruction on basic religious knowledge—not only the Pater Noster and Creed but the lives of the saints and biblical narratives—that could have far-reaching effects on their lives. The legendary humble backgrounds of figures like Maurice de Sully and Robert Grosseteste are a reminder that the "modest" religious instruction that every parent was responsible for conveying to a child, and every preacher to his parishioners, had the potential to become the basis for far greater and deeper learning; regardless of their historical actuality, such legends attest to a belief in the possibility of advancement through (spiritual) education.[32] Translating Latin learning, or "clergie," into the vernacular involved a transfer to the laity of the very quality whose lack supposedly distinguished them from their clerical teachers, and legendary cases like these imaginatively conveyed the potential for even the least among the laity to become the greatest in religious teaching.

While the "hardening of the distinction between the clergy and the laity" fostered by the Gregorian Reform of the eleventh century remained an issue through the next several centuries, as some of the canons of Lateran IV make clear, the picture shifts if we look less at clerical *status* as such, or at ecclesiastical hierarchies, than at the learnedness that was a defining element of that status.[33] Many texts, beliefs, and practices circulated across the supposed lay-clerical divide, and it is important to remember the "common culture" shared by laity and clergy.[34] An awareness of that commonality makes it easier to see how didactic works in the vernacular might imagine a spectrum that included teacher and student, rather than a division between them; the very existence of these works suggests that the learners have the potential to become learned. Repeatedly, as we will see, vernacular didactic and narrative works reflect on the mutual recognition, empathy, and assimilation that are part of the process of education, even if the gap or disparity between learner and teacher remains an important part of the picture. Similarly, the manuscripts that preserve these texts, with their varied contents and juxtapositions, can seldom confirm for us any specifically lay or clerical ownership or readership but rather indicate intense engagement with the project of religious education on the part of both clergy and laity and remind us of the "common experience of life" that they might share.[35] Taken together, they show the ways in which medieval readers of various, and often now irrecoverable, social and literate status were working on the problem of broadening education and considering its implications for "omnis utriusque sexus."[36]

The Low and the Middle

Such shared interests, of course, did not do away with the vexed issue of status; this reappears, in a number of texts, through the use of figures from a very different part of the social spectrum than the "aristocrats, gentryfolk, parish priests, and . . . urban laity" who probably formed the initial audience for doctrinal works: peasants, thieves, whores, and jongleurs. All of these groups had a wide range of associations, from the divided lesson provided by sinner-saints like Mary the Egyptian or the good thief on the cross, to the role of jongleurs in disseminating both secular and sacred literature, to peasants' labor of feeding the other orders even as courtly literature condemned them. Like their moral role, such groups' relationship to learning was not straightforward. Peasant literacy in the twelfth and thirteenth centuries may have been considerably more widespread than is generally acknowledged, and it has been suggested that "by the thirteenth century . . . parish priests were often of peasant, even servile, origins"; in such cases the famous *clerici/rustici* distinction would indicate a temporal difference rather than an innate one, as the rustic became learned.[37] From another angle, however, the identification of the *litterati* with the *clerici* meant that all *laici* were, by definition, *illiterati* and thus, by extension, *idiotae, rustici,* and so forth.[38] The knights and

aristocracy had, of course, their own ways of distinguishing themselves from
the *rustici*; the horror of peasants permeates courtly literature, whose fundamental social distinction is *courtois/vilain*.[39] But from a clerical point of view,
the laity could be regarded as one large mass of *illiterati*, while the court could
valorize noble birth above religious virtue. And in religious terms, as we shall
see, *vilain* could have a morally neutral or even virtuous association with the
humble and faithful *agricola* or with the "fool" who is wiser than those with
earthly wisdom.[40] The implications, in other words, of these binary divisions
were highly dependent on context, and they could thus be deployed to make
doctrinal points about the relationship of earthly and heavenly status.

To put it another way, the fluidity of such designations as *rusticus, courtois, laicus, vilain, clericus*, as well as their deep importance to the self-definition
of different groups, makes the discussions in the prologues of didactic works,
and the depiction of characters in imaginative works, more widely relevant
than they might at first seem. Peasants (*rustici, agricolae, vilains*) can stand, in
their unlearnedness, not only for the whole of the laity but also for the power
of simplicity itself. A striking example is the ax-wielding peasant or "churl"
who appears in the Lambeth Apocalypse (Lambeth Palace Library, MS 209).
This figure's ax, with which he is about to chop at the root of the Tree that
represents the World, is said in the words accompanying the image to symbol-
ize "the sentence of the Judgment or the preaching of the Gospel." As Jocelyn
Wogan-Browne observes, "Since the churl's label associates him with the
Judgment and the Gospel, we can perhaps understand his social class as ex-
pressive of the rhetorical *stilus humilis* of the latter. Perhaps he also signals the
intuitive access of the simple to Gospel meaning . . . while their superiors in
learning and in socio-economic status may enter with difficulty."[41] Terms des-
ignating the unlearned—*illiterati, rustici, indocti, laici, idiotae*—involve a
"double set of values" that "recogniz[es] the cultural norms associated with
literacy but justif[ies] . . . the sacred simplicity of the illiterate," an association
that, like the moral approbation the Church might direct at peasants for their
role in feeding society, offers a counterweight to the moral and social opprobrium heaped upon them in courtly literature.[42] As Paul Freedman points
out, there was another basis of potentially universal significance: the "penance" of peasant labor, which involved "both a positive or forward-looking
component (the hope of heaven) and a negative origin in sin (Noah's curse),"
is an echo of something "generally true of all humankind: all are lost with
Adam but redeemed with Christ, cursed but saved."[43] Peasants represent, in
other words, a focused instance of a universal human situation.

The social importance of peasants, their role as a foundational category, is demonstrated by their appearance—in the guise of Latin *agricolae* or Old French *vilains*—in early estates literature; alongside or overlapping with them, frequently, are "the married" or "men and women," the "omnis utriusque sexus" of Lateran IV.[44] While in early texts these less-exalted estates are often only sketchily addressed, their role (like that of other orders) becomes increasingly elaborated and detailed in the course of the twelfth and thirteenth centuries in consort with the growing effort to link confession to specific social situations and professions. I do not suggest that peasants were a focus of direct identification for wealthy lay readers; as the image discussed above indicates, they may have played an allegorical or exemplary role that an aristocratic reader could look at while still, as it were, imagining him- or herself in a different part of the picture. But the inclusion of peasants and other despised groups like jongleurs, thieves, and whores in both ecclesiastical and secular discussions of salvation keeps the issue of status before the eyes of the audience and serves as a reminder of the powerful motif of holy simplicity even as it works to make audiences more aware of, and more learned in, the rules of salvation.

The Unintended Consequences of Instruction

Particularly in combination with the ideas about status, humility, and mutual assimilation that often accompany it, the translation of basic doctrine that was intended for specific though deeply important purposes—to enable "good" confessions and appropriate reception of the Eucharist and to fulfill the priest's spiritual responsibility to his parishioners—laid the groundwork for (and at times anticipated) later vernacular translations and adaptations of more elevated learning. It is not that doctrinal encyclopedias and similar works have any deliberate radical intentions; "it is rather that the vernacularization of this oral form makes issues discussed in the interests of orthodox doctrine available for a range of listeners (who may or may not use them in the manner intended by their compilers)," as Jocelyn Wogan-Browne notes.[45] I would add that by depicting and commenting on the process of transmitting such doctrine these works draw attention to the particular situations, relationships, and capabilities of those who teach and those who learn, working against any idea of teachers/learners as reified categories. Rather than necessarily closing off or limiting the laity's access to "higher" doctrine, that is, such basic translations, and of course the preaching that they imitated and enabled, sped on its way the lay acquisition of learning that had such spectacular and richly studied manifestations in the fourteenth and fifteenth centuries and beyond.

Fiona Somerset has rightly noted the fast and slippery slope that leads from critique of clerical capacity to instruct, to the writing of manuals in the vernacular, to the composition of vernacular works that move well beyond "the minimum the laity are strictly said to require." But the very designation "surplus-to-pastoral instruction" assumes that pastoral requirements are limited; my claim is that Christian doctrine, once opened up for discussion—even the fictive and carefully controlled debate of dialogue texts or the comic backchat of fabliau and miracle tale—is inherently complex, paradoxical, and challenging enough that even a "basic" text will raise and have to deal with difficult theological matters.[46] "Moral theology," after all, is still theology; the tropological interpretation of Scripture is intimately linked with the historical, anagogical, and allegorical modes, part of the same project rather than a simplistic alternative. Moreover, translation itself inevitably draws attention to, and problematizes, the fact that teaching takes place by means of language; the fictive and frivolous associations of French verse in this period made this all the more visible, and it is instructive to see the varied ways in which a particular piece of "basic" doctrine might be conveyed. Just as William of Waddington's recasting of Augustine's sermon, with which we began, inevitably changes more than its language, so the handbooks as a group, not to mention the imaginative texts that take their teachings and run with them, shape the meaning of that teaching as well as its form.[47]

In the thirteenth century, schools for women or artisans or merchants were yet to come; formal schooling still addressed primarily those training for a clerical life, with some room for the aristocracy.[48] But the vernacular handbooks are in themselves a kind of school, early textbooks for do-it-yourself learners able—with the clergy's implicit blessing and probably in some cases their services as readers—to separate the process of their religious learning from the public experience of hearing sermons into a more intimate, self-directed, and textual mode. The handbooks' focus on their own orderliness, their explanation of forms of learning as well as its content—discussed in the next chapter—show them assuming an audience that was capable of acquiring the literal *in-struction*, internal formation or building, that the clergy provided and doing so without the physical presence of a teaching cleric. And narrative texts that depict the practical effects of such instruction at the point of death (or beyond) give us an idea of how such learning might have been put to work, and reworked, by its lay audiences.[49]

Having God to Hand

These texts, then, broaden our sense of the scenes and means of medieval teaching, and can help us place "basic" religious teaching in its fuller context as a developed mode of education. Seen in this light, doctrinal poetry has more in common than might immediately be apparent with the means and ends of classical instruction as discussed by Michel Foucault. His characterization of the subject's formation as relying on a "bond with the Truth rather than submission to the Law" is a helpful way to articulate some of our difficulties in thinking about medieval religious education (*instructio*).[50] If one turns away from the slightly obsessive focus on disciplinary confession as *the* goal of Christian teaching, it is easier to see in thirteenth-century teaching texts the attempt to bring the student to the master's level and allow him or her to form a "bond with the Truth" that entails and reflects a deeply personal and hard-won understanding of the teachings that will, ultimately, make the master himself dispensable by making the disciple his own master.

What has been called the "second wave" of penitential manuals, those written from around 1260 onward, focuses on the penitent rather than the priest and tries to instruct him or her "not just in how to confess properly but in how to combat sin, how to build up the self, how to develop cleanness of heart."[51] In fact, vernacular sermons and works of doctrine from the late twelfth century through the thirteenth often share this goal, and both echo the Greek and Latin terminology of subject formation as discussed by Foucault. He describes the practice or exercise (*askesis*) a student undergoes in order to form "a *paraskeue* [such that] the subject constitutes himself," and points out that *paraskeue* is translated by Seneca as *instructio*—a concept essential to Christian teaching and subject formation from an early period, with particular echoes in discussions of translation and access in preaching.[52] Foucault sees the self-constitutive instruction of classical *paraskeue* as made up of "discourses existing, acquired, and preserved in their materiality," things one has actually "heard or read, really remembered, repeated, written and rewritten" that, in order to function, must be, as he says, " 'ready to hand': *prokheiron*, which the Latins translated as *ad manum*."[53] This fierce attention to the *process* of learning, its material and embodied context, is echoed in a different key as the interlocutors depicted in dialogue texts mutually create such "discourses," and its idea of having knowledge *to hand* is precisely echoed in the term *manuel*, handbook, a word seemingly brought from Latin into French by William of Waddington in the *Manuel des pechiez*. William explains the title with care: "Le Manuel est apelé, / Car en main deit estre porté. / L'alme aprent recti- fier, / A chescun deit estre le plus chier" (It is called the "handbook," because it should be carried in the hand. It teaches one to correct the soul and should be very dear to each person, ll. 63–66).[54] What is "to hand" here is the book that teaches how to order the soul rightly, to *rectifier* oneself, as evoked also in the lines quoted in my epigraph. Books like William's aim to provide precisely the kind of *logoi* that one might have "heard or read, really remem- bered, repeated" and to dramatize or represent that hearing, reading, re- membering, repeating. They codify not only knowledge but the process of acquiring it.

In doing so, they provide further echoes of the idea of having religious learning or knowledge "to hand," in ways that remind us of the knowledge and practice *already* available to laypeople. Such existing knowledge informs the instruction offered by the handbooks, reminding us again of the interplay between lay and clerical forms and practices in religious teaching. In Maurice de Sully's vernacular sermons, for example, which circulated in France and England throughout the thirteenth century and which at times accompany the didactic handbooks (and the *Gospel of Nicodemus*) in manuscripts, the preacher discusses the meaning of the feast of Candlemas:

> Faisons issi la Candeler, que nos aions en nos iço que li cierge e les candeilles senefient, que nos avons au jor d'ui en nos mains. Li lu- minaries senefie la gloriose Deité Nostre Segnor, qui est pardura- ble . . . cil qui demaine bone vie e fait ces uevres que Deus aime, cil a Deu entre ses mains.[55]

> [Let us so celebrate Candlemas that we may have in ourselves that which the taper and the candles, which today we hold in our hands, signify. The light signifies the glorious deity, our Lord, who is eter- nal . . . he who leads a good life and performs the works that God loves has God between his hands.]

Maurice's explication links embodied practices familiar to his audience— holding a candle in memory of Mary's purification at the temple; participa- tion in a procession—with both their biblical antecedents and their tropological implications. To participate reverently in the procession at Can- dlemas *is*, through a kind of transitive process of meaning, to hold God in your hands: the knowledge that Maurice conveys gives new meaning to a practice already known.

The image of having God to hand is also invoked, albeit in reverse, in Pierre d'Abernon's *Lumere as lais*, from 1267. After the master in this dialogic text has explicated the articles of the faith as presented in the creedal prayer *Quicumque vult*, the disciple requests further explication of "Iceste saume" (this psalm). The master provides a careful account of what one should love, and in what order: God, one's soul, one's neighbor, and one's body. The passage is, as this might suggest, intensely concerned with right order and leads the disciple to provide an extended response in which he laments the many people who fail in their first duty, love of God, saying, "Dunt c'est pitié et grant dolur, / Ke si ordeinent lur amur / Ke, mes ke l'en chante utre eus la saume, / Deu lur faudra enmi la paume" (Thus it is a pity and a great sorrow that they order their love in such a way that, even if one were to sing the psalm fully for them, God will slip from their hands [lit. "will fail in the midst of the palm"]).⁵⁶ Here the disciple becomes, for a moment, the one who articulates Christian truth and who, by contrast with Maurice, emphasizes the disjunction between inner and outer forms: one may fully explain the Creed to such people, but without rightly ordered love and the good life it produces, God will slip from their fingers. The rhyme recurs later in the *Lumere*, when the master is criticizing those who do not adequately provide for their dead. He says, "Mes le siecle si est tut lur saume / Dunt chantent, ki faudra enmi la paume" (But the world, which is the whole psalm they sing, will slip from their hands, 2:164, ll. 12707–8). This second usage conveys the metaphorical idea of a psalm as the focus of one's efforts, religious or otherwise, and recalls the way in which a psalm—and certainly the creedal knowledge that is originally invoked under that name—would have been knowledge fully absorbed into the body by repetition that shaped one's orientation to the world.⁵⁷

Pierre's examples are in the negative, but he like Maurice and William suggests that a properly oriented will, of the kind needed to *rectifier* oneself, would lead to having God "to hand," and his book, like the others, strives to provide an orderly way to gain the knowledge and interior disposition that would lead to that end.⁵⁸ Such imagery suggests that these handbooks imagine the Logos being acquired in a way similar to the *logoi* of *paraskeue*, and for similar ends. The idea of having God to hand characterizes lay learning as more than a rote adoption of formulae; rather it is a kind of conversion or transformation, one that makes use of existing knowledge and practice but aims to give new meaning and depth to those existing forms.

In a discussion of how an "elite" might underestimate a public's ability to exercise discernment about the "products imposed on it," Michel de Certeau argues that this mistake rests on the assumption "that 'assimilating' necessarily means 'becoming similar to' what one absorbs, and not 'making something similar' to what one is, making it one's own, appropriating or reappropriating it. Between these two possible meanings a choice must be made."[59] But why must there be a choice? De Certeau's analysis seems in danger here of becoming merely an inversion of the approach it critiques. Texts that enact and simultaneously investigate the translation of *clergie* certainly suggest that the audience should assimilate to, indeed imitate, the teacher and his teachings. But they are at the same time acutely aware of the need for the student to make these teachings his own; of the reverse assimilation that the teacher and his teachings undergo, the way in which they collaborate with and assimilate to, as well as impose on, the audiences they address; and of the common end awaiting both teacher and learner. If it is, as de Certeau says, "always good to remind ourselves that we mustn't take people for fools," it is also good to remind ourselves that we are not the first ones to figure this out and that it is no more admirable for us to condescend to our objects of study than it is for medieval teachers to condescend to their students.[60] The texts considered here take seriously, as well as playfully, the idea that teaching is instructive and salvific for both teacher and student, and I have tried to enter into their spirit, embracing my own "docte ignorance" in order to learn more of what they have to teach.[61]

Chapter 1

The Face and the Mirror: Teachers and Students in Conversation

The transmission of *clergie* in thirteenth-century French works is innovative primarily in its means and forms rather than in its content. In particular, I will argue, the works in varied genres that aim to engage with the laity in the project of Christian learning are repeatedly characterized by a turn to dialogue or, to be more precise, by their attentiveness to a scene of individualized and interactive learning that may be imagined as a dialogue. While some catechetical or doctrinal texts, like the *Dialogue du père et du fils* and Pierre d'Abernon's *Lumere as lais*, take an explicit dialogue form, in others the address to and interaction with an audience are more implicit; this is the case in Robert of Gretham's *Miroir* (or *Évangiles des domnées*) and the *Mirour de seinte eglyse* of Edmund of Abingdon, where prologues and internal remarks convey the sense of a well-known and vividly present audience, whether or not that audience is given a voice in the text. Later chapters will turn to works where Christian teaching is conveyed through the presentation of dialogue between characters; here I consider the role of conversation and imagined interaction in works that serve as compendia of Christian teaching without a narrative element.

Throughout, I argue that such imagined dialogues are not simply an authoritarian monologism in disguise but serve to maintain the sense of exchange that serious and effective teaching has to incorporate. While it is possible to see dialogic didactic works as secretly monologic—as using their dialogue form merely to impose or enforce a unitary truth—such a view underestimates what they have to tell us about medieval Christianity's awareness of the unstable status distinction between teacher and learner. Attempts to depict "didactic" or "catechetical" questioning as ultimately monologic cast up any number of problematic exceptions, particularly in poetry, as we see in the work of H. R. Jauss; and even when the aim of the dialogue form is to reinforce a status quo, it inevitably represents, and thus preserves, challenges and disruptions to that process.[1] As Sarah Kay has noted, moreover, even much-maligned monologism is not necessarily "less radical" than multiplicity; and like the (later, and less religiously oriented) French didactic works she studies, the doctrinal poetry of the thirteenth century, despite its "pious agenda," acknowledges that "'oneness' is problematic, and 'one' meaning difficult if not impossible to assign."[2] Even if these dialogues encourage a unified point of view, the process they represent displays their awareness of the complexities involved in reaching—or trying to reach—that unity. It is also important that, like the classical and patristic dialogues Seth Lerer explores, the texts examined here "engage a future reading public . . . outside the circle of friends or students for whom the text was written" and enable readers "to measure themselves against both the student figure within the text, and the imaginary reader the text itself inscribes." Boethius wrote as Greek was dying out in Latin culture and as education moved from the public sphere of declamation into private reading and schoolroom colloquy; in the twelfth and thirteenth centuries, the authors I consider began to bring written Christian education into new vernaculars and tentatively reintroduce it to an arena outside the cloister, even if its reading audience remained limited.[3]

Some of the significance and the implications of imagined dialogue in this period emerge from the manuscript contexts of these works and the visual representations that accompany them. Medieval manuscript illumination includes a number of stereotyped images that serve to convey something about the genesis or transmission of the text they accompany, a kind of visual equivalent of the textual *Bildeinsätze* that provided the reader with a sense of what to expect from the work at hand.[4] Images of a preacher or teacher addressing an audience, of an author writing in solitude, or of an author visited by an inspirational figure are all familiar types. Another is the image of two individuals—usually master and disciple or father and son—face-to-face in conversation, holding the dialogue that gives the work its form. The extent to which such an image served as a generic indicator can be seen in Paris, BnF fr. 12581, a thirteenth-century manuscript, where essentially identical versions of this image are used to mark the beginning of the *Dialogue du père et du fils* (f. 344^r) (Figure 1), a teaching dialogue on the basics of the Christian faith, and, many folios later, the beginning of a French translation of Petrus Alfonsi's *Disciplina clericalis*, known as the *Chastoiement d'un père à son fils* (f. 408^r)

Figure 1. A father teaches his son in the *Dialogue du père et du fils*.
Paris, Bibliothèque nationale de France, fonds français 12581, f. 344ʳ.
By permission of the Bibliothèque nationale de France.

(Figure 2).[5] In both images, the father, seated higher and to the left, points to his left palm with his right index finger; the son, seated lower and to the right of the image, holds up his right hand as though speaking. Comparable images, with master and disciple rather than father and son, can be found accompanying such texts as the dialogic *Lumere as lais* by Pierre d'Abernon and even St. Edmund of Abingdon's *Mirour de seinte eglyse*, which is not in explicitly dialogic form, though it does contain occasional direct address.[6]

The association of the *Dialogue* and the *Chastoiement* by way of their opening miniatures in BnF fr. 12581 has particularly to do with their form; the varied and at times rather worldly instruction offered in the *Chastoiement* is of a different kind than the teachings on baptism and doctrine provided by the *Dialogue*. The latter, in fact, is more closely allied with the text that precedes it and of which, for the manuscript's scribe, it forms a part: a French translation of Honorius Augustodunensis's *Elucidarium*, known as the *Lucidaires*.[7] The *Dialogue*'s title, in this version, is "A dialogue between father and son on this same matter" (Uns dialogues entre le pere et le fil seur iceste meesmes matiere), namely, the "matter" discussed in the *Lucidaires*, which is indeed, like

Figure 2. A father teaches his son in the *Chastoiement d'un père à son fils*.
Paris, Bibliothèque nationale de France, fonds français 12581, f. 408ʳ.
By permission of the Bibliothèque nationale de France.

that of the *Dialogue*, the fundamentals of Christian belief. The *Lucidaires* too
takes the form of a dialogue, though here the participants are master and disciple rather than father and son. The text is lacking its beginning, so any
miniature that might have accompanied it is lost.[8]

The conjoining of a master-disciple dialogue and a father-son dialogue on
related topics, their form highlighted by mise-en-page in the form of initials
introducing each speaker and by the image that begins the inset *Dialogue*,
suggests the simultaneously hierarchical and cooperative nature of the conversation represented. The opening of the *Dialogue* reinforces this awareness of
the two parties' respective roles. As the father notes, a Christian used not to be
baptized until he was old enough to have "sen et discrecion" (sense and discretion) and knew "ce que il devoit croire, dire et faire come bons crestiens"
(what he ought to believe and say and do as a Christian); when he knew this,
he would immediately have himself baptized and "respond[re] pour soi" (an-
swe[r] for himself).[9] Now, however, since children are baptized before they

can possibly have learned all this, they are protected by the faith of their god-parents until they come of age. This brings with it a responsibility: if the child "retains foolish beliefs through their [that is, the godparents'] fault, since they did not do their duty to him, they shall pay dearly for it at the Day of Judgment"—as, of course, will the child himself (se il remaint en fole creance par leur defaute, que il n'aient fait vers lui ce que a eus en apartient, il le comparront chier au jor dou jugement, f. 344ᵛ). The same warning, as noted in the Introduction, applies to clerical teachers as well as to parents and godparents, making their students' moment of judgment a test for them as well.

In view of this imagined moment of mutual judgment, the dialogue form makes sense: it both reinforces the link between teacher and learner and performs for the reader the kind of interaction with "what [a Christian] ought to believe and say and do" that enables the necessary learning. Ernstpeter Ruhe has noted the internal variation of dialogue forms in the Middle Ages, pointing out the difference between catechism, in which the more learned party asks brief questions and the less learned party gives answers that demonstrate his or her knowledge, and "instructional dialogues," in which the disciple or child asks (usually brief) questions that allow the master to hold forth on the matter at hand—in the case of the texts studied here, Christian doctrine.[10] But as the *Dialogue du père et du fils* reminds us, these two types of dialogue are, in a religious context, deeply connected: the instructional dialogues present the teaching that the learner must master in order to be able to "respond for himself," whether in catechism or in confession. Such a mode of teaching is, of course, ancient, but it received new impetus in this period when "changes in pastoral conceptions of the sacrament of penance promoted dialogue as a practice fundamental to the exercise of the late medieval *cura animarum*," a context that highlighted the mutual responsibility of teacher and learner.[11]

The master's desire, as well as obligation, that the disciple attain the knowledge the master already holds, like the parallel between texts that present such interactions as a master-disciple conversation and those that imagine a father-son conversation, reminds us of the affection that is implicit in such teaching. Texts like the *Dialogue* or the *Lucidaires*—those that present basic Christian teaching with particular attention to how that teaching is formulated and conveyed—are the focus of this and the following chapter and the frame of this book. Even when not presented explicitly in dialogue form, they tend to address an audience directly and at times, as we will see below, to evoke that audience's presence in emphatic, detailed, and affective ways. The sense of close personal connection that they foster enables a transfer not only of the content of learning but of its process; by imagining the role of the lay learner as that of a disciple, such works "deploy dialogic form to posit the sharing of clerical understanding" in a way that has a lasting impact on lay spirituality in the late Middle Ages.[12]

Spreading the Word

Thirteenth-century doctrinal works in French form a crucial middle ground between the traditional spheres of laity and clergy, offering instruction both to the more learned among the laity and to the less learned among the clergy in a language that both could understand. Considering their importance in developing and enriching the spiritual formation of the laity and their breadth of distribution, they have been surprisingly underattended to by scholars in recent years, although the tide is beginning to shift.[13] While I consider here texts with varied manuscript histories, I focus most centrally on those that survive in ten or more manuscripts (including excerpts or fragments), as a way to indicate the reach of this tradition. The manuscripts that transmit these works show them, and the imaginative texts that often accompany them, as part of an ongoing process of interactive teaching that reaches beyond the text itself. Prologues are added, exempla imported or combined with extracts from other works, Marian or Christological material incorporated: these texts were received and responded to by audiences well beyond their immediate ones.[14] This is also evident in the variety of their addressees; different versions of a text, or even the same version, may at one time address the audience as "fils," at others as "seigneurs," "treschere soer," and so forth.[15]

While sometimes these works co-occur in large codices with varied contents, such as Cambridge, University Library, MS Gg.I.1, others survive in small manuscripts containing one or a few texts that a parish priest, for example, could have carried with him. Cambridge, St. John's College, MS F.30, from around 1300, measures about 10 x 7 inches. It contains only Pierre d'Abernon's *Lumere as lais*, a doctrinal handbook based on the *Elucidarium* among other works, and William of Waddington's *Manuel des pechiez* (in different hands but contemporary, and with Latin marginalia). New Haven, Yale University, Beinecke Library, MS 492 measures roughly 12 x 8 inches and includes (again in different but contemporary hands) the *Lumere*, the *Mirour de seinte eglyse* (a treatise on Christian knowledge and contemplation), and the *Petit sermon*, a verse sermon on loving and fearing God, with some English prayers and recipes at the end. Still other surviving manuscripts seem to have been designed as compendia that could include a broad range of texts conveying basic Christian learning in the vernacular and claiming at least a potential lay audience for their teachings. A striking example is London, British Library, Royal MS 20.B.XIV, a late thirteenth- or early fourteenth-century manuscript which suggests that such works of doctrine formed a reasonably coherent genre. It contains, in order, the *Manuel des pechiez* (which survives in twenty-eight manuscripts including this one); the *Mirour de seinte eglyse* (twenty-eight manuscripts); the self-explanatory *Exhortation to Love God* (two manuscripts); the *Roman de Philosophie*, by Simond de Freine, an adaptation of Boethius's *Consolatio Philosophiae* (three manuscripts); a poem titled *The Corruption of the World* (unique to this collection); Robert Grosseteste's *Chasteau d'amour*, a doctrinal allegory depicting Mary as a castle that protects Christians (nineteen manuscripts); the *Roman des romans*, a verse homily on the corruption of the world (ten manuscripts); a collection of *Miracles of the Virgin* (two manuscripts); and the *Petit sermon* (ten manuscripts).[16] This manuscript's generic coherence is somewhat unusual, but I provide its contents here to show both the range of topics that such a compilation might cover and the substantial popularity of many works in this genre.

Both the extent of these doctrinal works' transmission and their self-presentation argue for a substantial and varied audience, impossible though it may be to recover that audience's exact constitution. Certainly, however, the authors themselves envisioned their audiences as primarily those unversed in *clergie*, that is, in the Latin language and thus in higher learning. The sermon on the corruption of the world in Royal 20.B.XIV puts it succinctly: "Cest sermun est dist / Pur vus & escrist / Ki n'etes lettrés; / Vus ki n'etes mie / Parfund en cleregi, / Sovent le lisez" (This sermon is said and written for you who are not lettered; you who are not deeply learned, read it often, f. 87ʳ). The concluding instruction makes it clear that the primary audience addressed is literate in the vernacular, but not in Latin. The prologue to Robert Grosseteste's *Chasteau d'amour* takes a similar approach:

Tuz avum mestier de aÿe,
Mes trestuz ne purrunt mye
Aver le langage en fin
De ebreu ne de latin
Por luer sun creatur;
Ne buche de chanteur

Ne soit clos pur Deu loer
E sun seint nun nuncier.
Ke chescun en sun langage
Le conusse sanz folage
Sun Deu e sa redemptiun,
En romanz cumenz ma resun
Pur ceus ki ne sevent mie
Ne lettrure ne clergie.[17]

[We all have need of help,
but by no means everyone
can know, in the end,
the Hebrew or Latin language
in order to praise his creator;
nor should the mouth of the singer
be closed off from praising God
and announcing his holy name.
So that everyone might know
his God and his redemption
in his (own) language, without wickedness,
I begin my work in French
for those who do not know
either letters or learning.]

The acknowledgment that "we all have need of help" echoes the need for co-operation emphasized in Augustine's teaching that "God . . . cannot save us without us"; here, however, the focus is not on the need for the sinner to contribute to his own salvation but rather on the specific kind of help that someone who knows both Latin and French (and perhaps even Hebrew) can offer to those without higher learning, so that they too may know and praise God. Pierre d'Abernon, in his late thirteenth-century *Lumere as lais*, sees his book having a similar role. As he says, "sage en devendra ki suvent / Cest livere lit e garde en prent" (whoever often reads this book and takes heed of it will become wise), and he reinforces the point at the very end of his prologue: "principaument / L'ai fest pur lais veraiment, / E pur ceo le fis en teu langage / K'il en pussent estre plus sage, / E ke meuez conuistre nostre Seignur / Pussent, e aver ver lui amur" (indeed, I have made [this book] principally for laypeople, and therefore I made it in such a language that they might be made wiser by it, and might better know our Lord and love him).[18] This knowledge will make his lay readers "wise," will bring them toward the state of those who teach them.

The sense of these works as part of a coherent program of teaching, as conveyed by their manuscript context, and their insistence on teaching in a way that is *linguistically* accessible to a new audience are both in their own ways signs of a pragmatic desire for effective instruction that goes beyond the existing body of teaching. Neither written doctrine nor vernacular instruction is a novelty, but their combination—written religious instruction in the vernacular on a substantial scale—certainly is. The intense focus on communication implied by both dissemination and language is also visible in these works' attention to the interaction between teacher and learner, often depicted through the use of dialogue. What is new in these texts is not the dialogue form in itself—which goes back to such ancient models as catechism, Boethius's *Consolatio Philosophiae*, or Gregory the Great's *Dialogues*—or their content, but the attention they give to how the face-to-face interaction implied by the dialogue form or by a strongly imagined and specific audience shapes both the teaching offered and the relationship between the interlocutors. A shift in that relationship—and an evolving sense of how religious teaching needed to be positioned in order to be effective—is evident in teaching texts from the mid-twelfth to the late thirteenth century. I begin with a brief look at the *Speculum ecclesiae* of the prolific Honorius Augustodunensis, from the first half of the twelfth century; the satirical *Romans de carité* of Barthélemy, a Benedictine monk and recluse from Molliens, in Picardy, from the late twelfth century; and a handbook for preachers by Thomas of Chobham, an Englishman educated at Paris, from about 1217, before turning to a more detailed consideration of Robert of Gretham's *Miroir* or *Évangiles des domnées*, c. 1240, written for his patroness Aline de la Zouche, and Pierre d'Abernon's *Lumere as lais*, from 1267. The changes in circumstances of composition, the depiction of the relationship between teacher and student, and the modes of address in these works show new kinds of disciples taking up their place in the conversation.[19]

Teaching Across the Gap

The many and varied works of Honorius Augustodunensis, an older contemporary of Bernard of Clairvaux who wrote in the first decades of the twelfth century, became the bedrock of much lay instruction in the following centuries. Honorius's *Elucidarium*, for example, though it soon ceased to represent the cutting edge of Christian thought, was widely read in the centuries after its composition and translated into most of the European vernaculars (including both Continental and insular French versions), and its summary of Christian doctrine was influential, even if not definitive, particularly given its probable use by parish priests in their instruction of the laity.[20] While the *Elucidarium* plays an important role throughout this book, here I look to another of Honorius's many works of basic instruction, the model-sermon collection *Speculum ecclesiae*. Like the *Elucidarium*, this work shows Honorius to be deeply committed to effective teaching and by no means unaware of his audience; his model sermons include addresses to the imagined hearers acknowledging that they may be tired and cold and promising to be brief, and the text offers headings addressed to the potential preacher that suggest how the sermon may be extended if the audience is receptive: "End here if you like. But if time permits, add the following."[21] He also points to the need for vernacular translation: "In all sermons you should first say the verse in Latin, then explain it in the vernacular language [*patria lingua*]."[22] Even as he acknowledges the lay audience's needs and responses, however, Honorius tends to view that audience from a distance, as one might expect of a monk. He generally addresses his fellow monks or the clergy directly, and the laity only through them; even in his pastoral works, it is the priests, not their flocks, who occupy the center of the picture. Reflecting the inheritance of the Gregorian reform, he maintains a sense of separation between clergy and laity; as he puts it in a work on the preaching of monks, the monastic vocation is more exalted than that of the regular canon, which is by comparison "lower and nearer to the world."[23] His attitude toward his audiences has a similarly hierarchical tendency. Valerie Flint notes that one of Honorius's self-imposed tasks in many of his works is "resolving difficulties for the simple minded," and she later mentions his "desire to supply the needs of those struggling for improvement"; the note of gracious condescension derives from Honorius himself.[24]

Written for Honorius's fellow monks, the *Speculum ecclesiae* conveys the sense of a marked distinction between preacher and audience, teacher and learner. Describing the work as a "painting," he then gives an account of his title: "This little picture [i.e., his book] may be called 'The Mirror of the Church.' Let all priests therefore set it before the eyes of the Church, so that the spouse of Christ may see in it in what ways she may still displease her Spouse, and may shape her habits and her actions in its image [*ad imaginem suam mores et actus suos componat*]."[25] Later, concluding a section that discusses the Pater Noster, Creed, and a form of confession, as well as providing a series of prayers for various social groups—precisely the kind of basic teaching offered in many thirteenth-century texts—Honorius offers the familiar image of priests as a mirror, urging the preacher to instruct his listeners to "pray to God for our bishop, and for all priests, and for all those in holy orders, who should be the mirror of the Church, that almighty God may . . . so inspire them that they may fulfill in their works what they preach to the people in words, and see eternal life with him on the last day."[26] Both the teacher and the *Speculum* itself are "mirrors" for the faithful, but, as generally in Honorius, it is the difference between preacher and audience that is stressed, not their common ground: the priest is a mirror, but the role of the laity in using this mirror is hardly addressed; they are to pray and admire. We see a similar attitude in the famous "Sermo generalis" later in this text, a very early instance of the genre of *sermones ad status*, sermons to various social groups. At the beginning of the sermon about priests, Honorius says (speaking in the voice of the preacher), "We priests should be your tongue, and explain to you by interpretation everything that is sung or read in the holy office," and a few lines later he returns to the image of the mirror: "We should show ourselves, in our deeds, to be a mirror of what we teach in words."[27] Priests are, again, mirrors for their flocks as well as the speaking voice of those flocks; they speak to the faithful, and for the faithful, but there is no sense of a conversation, and the mirror is identical with the preacher, who alone can mediate doctrine and exemplary behavior to his listeners.

That this view was not limited to Latin literature is clear from the late twelfth- or early thirteenth-century *Romans de carité*, a widely popular sermonic estates satire (or satirical estates sermon) by Barthélemy, the "Renclus de Molliens."[28] Though like Honorius he speaks as one removed from the world—whether or not he was actually a hermit—he implicitly addresses a different audience through his choice of French verse rather than Latin prose. Nevertheless, he takes a similar tack in his depiction of the priest's role in relation to his flock: "Prestre, tu ies li mireours / Por mirer les fous pekeours; / Et se tu ies noirs et oscurs, / Ou se mireront il aillours?" (Priest, you are the mirror to which wicked sinners look; and if you are dark and obscure, where else shall they look?).[29] Later he admonishes, "Prestre, se lais hom est tes pers, / N'as pas de bonté grant foison" (Priest, if a layman is your peer, you have no great store of virtue), a critique that is reinforced in the following strophes, where the potential goodness of the laity is evoked primarily as a way to shame the clergy.[30]

The Renclus embraces the "angelicizing," reformist view of the clergy that emphasizes their need to distinguish themselves from the laity rather than their commonality with them.[31] The distancing effect is mitigated, in a sense, by the fact that he does not identify with the group he addresses; he is one of the "we" whom the preacher should defend. Nevertheless, the central importance of parish priests is conveyed by the many strophes designated to them, about a fifth of the work as a whole and by far the most devoted to any group. The laity, by contrast, are given only five strophes (150–54), which primarily exhort them to avoid covetousness and not to be too much attached to the world.

In the English subdeacon Thomas of Chobham's *summa* for preachers, written probably around the time of the Fourth Lateran Council, the focus has shifted toward the secular world in itself, rather than as a mere foil for the priest; Thomas speaks, unlike Honorius or Barthélemy, *as* a parish priest, and his attention is on the laity even as he addresses his colleagues.[32] Even as the "angelic" status of the clergy, their distance from ordinary lay life, was emphasized and reemphasized in the repeated attempts to institute clerical celibacy or to exalt the order of the priesthood, the clergy's responsibility to and engagement with their flocks were continually increasing, thanks in no small part to pressure from the laity itself.[33] The interaction between preacher and audience was visibly, for Thomas, a more complicated and less straightforwardly hierarchical one than it appears to be for Honorius or Barthélemy. Thomas's primary audience is one of potential preachers literate in Latin, and like Barthélemy but unlike Honorius he turns his analysis on the audience itself, rather than addressing the laity with or through them. Honorius's preacher is looked at, but only as an idealizing mirror for an admiring flock; Barthélemy's risks being a dark glass. Thomas's preacher, too, is a *speculum*—but with a difference. Where Honorius declares, "we should show ourselves, in our deeds, to be a mirror of what we teach in words," Thomas shifts the agency: "The preacher should be like a book and a mirror for his flock, that *they may read* in the works of their prelate as though in a book, and may see in a mirror what they should do," and goes on to quote Paul: "brothers, be imitators of me as I also am of Christ."[34] For Honorius and the Renclus de Molliens, the emphasis falls on the audience's unlikeness to the preacher; for Thomas, on their attempts to become like him—a subtle but important difference, especially since Thomas speaks in terms that place both preacher and audience in the elevated biblical context of the Pauline epistles. The image of the book, too, undergoes a shift here: rather than a text uniquely available to the preacher, which he must mediate to his flock, the book *becomes* the preacher, whom the laity may read for themselves and, implicitly, interpret. To extend the concept of reading in this way—to suggest that one may read a person, as well as a text—also extends the discussion toward learnedness rather than literacy: one may learn, and even read, without direct access to books.[35]

Humble Translation: Robert of Gretham's
Miroir or *Évangiles des domnées*

The work of the Renclus de Molliens shows that works in the vernacular could present a traditional or conservative view of the clergy-lay relationship; Thomas of Chobham's address to preachers demonstrates that works in Latin can be alive to the dynamic connection between preacher and audience. When the awareness and mutuality that we see in Thomas appear in a text in French verse, however, the whole discussion shifts: the very laypeople whose potential similarity to the preacher is at issue now have, at least in theory, direct access to the discussion by way of a text that is explicitly intended for lay readers (as many doctrinal works insist). This is all the more striking when, as is the case in some of the thirteenth-century doctrinal handbooks, those laypeople are the patrons and addressees of the text. As the laity become the primary readers, rather than the secondhand recipients of the clerical teacher's reading, the instruction becomes more self-conscious, attending explicitly to the relative status of teacher and learner, and emphasizing the capabilities of the latter. These texts aim, in many cases, to offer laypeople the intellectual means by which to correct themselves, rather than simply providing that correction directly.[36]

Such an approach implies a lessening of the disparity between teacher and learner, emphasizing their shared pursuit of enlightened faith. The move away from locating primary authority in the clerical teacher is evident in the way Robert of Gretham, a secular cleric writing probably in the 1240s for his noble patron, Lady Aline, uses the now familiar image of the mirror-book. His *Miroir* is no longer a metaphor for the preacher; it is poised to become his substitute.[37] As Robert himself says, "Si li auturs finist sa vie / Bon escrit ne poet finir mie; / Mais l'escrit par li parlera / Qu'avant mort e purriz serra" (If the author's life must end, good writing cannot end; but the writing will speak for him who will already be dead and rotting)—the book will survive the teacher, and circulate beyond his personal presence, in a way that gives a new independence to the viewers of the mirror.[38] In this way, the book both preserves the sense of "pastoral encounter" and allows it to become imaginary in a way that makes the lay recipient's role central to the functioning of the text.[39] Even as Robert demonstrates, as we will see, a strong sense of his audience, he, like other pastoral authors of the thirteenth century, is willing to write himself out of the picture, trusting in the abilities of his interlocutor. The humility and the confidence in the lay learner this suggests are evident in his text and show one way in which the hierarchical aspects of the relationship between teacher and learner could be, if not leveled, then nuanced by an acute sense of each side's contribution.

The emphasis on the reader as an active user of the text who needs to learn its methods is evident in Robert's nearly seven-hundred-line prologue. Here he takes care to elucidate his title:

Cist livres "Mirur" ad nun;
Ore oez par quele raisun.
Par le mirur veit l'om defors,
E par cest escrit, alme e cors.
Li mirurs les tecches presente
E cist les pensers e l'entente.
Li mirurs mustre les *mesprises*
E les chosettes mesassises;
E cist mustre en verite
Quanque l'em ad *mespris* vers De.
Li mirurs mustre *adrescement*
Del cors, del vis, del vestement,
E cist *adresce*, co sachez,
Pensers e diz e volentez.
Li mirurs est pur enseigner
Cument hum se deit *atiffer*,
Cist enseigne veiraiement
Des vertuz *l'atiffement*.

[This book is called "Mirror";
now hear the reason for that.
One may see his outward appearance in a mirror,
and through this writing, his soul and body.
The mirror presents outward qualities,
and this, thoughts and intention.

The mirror shows mistakes
and little things that are wrong,
and this [book] shows, truly,
whatever one has done wrong toward God.
The mirror shows the correct disposition
of the body, the face, the clothing,
and this, you should know,
directs thoughts and speech and will.
The mirror is for teaching
how one should adorn oneself;
this teaches truly
the adornment of the virtues.]
(Robert of Gretham, *Miroir*, ll. 151–68; emphases added)

This account takes the familiar and already widespread image of the book as mirror—widespread, that is, in Latin literature—and explicates it with formal care. Robert uses an activity that he may have seen as particularly appropriate to a noblewoman, the assessment of one's body, face, clothing, and adornment in a mirror, to familiarize her with the book's function, using verbal repetition to hammer home the equivalence between external and internal self-scrutiny. The description is not just an account of the book and its aims but a small lesson in metaphor and interpretation probably intended in this, the earliest *vernacular* "Mirror," to assist an audience less familiar with this literary image.[40]

The passage's carefully repeated exegetical form—the mirror does this, the book that—and formal repetition are echoed in the sermons themselves: in the sermon for the fourth Sunday after Trinity, for example, Robert explains how the parable of the lost sheep is played out in the events of sacred history: "Il quist l'ome verraiement, / Quant home devint charnelment; / E il sa berbiz retrovat, / Quant home de pecché sanat; / En ses espaules le posat, / Quant pur nos pecchez se peinat" (He sought man, truly, when he became a man in the flesh; and he found his sheep again when he healed man of sin; he put it on his shoulders when he suffered for our sins).[41] Some remarks later in the prologue affirm that while the preacher or cleric certainly has a role in offering exposition, the interpretation of Scripture is also a skill that the audience can learn and practice. Having said that trees, when in leaf, do not give up their fruit easily but must be shaken, Robert expounds his exemplum:

Alsi est de saint escripture:
La lettre pert obscure e dure,
Mais qui i mettrat sun purpens
Pur veer l'espirital sens,
E si l'escut cum par espundre
Le bien ke Deus i volt respundre
Mult i verrat pumettes cheres,
Co sunt sentences de maneres;
E mult li savura bien
La dulcur dunt ainz ne solt rien.

[So it is with Holy Scripture:
the letter seems dark and difficult,
but whoever applies himself
in order to see the spiritual meaning,
and shakes it by expounding
the good that God wished to conceal there
will see from it many good little apples,
which are guides to good conduct;
and the sweetness of which he previously knew nothing
will taste wonderfully good to him.]
(Robert of Gretham, *Miroir*, ll. 205–14)

Robert later offers further explication of such a reading method: "E si re-
devum purpenser / E les miracles revolger / Si nus i poüm rien trover / Ki a
nos almes eit mester; / Kar ço k'il fist ja charnelment / A nos almes trestut
apent" (And so we should think hard and search the miracles [to see] if we can
find anything there that may be necessary for our souls; for everything he ever
did in the flesh applies entirely to our souls).[42] As this makes clear, "even"
moral theology, tropology, is a subject for careful thought (*purpenser*), part of
the work of exposition described in the prologue. Through the careful explication of method, readers are given the tools they need to understand not only
its letter but its spirit, to begin to gain the skills of *clergie*. The exemplarity of
the preacher's words and deeds that Honorius envisioned, and that Thomas
characterized as a book to be read, has here become a mirror-text that allows
the reader to see and reform herself, at least partly in the image of her teacher.

In aiming to provide his lay reader with clerical tools, Robert is typical not only of his time but also of his pastoral role: early attempts to encourage lay audiences in gaining the skills of the cleric are often associated with household chaplains like Robert himself or with the canons, who lived a life both regular and secular—"lower and closer to the world," as Honorius put it. Jocelyn Wogan-Browne has argued that an Anglo-French translation of Gregory the Great's *Dialogues* by the Augustinian canon Angier of St. Frideswide, from the early thirteenth century, provides a truly vernacular *accessus*, and access, to its scholarly material; Angier is "equipping his audience for their own reading."[43] Morgan Powell makes a similar point about Old French "texts that aspire to offer a lay public the experience of the cleric's reading," as he argues is the case with the Old French *Eructavit*, a paraphrase-cum-commentary on Psalm 44 written for Marie de Champagne, possibly by her household chaplain, Adam de Perseigne. This text, which its editor calls "essentially an unsystematic manual of Church dogma, interspersed with exhortations and bits of exegesis," is a reminder, like Robert's *Miroir*, of the blurred lines between biblical translation and interpretive instruction that characterize many of the texts considered here.[44]

Other aspects of Robert of Gretham's prologue reinforce the sense that this book's primary reader, Lady Aline, and its many other potential users were in a less static and hierarchical relationship to their teachers than the one envisioned by Honorius or even Thomas. The prologue begins by chastising the "trechere dame" for her love of frivolous secular reading and characterizes the *Miroir* as a corrective to and substitute for that vain pleasure, but it soon turns to an alternative account of the book's creation.[45] Robert extends the common request for the reader's prayers in a somewhat unusual way; after asking Aline to pray for him, he explains,

> Kar lealment, sachez de fi,
> En vos prieres mult me fi;
> Kar bien le sai k'a bon entente
> Deus s'abandune e presente.
> E vus altre feiz m'avez dit
> Que jo feisse cest escrit;
> Pur co, sachez, ne l'ai pas fait,
> Mais nostre entente ke Deu veit;
> Vostre est li biens, vostre e li los,
> Kar sanz vus penser ne l'os.

[because truly, you may be sure,
I have great confidence in your prayers;
for I know well that God
commits and offers himself to a good intention.
And you have said to me before
that I should write this;
therefore, you may be sure, it is not I who have made it,
but our intention, which God sees;
yours is the good of it, and yours the praise,
for without you I would not have dared to think of it.]
(Robert of Gretham, *Miroir*, ll. 95–104)[46]

This account seems to reverse the causation of the initial claim about the work's genesis, but of course Dame Aline's interests in frivolous and in instructive literature are not mutually exclusive; as many an academic could attest, one can enjoy both dark and difficult reading and the lighter pleasures of frothy fiction. What this passage conveys is the complexity of a relationship in which each side had a kind of capital the other lacked: the power of patronage and social status on the lady's side; the claim to higher learning and moral authority on the cleric's.[47] Like the many works from this period in which holy laywomen or nuns cooperated with confessors who both authorized and admired them, Robert's *Miroir* is in a sense, as he indicates here, a collaborative composition: without Aline's encouragement, he would not have undertaken it; without her piety and vernacularity, there would have been no use for it; it is the product of their shared "entente."[48]

The credit here given to a patron might be seen as merely part of a modesty topos, but Robert's consistent emphasis on his own limitations alerts us to the complex power of humility and the different ways in which it could be deployed. In the sermons of Stephen Langton, for example, we similarly see the "traditional comment on the preacher's unworthiness" used as a way to urge the audience's own contribution: calling himself a "sterile tree" (*arbor sterilis*), Langton begs his "popular or mixed" audience to say the Pater Noster lest his discourse fall short as a result of moral deficiency ("Et ideo rogo vos ut unusquisque dicat 'Pater Noster' ne verba mea efficatiam suam amittant propter enormitatem vite").[49] Here the solicitation of the audience's contribution recalls the idea that everyone must participate in his own salvation; the individual Christian is not just "God's helper" but the preacher's as well. Robert extends this valuation of his addressee's participation by ennobling the role of the language they share, saying,

Point de latin mettre n'i voil,
Kar co resemblereit orgoil;
Orgoil resemble veraiement
Co dire a altre qu'il n'entent.
E si est co mult grant folie
A lai parler latinerie;
Cil s'entremet de fol mester
Ki verrs lai uolt latin parler.
Chescun deit estre a raisun mis
Par la langue dunt il est apris.

[I do not wish to put any Latin [in this book],
for that would seem like pride;
it truly seems like pride
to say to someone something he does not understand.
And thus it is great folly
to speak Latinity to a layperson;
he who wishes to speak Latin to a layperson
undertakes a foolish task.
Each person should be addressed
in the language he has learned.]
(Robert of Gretham, *Miroir*, ll. 79–88)

The equation of Latin with pride makes vernacular teaching, by contrast, a mark of humility and opposes it to the "folie" of a useless show of knowledge, a move that emphatically disavows any sense of vernacular writing as less worthwhile than Latin and gives the French-speaking audience the moral upper hand.

The danger of dismissing modesty topoi is highlighted by the role of humility in Christian theology. Since humility was, par excellence, the virtue embodied in Jesus' Incarnation, and pride the sin of Satan, the moral weight being brought to bear on the choice of the vernacular here is considerable. The power and adaptability of the "myth" of kenosis, Christ's humble self-emptying and assumption of human nature, made it available, as Nicholas Watson has suggested, for both conservative and radical uses, and it is this model of descent that lies behind (and ennobles) claims to lowliness.[50] The implicit association of the teacher's task with Christ's is only strengthened when we note that if the Incarnation was, as many commentators suggested, the supreme instance of humility, it could also be seen as the supreme instance of translation, "a Word given form and made available to human sensibility."[51] The teacher who talks over the heads of his students serves nothing but his own vainglory; the teacher who speaks their language can not only tell them about the Incarnation but even, in a sense, reenact it, becoming, like the Word made flesh, a "maens . . . covenable" (appropriate means or intermediary) by which knowledge of God, and thus salvation, may travel.[52]

Nor is the teacher's humility the only productive form of this virtue. Elsewhere in the prologue Robert praises "rusticity," littleness, and other traditionally "lay" characteristics, saying, for example, "Mielz valt vair dire par rustie / Que mesprendre par curteis[i]e" (It is better to speak the truth clumsily than to err through courtesy, ll. 111–12). Later he asserts,

> E l'em ne deit pas aviler
> La persone que l'om ot parler.
> De bordel poet prodome issir
> E de chastel malveis saillir,
> E queique la pe[r]sone seit,
> Cil est pruz ke bien fait.
> Nul ne dit mielz pur richete
> Ne nul pis pur sa povrete;
> Ne cherir un ne altre despire
> Quant l'espirit, qui volt, espire.

> [One should not revile
> the person one hears speaking.
> A good man can come forth from a hut,
> and a bad one spring from a castle,
> and whatever sort of person he may be,
> he *is* good who *does* good.
> No one speaks better because he is rich,
> nor anyone the worse for his poverty;
> one should not value one or despise the other,
> when the spirit breathes where he will.]
> (Robert of Gretham, *Miroir*, ll. 565–74).

Much of this, again, echoes standard modesty topoi, but the density of allusion to tropes of humility and equality is notable; in another instance, Robert compares himself to Balaam's ass—a standard figure for unlearned, and thus vernacular, wisdom (ll. 491–94).[53] He seems to embrace the way in which "the teacher as *maître à penser* also embodies a posture of humility": in emphasizing the value of humility, his own and others', he is conveying both the content of a Christian truth (that the lowly will be exalted) and a model for practicing that truth, by being open to teaching from whatever direction it comes.[54] The *Dialogue du père et du fils* echoes this lesson through another fundamentally important model of the humble teacher, the apostles themselves: "eslust Deu a ses disciples povre gentz et nice et foles des sens del siècle qui erent povere peccheurs" (God chose as his disciples poor and simple people, and foolish in the wisdom of the world, who were poor fishermen). The author points out the "scorn" (*eschar*) that the rich had for "such common folk" (*tiel rascaille de poeple*), echoing Robert's warning to anyone who might undervalue teaching simply because of its origin.[55] Both images focus attention on status in order to associate the teacher with a lowly, rather than an exalted, position.

Robert's delicate awareness of the status issues raised by teaching is also visible in his mini-exegesis of Lamentations 4:4, "The little ones have asked for bread but there is no one to break it for them." Robert, like many others, interprets the passage as a critique of clergy who do not teach, but he uses the standard image of the laity as "little ones" in ways that undermine the implied, and widespread, association between lay status and childlikeness:

D'itels dit bien Saint Jeremie
Od grant dolurs en sa prophecie:
"Li petit del pain demanderent
Mais ki lur depescast ne troverent."
Suvent pain en sainte escripture
La doctrine d'alme figure,
Kar pain sustent la charnale vie
E sainte escripture l'alme vivifie.
Li petit sunt la lai gent
Endreit de co qu'a l'ordre apent;
Il sunt petit, mais en Deu nun,
Mais en umble subjectiun;
Kar par regard est cil petit
Qui obeist a altri dit.
Le pain demandent li petit
Quant li lai funt tut lur delit;

El mund fichent lur espeir
E mettent l'alme a nunchaleir.
Kar en cest liu estot demander
Autant cum il en unt mester.

[Of such people St. Jeremiah speaks
with great sorrow in his prophecy:
"The little ones have asked for bread
but have not found anyone to break it for them."
Often bread in Holy Scripture
represents spiritual instruction,
for bread sustains earthly life
and Holy Scripture gives life to the soul.
The little ones are the laypeople
with regard to their order;
they are little, but not in God,
rather in humble subjection;
for in a sense he is little
who obeys what another says.
The little ones ask for bread
when the laity do whatever they like;
they fix their hopes on the world
and don't care for their souls.
For in this place people must ask for
as much as they need.]
(Robert of Gretham, *Miroir*, ll. 287–306)

First of all, Robert assigns the laity a taste for solid food (rather than the "milk" more condescending versions of this trope prefer), and he then tackles directly the question of "order" and status.[56] In a spiritual sense, he points out, the laity are "little" not in God's eyes but because they are in "humble subjection." While that humble subjection is presumably to God's representatives, the clergy, as well as to God himself, the passage does not assert this, and the reference to God's perspective reminds us that earthly humility and subjection are signs of exaltation rather than lowliness, or of lowliness as exaltation.[57] As the *Pastoralet*, an Old French translation of part of Gregory the Great's *Cura pastoralis*, puts it, "Quant li humble se degettent et tienent vil, il montent lors ansi come Nostre Sires monta" (When those who are humble cast themselves down and consider themselves lowly, then they rise just as our Lord rose); Robert echoes this motif later in his work when he notes that, after Satan's prideful fall, "[P]ur celel osche restorer / Volt Deus en terre home furmer, / K'om munte par humilité / Là dunt orguil s'est dejeté" (God wished to form man on earth to restore the heavenly host, so that man might rise through humility to the place from which pride was cast down).[58] Seen in this eternal context, humility and littleness, whatever their negative associations, become also a necessary means of ascent. When, in the prologue passage, the "littleness" of the laity is associated with their pleasure in the world, even this becomes an implicit demand for bread, a kind of cry for help, and Robert's final point is that the laity should ask more directly for the spiritual guidance they need, should participate actively in the process of gaining spiritual understanding.

The "bread for the little ones" passage is also quoted early in the *Miserere* of the Renclus de Molliens, but in a way that highlights the unusual aspects of Robert's explication. The Renclus writes,

En un autre liu truis lisant
Dieu par le prophete disant
Contre les enfruns panetiers:
"Li petit vont lor pain querant,
Mais n'est ki fraigne au famillant
Le pain dont il est grans mestiers."
Ja mais mes pains nen iert entiers;
As povres, come lor rentiers,
Fraindrai mon pain d'ore en avant.
Car j'en voi tant par ches sentiers,
S'il en manjoient volentiers,
Il me feroient mout joiant.

[Elsewhere I find in my reading
God speaking, through the prophet,
against the miserly bread-sellers:
"The little ones go looking for their bread,
but there is no one who will break the bread
of which those who hunger have great need."
My bread will never be whole;
from now on I will break my bread

for the poor, as the recipient of their dues.
For I see so many of them on these paths
who, if they would willingly eat it,
would make me very happy.]
(*Miserere*, 134, strophe 2)

Here, as in his comment on priests as mirrors, the Renclus shows a more
conservative view of the role of the "little ones," though he also associates
them with the poor, diminishing the infantilizing implication of the passage
and augmenting their moral status. He gives a nod to his own indebtedness
to those he teaches as their *rentier*, one who receives payment from them,
another reminder of the mutual dependence of clerical teacher and lay
learner; but his imagination of the "little ones" casts them as receivers of the
bread (or teaching), not as participants in its transmission. For Robert of
Gretham, the indebtedness is deeper and broader; for him as for Bernard of
Clairvaux, the teacher, "*insipientibus debitor*, stands 'in debt to the foolish' as
well as to the wise (Rom. 1.14), needing their need for interpretation, aware
that in them the text is to be fulfilled."[59]

The relationship of mutual indebtedness between teacher and learner repeatedly leads Robert to backtrack, to refine, to shift between the multiple
possible meanings of his terms in an ongoing response to his imagined audience. Although his work does not take an explicitly dialogic form, like some
others considered here, his powerful awareness of its reception creates a sense
of exchange that is by no means limited to a particular listener or reader; while
the text has its origin in his relationship to Lady Aline, his addresses in some
sermons to "seigneurs" and his awareness that the book will outlive him mean
that his attention to hierarchy and humility reaches beyond the immediate
situation. The particular patron-chaplain interaction that animates parts of
the prologue is simply one manifestation of the complex interdependence of
teacher and student, an interdependence that obtains for preacher and audience as well as for chaplain and patron. Moreover, since texts like Robert's in
England or that of the Renclus in France circulated quite widely, their rethinking of the "bread for the little ones" motif and their sense of the teacher's
indebtedness to his audience, whether financial, intellectual, or moral, reached
audiences beyond any immediate addressee.[60] And even as Robert's more extensive learning allows him to instruct Lady Aline and the others who will
read his work, he acknowledges their "littleness" and humility as a virtuous
check on his own potential pride and depicts them as readers on their way to

attaining the knowledge he already holds and as interlocutors who shape how he uses that knowledge.

He also acknowledges that he and his immediate audiences are part of a larger chain of transmission and explicitly affirms that those who learn from him may go on to teach others. The prologue says,

> [E]npres chascune lezcun
> Ki ad del ewangelie nun
> Ai mis del exposiciun
> Un poi pur mustrer la raisun
> Ke hom le ewangelie puisse entendre
> E li nunlettrez bien aprendre.
> E chascun ki siet lettrure
> E de franceis la parleure
> Lire i poet pur sei amender
> E pur les autres endoctriner.

> [Beside each lesson
> that takes its name from the Gospel
> I have put a little explanation
> to show the meaning
> so that one may understand the Gospel
> and may teach the unlettered well.
> And everyone who knows how to read
> and how to speak French
> can read there to improve himself
> and to teach others.]
> (Robert of Gretham, *Miroir*, ll. 429–38)

Since Robert has made it clear that Aline is one who "siet lettrure" and is thus able to read the book he creates, presumably she is among those who can learn from his "exposiciun" of Scripture and pass it along, improving herself and teaching others.[61] He makes a similar point near the end of the prologue: "Ore pri jo de quor parfunt / Tuz cels ki cest escrit averunt / Qu'il le present a delivere / A tuz cels k'il voldrunt escrivre. / Kar custume est del Deu sermun: / Plus est cher cum plus est commun" (Now I pray, from the bottom of my heart, all those who will have this book, that they willingly lend it to all those who want to copy it. For this is the custom with the word of God: the more common it is, the more precious it is, ll. 635–40). Robert may be playing on a rhyming Latin proverb, "omne rarum carum" (everything rare is precious), which Thomas of Chobham considered well-known ("dicitur vulgariter"); such reversal of a traditional hierarchy is in keeping with the rest of the prologue.[62]

Later Robert concludes a sermon on John the Baptist (from Matt. 11:2–10) with a striking address to his audience:

> E vus repoez angles ester
> Si co que oez de vostre prestre,
> U en essample, u en sermun,
> Recuntez en vostre meisun;
> Si vus as autres recuntez
> Le bien ke vus oi avez.
> Quicunke nume rien de De
> En tant est angle de verite,
> E le chemin fet aprester
> Par ki puissum a Deu aler.
> Pur co, seignurs, partut contez
> Le bien ke vus oi avez;
> Endreit sei chescun tant en face
> Ke tuz veum la Jesu face. Amen.

> [And you can be angels
> if what you hear from your priest,
> whether in a story or in a sermon,
> you repeat at home;
> if you repeat to others
> the good that you have heard.
> Whoever talks about anything to do with God
> is in doing so an angel of truth,
> and makes ready the way
> by which we can go to God.
> Therefore, lords, tell everywhere
> the good that you have heard;
> may everyone do so much, for his own part,
> that we may all see the face of Jesus. Amen.]
> (Robert of Gretham, *Miroir*, ll. 1440–53)

The idea that laypeople can take what they have learned from sermons and repeat it to those at home is not revolutionary, but in the context of the prologue, which imagines the *Miroir* being transmitted through various combinations of speech and writing, it becomes part of a far broader effort at education performed jointly by clergy and laity—all the more so in its association of the laity with angels, messengers, and John the Baptist. Indeed, Robert has described his own role in terms very similar to those he uses to characterize his reader's: "Bien sai tant est grant la matire / Que jo ne pus a tuz suffire; / Mais mielz valt partie tucher / Pur mei e altres amender" (I know well that the material is so great that I cannot deal with it fully, but it is better to touch on it in part to improve myself and others, ll. 439–42). He and his audience are engaged in the same project of improving themselves through learning, whether heard or read, and then passing the lesson on to others, through writing or through speech. It is by mutual effort and a concerted willingness to make the word of God more precious, because more common, that teaching on earth enables both teachers and learners to face God.

Dallying with Friends: Pierre d'Abernon's *Lumere as lais*

Written some thirty years after Robert's *Miroir*, Pierre d'Abernon of Fetcham's *Lumere as lais* derives its title from its source, Honorius Augustodunensis's *Elucidarium*, rather than from the "Mirror" tradition, but like Robert's text it is notable in its attention to the lived encounter between teacher, student, and doctrine. Pierre, too, is closely connected with a lay audience; he was an Augustinian canon, a member of the "lower" and more secular group to which Honorius refers, and takes his surname, d'Abernon, from the lay patrons of the Fetcham living, to whom he may have been related. They may also have been among the "friends" for whom he wrote his *Light for the Laity* around 1267.[63] The presence of these nameless *especiaus amis* shapes his instruction; if Robert's prologue and sermons are attentive to the shifting status distinctions between himself and his patron, and emphasize the necessary humility and the joint endeavor that bind teacher and student, Pierre adopts even more equalizing terms, imagining the disciple as a fellow learner and emphasizing his affection for both that imagined speaker and the other "friends"— ultimately, all the book's readers—that he represents. In his affection and his desire to instruct, the teacher is again an imitator of Christ, whose similarity to humankind Pierre stresses as a means of knowledge. In answer to the disciple's question as to "why the Word was made flesh," the master says,

> Pur ceo ke humme charnel esteit
> Ne n'ama ne ne cunust a dreit
> For chose ke fust a li semblable;
> Pur ceo, pur amender, sanz fable,
> Sun estat, le fiz Deu prist
> Char, k'est sa parole dit,
> Ke cunuistre le pust [e] amer,
> Ke par tant pust sa joie aver.

> [Because man was fleshly
> and did not love nor rightly know
> anything but what was similar to him;
> therefore, in order to improve, in truth,
> his condition, the son of God took
> flesh, which is called his Word,
> so that one might know and love him,
> and could thereby have his joy.]
> (Pierre d'Abernon, *Lumere*, 1:138, ll. 4503–10)

Like Robert's association of the teacher with the sublime virtue of humility,
Pierre's evocation of Christ's likeness to humankind as the essential means to
"loving and knowing rightly" resonates with the teacher's assimilation to his
student and vice versa. That Pierre imagines the Incarnation in terms of likeness and even friendship—he later says that Christ was "semblable e ami / A
Deu e a humme ausi" (fellow and friend to God and also to man, ll. 4681–
82)—is in keeping with his *Lumere* as a whole, which envisions a teaching relationship grounded in these qualities.

   Like Robert, Pierre begins with a lengthy prologue that details his work's
form and intentions and highlights the complexities of vernacular *doctrina*.
He takes particular care to discuss the text's dialogue format, borrowed from
Honorius, whose *Elucidarium* takes this form; but Honorius makes only the
briefest of comments on his own dialogic mode, saying that he has "taken care
to transmit to posterity, in writing, the matters debated [*disputata*]."[64] Pierre
provides a more extensive account of the form of his work to enable the reader
to follow it; in this he adheres to current scholastic practice, as do some other

didactic works.[65] Immediately after explaining that the *Lumere* is divided into six books, and each book into chapters and distinctions, which are rubricated, Pierre describes the work's dialogue form: "Dunt cume deciple muef questiuns, / E pus cume mestre en faz respuns / Solum ceo ke Deu m'enseine / Par escripture, [e] reisun meine, / Kar plus i ad solaz, ceo semble, / Quant deus s'entredalient ensemble" (As a disciple I ask questions, and then as a master I give answers to them, according to what God teaches me in Scripture and as reason leads me, for there is more pleasure, it seems, when two people converse together, ll. 621–26). If Honorius's "disputata" assumes the audience's knowledge of the disputation/dialogue form, Pierre's careful explication of that form's mechanism makes it clear that he is presenting not only his ideas but their mode to an audience potentially unfamiliar with it. Like Robert of Gretham's discussion of how his metaphorical mirror works, Pierre's explanation is a reminder of the "intensely active and intensely self-aware" representation of teaching in medieval didactic texts and a further indication of the changing audience for such texts.[66] Pierre was not alone in feeling the need for such an explanation; a few manuscripts of the Continental *Dialogue du père et du fils*, for example, make a similar attempt to explicate their form, noting, "Cest livret est apelé dialogue pur ce que il est fait et ordené des paroles de deus, c'est dou pere qui son filz enseigne et dou filz qui au pere demande ce que il ne set" (This book is called "Dialogue" because it is made and arranged out of the words of two people, that is of the father who teaches his son and of the son who asks the father about what he does not know).[67]

The "solaz" that Pierre evokes also hints at a new audience and is clearly important to his sense of what he is doing; it appears again later in his account of the work's addressees and has already been used to sum up the book's aims: "Par iceste reisun cest livere faz, / Ke l'en put aprendre tut par le solaz" (I have made this book for this reason, so that one may learn with great pleasure, ll. 525–26).[68] Equally striking is his phrase "quant deus s'entredalient ensemble": the insistence on the duality of the encounter—"when two talk to one another together"—conveys in a compressed form the central importance of engagement between the interlocutors and the fundamental role this plays in teaching. The responsiveness to an interlocutor that we see in Robert of Gretham, the deep sense of responsibility, cooperation, and humility, here becomes an almost playful account of the instructive dialogue of master and pupil: the primary meaning of *entredalier* is "to debate," but its range of meaning also includes "to joust" and even "to embrace."

On one level, of course, the affectionate disputation is a fiction, as Pierre has openly acknowledged: "As a disciple I ask questions, and then as a master I give answers," he says, explicitly casting himself as both teacher and student. This dialogue-for-one-voice recalls the internal dispute that, as Stephen Justice has shown, constitutes Aquinas's sense of how belief itself works. As Justice puts it, "in belief, thinking accompanies the assent, remains continually vocal within it: the self is always potentially talking to itself, confronting assertion with doubt and doubt with assertion."[69] Dialogue texts acknowledge and represent that interior conversation, conveying Christian belief not as a finished or closed-off product but rather as a continuing process. In imagining the interlocutors as master and disciple (or father and son), however, they make the "bringing together of one thing with another" into a concrete scene, of a kind long found useful in Christian teaching.[70] Pierre's use of dialogue as a deliberate choice for Christian teaching, while based on his use of the *Elucidarium*, also looks back to Gregory the Great's *Dialogues*, in which Gregory praises his disciple Peter for asking simple questions. Gregory says that in "taking on . . . the feeling of the disorganized crowd" Peter is following the model of the "outstanding preacher" Solomon, in the book of Ecclesiastes, who similarly "impersonates" his audience in order to bring them "into harmony."[71] Pierre's self-conscious acknowledgment of the dialogue form also, of course, aims to show not the dissonance but the "harmony" of the topics the dialogue addresses. But because, unlike Gregory and Peter—who, like Honorius and his interlocutor in the *Elucidarium*, are both monks—Pierre's master and disciple are simultaneously lay and clerical, Latin speakers and French speakers, his adoption of the dialogue form is in a sense more beholden to, and more thoroughly shaped by, its disparate constituent voices.[72]

Any sense of "entredaliance" as an empty gesture toward cooperation is further undermined by the remainder of Pierre's prologue, which foregrounds the duality, the encounter, that the dialogue form inscribes in the text and uses this to frame an account of the differing kinds of knowledge or expertise among his imagined audience. Regarding the "general intention" (*fin generale*) of his work, he says it is "ke tutte gent / En fussent tretuz amendez / Ki l'averunt oi ou regardez" (that all people who have heard or seen it may be entirely improved by it, ll. 656–58) and then goes on to specify the "particular intention": "L'especiale fin, mun quer sent / Est pur solaz e amendement / De mes especiaus amis — / C'est la reisun pur quei le fis" (the particular intention, I say sincerely [lit. "my heart feels"], is for the pleasure and improvement of my particular friends—that is the reason I wrote it, ll. 659–62).[73] He finishes by saying that the "propre fin" for which he writes is to gain remission of his sins

from God and to have grace in his sight. Thus his purely self-interested mo-
tives are intertwined with his desire for the general good and his personal investment in his "especiaus amis," whose precise identity is never specified. If
the *Lumere* does not serve its "general" and "special" ends of improving both
its broad audience and Pierre's immediate audience, then presumably it will
not stand him in good stead with God; his own spiritual progress and reward
are interdependent with those of his audience.

While the immediate conversation of the *Lumere* reflects the sense of intimacy evoked by the references to *especiaus amis*, Pierre is clearly imagining
an audience beyond them, and one that at times is strikingly diverse for a text
of this complexity. He asks at the end of his text, "quanke orunt volunters cest
romanz, / Veux e jufnes, femme[s] e enfanz, / 'Amen' die devotement / A ceo
chescun" (let all those who willingly hear this work in French, old and young,
women and children, each devoutly say "Amen" to this [i.e., the prayer for the
author's soul], 2:199, ll. 13953–56). A deluxe early fourteenth-century manuscript of the *Lumere*, British Library, Royal MS 15.D.II, picks up on this varied
sense of audience. The initials of some of the work's chapters show the familiar
image of master and disciple in conversation; others depict various individual
faces, lay and clerical, male and female. Aden Kumler notes both the "partic-
ularized" quality of these representations—"Tonsured clerics, youths, bearded
laymen, young women with elaborately braided hair topped by floral chaplets,
and older matrons in veils"—and their size: "Unusually—even startlingly—
large, these inhabitants of the vernacular letter are masters and mistresses of
all they survey."[74] Even manuscripts less gorgeously illustrated than Royal
15.D.II, however, point to a lay readership, compiling the *Lumere* with works
whose lay audience is carefully specified or evoked. While it is impossible—
even for the author—to be certain of any given author's precise audience,
both Pierre's explicit comments in the *Lumere* and its early manuscript contexts suggest that his work, like Robert of Gretham's, genuinely had the potential to appeal across the lay-clerical spectrum, and not necessarily only to
readers wealthy enough to commission deluxe manuscripts. In Oxford,
Bodleian Library, MS Bodley 399, for example, the *Lumere as lais* appears
alongside (in a different, though contemporary hand) the emphatically lay-
directed *Kalendar* of Ralph of Lenham and Robert Grosseteste's *Chasteau
d'amour*; and British Library, Royal MS 16.E.IX contains an abbreviated version of the *Lumere* that begins with its critique of "rich people who do not
wish to serve God" ("De la riche gent ke nunt talent de servir deu," f. 3ʳ). The
potential for such texts as the *Lumere* to address the clergy is clear, and has

often been noted, but there seems no reason to disregard the work's own statement of its intended audience, and there were, as Ian Short has pointed out, "many areas of overlap and interdependence between what for our own convenience we categorise as the learned and lay cultures."[75] Works like Pierre's or Robert of Gretham's can help us see that interdependence in action and gain a sense of the emotional and intellectual energy that animated it.

The varied and interacting audiences that we sense in the prologue and in the manuscripts of the *Lumere* are further apparent in Pierre's discussion of his work's title. Here, even more forcefully than in the account of his intentions, we see the larger implications of his attempt to address and enlighten both "particular friends" and the faithful in general, as he turns to the crucial pairings of lay and clerical, Latin and vernacular. He writes,

"Lumere as Lais" l'ai numé
Pur [ceo] k'en puent estre esluminé,
Ne mie pur ceo, veraiment,
Ke clers ne puent ensement
Estre esluminé par regarder
Endreit de saver e endreit de amer,
Kar duble i ad esluminement,
De saver e de amer ensement.
De saver, kar meint en savera
Choses k'avant aparçu n'a;
Esluminé put estre de amur
Ki en quer le prent ver nostre Seignur;
Pur ceo en puent, en veritez,
Clers e lais estre esluminez.

[I have called it "Light for the Laity"
because they can be enlightened by it,
not, indeed, because
clerks cannot also
be enlightened by looking [at it]
as regards knowing and loving,
for there is a twofold enlightenment:
through knowledge and through love.
Through knowledge, since many will know by this
things that they have not before perceived;

those may be enlightened by love
who take it to heart as regards our Lord;
thus, indeed, may
both clerks and laypeople be enlightened.]
(1:19, ll. 671–84)

As is the case also for Robert of Gretham, the categories "lay" and "cleric" seem here to have an uneasy, though by no means antagonistic, relationship. The repetitions of the passage and the double negative ("not because clerks cannot also be enlightened") hint at the potential tension of the lay-cleric relationship, offering an attempt at balance that looks nervously toward imbalance. The somewhat awkward way in which Pierre interrupts his rationale for naming the book in honor of the laity, in order to assure us that the clergy may also benefit from it, suggests his attempt to manage both the history of instruction in which he stands and that provides his title and the pastoral circumstances in which he finds himself, which have determined the shape of his work. As in the *Miroir*, written instruction in the vernacular has the inevitable, if implicit, effect of drawing the laity toward a clerical stance by giving them the opportunity to ponder and interpret doctrinal material.[76]

Moreover, the pairing—not, we may note, the opposition—of *amer* and *saver* in this passage further resists any sense of definitive hierarchy; while the clergy might have wanted to lay claim to knowledge, they would surely not have wanted to cede love to the laity. In a sense, the two terms' relationship is one of dynamic fluidity, recalling the similarly dynamic relationship between languages in this period.[77] Pierre treats love and knowledge as coexistent and, it would seem, mutually reinforcing—"duble i ad esluminement"—though the placement of this assertion implies that it is *because* enlightenment is not simply a matter of the intellect that the *Lumere* is appropriate for clerks. And while Pierre is careful not to suggest any sort of hierarchy between the terms, there can be no question that, if there must be a hierarchy, from a Christian perspective love will prevail: "If I speak with the tongues of men and angels and have not love . . . I am nothing," as St. Paul says (1 Cor. 13:1). The entirety of Pierre's work, however, generated out of his love for his particular friends, insists on the conjoining of love and knowledge, even when—as here—it acknowledges the difficulties raised by their conjunction.

Pierre's slightly anxious efforts to account for both clergy and laity, love and knowledge, are echoed in other, similar works. Consider the beginning of

Adam of Exeter's French exposition of the Pater Noster, probably from the
first quarter of the thirteenth century:

> Suvent avient ke amur crest par conisance, kar ço ke nul ne seit ne
> purra legerement amer. Dunc sachez ke home taunt cume il entent
> e veit plus de la verité e del ben, taunt plus l'eime e plus en a joie.
> Por ce sunt gent de religiunt ki clers sunt mot a eise quant il enten-
> dent les paroles k'il dient en lur oreisuns. E vus femmes de religion
> avez a la fiez en ce defaute quant vus n'entendez pas ceo ke vus dites
> en vos oreisuns. Nel di pas par ceo ke vus n'eez autant joie e devo-
> ciun en vos oreisuns cume les clers, einz crei vereiment ke vos en eez
> autant u plus, kar joie espirital ne vent pas de saver, ainz fet d'amer
> nostre tresduz Seignor Jesu Crist. Einz le di pur ceo ke, quant vos
> preez nostre tresduz Seignor Jesu Crist, mot vodriez volentiers en-
> tendre en vostre quer ceo ke vus dites de buche pur la amur ke vos
> avez a nostre tresduz Seignor a ki vus parlez.

> [It often happens that love grows on acquaintance, for no one can
> easily love that which he does not know. So you must see that the
> more a man understands and sees truth and goodness, the more he
> loves and rejoices in it. This is why religious who are educated are
> very pleased when they understand the words they speak in their
> prayers. And you religious women sometimes have this shortcom-
> ing, that you do not understand what you say in your prayers. By
> this I do not mean that you have less joy and devotion in your
> prayers than the clerks have; I truly believe you have as much or
> more, for spiritual joy does not come from knowledge, but rather
> from loving our dear Lord Jesus Christ. Rather, I say this because
> when you pray to Our Lord Jesus Christ, you earnestly wish to un-
> derstand in your hearts what you are saying with your lips, for the
> love you feel for our dear Lord whom you are speaking to.][78]

I quote at length because this passage takes such care to balance the claims of
love and knowledge, and to address, implicitly, the questions they raise: if love
must prevail, then why bother with knowledge? If knowledge is important,
does that lessen the stature of those who have only love? Adam's words to the
"femmes de religion" who are his primary addressees suggest how a particular
audience might have received the attempt to articulate the relationship of love

to knowledge—possibly, it seems, by taking offense at the suggestion that their limited knowledge impinges on their love. Adam resolves this by making knowledge both grow out of and contribute further to love, in an endless and productive cycle.

Adam argues for knowledge as enabling and deepening an already existing love on the part of those schooled at least in the verbal repetition of doctrine. But the role of knowledge arises all the more pressingly for those cut off from such learning. This is the focus in one manuscript of the *Petit sermon*, another didactic work in French verse from the first half of the thirteenth century. British Library, Cotton MS Domitian A.xi. has a unique prose prologue that reads,

> Pur ceo ke la rien ke seit ke homme put fere en ceste vie dunt
> homme put melz plere a Dieu si est amour ordiné adreit, sicum
> Saint Poul li apostle e autres seintes tesmoynent en le evangel, meis
> laye gent ne entendent pas le evangel pur ceo ke ceo est latin, si est
> le evangel translaté hors de latin en franceys al aprise de lay gent,
> sanz quele aprise nus homme put ester salvé.[79]

> [Since the thing most pleasing to God that a man can practice in this
> life is rightly ordered love [*amour ordiné adreit*], as St. Paul the apos-
> tle and other saints bear witness in the Gospel, but lay people do not
> understand the Gospel, because it is in Latin, thus [here] the Gospel
> is translated out of Latin into French for the instruction [*aprise*] of
> lay people, without which instruction no one can be saved.]

This prose prologue both anticipates and attempts to contextualize the first lines of the *Petit sermon*, which give a loose translation of 1 Corinthians 13:1, by clarifying their ultimate goal (rightly ordered love of God) and accounting for the work's French form. The text itself (which appears without prologue in the other nine manuscripts) begins,

> Seynt Poul li apostle dit—
> Sicum nus trovum en son escrit—
> Il dit, si homme ust chescun bien
> Si amour ne ust ne serreyt rien,
> Kar ja ne eit homme tant des vertuz,
> Sil n'eit amur, trestut est muz. (f. 89[ra])

[St. Paul the apostle says—
as we find in his writing—
he says, if a man had every good quality
and did not have love, he would be nothing,
for no matter how many virtues a man has,
if he does not have love he is completely mute.]

The supreme importance of love is acknowledged once again but turned to a slightly different purpose through the prologue's implication that a lack of knowledge can lead to "disordered" love. As for Adam of Exeter, love is the justification for knowledge, but here that knowledge is being made available to a different audience, the laity who, as much as professed religious, need love informed by knowledge.

The emphasis on rightly ordered love and its grounding in instruction in the *Petit sermon* resembles Pierre's presentation of the *Lumere* as "ordered" both formally and spiritually. Discussing the work's structure, he accounts for its main sections, then notes, "Les parties principaus noumez / Ai en sis livres ordinez" (I have arranged these principal parts into six books, *Lumere* 1:16, ll. 581–82), and he makes clear that both the book's content and its form are organized around "Jhesu Crist nostre Seignur": "A lui cum chef est ordiné" (it is ordered with him as its head, l. 568). This is both because Christ is creator and creature, and thus contains in himself all that the book might touch on, and because the book orients itself toward him by teaching one to avoid sin and pursue virtue (ll. 553–60, 569–70). "Dunt tut receit ordeinement / De Jhesu Crist, quanke al livere apent" (Thus everything that belongs to this book receives its arrangement from Jesus Christ, ll. 571–72): this is true both of everything as it appears within the text and simply of *everything*, since the work aims to capture the entirety of Christian knowledge. The book replicates the world, imitating and attempting to further the ordering of the world according to God.[80] The emphasis on right order refers ultimately not only to the orderliness of the book itself—important in both the *Manuel des pechiez* and the *Lumere*, among others—but also to the orthodoxy of its teachings and to the need to convey them as widely as possible. As Isidore of Seville wrote, "Orthodoxy is believing rightly [*recte*], and as one believes, living rightly."[81] If laypeople are to live rightly, to have rightly ordered love, as the *Petit sermon* says, then they must have rightly ordered teaching.

This centrality of order is another inheritance from the twelfth century, when, as Bernard McGinn puts it,

The theme of the ordering of love (or better, the "reordering" in our present fallen state of the love that should have been ours) took on a heightened importance. . . . To set charity in order was both a theoretical task and a practical task, involving knowing both what needed to be done and how to do it. Thus, the ordering of charity depended on grasping the proper relation between love and knowledge.[82]

Thirteenth-century works of doctrinal instruction for the laity could be seen as the fullest extension of this theoretical and practical task, as charity demanded that love and knowledge be exercised jointly to produce orderly and rightly directed biblical or doctrinal translation into French verse, a clerical mode turned into a vernacular one. These authors go further, however, not merely practicing the conjoining of love and knowledge but producing, for their lay audiences, meditations on these paired terms that saw them as mutually informing.

Pierre returns to this crucial pairing in a section of his work that discusses whether we can know what would have happened if there had been no Fall. Here and elsewhere, he casts a wistful eye at the possibility of knowledge without study, which he has earlier identified as a characteristic of angels: "Sanz travail e sanz estudie / Les ars seivent e ph[i]losophie" (without labor or study they know the arts and philosophy, *Lumere* 1:42, ll. 1355–56).[83] He asserts that had there been no original sin, "Scien[ce] eust eu humme e cointise / En tuttes choses sanz aprise" (Man would have had knowledge and awareness of all things, without instruction, 1:79, ll. 2509–10). The remainder of this lengthy response by the master on the consequences of original sin returns repeatedly to the loss of knowledge as one cataclysmic outcome, part of a larger loss of effortlessness: we cannot recover the "estat" that Adam lost for us without a combination of God's grace and "grant labur" on our own part, and the recovery will only be in the next world:

Ne pleinement n'i avendrum mie
Tant cume sumus en ceste vie,
Kar avant ceo ke ici pussum saver
Clergie, covient mut travailier,
Mes ja pur quanke nul purra
Travailier, ja ne savera
Quanke est a saver a dreit,

Ja de si bon engin ne seit,
Ne ja tant ne vive lungement
Ke pust aprendre quanke i apent.

[Nor will we fully have [Adam's state]
so long as we are in this life,
for before we can be learned here
a great deal of work is required,
but no matter how much one may work
he will never know
what it is to know truly,
no matter how clever he may be,
nor will he ever live long enough
to be able to learn all that belongs to it.]
(1:80, ll. 2543–52)

The passage laments both the difficulty of obtaining knowledge in our fallen
state and its inevitable inability to save us: it is a necessary but not a sufficient
condition. The only solution, the master emphasizes, in a passage of unusually
sustained anaphora, is to take great pains to combat the evils of the world "Par
repentance e orisuns, / Par penance e confessiuns, / E par amoune suvent
duner, / Par fei, par espeir, par Deu amer, / Par ces choses si entera / En bonté
cil ki bien lé fra" (by repentance and prayers, by penance and confessions, and
by frequent almsgiving; by faith, by hope, by loving God: through these, he
who does them well will enter into blessedness, 1:81, ll. 2561–66). The detailed
focus on right *practice*, rather than right knowledge, is unusual in Pierre's text
and implicitly reinforces the limits of knowledge; yet it is only through perfect
knowledge, the master goes on (in reply to a further question from the disciple), that we attain perfect love: "nul ne l'aime pleinement / For cel ki pleinement l'entent, / Kar de la pleniere cunisance / Plenier amur vient, sanz
dutance" (none loves him fully except him who understands him fully, for
from fuller knowledge comes fuller love, without doubt, ll. 2591–94). And the
pursuit of such knowledge requires both labor and love.[84]

Perfect knowledge, of course, remains out of reach here, for "ici nostre
Seignur / Ne veum, for cum en mirur / Ki fust mis en un oscurté / Ne mie
pleinement en clarité" (here we do not see our Lord, except as in a mirror that
is placed in darkness and not in full clarity, 1:82, 2599–2602), and so we cannot love God fully; but "au ciel le verum, si li plest, / Face a face sicume il est,

/ E dunc l'amerum parfitement, / Par unt bons serum pleinement" (in Heaven we will see him, if it pleases him, face to face just as he is, and then we will love him perfectly, whereby we will be fully good, ll. 2605–8). There is a note of longing throughout this section that powerfully conveys the emotional importance, for Pierre, of learning, knowledge, *clergie*—and the simultaneous awareness that these things are valuable as means, rather than ends, and that their true end is not available in this world. Both in the limitations of his learning, which are inevitable in earthly life, and in his need for love, which is a quality equally available to clergy and laity, the master is assimilated to his disciple; together they look, and travel, toward a moment of fulfillment. The evocation of the effortless knowledge and perfect love that souls will have in Heaven echoes the similarly intense entwining of love and knowledge in the prologue to give a glimpse, for a moment, of the master's own desire, the love of God that depends on knowledge and that, joined with love of "particular friends," drives him to teach.

The need for both clergy and laity to strive for knowledge as complete as possible, as a means toward a fuller and truer love, is the driving force of the *Lumere*, and Pierre does not just pay lip service to his lay audience's capacity for enlightenment. In his wholesale importation of scholastic modes into his lay text—which Glynn Hesketh calls "very probably the first work in French to apply these methods to theological writing in the vernacular"—and also in the topics that he treats, Pierre is willing not only to give his readers implicit credit but to allow them access to material often considered off limits in texts addressed to laypeople.[85] While many works of "basic" instruction offer subtle insight into such fundamental theological complexities as the Incarnation, the Redemption, and the workings of grace, Pierre goes further, tackling even such admittedly tricky issues as God's foreknowledge of salvation and damnation. The disciple raises this matter, in an unusually lengthy question (1:27–28, ll. 907–36), and the master at first demurs, but quickly gives way:

Saciez ke ceste question
Must est fort en desputeisun.
Pur ceo n'oi avant en penser
A la[i] ceste questiun ren tucher,
E si vodrai meuz autri reisun
Oir e lur solusiun
Ke respundre devant lai gent
Ce ke a pure clerigé apent.

. . . .
Mes pus k'il vus veint a pleisir,
Pur vostre volunté acumpler
Une respunse vus tucherai
Cume en franceis meuz purrai;
[E si en suy mut plus hardi
Pur ceo k'en vostre bon sen m'afi,
Kar ne eusiez ceste questiun
Muwe si ne eusez grant reysun].

[You should know that this question
is hotly disputed.
For that reason, I did not plan
to discuss it at all with a layperson,
and I would prefer to hear other questions,
and their solutions,
than discuss before laypeople
what is a matter of pure clergy.
. . . .
But since it pleases you,
to fulfill your wishes
I will sketch an answer for you
as best I can in French;
and I am the bolder in doing so
because I have faith in your good sense,
for you would not have asked this question
if you did not have a good reason.]
(1:28–29, ll. 937–44, 947–54)[86]

This elaborate framing of what was, indeed, a hotly disputed question is the more striking in that the chapter "shows every sign of being an original interpolation," so that not even the faint pressure to be faithful to a source can account for its presence.[87] Apparently Pierre wanted, for whatever reason, to put this material into French.

At the end of the chapter, having offered a reasonably coherent Boethian answer to the question that emphasizes each individual's responsibility for his or her own fate, he concludes, "[A]utre sentence meuz vodraie / Ici entur oir ke la meie, / Dunt si de bon clerc e de bon devin / Le mei enveez en latin, / Mut volenters le translaterai / En franceis al meuz ke jo sai" (I would prefer to hear another opinion about this than my own, so if you send me one by a good clerk or theologian in Latin, I will very willingly translate it into French as best I can, 1:31, ll. 1051–56). The attention to translation that begins with the prologue and surfaces again here continues elsewhere in the work; at a later point, the disciple says, "Mestre, si vus vient a talent, / Dite mei entendablement / K'est a dire 'contemplacion,' / E ceo ke vus apelez 'action,' / Ke il me semble, par mun devin, / Ke c'est un franceis latin!" (Master, if you would be so kind, tell me in terms I can understand what "contemplation" means and what you are calling "action," because it seems to me, in my estimation, that this is Frenchified Latin! 2:4–5, ll. 7181–86). The master acknowledges the alleged neologism, which touches on an area sometimes deemed too advanced for lay readers, but again, after this disclaimer, goes on to give an approximation.[88]

Pierre seems, that is, acutely aware of the implications of translating into the vernacular but also quite willing to expose "pure clergé" to the inquiring gaze of a vernacular audience—precisely, he says, because he knows and has faith in the disciple's good sense.[89] While a limited address to a single, known interlocutor would arguably mitigate the dangers of treating such explosive issues, the fictional aspects of that address, and the written work's ability to move beyond its original context, suggest a broader faith in whatever audiences the text will eventually reach. In a similar vein, the passage shows again the impossibility of disentangling the work's clerical and lay audiences and addressees: if the interlocutor's "real" clerical status is betrayed by the request that the disciple send a better Latin version, the existence of an audience interested in and capable of appreciating fine points of doctrine, but only in the vernacular, is also assumed. At the same time, Pierre, both in his role as inquiring student (when he speaks as the disciple) and in his offer to be corrected (when he speaks as the master/author), reminds us of his status as one who has, in his time, been the disciple and who continues to engage with that role—in part by acknowledging the limits of his own learning—as well as taking his place as a *magister*.[90] The author's dual identity and its implications for the role of the disciple (as one who is and is not identified with the master) point again to the openness of dialogue as a form that allows a reader or hearer to identify with either position in the conversation. As Jean-Claude Schmitt observes,

At least in theory, the conditions of the "*majores*" and "*minores*" were not fixed, since "the succession of times" seemed marked by a growing explication of faith: here again the model, borrowed from

Gregory the Great . . . was initially historic, but it applied also to the progress of the faith in the life of a single person. . . . This "progressivist" conception of the faith could not but encourage the apostolic efforts of the Church in the thirteenth century.[91]

Pierre d'Abernon's use of dialogue to present both an ordered overview of Christian history and an inquiry into the aspects of Christian belief that might attract the interest of an eager learner conveys a similarly "progressivist" view of his audiences, known and yet to come. In both form and content, he displays the love of knowledge and the knowledge of love that ideally link teacher and student.

As we saw above, Pierre imagines the interdependence of love and knowledge culminating in the moment when one sees God face-to-face, a moment that remains always beyond reach. The image conveys, as do the ends of many of his chapters, how powerfully present this moment was to his imagination and how strongly it motivated his teaching.[92] That the emphasis here falls on love, rather than on fear, presents the teaching project of the thirteenth century in a hopeful mode that, I suggest, we must recognize as an essential counterbalance to its better-known minatory forms: learning comes "by faith, by hope, by loving God," as Pierre puts it. Like Robert of Gretham's rejection of the prideful use of incomprehensible Latin, or his evocation of the value of littleness, the emphasis we see in Pierre, or Adam of Exeter, or the *Petit sermon* on love as a companion to knowledge, knowledge as a means to love, echoes the closeness and exchange between laity and clergy that shaped the pastoral efforts of the thirteenth century. Depicting the process of learning that which cannot truly be known, these texts insist on that process as a cooperative and mutually responsive one in which the laity begin to take on a new role and status as educated Christians, even if their spiritual progress, like that of their masters, can never reach its ideal fulfillment in this life. As we will see in the next chapter, however, the bond between teacher and student that these instructional texts insist on can—like the book that outlasts its author—extend to, and even beyond, the moment of death.

Chapter 2

Teaching Death: Narrative Assimilation and the Point of Distinction

The sense of connection and even assimilation between teacher and learner that we see embodied in many doctrinal and didactic texts of the twelfth and thirteenth centuries presents the project of learning as in many ways a hopeful one. Even as these texts emphasized the face-to-face moment of teaching, however, they looked implicitly toward another such moment, the moment of death and individual judgment when every person comes face-to-face with God. This confrontation could be characterized, as it is in 1 Corinthians 13:12, as the perfection of knowledge: "We see now through a glass in a dark manner; but then face to face. Now I know in part; but then I shall know even as I am known." Before the advent of such perfect knowledge, however, those on earth remained uncertain not only about their own fate but about the fate of those gone before. Discussing suffrages for the dead, the late twelfth-century theologian Raoul Ardent emphasizes this lack of knowledge: "But we, brothers, who do not know who has need [of prayers and suffrages] and who does not . . . we must offer prayers, alms, and masses for all, including those for whom we have no certainty."[1] The careful attention to this topic in the twelfth and thirteenth centuries points to a broad desire for knowledge of death and the afterlife, a curiosity about hidden things. This desire is clearly part of a larger push for the accumulation and categorization of knowledge in the period and is attended to in works that, like the secular encyclopedias that examined earthly categories and phenomena, aimed to organize religious teaching. Strikingly, however—though perhaps unsurprisingly, given the uncertainty that necessarily attends the topic—the nature of death and judgment is most consistently explored by way of narrative.

The usefulness of stories in this context suggests how easily the general wish for greater certainty about (and ability to categorize) the status of the deceased could become focused on particular cases, since every living person had a stake in this question. Medieval religious teaching represented the scene of death and judgment, the point at which the individual's salvation or damnation was decided, not only as its own ideal supersession—the moment when all teaching is subsumed in perfect knowledge—but as its motivating force: one must learn here on earth so that one may be saved at the moment of judgment. The individual judgment and its aftermath, the mysteries of salvation and damnation, repeatedly feature in didactic and imaginative texts that convey Christian doctrine. Their presence there could be attributed to a desire to terrify and discipline the laity, but surely it is also possible that there was a desire to receive as well as impart such knowledge; perhaps the only thing worse than knowing about Hell is *not* knowing about it. This possibility is reinforced by the way in which the individual's death and judgment are portrayed: rather than insisting on terror and solitude, or on beatitude and community, these depictions often present a meeting between individuals, a scene of instruction in which the desire to know more, the desire for certainty, is answered by a familiar interlocutor or modeled by an exemplary figure. Such narratives draw attention to the relationship between formal and informal education, asking what modes of instruction are most effective and who can offer such teaching. Since the perfect understanding granted by death inevitably surpasses any earthly knowledge, they can also upend the earthly status distinction between two people, particularly if they were master and student on earth.

The question of earthly versus heavenly status and the relationship of master and pupil in the light of eternity are exemplified in a widely told late medieval revenant story. A version appears in the trilingual miscellany Bodleian Library, MS Laud miscellaneous 471, from the late thirteenth or early fourteenth century, which contains a variety of didactic and devotional texts, including Robert Grosseteste's *Chasteau d'amour* and some of Maurice de Sully's French homilies; the short Latin narrative is marked by a pointing hand in the margin of the manuscript. It tells of a Paris master of arts who

> begged a sick student very dear to him to return, if possible, after his death, in the meadows of Saint-Germain at a certain day, place, and time. In the appointed place the master saw him dressed in a cape of parchment minutely covered with letters. He asked him

about his condition [*statum suum*], and the student replied that he was gravely afflicted because the smallest letter was heavier than the towers of Saint-Germain, "And if you wish to know how severe the punishment is, you can feel a part of mine from the fire in which I burn: just feel a drop of my sweat." Stretching out the master's hand, he cast on it a drop that pierced it faster than a sword, and all his life this hole was visible and could not be cured. And the master made these verses: "I leave croaking to the frogs, cawing to crows, and vain things to the foolish. I hasten to the logic that does not fear the 'therefore' of death." And returning home, he immediately entered the Cistercian order.

[Quidam magister arcium parisiensis] rogavit discipulum egrotantem sibi valde carum ut si posset esse rediret ad eum post mortem in pratis sancti Germani, prefixa die, loco, et tempore. Loco dicto, vidit eum magister indutum capa de percamena minutissim[e] litter[ata]. Quesivit ab eo statum suum, qui respondit se ita graviter affligi, quod minima littera erat gravior quam turris sancti Germani, "Et si vis scire quam gravis est pena, meum de igne quo ardeo poteris sentire aliquid: sed guttam de sudore meo senties." Et porrecta palma, projecit sibi guttam, que velocius telo manum perforavit. Et in tota vita eius apparuit foramen nec potuit sanari. Et fecit hos versus: "Linquo coax ranis, [cras] cornix, vanaque vanis. Ad logicam pergo [que] mortis non timet ergo." Et domum rediens, statim intravit ordinem cister[ci]ensem.][2]

Such a story falls easily into the category of those that sought to convey the inexpressible horrors of Hell and Purgatory as a way to frighten the faithful into good behavior; recent scholarship might also encourage us to see in it the punitive aspects of medieval teaching, the marks it leaves on the body.[3] The tale clearly also offers a critique of the worldly learning of the schools as against the greater wisdom of religious devotion. But it has another aspect, perhaps the more visible in light of the works discussed in the previous chapter, that is equally or more important to its meaning: the affection that links teacher and student, emphasizing the importance of experience and personal connection in teaching even as it denigrates the dangers of "empty" learning. It demonstrates the irrelevance of earthly status while insisting on the persistence of earthly affections: the student's status is now eternally fixed but in a way that enables him to help others escape the same fate; he becomes, through painful experience, his teacher's teacher.

To consider medieval instruction about the moment of death and its aftermath in light of the relationship between student and teacher is to see a more hopeful vision of the "last things"—death, judgment, Heaven and Hell—than is usually attributed to the Middle Ages. Since any religious teaching had the ultimate goal of salvation, it was only at the moment of an individual's death—a moment that became an increasing focus of attention in the twelfth and thirteenth centuries—that teaching could truly be judged. At the same time, most teaching took place, of necessity, prior to that moment and could invoke it only as an event of uncertain temporal proximity. As a result, death is in a sense the ultimate "teachable moment," both the subject of much instruction and the imagined scene of its completion, and its links to teaching are deep and indissoluble. The story of the student returned from Hell, while it invokes the unspeakable torments there, does so as part of a lesson that is about love as well as death, about the ability to reach across a boundary to instruct, and save, another person.

If we take death and terror to be the focus of medieval instruction, that is, we mistake the means for the ends; as Jane Gilbert has observed, damnation is an important concept for medieval people, but "it by no means dominates medieval literature in French and English."[4] The story above, and many others like it, concludes not with death and torment but with rescue by teaching: instruction is as crucial an element of medieval conceptions of death as death is of instruction, and it is teaching that has the last word. The many scenes of deathbed conversion, visions of the afterlife, and accounts of last-minute rescue that we find in medieval texts, and especially those of this period, need not point exclusively to a culture of "sin and fear."[5] They can serve, instead, as a kind of thought experiment, one that places the audience of such a story in a paradoxical position: in order to function, depictions of death must simultaneously invoke the listener's similarity to as well as his or her difference from the protagonist of the story. By presenting as teacher a familiar figure, one who has shared the experiences of his or her still-living student, these tales use similarity to create a different ending, a different fate for the survivor than he or she might otherwise have had. In evoking this simultaneous similarity and difference, they also draw in—like the story of the master and his disciple—the question of how the story's teller, the actual teacher, is implicated by the narrative, in what way he too might be like or unlike the figures in the story, like or unlike his hearer.

The ability of death to highlight the problematic issue of earthly status is not limited to didactic texts; Neil Cartlidge observes, in a discussion of the thirteenth-century romance *Amadas et Ydoine*, "The difference between life and death . . . might be just as much a matter of degree and purpose as the difference between the various 'orders' or estates of medieval society." As he points out, "the possibility of collapsing some of the fundamental categories of existence" by questioning the distinction between life and death "is possibly not quite so unmedieval as it might seem, for the disruption of those categories is essential to the narrative of Christianity itself, which insists on the eventuality of resurrection in a way that is deliberately oxymoronic."[6] That essential duality or instability of death in Christian theology and thus in Christian teaching, the ability of death to turn back on itself and become life, relies, for the individual believer, on effective instruction. Death is generative, but it can become so only if it is brought before the face of the learner, if it is made visible. And the most effective way of making it visible, it would seem, is by confronting the audience with a familiar, or at least a recognizable, face.

Recognition, of course, can be both reassuring and menacing. A narrative from the *Manuel des pechiez* emphasizes the positive aspects: here we are told of two knights who "cherement se entre ameient" (loved one another dearly). One dies but returns, on a moonlit night, to find his friend lying awake; the scene of their confrontation is depicted in Princeton University Library, Taylor MS 1, which contains an illustrated *Manuel des pechiez* copied for a noblewoman (Figure 3).[7] The surviving knight, seeing a ray of light that resembles "celuy qe aveit si chier" (him whom he had held so dear), wonders if it is a phantom, but the friend "qe il ad tant amé" (whom he so loved) comforts him, saying that he has only come to ask for help in alleviating his torments.[8] The living friend promises to do so and the dead man touches his arm to help him remember, piercing it to the bone; the wound, though incurable, does not hurt the survivor. This narrative, unlike the one with which I began, emphasizes the departed friend's "estat" and request for help rather than the conversion of the survivor, but like that other it makes death a porous boundary across which those who love one another can still provide instruction or aid; indeed, the story specifies, "Mult li valust le visiter, / Sachez, del mort chivaler, / E al mort, autresi, / Car le vif fist prier pur li" (The visit of the dead knight helped him [i.e., the survivor] very much, you may be sure, and also [helped] the dead man, for he caused the living one to pray for him, *MP* Roxburghe ll. 2719–22, *MP* EETS ll. 2745–48). Such episodes are characteristic of the effort to establish the doctrine of Purgatory, and the need for the living to lighten

Figure 3. A knight returns from the dead to visit his beloved friend.
Manuel des pechiez, Manuscripts Division, Department of Rare Books and Special Collections,
Princeton University Library, Taylor MS 1, f. 31ʳ (detail).

the suffering of the dead through prayer, but comparison with the story of the master and student and the assurance here that the visit benefits the living as well as the dead friend remind us that such exempla are also part of a larger body of teaching in which death becomes a source of instruction and a means to express the strength of an affective bond.[9]

The instruction enabled by death and eternal fate does not always promise help to the sufferer, however, or emphasize Purgatory; a key example here is the story of Dives and Lazarus, also included in the *Manuel*. Like the story of the two knights, it is equipped with a marginal image in Princeton University Library, Taylor MS 1. Dives, in the lower right corner of the folio, looks up at Lazarus, who is tucked in the bosom of Abraham like a baby in a sling (Figure 4). Lazarus looks off to one side or perhaps up at Abraham, Abraham straight ahead and slightly upward, neither of them regarding Dives at all. Recognition after death is not enough; conversion or rescue depends on a bond created in life. Here it is not Dives, who comes to true recognition too late, but the viewer for whom this familiar story puts a face on the need for a

Figure 4. Dives looking at Lazarus
in the bosom of Abraham.

Manuel des pechiez, Manuscripts Division,
Department of Rare Books and Special
Collections, Princeton University Library,
Taylor MS 1, f. 59ʳ (detail).

virtuous and charitable life. The depiction—verbal or visual—of Dives and
Lazarus also personalizes an abstract concept, the idea that those in Hell could
see those in Paradise, and in this way as well makes the afterlife more easily
apprehensible.[10]

The face-to-face scene of instruction emphasized by the miniatures that
head many dialogue texts, then, is echoed in the narratives that depict confrontations at the point of death or even beyond. Death enables a scene of
encounter, in which the move from this world to the next (or, indeed, back to
this world) is depicted not as a departure or a conclusion but rather as a

conversion. In its emphasis on conversion and change, on "ceasing to be one kind of person and becoming another," it corresponds across time with the scene of instruction; the two are mutually informing and are linked by the images of the mirror (as explored in the previous chapter) and of seeing face-to-face.[11] The earthly mirror can reflect the truth only partially and dimly but is also, as works like Robert of Gretham's *Miroir* discussed in the previous chapter or the many instructive *Specula* suggest, an essential part of the journey toward the moment when one sees God face-to-face.[12] The scene of instruction, an interaction that is intended to guide the faithful soul on its way, anticipates, in its intimacy, the moment in which knowledge will be infused rather than taught.

Pearls Before Swine? Access to Knowledge in Twelfth-Century Teaching

If stories like that of the master and the disciple or the two knights convey the instructive importance of recognition and affection up to and even beyond the point of death, the branch of this tradition that casts the interlocutors as scholars points, as noted above, to another concern central to the teaching imperative of the thirteenth century: the question of the ultimate value of learnedness for salvation. This issue became more pressing as the audience for religious teaching broadened in the course of the twelfth and thirteenth centuries, and was sharply articulated in the battle over the teaching of Peter Abelard, which, as Gillian Evans has noted, "marked a key stage in the uneasy story of the relationship between theological scholarship and the teaching office of the Church."[13] Abelard's opponents repeatedly objected to what they saw as his tendency to stray beyond the appropriate limits of human knowledge: "He ascends even to the heavens, and descends even to the abyss. Nothing may be hidden from him, whether in the depths of Hell or in Heaven above."[14] And this excessive inquiry not only affects his immediate students, they warn, but is in danger of spreading to the entire population, in towns, villages, and castles; the literate, children, the simple, and even fools are listening to disputations about the nature of the Holy Trinity and many other matters—potentially including, as Virginia Brilliant points out, the "explicit discussion of a *iudicium* at the moment of death."[15] The anxiety, that is, involves both what is taught and who is taught. Bernard of Clairvaux embraces both of these concerns, lamenting that Abelard's "theology"—a newfangled term at that time, though one used also by Honorius Augustodunensis—is really "foolish talk" (*stultilogia*) that overvalues abstruse thought for its own sake and wrongly initiates "green young students . . . and those who are barely able to keep down, so to speak, the first solid food of the faith" into the mystery of the Trinity, "seeing nothing through a glass darkly but looking on all things face to face."[16] In other words, Abelard teaches things that should remain hidden to those from whom they should remain hidden.

In a sense, we might say that what Bernard and others are concerned about is Abelard's tendency to treat his students as equals. One point on which Abelard's supporters and his opponents could agree was his enormous appeal as a teacher—an appeal also conveyed in the complaint, noted above, that the questions he raised were of interest to people of every social and intellectual level. His willingness to question and dispute anything, which was the basis of the objections against him, seems to have drawn students in, and his work and thought in turn developed through his teaching.[17] His *Sic et non* evokes disputation, and his *Soliloquium* takes the form of a dialogue between "Peter" and "Abelard": like Pierre d'Abernon in the next century, Abelard acknowledges that he plays both roles in the conversation, even as he offers up both roles as potential models for his audience. And like Pierre, he seems to have found personal connection to be an essential part of teaching—but whereas with Pierre the evidence, as discussed in the previous chapter, derives from his own writings, with Abelard we can trace his friendships and his influence as a teacher through the records of his disciples and supporters.[18]

Abelard, in other words, despite his famous arrogance, was willing to make the questions he addressed widely accessible; and he repeatedly challenged his own teachers, showing little regard for a hierarchy of teaching. Bernard's remark about "green young students" and his use of Paul's letter to the Corinthians suggest that he was much less willing to countenance such aggressive inquiry in those he considered unprepared for it. Yet the full passage in 1 Corinthians 13 is a reminder that the limitations of human vision are temporary: "We see *now* through a glass in a dark manner; but *then* face to face. *Now* I know in part; but *then* I shall know even as I am known." Just as students may one day be able to grapple with, even if not penetrate, the mysteries of the Trinity, so all Christians will one day possess perfect knowledge, perfect recognition, as they see God face-to-face. Bernard himself, of course, in the Pauline context, can only be one of those who do not *yet* see face-to-face; but without the explicit temporal reference (and first-person plural) of the epistle, his use of the image emphasizes his distinction from these students, their unworthiness of learning that he feels able, however cautiously, to engage with. When he thinks of the intellectual debate, then, Bernard implies that students are getting ahead of themselves in terms of both their earthly status as students and their eternal status as those not yet admitted to the beatific vision. Despite its potentially equalizing qualities (since no one yet sees "face-to-face"), his use of this image emphasizes current disparity and thus aims to prohibit certain kinds of teaching.

A similarly ambivalent attitude is evident in his first sermon for the feast of All Saints, for which his text is Matthew 5:1–12, the Sermon on the Mount. On the one hand, just as the idea of seeing face-to-face is ultimately available to all Christians, so this sermon emphasizes the welcoming nature of Christ's preaching. Bernard evokes early on the "universal" nature of the feast day and its consequent importance, and he also mentions the "worldly people" (*saecular[es]*) who are accustomed to turn out in their finery for feasts. The opening of the sermon, that is, emphasizes earthly as well as heavenly community, and the biblical text reinforces the accessibility of Jesus' message.[19] In Bernard's terms, the feast, like the Sermon on the Mount, is addressed not only to those who are already saints but to those who may become saints, to all of the faithful; it encompasses the temporal disparity that is so central in his discussion of theological teaching. As he writes,

> Jesus, seeing the crowds, went up on the mount—seeing with a gaze of compassion, for they were like wandering sheep, having no shepherd. Why, before beginning to teach, did he go up on the mount, if not because by this very action he taught that preachers of the word of God need to attend to sublime things through spiritual desire and holy life, and to ascend the mount of virtues? And when he had sat down, his disciples approached him. When he had sat down, it says. Otherwise who could approach that immense height? Most kindly indeed he lowered himself, and humbled [*exinanivit*] himself so far as to sit, just as if he said to the Father: You have known my sitting and my rising (Ps. 139:2). He sat so that even publicans and sinners might approach him whom, when standing, the very angels had not been able to reach; so that publicans and sinners might approach him, Mary Magdalene might approach, and the thief from the cross.[20]

The passage depicts teaching as a form of simultaneous exaltation and humility, in which the teacher must both raise himself above those to whom he teaches and lower himself to give them access; Bernard turns repeatedly to the verb *accedere*, the root of "access," to describe the teacher's relation to his audience.[21]

Even as it emphasizes the status distinction between preacher and audience, however, the sermon insists on Jesus' "humble" descent toward those he teaches, the inclusiveness of his message, and this is reinforced by the final invocation of famous sinner-saints like the publican, Mary Magdalene, and the thief on the cross. They serve as a reminder that earthly status is no determinant of heavenly status and that things may be different in their ends than in their beginnings. This point could be made argumentatively, but one of the most familiar ways it is made in medieval teaching texts is precisely as Bernard makes it here, through the invocation of well-known figures whose turns of fortune make them—like Dives and Lazarus—immediately apprehensible reminders of the unknowability of eternal fate. Indeed, the pastoral usefulness of these sinner-saints was such that they were incorporated into synodal decrees: a chapter added to the Paris statutes of the early thirteenth century says, "a confessor should not alarm the one confessing concerning particular sins, but lure the viper from its den with a pure heart, persuading by the examples of David, St. Peter, Magdalen and the thief and so on."[22] For a medieval Christian, these sinners who were encouraged to approach by Jesus' humility were, of course, now numbered among "all saints," offering both recognition and an assurance that the sinful can be forgiven and the humble exalted.

At the same time, just as Bernard's account of Jesus' preaching insists on distance as well as proximity, his examples of those able to approach Jesus in spite of their lowliness are all temporally distant and already exalted figures, well-known sinner-saints now firmly established as part of the heavenly court rather than contemporary figures whose elevation might prove a more problematic model. In addition, these saints' virtue lies, in most pastoral accounts, not in their intellectual attainment but in their moral quality, their saving humility; redeemed sinners who can nonetheless approach God, they exemplify the opportunity for moral rather than intellectual progress. Bernard is willing, in other words, to offer full access to seemingly unworthy students when the teaching in question is tropological rather than theological; and he is more comfortable imagining them from a considerable temporal distance.

Abelard's teaching and its broad appeal, however, had already signaled the difficulty of divorcing theological inquiry from moral questions, and the proximity or overlap of the two realms remains in question throughout the next several centuries.[23] Bernard inadvertently provides a motto for the vernacular handbooks of the thirteenth century when he depicts Abelard asking, "What is the use of talking about teaching if what we wish to teach cannot be explained so as to be understood?" The question echoes in Abelard's extensive influence on the dissemination of doctrine, his role as "the greatest of medieval *vulgarisateurs*."[24] Indeed, Bernard complains of Abelard's teachings "on Christ's Descent into Hell, on the sacrament of the altar, on the power of binding and loosing, on original sin, on lust, on sins of pleasure, on sins of weakness, on sins of ignorance, on the workings of sin, on the will to sin"—all topics that (in a suitable form) are mainstays of the instructional literature of the thirteenth century.[25] The uncertain boundary between theological investigation and moral instruction is echoed by the uncertain boundary between those who may and those who may not inquire, and Bernard's own view of the *fideles* is somewhat incoherent, since he "complains both that Abelard thus lays sacred things before those unfit to see them and that he corrupts the faith of simple people; these simple people appear to be both the faithful and the 'swine.'"[26] The paradox betrays a dual attitude toward *simplices* that is as old as Christian teaching: it is good to learn, but only if you learn the right things; it is acceptable to be a holy fool (*idiota, indoctus, rusticus*), but not to be a fool *tout court*.

The question of what kinds of knowledge are universally worthwhile is part of the point of the tradition with which I began, of which the story of master and disciple is one version. This tale's repetitions with variations had a certain vogue in Latin literature in the twelfth century and especially the thirteenth; versions of the story appear in the works of William of Malmesbury, Odo of Cheriton, Robert of Sorbon, Jacques de Vitry, and Étienne de Bourbon among others.[27] As a group, they address three central themes, any of which may be emphasized in a particular version: the contrast between useful and frivolous learning; the affection between the main characters; and curiosity about death. Attending to the learner's desire for knowledge, the relationship between teacher and student, and the value of different kinds of learning, they respond to important questions in this period when the nature, means, and methods of instruction were all shifting as lay learners and widespread doctrinal teaching gained a new importance in medieval education.

As in the story from the *Manuel des pechiez* discussed above, where both characters are knights, some versions of the tale cast the main characters as equals, one of whom becomes the teacher through the experiential knowledge granted by death. The Cistercian monk Hélinand of Froidmont, writing in the early thirteenth century, tells of two clerics, learned in letters but not yet priests, who were very fond of one another (*inter se multum amici*). They agreed that whichever of them died first would return and report to the survivor, answering the desire to know more—to "descend into the abyss," as Bernard put it, if only in imagination. While in this version the friend who dies first does as usual recount his dire torments, his attachment to frivolous learning is not mentioned, and he refuses prayers and suffrages as useless, but advises his friend to "change his habit" and become a monk, which the friend duly does.[28] In this case, that is, the story benefits only the living friend; while it is clearly designed to convey the horrors of Hell, its ultimate goal is the salvation of both the intradiegetic and the extradiegetic audience, achieved through a combination of curiosity and friendship.

Since Hélinand recounts the story as part of a chronicle, rather than in a sermonic context, it lays claim to historical as well as exemplary authority, a quality typical of many "visits by the living to the dead . . . [and] by the dead to the living" in this period.[29] Another version, told by the distinguished preacher Robert of Sorbon (1201–74), asserts its historicity by means of personal witness and offers considerable detail:

> In the time of blessed Bernard, when he was preaching at Paris, there were in Paris two English masters, masters in arts, one of whom was called Cello [i.e., Serlo of Wilton], the other Master Richard. The latter died and afterward appeared to Cello, his companion, and had a clasped cape, woven with logical puzzles [*sophismata*], and told him that the cape weighed on him more than the towers of Saint-Germain, and said, "These writings signify vainglory, for I used to talk and dispute to show off." And he said, "Do you see how this cape burns?" And he dropped a drop on [Cello's] hand and his hand was pierced; and lighting a candle [Cello] saw his pierced hand and ran to St. Bernard and entered the order, and said, "I leave croaking to the frogs and cawing to the crows and vain things to the foolish; I hasten to the logic that does not fear the 'therefore' of death."

> [Tempore beati Bernardi, quo praedicabat Parisius, fuerunt Parisius duo magistri Anglici, magistri in artibus, quorum unus vocabatur Cello, alter magister Ricardus. Hic mortuus fuit et post apparuit Celloni, socio suo, et habuit capam clausam, contextam sophismatibus, et dixit ei, quod illa capa magis eum premebat quam turris S.

Germani, et dixit quod "Illae scripturae significant vanam gloriam, quia ad ostentationem loquebar et disputabam." Et dixit, "Vis videre, quomodo haec capa exurit?" Et instillavit ei guttam in manum, et perforata est manus ejus; et accedens candelam vidit manum perforatam et cucurrit ad sanctum Bernardum, et intravit in ordinem, et dixit, "Linquo 'coax' ranis, 'cras' corvis, vanaque vanis; ad logicam pergo, quae mortis non timet 'ergo.'"][30]

The view of learning and of the Cistercian order here seems to be one that Bernard might have favored; and certainly his distrust of Abelard's "sophismata" and ostentation led him to suggest a similar fate for his opponent. Yet the story's persistence also serves to convey the continuing curiosity about death that, at least in imagination, characterized students and masters, clerics and laity alike. If Bernard's mistrust of higher learning is clearly acknowledged and shared by some of these retellings, so are the affection and the desire for instruction that characterize Abelard's teaching. The need to put a face on death, to preview one's own mortality, is evident throughout the teaching of the twelfth and thirteenth centuries.

The Faces of the Faithful: Uncertain Examples in Honorius Augustodunensis

In becoming learned, in desiring to see "face-to-face" to the extent possible in this world, Abelard's students and their successors challenge temporal hierarchies and the stability of status categories, including the distinction between student and teacher. The uncertain relationship of earthly and heavenly status, and the role of teaching in establishing and affecting both, are put front and center in the *Sermo generalis* of Bernard's contemporary Honorius Augustodunensis. This text, which forms part of his *Speculum ecclesiae*, is the earliest collection of *sermones ad status*, sermons to particular groups or professions. Bernard, in considering the effect of preaching on eternal status, looked to distant and canonical exemplars; Honorius's own *Elucidarium*, a dialogue on basic Christian teachings directed to his fellow monks, consigns various groups more or less en masse to (usually) the fiery pit or (less frequently) the choirs of angels. In the *Sermo generalis*, which provides model sermons for use with lay audiences, the intersection of earthly teaching with eternal fate is addressed through narrative. The stories depict one member of the estate they address, with the explicit intention of influencing the behavior and, ideally, the eventual fate of other, living members of that estate—a move that has the effect of creating a link between living and dead members of a given estate, an impulse seen also, usually on a more individual level, in treatments of Purgatory. In this way such exemplary tales put a face on the message that, in the *Elucidarium*, is conveyed in more impersonal terms and in doing so give greater presence to the lay audience.

Recent work on medieval exempla has emphasized their potential to exceed the "univocal and explicit" lesson that they seem designed to convey, to be (like pedagogical dialogues) inherently unstable means of transmitting authority.[31] As a means of teaching that asserts a relationship between the universal and the particular—from this particular case, one may infer and apply a general point—they encourage close attention to how the recipient might interact with a broader world of instruction. When a teaching relationship is modeled within an exemplum, the comparison between the extra- and intradiegetic worlds has the potential to become even more striking: the audience of an instructive exemplum finds itself learning simultaneously from a figure or figures within the story and from the person telling the story. In narratives that focus on death, the effect is intensified by the universal application of such a lesson: a priest or preacher may not be implicated by a story about merchants' sharp practices or peasants' withholding of tithes, but no one is immune from a lesson about death. Finally, many medieval death-and-judgment narratives involve reversals and unexpected outcomes; such ultimate uncertainty calls into question the present status of listener and teller.

The central focus on a lay audience in the *Sermo generalis* encourages attention to the relationship between preacher and audience, which is more pointed than what we see in the *Elucidarium*. In the latter, the sins of priests and other religious are seldom imagined as failures of teaching. Only once in the *Elucidarium* does Honorius briefly link the fate of the preacher with that of his audience, when he modifies Psalm 48:14, "Sicut oves in inferno positi sunt, mors depascet eos" (like sheep they are placed in Hell, death consumes them), to read, "Ut oves, sic et pastores in inferno positi erunt: mors depascet eos, quoniam Deus sprevit eos" (like the sheep, so will the pastors be placed in Hell: death will consume them, for God has spurned them).[32] In the *Sermo generalis*, however, the sermon on priests explicitly makes this connection; Honorius says, "If . . . we preach the word of God to you, we acquit ourselves and make you greatly obliged to us. If, however, we do not proclaim to you the salvation of your souls, and you die in your crimes, your blood will be demanded at our hands, as if we had killed you." Similarly, if preachers preach well but live badly, "Thus we call the people to joy, and ourselves hasten toward lamentation."[33] The context of preaching, and particularly the estates sermon's social emphasis, draws attention to the interlinked fates of preacher and audience that echo their proximity in teaching: the instruction provided in life, if rightly presented, understood, and followed, promotes the salvation of both teacher and student.

Honorius's sermon on priests, as discussed in the previous chapter, insists on the distinction between priest and audience even as it acknowledges their entwined fates; not only do priests begin the list of estates, in a mark of their exalted status, but also the exemplum appended to this sermon depicts an idealized priest who, after his virtuous life, is granted a celestial vision and is able to announce to his brethren his forthcoming ascent to the choirs of angels. Most of the exempla, however, depict a less straightforward path to salvation. In his sermons to judges, the rich, the poor, knights, merchants, farmers, and married people Honorius gives a brief account of the estate's religious and in some cases secular duties, followed by an exemplum designed to fix the preacher's instructions in the memories of his audience.[34] Such exempla could—as we see in other texts—address events at any point in a character's life, but in the *Sermo generalis* they treat, consistently, the death and final reward of a member of each estate.[35] Often this address is made in terms particularly suited to that estate, as when Honorius exclaims of a virtuous merchant who leaves his profession to become a hermit, "O how fortunately he bargained, who purchased for himself such heavenly things" (866A). The language transforms the earthly characteristics and practices of a profession into a celestial equivalent, linking and assimilating the audience's present and future.

These brief stories cover a considerable range of familiar narratives about death and judgment; a summary will demonstrate how many involve a personal interaction that bears on the outcome. After the story of the virtuous priest, we hear of the pagan judge who promised justice to a widow and whose postmortem suffering was alleviated, many years later, by the tears of Gregory the Great. In the exemplum concluding the sermon "Ad pauperes," which serves also as the narrative for "Ad divites" immediately preceding it, Honorius tells of a hermit who asked—in an echo of the master and student with whom we began—for a revelation concerning "the end of a good man and of a bad" (*de fine hominis boni et mali*). Going out into the street, he sees a pauper breathing his last and being collected by a troop of angels, and a rich man on his deathbed asking God's help as he is attacked by a crowd of demons, only to be told that he has remembered God too late (864A–865A). In a slightly different take on this motif, the sermon to knights tells of one who, sick unto death, is urged to repent by the king he serves but refuses to do so lest he recover and other knights laugh at him; after demons appear with a list of his sins and drive off the angels who had appeared with an all-too-brief list of his good works, he despairs and is dragged to Hell.[36] The latter two stories, both of which involve an onlooker granted privileged knowledge of death, emphasize the lesson learned within the story as well as the one directed at the sermon audience. The tale of the knight also makes it clear that the intervention of an affectionate friend is not always sufficient to provoke conversion: the king does his best, but the knight is still too much focused on earthly reputation to consider eternity.

In the story of the merchant noted above, we see another familiar theme, that of the unpredictable relationship of earthly and heavenly status. Here a hermit asks God to show him with whom he might be compared in terms of eternal reward. God replies that the hermit has not yet reached the spiritual level of a virtuous merchant currently on his way to visit him; the merchant's custom is to offer his best goods to the servants of God and then visit the monks. The hermit runs to urge the merchant to leave the uncertainties of the sea for the "sturdy house" (*firma mansio*) prepared for him in Heaven, which the merchant duly does.[37] Taken together, Honorius's exempla insist on several familiar lessons about death—the need to repent in time, the potential for help from those still living, the importance of recognizing sanctity wherever it manifests—in a way that emphasizes the need to gain knowledge of this unknowable moment, and they dramatize that need by depicting a character who learns the lesson within the frame of the story.

The last and longest exemplum Honorius tells, in his sermon "Ad agricolas," brings together themes from several of the others: the uncertainty of earthly knowledge about eternal fate; the possibility of reversed expectations; the importance of witness. This narrative also plays out, in a sense, the drama of exemplarity itself, the fact that one may not always know how to interpret a given narrative or whose example to trust. Intriguingly, the sermon that contains the exemplum begins with an unusual moment of identification on the part of the preacher, who addresses his rustic audience as "fratres et socii mei" (my brothers and companions), reaching all the way across the estates so far presented, from priest to peasant. The address may reflect preachers' role as sowers of the Word or the traditional depiction of both preachers and farmers as the feet of the Church, and its emphasis on commonality is reinforced by the virtuous nature of both groups as depicted here.[38] The sermon begins with praise and an emphasis on obedience to the clergy, tithing, and similar topics. Its exemplum treats a taciturn farmer, afflicted by illness, who nevertheless supports his family as best he can. At his death, there is a tempest so terrible he cannot be buried but has to be thrown out the door after three days when the stench becomes too dire. The man's wife, on the other hand, is in excellent health but gives herself over to adulterous affairs, neglects her family, and is so garrulous "that every one of her limbs seemed to be a tongue." Upon her death the heavens are clear and pleasant. Their daughter, still young, wonders which parent she should imitate, ultimately deciding that her mother's apparently better fate makes her the preferable model. As the girl sleeps that night, she is visited by a being with a fiery countenance, who elicits an account of her dilemma and then leads her to see her parents in the afterlife: her father, surrounded by beauty and sweet fragrances in Heaven, embraces her but cannot allow her to stay with him; he says, however, that if she imitates him she will come to that place in her turn. She is then led off to see her mother, who lies at her left hand in a valley of inexpressible horror, submerged up to her neck in a fiery furnace and encircled by burning snakes sucking at her breasts. She begs her daughter for help, reminding her of all the care she had given her. The daughter bursts into tears and wakes in her bed; though unable to help her mother, Honorius reports, she lived so religiously thereafter that there can be no doubt she followed her father to Heaven (866A–867C).[39]

Like the many visions of and journeys to the afterlife that populate Christian literature, especially in the twelfth and thirteenth centuries, this narrative demonstrates an interest in witness: here, as in the story of the student returned from Hell or the hermit who sees the deaths of the rich and the poor man, there is an observer within the story, a person to whom the scene of individual judgment or its outcome is displayed. The effect is to create a kind of *mise-en-abîme*: the hearer of the sermon watches the witness in the story learn about the events that surround or result from an individual's death. Sometimes the person being judged is the focus of the narrative; but often the protagonist is, like the exemplum's audience, an observer rather than a participant. In either case, however, the distancing effect of the layers of witness emphasizes the story's teaching function. The implication of such individual-judgment exempla is that the person who hears or reads them both is and is not the protagonist: that is, both the ability to identify (here heightened by the estates emphasis and, in this specific exemplum, by the witness who, like the audience, is trying to learn how to live virtuously) and the crucial nonidentity are necessary for the exemplum to function. As Hugh of St. Victor puts it, commenting on the term "tropology," "we certainly turn around the language of a story about other people when, having read of others' deeds, we adapt our way of living to their example."[40] The point-of-death exemplum, in a sense, brings the moment of (its own) teaching and the moment of death it represents into conjunction: because the hearer too will die, and face judgment, he or she must pay careful attention to the fate of this predecessor; but because he or she has yet to face that moment, the exemplum can perform its teaching function. Setting the moment of death before the eyes of a living audience makes death's terror into a means rather than an end: the listener is still in a position to affect the form and outcome of his death, to avoid the end with which he has been presented by the story.

Honorius, then, when faced with a living audience, immediately addresses the question of their death and judgment by turning to stories, often to stories that depict the desire for knowledge about salvation on the part of a living observer. His sermons to various earthly *status* become, that is, sermons about eternal status and about how the two might be connected. This format's guiding principle, that every individual, whatever his or her earthly categorization, ultimately faces the same moment of death and judgment at which he is subject to a different kind of categorization, is a reminder of the subjection to death that unites teacher and student. And while the estates approach may seem to suggest that one's chances of salvation are partially determined by profession, the exempla work against this both in their insistence on particularity—that of the figures within the story and of those who hear and must apply them—and in their repeated attention to reversal and uncertainty. In doing so, they challenge the stability of status that estates categories, with their hierarchical format and lumping together of individuals, may initially suggest and bring preacher and audience onto the same footing, as individuals who must learn how to confront death. Honorius, of course, does not acknowledge or embrace this similarity; as his sermon to priests makes clear, in his view preacher and audience remain very much "we" and "you," two distinct groups, and the eternal fate of priests is the tidiest and least interactive of all those represented. In the thirteenth century, however, the desire for narrative that we see already in the *Sermo generalis* as a means of confronting death becomes more self-consciously a way to address issues of status and hierarchy that were fiercely relevant, and inevitably unstable, not only in the moment of death but in the scene of teaching that looked toward and responded to that past and future moment.

Facing Death in the Thirteenth Century

Discussions of death and its relation to teaching in thirteenth-century pastoral texts show the changes that took place as the thinking of figures like Abelard, Bernard, and Honorius Augustodunensis—all of whom were deeply concerned with teaching, but all of whom addressed primarily an already-learned audience of monks or scholars—began to reach new audiences. In the course of the twelfth century, those interested in teaching turned their attention increasingly toward pastoral care, toward a relationship between preacher and flock that could explicitly encourage "the elect and the lowly . . . to learn from each other."[41] The shift that took place over the course of the twelfth and into the thirteenth century did not primarily involve the content of teaching, since the subjects that animated these thinkers, and often the very stories they told, continued to be those that drew attention in later periods; rather, there is a change in the actual and imagined audiences of instruction. The link between the fate of the teacher and that of his audience and their shared desire for knowledge of the moment of death, already evident but downplayed in the *Sermo generalis*, becomes a more central focus in the later twelfth and early thirteenth centuries, with the renewed emphasis on widespread preaching promulgated by the circle of Peter the Chanter at Paris.[42] Stephen Langton, one of that circle and later archbishop of Canterbury (1207–28), conveys the similarity of teacher and learner when he says in his inception sermon that the student of Holy Scripture needs "purity of life, simplicity of heart, attentiveness of mind, humility, and gentleness"; the teacher needs "knowledge, life, humility, and gentleness."[43] The imagined student here, like the teacher, is a cleric, but the virtues ascribed to the two figures have nothing exclusively clerical about them; the only one that might seem to, purity of life, is attributed solely to the student.

As the sense of commonalities between teacher and student begins to reach beyond the cloister or the university and into the instruction of the laity, as we saw in the previous chapter, it intensifies the sense of the bond between them. This bond's power and potential danger are reinforced by the consistent emphasis on the preacher's moral responsibility for his flock's knowledge and thus their eternal fate. One of the Chanter's students, the English subdean Thomas of Chobham, faces squarely the conjunction of teaching and death when, echoing Honorius, he articulates the consequences of the preacher's failure: "Whoever takes on the care of souls takes on the obligation of preaching to them, and if any of his flock [*aliquis subditis*] perish through the negligence of the priest, God will demand his blood at the hand of the preacher."[44] Here the death of the "sheep" for whom the preacher bears mortal responsibility and that of the preacher himself are superimposed; the judgment on the flock becomes a judgment on the pastor. This is not to say that Thomas wanted to break down the distinction between preacher and audience; indeed, I have argued elsewhere that he is in some ways eager to reinforce it precisely because he was aware of the two groups' proximity.[45] His sense of both the distinction and its fragility shapes his descriptions of the moment of death and how the preacher should present it.

Like the story of the master returned from Hell, Thomas's preaching on death seems at first to conform to the well-known narrative of the Middle Ages as a culture of guilt and fear. Having declared preaching to be twofold, directed to the fear and love of God, he immediately connects these to eternal fate, exhorting, "the preacher should always inspire in his hearers the fear of God by way of the pains of Hell, and on the other hand encourage them to the love of God by way of the reward of glory" (28). He then offers a fairly brief discussion (about four pages in the modern edition) of "How listeners should be encouraged to love God," which consists largely of instructions to be merciful as a way of being worthy of God's mercy, followed by a much longer section (about twenty pages) on "How listeners are to be terrified [*absterrendi*]," which focuses on death, judgment, and Hell, beginning with the latter. Even here, Thomas offers some consolation, urging the preacher to remind his flock of the benefits of frequent confession—the more, the better. Like exempla of death and judgment, this points to the fact that there is still time for amendment. Thomas formally reinforces the lesson that Hell is not yet inevitable by reversing time in this section: beginning with a general treatment of Hell and its pains, he moves next to the terrors of the scene of individual judgment and finally to the moment of death. The implicit next step, of course, would be to the present moment in which the preacher addresses his audience.

Thomas's discussion of Hell is descriptive; it is not until he comes to judgment and death that he turns to dialogue and dramatic action to convey his lesson, as Honorius had turned to exempla in order to convey the individual judgment. The forms Thomas chooses are ones that have an independent life in vernacular as well as Latin literature: he begins with a miniature dialogue between soul and body, a widely popular and ancient topos that came to have an association with "the passing of the Particular Judgment, and the consignment of the soul to a place of reward or punishment."[46] The dialogue form Thomas uses echoes the efforts to make doctrine lively and accessible that we see in many teaching texts of the period, and Continental and insular French versions of such debates circulated in manuscripts alongside such texts as the *Manuel des pechiez*, the *Mirour de seinte eglyse*, and the *Lumere as lais*.[47] Thomas's body-soul debate leads into another favorite scene, that of angels and devils attending upon the soul's exit from the body, a motif already noted in Honorius's exempla and that gets considerable play in fabliaux and Marian miracles, as we will see in later chapters. Only then, continuing backward in time, do we come to a depiction of the newly freed soul suddenly in the possession of full knowledge, particularly whether it is destined for salvation or damnation. This knowledge will be accompanied, Thomas asserts, by a vision of Christ, "for then, they say, he will appear to us in the form of the Crucified": just so did he appear to his mother and to St. John (50–51). At this humanizing and hopeful moment, with the invocation of two of the figures most closely and positively associated with Jesus (and visible on innumerable rood screens), the careful detailing of the terrors of death, the structure of authority and quotation that Thomas has followed throughout most of this section, gives way definitively to storytelling.

Thomas's narratives, all of which evoke saintly authority in a more embodied way than do his earlier discussions of Hell and judgment, abandon the dire warnings intended to terrify hearers and instead offer, finally, comfort in the stories of those who have gone before. One may read in "many hagiographical writings," Thomas says, that many saints at their deaths had angels and devils contend for them. The first "saint," however, proves to be one only after a discouraging beginning: a rich man who never gives alms, when begged by an enterprising pauper for the bread he is carrying from the oven, throws a piece in his face with the words, "May you never have joy of that bread." Lo and behold, when the miser later lies on the verge of death, with the devils waiting to snatch his soul, an angel appears holding the piece of bread and restores him to life (51). The reversal of audience expectations—this is not how stories of the avaricious rich usually conclude, and the unfortunate Dives would surely have come to mind—is achieved through the reversal of the miser's fate. And since our expectations have been shaped in part by the various terrors that precede this story, it offers a rescue to the reader analogous to that provided to the rich man—a rescue by the thinnest of threads but one that, improbably, leads this sinner to be classed among saints. The story of the miser suggests that even a narrative lacking the spectacular conversion most sinner-saints achieve can offer encouragement to good deeds.

There follow similar stories of how small good deeds (the gift of a cup to St. Lawrence's church, the composition of a life of St. Nicholas) as well as larger ones (Charlemagne's building of churches in honor of St. James) are sufficient to save their authors from the clutches of the demons. The last tale involves a saint as the soul in jeopardy, rather than as rescuer: St. Martin, having once dropped a coin from the offering and lost it in a corner of the altar, is accused upon his death of avarice. The implication, which Thomas soon makes explicit, is that just as small good deeds can help the soul, small bad deeds can be grounds for a diabolic threat—but since Martin's salvation is hardly in doubt, the menace is greatly diminished. With this story, the transformation is complete; the worldly, selfish miser has become, through a series of narrative steps, the equivalent of the saint, and the preacher is reminded, in the final words of this chapter of the *Summa*, to admonish his anxious listeners that they should always have "some familiar saint" to honor, "so that at their deaths he may be ready to help them" (ut in exitu sit paratus ad ei subveniendum, 53). This was, of course, an ancient part of saints' role in Christian practice, but Thomas's presentation links it closely to an imagined scene of judgment.[48]

The reminder that saints can offer help at the moment of death is also present—like so much of what comes later—in Honorius's *Elucidarium*, which again invokes the good thief mentioned by Bernard in the sermon discussed above. The disciple asks, "Those who were caught committing crimes, and condemned by the judges to the rack or to another torment, and who repented on the very point of death [*in ipso mortis articulo*]: is there any hope for them?" Rather unusually, the master responds comfortingly to this question: "Great hope: for some are purged through that torment, and are saved as the thief on the cross was; some are freed from pains by prayers of the saints."[49] The latter case, as we will see in later chapters, was frequently invoked in Marian miracles, where Mary and other saints play a major role at the point of death. Thomas's examples, or the story of the good thief and others saved at the last moment, serve as a reminder that part of the reason such saints can help in extremis is that they have already faced that moment themselves and navigated its terrors. A sermon by Stephen Langton on the clergy's responsibility for the laity extends this lesson in another direction: citing the example of Peter's denial of Christ, he says even one sent by God fell "so that he might know, by his own weakness, how to come down to the level of others [*ut sciret ex propria infirmitate aliis condescendere*]. Thus you [priests] too should remember your own weakness so that you may know how to have compassion for others."[50] Priest, saint, and lay audience are linked by their weakness, and their shared fate, in ways that recall but extend Bernard's discussion of the Sermon on the Mount. Langton ends this sermon to a group of clerics in an unexpected way: "I wish to conclude my remarks with a common example on account of the simple," he says, blurring any hard line between the *simplices* and the *clerici* even as he reminds his audience that their eternal fate depends on their care for their flocks.[51]

Langton invokes his examples, as Honorius does, to bring home his message and fix it in his audience's minds; in his case, the message is one of warning, or at least a reminder of the clergy's need to recognize their similarities to the laity if they are to perform their duties adequately. As we see in Thomas of Chobham, however, the stories of saints who slipped could also encourage a lay audience to see themselves in those saints and to gain hope from the identification. Both the saints' prior experience and their own recognizability impart some familiarity to the ultimate unfamiliar, the moment of death; they give a face and a name to that dark moment and in so doing lessen its darkness. Although Thomas begins by structuring his work via the love and fear of God, the discussion of the fear of God eases, through narrative, into an account of the hope that makes that fear bearable. The order in which these matters are presented partly echoes the concept that, as St. Bernard put it, "The beginning of wisdom [is] the fear of God; the middle, hope; and love, the fullness": Thomas begins with love, rather than ending there, but his account of the usefulness of fear modulates into stories that emphasize hope, presumably to address the audience of the *non valde boni* and *non valde mali* (neither very good nor very bad), or at least those who might see themselves that way.[52] In his sermon, moreover, Bernard "equated each grade with beginners, learners, and perfect" (*incipient[es]*, *proficient[es]*, *perfect[i]*): it is thus the "proficientes," those learning or making progress—like Thomas's audience, one might imagine—who are associated with hope.[53]

While Bernard's scale might seem to offer a more secure position to those teaching about death than those learning about it, we have already seen how frequently exempla about death and judgment insist on the potential for status reversal and use this to reinforce their instructive power. Those that explicitly represent an instructive scene, like the story of the teacher/student returned from death, also make it clear that the point at issue is not simply learnedness or unlearnedness but the importance of face-to-face teaching. Such narratives reinforce the need for death, like divinity, to be personalized or embodied in order for its implications to be understood, even as they undermine any claims of the learned to be exempt from their own lessons. In his *Évangiles des domnées*

(c. 1240), for example, the chaplain Robert of Gretham recounts the story of "un riche home . . . / K'om el siecle mult sage tint, / Tant ert de scïence prisez / Ke de clergie ert mult amez" (a rich man . . . whom the world considered very wise, he was so greatly prized for his knowledge and loved for his learning).[54] The man falls ill and is at the point of death, but he cannot believe in the soul or the resurrection until visited by a dead friend in a dream. The story's initial emphasis on the great "clergie" that is not enough to persuade the wise man of an essential truth echoes the conjoining, in teaching texts, of *scïence* or *clergie* with what a later author would call "kynde knowynge," knowledge incorporated into the self through humility and love, and often with the help of face-to-face encounter.[55] Here, Robert of Gretham lightens the emphasis on the dangers of worldly knowledge, transmuting it so as to convey not the cloister's superiority over the schools but the insufficiency of learnedness alone to teach the most important lessons. Like Thomas of Chobham's stories of saints likely and unlikely, it serves to suggest that once a soul achieves, through death, what Thomas calls "unrestricted control of its knowledge" (*liberam potestatem scientie sue*), it attains an impressive ability to instruct others.[56]

Teaching Across Time: Now and Then

The power of the dead, of whatever earthly estate, to instruct the living not only participates in the persistent Christian emphasis on holy simplicity or status reversal; it also plays on the simultaneous connection and unlikeness between teacher and student. It is because of what he and his friend have shared and what now distinguishes them that the revenant is able to serve as a teacher. The dead friend makes concrete not only the pains of Hell but the future of his living companion: the deaths of the saints, however familiar, can never be as proximate as those of a contemporary. By bridging one gap, between the lived present and the uncertain future of death, the revenant also makes it possible to contemplate a still greater gap, that between time and eternity, and to direct the audience's attention to the end of time itself, the Day of Judgment. While "the day of death [that] is each person's day of judgment" is the characteristic focus of much preaching and didactic literature, the final Judgment, as the ratification and eternalization of that personal judgment, can reinforce the implication that visiting the "then" of judgment can and should have an effect in the "now" of the audience.[57] Understanding this ultimate distinction, and judging for oneself where one will stand in eternity, becomes an important means by which, as with exempla, the audience assesses its own likeness and unlikeness to an ideal.

The account of Judgment given in Matthew 25:31–46, the parable of the sheep and the goats, makes the conjunction of times and the personalization of the lesson of death a foundational part of Christian teaching. The *Manuel des pechiez* takes up this passage in discussing the eleventh article of the faith, the resurrection of the body. It depicts Jesus telling the blessed,

> A manger me donastes a mun mester,
> E a beivre pur ma seif estancher;
> Nus estoie, et vus me vestistes,
> En prisun, a moy venistes,
> Sanz hostel, et me herbegastes,
> Malades, et vus me visitastes.[58]

> [You gave me food when I needed it,
> and drink to quench my thirst;
> I was naked and you clothed me,
> in prison and you came to me,
> without lodging and you sheltered me,
> sick and you visited me.]

As in Matthew, the blessed ask, "Sire, qant vus veumes meseisez, / E tiels eovres vus feimes de pité?" and Jesus replies, "Quant a un des miens avez doné, / E a moy donastes pur verité" ("Lord, when did we see you in trouble, and do such works of compassion for you?" "When you gave to any one of mine, you gave to me, in truth," *MP* Roxburghe, 424, ll. 831–32, 834–35). The damned receive the same lesson in reverse. Here, the recognition that enables the stories of revenants occurs belatedly: only in the light of Judgment can the almsgivers (and refusers of alms) realize with whom they interacted and in doing so fully recognize themselves.[59]

William of Waddington concludes the discussion by pointing to its implications: "Pur ceo des povres eiez pitez, / Car, solun nos eovres serrum jugez; / Ki poi de almoine fet avera, / Mult cherement dunc li peisera" (Therefore take pity on the poor, for by our works we will be judged; whoever has done little almsgiving will then dearly regret it, 425, ll. 853–56). Another manuscript of the *Manuel* makes this point even more succinctly: "Pur coe tant cum en le secle demorez, / As poveres ben fere enpensez" (Therefore, while you remain in the world, take care to do well by the poor).[60] Both the future perfect of "Ki poi de almoine fet avera"—literally, "whoever will have done little almsgiving"—and the faintly threatening "tant cum en le secle demorez" (while you remain in the world) emphasize the link between present and future, and ask the audience to see themselves simultaneously as present almsgivers and as future subjects of judgment. In a sense, they experience the "then" of judgment and its intimate, almost time-traveling link to the "now" of ethical action; the story imagines them face-to-face not only with Jesus but with their own actions. It also, like the story of Dives and Lazarus, implicitly calls to mind their own earthly, face-to-face encounters with those less fortunate than themselves and asks them to recognize both the personal implications of their actions and their eternal meaning. Each recipient of the works of mercy becomes, in this multitemporal perspective, God himself; the future is the present, and shapes it, just as the present determines the future.

William is greatly concerned with the need to impress an awareness of time on his hearers; in part of his lengthy discourse on the sin of laziness—a sin naturally connected to time—he imagines

> cum il [the lazy one] se repentira
> Al drein jur quant il murra . . .
> Dunc purra dire, allaz,
> Qe il ne ust lessé sun gas,
> E plus amé seinteté,
> E bone vie, & verité;
> Trop est ore tard, trop est ore tard;
> Ore sum lyé en le hard,
> Pur estre en enfern dampné.

> [how he will repent
> on the last day when he dies . . .
> then he will say "alas!"
> that he never left his frivolity
> and loved holiness more,
> and good life and truth:
> "Now it is too late, now it is too late,
> now I am caught in the noose,
> to be damned in Hell."]
> (*MP* EETS, 146, ll. 4151–52, 4154–62; *MP* Roxburghe, 137, ll. 4115–
>   16, 4119–25

The importation here of what sounds like a secular lyric ("Trop est ore tard")
may have served to familiarize the lesson that William tries to convey: that
time is short, that the future is upon us.[61] This dangerously abstract concept
can be put across most effectively, it seems, by imagining face-to-face encounters: between the living and the living, the living and the dead, the dead and
God—and indeed, the living and their future selves.

The sense of an intense personal relationship that, as argued in the previous chapter, shapes Pierre d'Abernon's *Lumere as lais* creates in that text a
subtly different arena for consideration of death and judgment. Pierre's willingness to allow the disciple, and thus implicitly the work's audience, a status
and understanding more equal to that of their teacher enables him to explore
more directly the mechanics of making intellectual connections. Like other
parts of his prologue, his discussion of various kinds of *ends* shows him working through the ways in which the text's structure itself serves to teach its
readers. The subject (*sujet*) or matter (*matire*) of the book, Pierre says, is Jesus
Christ,

> Kar kanke est [en] cest livere trové
> A lui cum chef est ordiné,
> Kar les pecchez enseine pur eschiwre,
> E les biens k'enseine deit um siwre.
> Dunt tut receit ordeinement
> De Jhesu Crist, quanke al livere apent;
> Dunt les pecchurs au derein punira,
> E as bons reguerdunera.
>
> [For whatever is found in this book
> is ordered with him as its head,
> for it teaches the sins so that one may avoid them,
> and teaches the virtues that one should follow.
> Thus everything that belongs to the book
> it takes in an orderly way from Jesus Christ;
> according to it he will punish sinners in the end,
> and will reward the good.]
> (Pierre d'Abernon, *Lumere*, 1:16, ll. 567–74)

Such orderly orientation toward an end ("au derein") makes it suitable that
the "derein livre" (last book, 1:17, l. 608) of the work should treat the "derein

jur de jugement" (last Day of Judgment, l. 607) and the pain or reward it will bring.[62] Turning to his own work's "goal" or "end" (*fin*), Pierre addresses three aspects of it: the "fin generale" (general aim, 1:18, l. 651), "especiale fin" (particular aim, 1:19, l. 659), and "propre fin" (personal aim, l. 663). The latter is "Ke Deu me face remissiun / De mes pecchez, e ke meilure grace / En pusse aver dever sa face" (May God grant me remission of my sins, and may I have better grace in his sight, ll. 664–66). Here we have an echo of the idea that the preacher or teacher will answer for the souls of his students at judgment, imagined in terms of the author's face-to-face meeting with God. Both the readers of the book and its writer, in other words, should understand its teachings to be oriented, finally, toward the moment of death and judgment, and Pierre's close association of the Last Day with the end of his book in both senses—its conclusion and its goal—encourages the audience to make connections between the text before them and the final encounter for which it aims to prepare them.

As the work moves toward this conclusion, it revisits many of the concerns about death and judgment we have seen in other works, but often in a distinctive way. Despite Pierre's emphasis on finality—the last book, treating the last day—he includes a substantial discussion of Purgatory, whose very existence is in a sense a deferral of that finality and signals the difficulty of making orderly distinctions. This discussion of Purgatory stands out as especially notable because it offers, in a poem of almost fourteen thousand lines that emphatically claims a lay audience, the work's sole foray into nonbiblical narrative. Having begun that foray, however, it pursues it at length, retelling in considerable detail three exempla from Gregory the Great's *Dialogues* designed to persuade hearers of the existence of Purgatory.[63] Like their patristic source, Pierre's stories place less emphasis on personal knowledge than do the exempla discussed above. Each of the first two presents an encounter between the figure in Purgatory and the living person to whom he tells his story, but not a preexisting friendship. In both cases, the dead man appears to the living one in a bath (this being, apparently, a good place for revenants) and the recipient of the story goes on to pray successfully for the relief of the sufferer, but no personal relationship is emphasized and in the second story the two men had never met in life. In the final story, the point is simply that a man on the verge of death sends a message to a friend—who turns out also to be about to die—that the boat is waiting to take them to Sicily: in the isles of Sicily, Pierre says, as everyone knows, there are cracks in the earth filled with fire. The dying man, in other words, has a preview of Purgatory.[64]

What makes Pierre's exempla striking is not their emphasis on the personalities within the story—since, as noted, little attention is given to the relationships between the figures—but rather their mere presence at this point in the *Lumere*. Since Pierre has so strictly avoided narrative, despite addressing an audience that was supposed to be particularly susceptible to this method of teaching, his move here suggests that stories are the *only* adequate way to convey the doctrine of Purgatory. As he goes on to say, the eternal fate of the "bons parfitement," the *valde boni*, is of course Heaven; that of the "mauveis," the *valde mali*, is Hell. Purgatory, however, is the place for the "bons meinement," the *mediocriter boni* (2:153, ll. 12315–20).[65] Clear-cut rules and designations may suffice for those at either end of the spectrum, but in the messy middle, story may be the only form of argument one has. Pierre is happy to leave this uncertainty behind, however, moving from the stories themselves to the question of the "distincteisun," differentiation, between Hell and Purgatory. This term, one he also uses for the divisions of his book, brings the discussion back to the scholastic mode in which Pierre feels most comfortable and in which he is happy to include his audience.

For Pierre, indeed, a key point of contact between author and audience, teacher and student, seems specifically to be the task of making distinctions—textual, moral, spatial. Shortly after the purgatorial exempla, the disciple inquires into whether one can help the dead with good works, pointing out that the bad hardly deserve it, while the good do not need it. The master replies,

> A soudre vostre question
> Covint fere destinctiun
> Des bons e mauveis ensement,
> Ke ne sunt pas teus oelement;
> Ke les uns sunt bons parfitement,
> E les autres sunt bons maenement,
> E les uns sunt mauveis pleinement,
> E les autres le maen tenent sovent.
> Pur ceo covint il destincter
> Pur ki l'en deit a dreit prier.

> [To resolve your question,
> one must make a distinction
> among both the good and the bad,
> who are not [all] equally so [i.e., good and bad];

for some are perfectly good,
and others are moderately good,
and some are fully bad,
and others often hold to the middle.
Therefore one must distinguish
for whom one should rightly pray.]
(2:162, ll. 12651–60)

Here the "distinction" (which reinstates the *non valde boni* and the *non valde mali*, rather than lumping them into the *mediocriter boni*) is both the difference between these souls and the ability to see that difference, to distinguish—with the aim of acting on that distinction in deciding for whom to pray.[66] The surface similarity of the six-line rhyme on "-ent" and the syntactical repetition of "les uns sunt . . . les autres sunt . . . les uns sunt . . . les autres" play with the potential difficulties of distinction between groups: the beginnings of these lines echo each other, but while they all come to the same end (-ent) they do so in ways that make a crucial difference. The disciple, and all those who wish to pray correctly, must learn how to differentiate between endings; that ability to distinguish, though initially held by the master, is transmitted, through his orderly text, to the disciple. Here, the teaching of moral behavior and the theological lessons implicit in it are no longer divided, as Bernard had imagined, but have come together as the master and disciple jointly consider the point of death, united by their common inquiry rather than, or as much as, by their common fate.

The shift in the mode of teaching that we see in the *Lumere* is all the more evident in Pierre's treatment of Dives and Lazarus, which immediately precedes the discussion of those for whom one should pray. The *Manuel des pechiez*, as noted above, tells this story in a form that is easily visualized and could indeed be painted, as it is in Princeton University Library, Taylor MS 1. In the *Lumere as lais*, however, the disciple raises concerns about such a visualization: how could Abraham put Lazarus in his bosom, he asks, when he was not wearing any clothing? How could Lazarus refresh the tongue of Dives with a drop from his finger, when, they being spirits, Lazarus had no finger and Dives no tongue? And how could Abraham, being (as previously established) in a place of darkness, give any solace to one deep below the earth? The master responds to these appealingly literal questions with great seriousness: "Saciez ben en bone fei / Ke ces questiuns sunt fort a mei, / Mes sulum le Deu enseinement / Vus en dirai ceo ke je sent" (You should know well, in good faith, that these are hard questions for me, but according to God's teaching I will tell you what I think, 2:161, ll. 12603–6). He goes on to suggest that Abraham's bosom is the place where both Abraham and Lazarus are, which has at least hope even if no light; and while it is true that spirits have no bodies, still Augustine says they have the semblance of corporeality and can be tormented in appropriate parts of it, as Dives is for gluttony. The familiar exemplum of Dives and Lazarus here becomes not an iconic account of eternal reward and punishment but the grounds for a theological investigation in which the master claims no special expertise, only a willingness to do the best he can (a recurrent feature of his teaching throughout the work). One thing remains, however, from the traditional emphases of the story. The rich man, the master says, perceived the hope that distinguishes the bosom of Abraham, "[d]unt il desira acun refu / Par celi ke dunke cunisseit / K'en siecle conustre ne voleit" (whence he desired some help from the one he then recognized, whom in the world he did not wish to know, 2:161, ll. 12616–18). High theology is important, but the story returns at last to the familiar face—friendly or otherwise— to drive the lesson home, and it is after this that the disciple raises the very personal question of how one knows for whom to pray.[67]

Pierre's text does not represent the end of an evolution, of course; its composition predates both the miniature in Princeton University Library, Taylor MS 1 and the Latin exemplum in Bodleian Library, MS Laud miscellaneous 471. Taken together, however, the twelfth- and thirteenth-century accounts of the moment of death considered here convey the emergence of a pedagogy that is grappling with the distinction between teacher and audience and attentive to the personal relationships and particular applications involved in teaching. Honorius's estates sermons in the *Sermo generalis* acknowledge the curiosity and uncertainty that attend upon death and judgment, while maintaining a certain magisterial distance between preacher and laity, but the works of Thomas of Chobham, Robert of Gretham, and Pierre d'Abernon engage more closely with the implications of such stories for the practice of teaching. The inclusion of the preacher or teacher in the scene of death, the questioning of earthly *science* and *clergie* as grounds for salvation, the uncertainty of eternal status until the very moment of judgment all work to assimilate teacher and student, and to give a sense of a world where the *mediocriter litterati* and *mediocriter boni* could, as the *Lumere* suggests, begin to pursue learning alongside their teachers, to ask questions and make distinctions for themselves. The role of death as simultaneously the most solitary and the most universal of human experiences is part of what makes it such a central aspect of these early attempts at universal education; the desire for a knowledge that will surpass earthly learning and for certainty about eternal status also makes stories of death and judgment powerful instruments for investigating the relation of teacher to student. As we will see in the next chapter, one particular and fundamentally important death, that of the good thief whose last-minute rescue echoes those of other exemplary sinners, gives a very human face, and ultimately a teaching voice, to a figure who embodies the reversals that a Christian death can enable.

Chapter 3

Last Among the First: Salvation, Status, and Reversal in *L'Évangile de Nicodème*

The narratives about the moment of death and individual judgment discussed in the previous chapter ask their readers or hearers to think forward to their own future deaths by way of the death of another, to use familiarity and intimacy as means of understanding that link past, present, and future. The stories I turn to in this chapter also call on familiarity as a means of learning from and about death, but here the deaths narrated are ones that precede even those of the well-known sinner-saints mentioned by St. Bernard or the figures evoked by Thomas of Chobham. These are two deaths that stand at the hinge of Christian history, those of Christ and of the "good thief" crucified at his right hand who, according to the Gospel of Luke, becomes the first saved *Christian* to enter Heaven; between the thief's death and his entry into Paradise comes the apocryphal episode of Christ's Descent into Hell, from which he rescued the souls of the just, often known as the Harrowing of Hell. The connections between the good thief's story and the Descent, and the implications of their conjunction, are most fully addressed in the widely disseminated, apocryphal *Gospel of Nicodemus* or *Evangelium Nicodemi*, whose Old French and Anglo-French retellings I consider here. The *Évangile de Nicodème* can be seen as an elaborate and extended episode in a long process of question and response in the development of Christian doctrine. Its central concerns are rooted in the difficult doctrine of the two natures of Christ: the story of the Harrowing of Hell and the entry into Heaven of the first saved souls, as recounted in the twelfth- and thirteenth-century French versions, can be seen as an attempt to understand, imaginatively, the implications of those natures and their salvific force. The history of this apocryphal gospel effectively conveys "the indispensability, to true faith, of parabiblical literature" and in so doing enshrines the role of the recipient in the text that teaches him.[1]

The *Évangile de Nicodème* is linked to "basic instruction" in Christian belief from two directions: as part of the "medieval popular Bible" and as the imaginative elaboration of an element of the Apostles' Creed.[2] A foundational sequence memorialized in foundational texts, the death of Christ between two thieves, his Descent into Hell, and the advent of the first saved souls into Heaven stood at the very heart of what most Christians would be required to know; the entwining, in this sequence, of learning, death, and status reversal puts those issues at the heart of Christian understanding. The didactic and doctrinal compilations considered in previous chapters provide an intensely personal and affective account of how the relationship between teacher and learner shaped and responded to the equalizing implications of Christian teaching; the story of the good thief as told in the Gospel of Luke and the *Gospel of Nicodemus* depicts a learner becoming a teacher and displays the conjunction of death, status, and instruction to a very wide audience indeed.

The pastoral efforts of the twelfth and thirteenth centuries reflected the belief that "moral reform . . . required a foundation in faith, for right under-standing and right behavior to support one another."[3] For the thirteenth century that foundation involved, at a minimum, knowledge of the Pater Noster, Apostles' Creed, and Ave Maria, and more broadly, as laid out in episcopal legislation of the thirteenth century, the twelve or fourteen articles of the faith (largely overlapping with, and often associated with, the Creed), the ten com-mandments, the seven deadly sins, and the seven sacraments. Detailed in-struction on such topics is a mainstay of doctrinal compilations like the *Lumere as lais*, *Manuel des pechiez*, and *Dialogue du père et du fils*, but even those without the means to own manuscripts or the ability to read them would have known the Creed, whose mention of Christ's Descent into Hell acknowledges and attempts to account for the mysterious period between Christ's death and his Resurrection.

This period also saw the beginnings of widespread Bible translation into French.[4] While the Latin Bible was disseminated by way of sermons and cat-echetical instruction, "the Bible" was by no means a stable or bounded entity for twelfth- and thirteenth-century readers, especially in its vernacular mani-festations; "a quantity of vernacular material in prose and verse existed from the twelfth through fourteenth centuries whereby a lay person in France or England could derive considerable biblical knowledge" even beyond that con-veyed in sermon form. This material included apocryphal sources like the

Évangile de Nicodème; many authors of "biblical" works "appropriated and recycled large chunks of [apocryphal, native, or rabbinic] material without perhaps clearly knowing, or caring about, their origins."[5] The biblical paraphrases that formed an important part of this transmission offered one way of bridging the gap between clerical and lay cultures that the Gregorian reform had tried to institute, and apocryphal gospels show how "les formes et les matériaux de l'enseignement traditionnel se sont enrichis de sources jusqu'alors inexploitables dans l'expression écrite."[6] The paraphrases, translations, and other works directed at aristocratic lay readers drew on such resources as the *Historia scholastica* of Peter Comestor or on Peter the Chanter, a strong proponent of pastoral instruction and "the first master at Paris to produce a systematic commentary on all of the books of the Old and New Testaments" in the late twelfth century; previous medieval theologians had emphasized the Psalms and the Pauline epistles.[7] Such biblical and apocryphal histories, that is, find their place in the larger history of expanding pastoral instruction and, indeed, expanding instruction more generally: it is also in the thirteenth century that the first *complete* Bible in Old French appears, part of a larger wave of vernacular translation that included legal, medical, scientific, and other works.[8]

The *Évangile de Nicodème* thus represents a broadening vernacular biblical tradition; one of its anonymous prose versions, for example, consistently forms part of large biblical-hagiographical compilations (many of them closely related to one another).[9] The various versions of the *Évangile*, in fact, all tend to appear in manuscripts alongside other works aimed at inculcating a basic knowledge of the faith. The prose version mentioned above, for example, appears in BnF fr. 187, which also contains, among its eight works, French translations of Maurice de Sully's sermons and Honorius Augustodunensis's *Elucidarium*. Cambridge, Emmanuel College, MS 106, which contains the *Mirour de seinte eglyse* and *Dialogue du père et du fils*, concludes with another prose *Évangile* (here incomplete), while the Nuneaton Book (Cambridge, Fitzwilliam Museum, McClean MS 123) begins with Grosseteste's *Chasteau d'amour*, followed by the section of Edmund of Abingdon's *Mirour de seinte eglyse* that treats the Pater Noster and then a verse *Évangile* by the poet Chrestien.[10] Like the twelfth-century Psalm paraphrase *Eructavit*, the *Évangile* contributes to, or expands on, biblical knowledge by offering an imaginative retelling in French of a particular episode and incorporates that knowledge into a larger teaching tradition.[11] As a story about the most important individual death in the Christian tradition, that of Christ, and of one that accompanies and in some ways mimics it, that of the good thief, it resonates with the stories discussed in the previous chapter but changes their emphasis by having narrative incorporate episodes of instruction, rather than the reverse. In the *Évangile*, that is, didactic instruction arises out of a story rather than being supported by it.

The figure who makes this possible is the good thief; the evangelist Luke's treatment of him makes him a crucial exemplar of distinction at the point of death—of the problem of individual judgment—while later treatments show how the conjunction of opposites in both Christ and the good thief encourages audiences to engage with the contradictions of Christian doctrine and of their own position in relation to it. The ways in which the good thief is associated with and differentiated from his opposite, the bad thief at Christ's left hand, as well as his likeness to and difference from Christ himself, show his development as a figure of Christian learning, as one who grasps the most essential and basic knowledge a Christian can have: that Christ is both God and man. It is his ability to convey this lesson at the very point of death, and beyond, that makes him such a useful exemplar of Christian instruction; at the same time, his simultaneous lowliness and exaltation echo those of Jesus on the Cross and give another means of access to the central paradox of Christianity.

Between Two Thieves

In the Gospels of Matthew and Mark, passersby, priests, and scribes mock Jesus on the Cross, urging him to save himself if he really is the son of God; both Gospels say that the two thieves crucified on either side of him joined in their scorn (Matt. 27:38–44, Mark 15:27–32). Mark notes that the thieves' presence fulfills the prophecy of Isaiah 53:12, "he was counted among the wicked" (*cum iniquis reputatus est*); it is one of the many signs of Jesus' utter degradation at the point of death, which the universal mockery reinforces. The Gospel of Luke, however, makes a striking departure from this scene. Like Matthew and Mark, it recounts that Jesus was crucified between two thieves. The one on his left echoes the passersby, scribes, and priests in the other two versions, taunting, "If you are Christ, save yourself and us."[12] The one on the right, however, rebukes his counterpart: "We deserve our punishment for our deeds; he has done nothing wrong. Lord, remember me when you enter your kingdom." Jesus responds, "Truly, I say to you, today you will be with me in Paradise" (Luke 23:38–43).

It is thus the Gospel of Luke that begins the exploration of a character who will eventually play a notable role in the *Evangelium Nicodemi* and its vernacular offspring.[13] In distinguishing the thieves from one another, Luke implicitly points to death as a moment for essential distinctions; by making the good thief himself the agent of that distinction—through his confession of his wrongs and his appeal to Jesus—he provides an early, and fertile, instance of last-minute learning and repentance. If the narratives of beloved visitors from beyond the grave call attention to temporal distinctions, drawing on past affection as they display a potential future, the two thieves provide a synchronic juxtaposition of possibilities, one emphasized in the many visual depictions of the Crucifixion. Rather than visiting his double from beyond the grave, the good thief warns him in their shared present, presenting a decision point: "Do you not fear God? for you are under the same judgment." His first distinctive action is to appeal—as the revenant teachers do—to both similarity and difference: the thieves and Jesus are under the same condemnation, but in one case justly, in the other unjustly. And the thief's ability to make this distinction, to see the ways in which he and his fellow are both like and unlike Jesus, points to a central quality of the second person of the Trinity—that he is like and unlike humankind—and distinguishes the thief himself. He breaks away from the mass of jeering spectators by acknowledging both of Jesus' natures, his undeserved human suffering and his divine lordship, and as soon as he does so, he becomes a teacher—initially, an ineffective one, but as we will see this moment sets the stage for a later and more successful instructive episode.

By presenting the likeness/unlikeness dichotomy that we have seen in other contexts (teacher and student, dead friend and living friend) and by making both similarity and difference apply in two directions—from the good thief both to the bad thief and to Jesus—this scene highlights the thief's paradoxical qualities as one who is simultaneously a good man and a bad one, a paradox that, again, echoes that of Jesus' own two natures. We see this likeness and difference imaginatively realized in a manuscript from the early fourteenth century, the Holkham Bible (British Library, Additional MS 47682, c. 1320–30), which conveys biblical history through pictures accompanied by Anglo-French text. In an image representing several moments from the Gospels (particularly Luke 23:42–43 and John 19:26–27), we see Christ on the Cross, hanging between the two thieves (Figure 5).[14] He is depicted notably larger than the thieves, whose proportions and postures resemble one another: they have their arms pulled back over the crosspieces of their crosses and pinned behind them, while Christ's arms are stretched out to the sides. Both

Figure 5. Christ crucified between two thieves.

thieves' knees point outward, toward the edges of the page, but while the bad thief's face is also turned away from Christ, the good thief looks toward him; they thus form partial but imperfect mirror images of one another. The precise object of Christ's gaze is difficult to ascertain, due to damage to one of his eyes, but his head is turned in the direction of the good thief and he gazes toward him and the other figures on his right, including John the Evangelist and the women at the Cross.

The picture is crowded with speech scrolls that, unlike the explanatory French text on most pages, quote the Latin Bible, emphasizing the canonicity of these words. The bad thief's reads, "Si filius Dei es, salvum fac teipsum et nos"; the good thief's, "Memento mei Domine dum veneris in regnum tuum." From Jesus there extend two scrolls: one of double width, curving down toward John and the women, that contains the words by which he commends his mother into the Evangelist's keeping (John 19:26) and another, never filled in, that curves over the head of the good thief and was surely intended to contain his reply ("Amen dico vobis"). The bad thief's eyes are turned toward Jesus, though his face is not; he is further separated from him by the blank space between them (his speech moves away from Jesus, and Jesus does not answer him) and by the very shape of his body. The good thief not only turns his face toward Christ, in a pictorial echo of his conversion, but the shape of his body mimics that of Christ, and the unfilled scroll prepared for Christ's address to the thief echoes the shape of the thief's speech to him. The image thus makes clear the distinctiveness of Christ, as the largest and central figure, but also allows the good thief both to imitate him (in the shape of his body) and to come face-to-face with him. At the same time, as noted, the good thief is in some ways assimilated to his wicked counterpart, and a work of similar date to the Holkham Bible picks up this part of the lesson. The *Ci nous dit*, a Continental French compilation of moralized narratives, biblical and otherwise, observes that we are all thieves: "Nos ames sont Nostre Segneur; et toutes foyz que nous pechons nous aemblons ce qui est sien. Et pour ce fu li un des larrons bons et il autres mauvaiz, *en senefiant* que nous estions tuit larron, bon et mauvaiz, *larron repentant et larron perseverant*" (Our souls are our Lord's; and every time we sin we steal what is his. And for this reason one of the thieves was good and the other bad, signifying that we are all thieves, good and bad, the repentant thief and the thief who perseveres).[15] Even as the good thief presents an example to follow, the bad thief offers a reminder of the sinful nature that makes the lesson difficult to learn.

If the Crucifixion scene in the Holkham Bible makes clear both the thieves' similarities and their essential difference, it also uses pictorial representation to emphasize their responses to their shared *damnatio*. This depiction contains only the good thief's speech to Christ, though space is made for Christ's reply; it does not represent his speech to the bad thief. In a sense, however, the work of that speech, wherein the good thief makes clear his recognition that Jesus is man and God and urges the bad thief to embrace this knowledge, is performed here by the image itself. The fact that the bad thief's eyes are turned, in a somewhat contorted way, toward the figure of Christ even as he faces the other way suggests a certain awareness of the conversion that he will not make. Interestingly, there is a hint of the good thief's teaching role on the previous, facing folio (Figure 6), whose upper panel represents Christ being nailed to the Cross. Here, as in the Crucifixion image, Christ's body is larger than that of the thieves. They stand together and their similarities are evident, as in the following picture, but one can distinguish them by

Figure 6. The two thieves, carrying their crosses, see Christ being put on the Cross.
© The British Library Board. Holkham Bible Picture Book,
British Library, Additional MS 47682, f. 31ᵛ (detail).

the fact that here, as at the Crucifixion, the good thief is given reddish-brown hair while the bad thief's is black.[16] The good thief stands closer to Jesus and seems to be gesturing toward him as he looks at the bad thief, who draws back almost fearfully. While there is no speech scroll, it seems likely that an audience familiar with the Gospel narrative would have remembered the good thief's words to his companion and the latter's resistance.

By the time the Holkham Bible was created, the high and late medieval interest in the historical events of the Crucifixion was well established. That interest draws, of course, on older traditions, and in the *Glossa ordinaria* and its sources we can see the interpretations that contributed to depictions like that in the Holkham Bible or the *Évangile de Nicodème*. Bede, for example, a major source for the Gloss, acknowledges the ways in which the scene presents a similarity between Jesus and the thieves, recalling Isaiah 53:12, "he was counted among the wicked" (*cum sceleratis reputatus est*). Bede goes on to connect this with Christ's Descent into Hell: "then indeed he was counted among the wicked, when he descended to Hell, and called back to the heavens those of his own whom he found there."[17] Central to the episode, however, is the way in which this similarity between Jesus and the thieves is both undeniable—they suffer the same fate—and misleading, and this is the focus of the good thief's words in Luke. The good thief's goodness derives not from any remorse he feels or any restitution he is able to make for his evil life but from his sudden ability to recognize Christ as *not only* a fellow sufferer *but also* God. As Bede puts it, thanks to this "sudden grace" (*subita . . . gratia*) the thief has faith, hope, and charity (referring to 1 Cor. 13:13):

> For he had faith when he believed that God, whom he saw dying at
> the same time along with him, was soon to reign. He had hope
> when he begged admittance into his kingdom. He also retained
> lively charity even at his death, when he declared to his brother and
> fellow-thief, dying for the same crime, his iniquity, and preached to
> him the life that he had come to know [*vitam quam cognoverat prae-
> dicavit*]. Behold how he, who came to the cross out of guilt, de-
> parted from the cross out of grace. He confessed the Lord whom he
> saw dying with him in human infirmity, when the apostles denied
> him whom they had seen acting with divine power.[18]

Coming face-to-face with God, the good thief experiences a moment of knowledge (*cognoverat*), of recognition of both himself and Christ, that reverses both his own earlier life and the series of people who, in this chapter of Luke, have mocked Christ in the belief that he has only a human nature. As the good thief distinguishes himself from the bad, doubling their role, he acknowledges and proclaims both Christ's two natures and their implications for himself and others. François Bovon points out that this scene is "unique in the Gospels. Jesus is present, but he is silent and inactive" during the conversation between the thieves, and it is the good thief, rather than Jesus himself, who becomes the teacher and "preacher" to his counterpart.[19]

The centrality of teaching to this scene is brought out in the twelfth-century *Tractatus de septem verbis Domini in cruce* of Arnold (or Ernald), abbot of Bonneval, a friend and biographer of Bernard of Clairvaux. In its focus on the seven last words of Christ, Arnold's treatise is an early entry in the imaginative elaboration of the events of the Crucifixion; devotion to the seven last words flourishes from the twelfth to sixteenth centuries, but he is the first whose work on the subject survives.[20] In his preface, Arnold writes that in the seven words

> Christ recapitulates all his teaching: the things previously preached so diffusely, He reduces to short headings, so that in this compendium of words, the nature of Christian faith shines forth, and from this small seed an immense harvest grows up to benefit all the faithful. For the more briefly they were said, and the fact that they were said in that moment in which the circumstances of things demand that serious and necessary things be treated, the more diligently they should be investigated.[21]

The emphasis on "that moment" (*illo articulo*) as a guarantee of the seriousness and necessity of what is said reiterates the power of the moment of death as a teaching tool for the entire audience, not just the thief. And the words to the thief take a privileged place in this preface: Arnold depicts Christ's promise to him, spoken with power and authority, as "this last subtle teaching" (*ultima schola subtilitatis*) that is "the fundament of faith" (*fundamentum fidei*) because it displays the simultaneous humanity and divinity of Christ. He also invokes kenosis, saying, "humility and sublimity divide between themselves, in a kind of alternating manner, the form of God emptying himself, and the form of a servant taking the name that is above every name" ("et vicissim humilitas et sublimitas quibusdam revolutionibus inter se partiantur negotium, forma Dei se exananiens, et forma servi nomen quod est super omne nomen accipiens,"

PL 189:1680A; cf. Phil. 2:6–7, 9). The thief's ability to grasp this ultimate lesson puts him in possession of the "fundament of faith" and enables him both to become part of the narrative of Christian truth and to convey it to others.

The theme of contrast that Arnold here evokes with regard to Christ reappears with reference to the thieves in his discussion of Luke 23:39–41. He says that the bad thief considered it "foolish to believe Him king or God who was oppressed by the same opprobrium and torment like his own," casting his rejection of Christ's divinity as, in effect, an inability to understand the balance of likeness and difference between himself and Jesus.[22] The effect, of course, is to differentiate him absolutely from the good thief—"Thus one was a mocker, the other a confessor; one a vilifier, the other a venerator; this one hoping, the other despairing; this one loving, the other disdaining"—not only in the present moment but eternally: "The judge of this controversy was present who, having sentenced the blasphemer to hell, promised the believer the kingdom."[23] Christ does not sentence the bad thief to Hell in the course of the Gospel scene; here the author points to the implication for their eternal fate of the placement of the thieves at Christ's right and left hand (which, as noted above, echoes Matt. 25:31–46). Like the good thief, the audience is asked to understand that implication, for themselves as well as for others.

What is so striking about the role of the good thief is its combination of several themes: attention to the central truth of Christianity, Christ's divine and human natures; the connection between Christ and the individual believer, which reflects both the likeness and difference enabled by Christ's two natures; and a demonstration of the teaching enabled by that connection. It is significant that the scene contains both the good thief's performance as a preacher to the bad thief and the "private conversation" between the good thief and Jesus: while here the order of those is reversed from what we might expect (that is, the good thief speaks first to the bad), this only foregrounds the importance of the good thief's interior comprehension. Arnold emphasizes the authoritative teaching voice this comprehension enables, insistently presenting the good thief as a kind of *magister* who puts forth arguments and disputes in a new mode ("in auditorio publico fidei protulerat argumenta, et novo philosophandi genere . . . justitia disputabat," PL 189:1690A); he points to the way in which the thief philosophized, preached, and became an "illustrious speaker" ("philosophatur, et praedicat," col. 1690B; "illustris concionator," col. 1691A). For Arnold, as in the image from the Holkham Bible, it is specifically the bad thief's recalcitrance and blasphemy that provoke and enable this magisterial performance; resistance elicits faithful teaching, making the bad thief necessary to the good even as the narrative asserts their disparity.

The order of the speeches—first between the two thieves, then between the good thief and Christ—also draws our attention to the fact that the good thief converts not because Christ has preached to him but because he has been able to see past the appearance of (mere) humanness to what it conceals. As in the Eucharistic miracles discussed by Steven Justice, this ability to see past what seems an obvious truth—that Jesus is a condemned criminal dying a painful and humiliating death—does not seek simply to reassert or impose belief but to acknowledge the persistent difficulty of Christian doctrine. Here, through the figure of the good thief, the believer is confronted with the horrifying truth of torture and death that the Incarnation and Redemption require, as the people in Eucharistic stories must confront the horrifying truth of the real presence. These two difficult doctrines are deeply connected, as Justice notes: in one account, it is precisely a belief in the Incarnation that leads a woman to resist belief in the Eucharist.[24] An important difference, of course, is that the unseen truth the thief grasps is a comforting one, compensating for the horror of the visible, while in the Eucharist the seen is comforting, the unseen appalling. In both cases, however, the narrative insists on the need for a simultaneously cognitive and emotional engagement with a central doctrine, and in the good thief's case, it is precisely the barriers to accepting that doctrine—personified in the bad thief's reaction—that make it possible and necessary to understand and to teach it.

The episode thus represents, dramatically, the process and effect of an individual's comprehension of Christianity's central truth, one that is highlighted and made urgent by the imminence of both his own and Jesus' death, and in so doing it points to the need for each Christian to attain this same knowledge. The growing devotion to the seven last words, like images of the Crucifixion that show the thieves on either side, made this moment and its lesson available in an immediately apprehensible way for medieval Christians. The attention to "divine humanity" and "Christ's love for man" so important to Arnold of Bonneval plays out further, as we will see, in the related account of the Descent into Hell. Here kenosis, the divine self-emptying that lifts up humankind, is again the mystery at center stage. The thief's move from bad to good, or rather his simultaneous embodiment of good and bad, is a kind of echo of Christ's simultaneous highness and lowness, on display in the Gospels and played out further in the *Évangile de Nicodème*.

The Creed and the Descent

If Luke's Gospel provides one key component of the *Evangelium Nicodemi*, another seems to arise ultimately out of the Apostles' Creed. As noted above, Bede associates these two episodes through their shared counting of Christ among the wicked, reflecting their shared focus on Christ's two natures, which is in turn a central concern in the *Evangelium*. The whole text might be seen, in a sense, as a response both to the desire to understand more fully and imaginatively how God can die and not die, can be both human and divine, and to an eagerness to know more about the mysterious gap in Christ's biography, the three days between his death and his Resurrection. That gap, with the support of biblical texts like Ephesians 4:8–10 and 1 Peter 3:19–20, gave rise to the story of the *Descensus ad inferos* or Harrowing of Hell, in which Jesus descended to Hell in order to rescue the souls of "his own," as one version puts it. As this formulation suggests, the exact identity of those rescued is somewhat unstable, but in most medieval versions it consists essentially of the patriarchs and prophets—even as the concept of "Christ's own" clearly appeals to a Christian audience that could see itself in similar terms.[25]

Like the account of the good thief in the Gospel of Luke, the story of the Descent emphasizes the conjunction of lowliness and exaltation, as I will discuss below, and it is surely no accident that these two stories are combined and imaginatively expanded in the *Evangelium Nicodemi*. First, however, I want to consider the emergence of the *Descensus ad inferos* section of the *Evangelium*. The history of this narrative makes it clear to what extent it was what we might call an elicited text—elicited, in this case, by the desire of the faithful to understand all of salvation history, particularly the earliest workings of salvation, and to gain reassurance about the mystery of death and the afterlife. D. D. R. Owen suggests, "It was on the events recounted by the *Gospel* that [the] Christian based his own hope of personal salvation"; in light of this, it is not surprising that, since the *Gospel of Nicodemus* did not originally exist, it was found necessary to invent it.[26] While the story of the Descent is surely an attempt to grapple theologically with an important moment for understanding Christ's sacrifice and Resurrection, it also reflects, like the legends that sprang up regarding the life of Adam and Eve after the Fall, a desire "to know, in crude terms, what happened next."[27] The "high" theological investigation of this moment and the "crude" wish for more information, for a fuller account of important events, are not unrelated impulses, and both contribute to the rise of apocryphal works.

The forms and traditions that, over the course of centuries, gave rise to the several Old French and Anglo-French versions of the *Évangile de Nicodème* demonstrate the continuing desire for further knowledge that makes this collection of texts an apt representative of the lay-clerical interaction and cooperation that characterize French didactic works of the thirteenth century. The *Evangelium Nicodemi* was probably composed in the fourth century; the *Descensus* section was added perhaps a century later.[28] This move—the addition of further information on a point of interest (in this case, Christ's whereabouts and activities during the three days between the Crucifixion and the Resurrection)—is a recurring motif in the traditions that ultimately give rise to the *Évangile*. For if the *Descensus ad inferos* was an addition to the *Evangelium*, that apocryphal gospel itself serves as a kind of imaginative expansion of a section of the Apostles' Creed, which declares that Jesus "suffered under Pontius Pilate, was crucified, died, and was buried; he descended into Hell; on the third day he rose from the dead."[29] And the brief note "descendit ad inferna" itself was not a stable part of the earliest Latin creeds; it does not appear either in the so-called Roman Creed of the fourth century or its posited antecedent of the early third, the "proto-*R*."[30] So both in the *Evangelium* and in the Creed Christ's Descent into Hell is a belated addition, reflecting its problematic but desirable nature: it acknowledges that the Crucifixion has not only not saved everyone (as we know already from the bad thief) but left the fate of some of those "deserving" of salvation in a state of uncertainty. The *Descensus ad inferos*, in fact, did not become a stable part of the Creed until the pontificate of Innocent III in the early thirteenth century and is not, for instance, part of the Creed as expounded by Maurice de Sully in his widely disseminated French sermons of the late twelfth century.[31] It is surely no accident that it was the thirteenth century that saw the official inclusion of "descendit ad inferna" in the Creed; it reflects the curiosity about the afterlife that fueled the production of so many (other) visions of and visits to Heaven and Hell in medieval culture, as well as of course the famous "birth of Purgatory" discussed by Jacques Le Goff.[32] The episode's increasing canonicity speaks to its usefulness in the teaching of Christian history.

It is not until the *textus receptus* of the seventh century that we first find "descendit ad inferna" as a fairly regular part of the Creed, even if not one that is reliably present in all versions from then on. The paired descent/ascent that this element creates in the language and imagery of the Creed ("he descended into Hell; on the third day he rose"), the conjoining of death and the transcendence of death, recalls the lesson intuited by the good thief, that at his

moment of greatest powerlessness Christ is simultaneously at his most powerful. In a sense, the *Descensus* episode in its extended form is an elaborated and,
as it were, historiated meditation on Philippians 2:5–11 (which, as we saw
above, Arnold of Bonneval links also to Christ's death on the Cross):

> For let this mind be in you, which was also in Christ Jesus: Who
> being in the form of God, thought it not robbery to be equal with
> God: But emptied himself, taking the form of a servant, being made
> in the likeness of men, and in habit found as a man [*semet ipsum
> exinanivit formam servi accipiens in similitudinem hominum factus*].
> He humbled himself, becoming obedient unto death, even to the
> death of the cross. For which cause God also hath exalted him, and
> hath given him a name which is above all names: That in the name
> of Jesus every knee should bow, of those that are in heaven, on
> earth, and under the earth [*caelestium et terrestrium et infernorum*]:
> And that every tongue should confess that the Lord Jesus Christ is
> in the glory of God the Father.

This passage is the locus classicus for the concept of kenosis or self-emptying,
of Christ's humility as a model for Christians—a model with important implications for teaching, as noted in Chapter 1, and for the related ideas of
docta ignorantia and holy simplicity—and it shows the descent-ascent, humil-
iation-exaltation motif echoed in the Creed.[33]

The episode of the Descent can serve as a kind of narrative working-out,
an unfolding in time of the eternal juxtaposition of exaltation and lowliness
presented by the passage in Philippians. Peter Lombard, writing on the Epistle
to the Ephesians, makes the connection clear:

> the same person who descends is also he who ascends; that is, it is
> the same one who descends into Hell and who ascends above all
> heavens. . . . But what does it mean that the humanity ascends, that
> is, how could the humanity ascend, unless it were because the God-
> head first descended into the parts of the earth which are below the
> air, so that it might be united with human nature? The Godhead
> descended, indeed, not in a particular place, but through self-
> emptying [*non localiter, sed per inexanitionem*]: and since he had said
> that the humanity ascended, and the Godhead descended, lest there
> should therefore seem to be two, he adds: He who descends, that is,

God, and who ascends above all heavens, that is, man, is Christ
himself, that is, one and the same person.[34]

While in their full meaning Christ's descent and ascent do not take place "lo-
caliter," the story of the *Descensus ad inferos* does offer a specific, concrete, lo-
calized way to envision that descent and its effects. As such, it creates, like
stories of death and judgment, a space in which to consider how the originary
status reversal of the Incarnation might be understood by, and shape the lives
of, Christians in later times. And the story of the good thief, who is able to
grasp the impossibility that so many others reject in that Gospel sequence—
that Christ has two natures—plays out dramatically a version of resistance to
and ultimate embrace of the Incarnation, also of course the subject of fero-
cious theological debate in the early Church, with which this passage from
Philippians grapples.

The fundamental importance, for an understanding of Christ's two natures, of the imagery in Philippians 2:5–11 is asserted in the so-called *Tome of
Leo*, the letter written by Pope Leo I in 449 to combat the priest Eutyches,
who had denied Christ's human nature (the Monophysite heresy); this letter,
ultimately read aloud and accepted as orthodox doctrine at the Council of
Chalcedon in 451, became an important basis for patristic and medieval Chris-
tology.[35] Leo's letter exemplifies the conjoined elements that recur throughout
the history of the *Evangelium Nicodemi*: basic teaching, investigation of the
nature of Jesus, and interest in the human events of his life. Leo begins by
expressing his consternation about those who, "not being pupils of the
truth[,] . . . turn out to be masters of error" ("magistri erroris existunt, quia
veritatis discipuli non fuerunt") and depicts Eutyches as "[a] man who has not
the most elementary understanding even of the creed itself. . . . This old man
has not yet taken to heart what is pronounced by every baptismal candidate
the world over!" He goes on to present both confessional statements and biblical teaching as clear refutations of Eutyches' position, saying that if Eutyches
was unable to garner the truth from "the common and undivided creed by
which the whole body of the faithful confess," then "he should have subjected
himself to the teaching of the Gospels."[36] The language of instruction throughout the letter's first section is notable: Eutyches is urged over and over to be
sure he has learned well before he presumes to teach. The insistence on the
"basic" nature of this teaching is, of course, polemical; by claiming it as self-
evident to even the simplest Christian, Leo evades the inherent mystery and
complexity of the contested doctrine.

Having dispensed with these preliminaries, Leo then launches into an impassioned account of Christ's two natures: "Lowliness [*humilitas*] was taken up by majesty, weakness by strength, mortality by eternity. . . . He took on the form of a servant [*Assumpsit formam servi*] without the defilement of sin . . . that self-emptying [*exinanitio*] by which he, invisible, showed himself visible" (one of several references to Philippians).[37] Throughout Leo works by juxtaposition and paradox, evoking the "lowly cradle" and the angelic song, the attack of Herod and the "bended knee" of the Magi, and so forth. Turning to the Crucifixion, he notes that "it does not belong to the same nature to . . . hang on the cross and, with day changed into night, to make the elements tremble; or to be pierced by nails and to open the gates of paradise for the believing thief."[38] Throughout, Leo's desire seems to be to make the two natures of Christ accessible, comprehensible, and indivisible, in a kind of mimicry or repetition of the Incarnation itself, in which, as he puts it, "The ungraspable willed to be grasped" (*incomprehensibilis voluit comprehendi*).[39] That Leo mentions "descent" only in the context of how Christ, "descending from his seat in heaven . . . enters this lower world"—that is, the fact that his account, despite its detail surrounding the Crucifixion, does not mention the Descent into Hell—is another sign of that story's intermittent role in conceptions of Christ's life, though certainly the Descent was thoroughly explored by other patristic commentators.[40] But Leo's letter, while not addressing the Descent itself, echoes the *Evangelium Nicodemi* in its interest in the two natures of Christ; it draws on many of the same scriptural moments and on similarly paradoxical language to imagine Christ's earthly history and make the Incarnation accessible to the audiences who needed to "grasp" its true complexity.

The link between basic teaching, baptism, and Creed was well established already, of course, by Leo's time, and here it is striking to note—tracing the traditions back further—that the Creed itself may have developed out of an embryonic account of the role of Christ in Christianity. Liuwe Westra suggests that the Creed emerged from a process whereby, in the second and third centuries, a continuous statement of belief was created from the "fusion" of "Christological formulae" and "threefold baptismal questions."[41] Those questions took the form, "Do you believe in God the Father Almighty? –I believe. Do you believe in Jesus Christ, the Son of God? –I believe. Do you believe in the Holy Spirit? –I believe." The "Christological formulae" permitted an expansion of the central section of this sequence, the question about Christ, so that the large middle section of the Creed that eventually emerges reflects an attention to Christ's two natures reminiscent of that which we see in the *Tome of Leo* and no doubt similarly intended to exclude certain views of their relationship. This attention, combined with the moment of dialogue and conversion represented by baptism, ultimately gives rise to the *Credo*.

Margaret Nims calls Christ the "supreme instance of a *verbum translatum*," but that translation can be difficult to interpret.[42] The recurrent attempts to make it comprehensible, to narrate and imagine it, aim both to confine interpretation of the Incarnation and, in a sense, to imitate it. The fact that so many of these attempts, and certainly those represented in the *Evangelium Nicodemi* (or in Leo's *Tome*), are framed as debates, dialogues, exchanges between two figures draws our attention to the way in which articulation of Christ's two natures both roused controversy and attempted to draw the student into a closer similarity with Christ—a dynamic that we have seen already in the interactions of the good and bad thieves. Both the dialogic form and the alternation between the familiar and the unfamiliar, the exalted and the humble, the divine and the human work to pull the listener or student into the picture, to engage his or her person in the understanding, and ultimately the imitation, of Christ himself. At the same time, there is a repeated pattern in the history of the *Evangelium* and the Creed whereby a minimal account of a complex and alluring doctrine—the two natures of Christ, the Descent into Hell—gives rise to an extended explication. Again, such a move seems to reflect not only the ecclesiastical hierarchy's desire to control the terms of Christian belief but also the desire of the faithful for fuller knowledge. If the quashing of heresies and the establishment of a unified orthodoxy was one important spur to the development of doctrines, surely curiosity, among both clergy and laity, was another.

Drama, Doctrine, and Dialogue in the *Évangile de Nicodème*

Both the story of the good thief and that of the Descent into Hell were eventually recounted, along with the trial of Jesus and the Crucifixion, in the apocryphal *Gospel of Nicodemus* or *Evangelium Nicodemi*.[43] In the *Évangile*, or rather the *Évangiles* (since there are six to eight distinct versions in Old French verse or prose, most with several exemplars), the section that particularly interests me derives from the *Descensus ad inferos* section of the Latin *Evangelium Nicodemi*, which ends with the reappearance of the good thief.[44] The central importance of dialogue as a way of conveying and understanding Christ's nature is reinforced in the *Evangelium*, and thus the *Évangile*, which ring many changes on the theme of recognition and misrecognition already evident in Luke 23:27–43 and the other passages where Christ's identity is in question. Repeatedly, such scenes in the apocryphal account, like those in the canonical ones, engage with and repeat biblical texts in a recursive way that offers a model for audiences; once translated into French (or other vernaculars), they perform and practice this repetition for a new, lay audience.

The moments in the story I particularly emphasize here are those that, like the narratives in the previous chapter, depict a moment of face-to-face meeting and, with it, the problem of recognition or misrecognition. The scene at the Crucifixion is a key instance of this, since it dramatizes the good thief's accurate recognition of Jesus as God, but in fact the issue arises from the first moment of the *Evangelium Nicodemi*: the story begins when the Jewish leaders bring an accusation against Jesus before Pilate. Their first words indicate the battle over his identity and over the possible ways of recognizing him that will recur throughout the text: "We have known this man as the son of Joseph the carpenter by Mary and he says he is the son of God and a king."[45] The *Gospel* as a whole revolves around this central uncertainty, an apparent point of either/or that of course, for a Christian, was both-and; the story plays out various ways of coming to terms with the confusing, and status-destabilizing, implications of the Incarnation and rehearses in narrative form theological contests over the nature(s) of Jesus. The *Descensus ad inferos* and its vernacular offspring offer recognition as a means of resolution, and that recognition, it is clear, is both textual and dramatic: textual, in that the *Evangelium* from its earliest moments, and with particular density in the *Descensus* section, rehearses the language and events of the Bible; dramatic, in that this rehearsal is performed by characters in the story as part of their unfolding experience of the Passion and Resurrection, the point when literally everything in Christian history—past, present, and future—is seemingly up for grabs.[46]

We see the importance of the past from the beginning of the *Descensus* section (and here I turn to the French versions of the story). The resurrected sons of Simeon, Karinus and Leucius, relate that while they, with the patriarchs and prophets, were in the depths of darkness, there suddenly came a brilliant light, which immediately began to draw from those assembled repetitions of their own prophecies and biblical histories. Thus Isaiah, for example, cries out,

"Ce est li fiux Deu ki ci vient. Je le dis bien quant je estoie vivans
sor terre. Je prophetizai: 'Populus qui sedebat in tenebris vidit lucem
magnam habitantibus in regione umbre mortis. Lux orta est eis. Li

puepes ki seoit en tenebres vit la grant lumiere; et a çaus ki estoient
es tenebres d'Infer vint la grant lumiere et est espandue sor eux.'
Ore est venue cele lumiere," dist Ysaïes, "ce est cele ki la vient."[47]

["This is the son of God who comes here. I said as much when I was
alive on earth. I prophesied: 'Populus qui sedebat in tenebris vidit
lucem magnam habitantibus in regione umbre mortis. Lux orta est
eis. The people who were in darkness saw the great light; and to
those who were in the darkness of Hell came the great light and
shone upon them.' Now that light has come," Isaiah said, "it is this
one that is coming here."]

Similar self-quotations and recapitulations of biblical events are performed by
Simeon, John the Baptist, and David; their appearance here is in a sense an
answer to or fulfillment of the *Ordo prophetarum* of liturgical drama, where
each prophet is led away to Hell after speaking his piece.[48] In the prose version
of the *Évangile* with the most manuscript survivals (Ford's version B), which I
use here, these passages are quoted in Latin, often rubricated, and then translated into French by the speaker; this tradition is probably slightly later than
the prose version entirely in French and may suggest that the ability to access
the Latin more directly came to be of increasing interest. We see a similar transition from the French text of Robert of Gretham's *Miroir*, which includes no
Latin, to its fourteenth-century Middle English translation, which does; and
Margriet Hoogvliet has noted the highlighting of Latin biblical material in
some fourteenth- and fifteenth-century French manuscripts.[49] In the *Évangile
de Nicodème*, the importation of Latin allows one striking choice: when, in the
course of these recounted prophecies, Adam asks his son Seth to tell how the
Archangel Michael promised him that his father would be saved after 5,500
years, the passage—which is apocryphal—is given only in French, though it
does appear in the Latin of the *Evangelium Nicodemi*.[50] This suggests that in
addition to providing a scriptural lesson, the text was maintaining for its readers a distinction between canonical and noncanonical scriptures and thus
building upon the biblical education implicitly provided by the text itself.

Accompanying this textual recognition, as noted above, is dramatic recognition. While the recitations of the patriarchs and prophets are rather static,
serving primarily to reembody and recall biblical texts and to show the fulfillment of prophecy, the lengthy and somewhat panicked debate between Satan
and Enfer that follows brings the dilemma of proper recognition vividly to

life. The infernal powers argue about who, exactly, is on his way, and their disagreement in essence repeats the seemingly dichotomous possibilities that the Jewish leaders set out in the beginning: is Christ (only) a man, or is he (also) God?[51] The scene begins when Satan appears and exultingly tells Enfer,

> "Enfers, apareille toi de recevoir Jhesum ki dist ke il est fiz Deu, et si est hom, et crient la mort quant il dist: 'Tristis est anima mea usque ad mortem. M'ame,' dist il, 'est triste dechi a la mort.'"

> ["Hell, prepare yourself to receive Jesus who says that he is the son of God, and is also a man, and fears death when he says, 'Tristis est anima mea usque ad mortem. My soul,' he says, 'is sad even unto death.'"]

Hell, unlike Satan, is immediately suspicious, asking,

> "[K]i est cil ki tant puet par sa parole, ki teus vertus fait con tu m'as dit, et hom est et mort crient? . . . Et ki est or cist ki est si puissans et si contraires, et est hom et mort crient? . . . Et s'il dist k'il crient mort, dont se veut il celer."[52]

> ["Who is this who can do so much through his words, who does such feats as you have told me, and is a man and fears death? . . . Who is this, now, this man who is so powerful and so hostile to us, and is a man and fears death? . . . And if he said that he fears death, then he wants to hide himself."]

These questions introduce yet another mode of recognition: the fear of death is what most tellingly—and thus most persuasively—marks Jesus as human in Satan's eyes; even in the greatest fear of death, then, humans can remember that this, too, is a link to Jesus. Satan resists Enfer's interpretation (which refers to an influential view of the Incarnation as, in essence, a trick), but the point is made moot by the arrival of Jesus himself, announced by David in Latin: "Tollite portas, principes, vestras, et introibit rex gloriae": "Cast up your gates, o princes, and the king of glory will enter."[53]

Jesus enters and illuminates the darkness and the captives. Hell and Satan cry out and acknowledge their defeat but then revive the question that has recurred throughout this dialogue-heavy text: who *is* this intruder?

"Ki iés tu ki sans pechié et sans corruption et par majestés as en despit nostre seignorie? Ki iés tu ki iés si grans et si petis, si humles et
si biaux chevaliers, empereres sambles et hom, sers de pechié, si iés
si fors batellieres de rois de gloire, et mors fus et ore iés vis?"[54]

["Who are you who, without sin or corruption and with majesty,
despise our lordship? Who are you who are so great and so small, so
humble and so glorious a knight, seemingly an emperor and a man,
slave of sin, yet you are so strong a champion of the king of glory,
and were dead and now are alive?"]

Or as Chrestien's verse version of the *Évangile* puts it, echoing Philippians
2:7–8, "Humbles ies en trés grant hautesce. . . . En forme de serf as victorie"
(You are humble in all highness. . . . In the form of a slave you gain victory).[55]
The intruder's power and glory get most of the attention in the passage as a
whole, but confusion arises from the apparently contradictory smallness,
humbleness, and servitude he also embodies—theologically, a surprising feature, since the medieval Church taught that Jesus descended into Hell in the
spirit rather than in the body.[56]

In a sense, the basic paradox of the Incarnation is here given renewed
force through its articulation by those whose incomprehension reflects their
spiritual incapacity; ordinary Christians hearing the story would, by contrast,
have had no confusion whatsoever about who this figure humble in his greatness, victorious in his servitude might be. As C. W. Marx says, speaking of the
Latin *Evangelium Nicodemi*, the Christian audience "is by implication being
encouraged to supply the meaning of various biblical episodes . . . [as] a device for reinforcing and fixing the received tradition of interpretation of the
life of Christ," while "failure to invest episodes with their true significance"
becomes associated with the Devil.[57] This does not remove the difficulty that
is confronted here; the need to retell and replay resistance to the Incarnation
suggests the way in which "many different testimonies" may be required to
produce "the sensation of knowing" the truth of something that on the face of
it is unbelievable.[58] In replaying and reexperiencing that scene, however, the
believer becomes, in imagination, a witness to the truth proposed.

If the demons' incomprehension functions as a spiritual lesson across time,
however, it also—like the biblical quotations that recall past events and foretell
future ones—reflects the pivotal role of this particular story in Christian history: this is precisely the moment when the stakes of the Incarnation become

clear. Marx has explored how the complex theology of the Redemption is represented in vernacular literature of thirteenth- and fourteenth-century England; the *Évangile de Nicodème* plays its part in this story through its use of the motifs of trickery and deception. Thus another verse version of the *Évangile*, by the Norman poet André de Coutances, probably from the late twelfth century, presents the introductory conversation between Satan and Hell about who is coming as follows: "'Enfer,' dist Sathan, 'ce n'est rien; / Mort est Jhesus par mon engien. / . . . quant mort est & confunduz / Donc n'est sa poesté alée?'" ("Hell," said Satan, "this is nothing; Jesus is dead through my cunning. . . . When he is dead and destroyed, then is his power not gone?").[59] The idea that Jesus is "destroyed" by death and his power eliminated is, of course, turned back on the infernal powers later, but more striking here is Satan's description of his victory as coming through "engien," cunning or trickery; a longstanding view of the Redemption—one that motivated Anselm of Bec's critique in *Cur Deus homo*—held that the Incarnation itself was, precisely, a trick intended to lure Satan into overstepping the bounds of his power, his rightful claim on sinful humankind, and thus invalidating that claim. Satan's tricking of Christ, in other words, is actually Christ's tricking of him and results from Satan's misrecognition, his inability to understand that what is humble may also be exalted—a characteristic error for a figure defined by his sinful pride. Like the parable of the Pharisee and the publican (Luke 18:9–14) or the account of the good thief, these exchanges in the *Évangile de Nicodème* dramatize the downfall of pride, the flip side of the power conferred by embracing humility, by recognizing one's own weakness or sinfulness.

Throughout the various versions of the *Évangile de Nicodème* that lesson is conveyed by means of (mis)recognition and paradox. The first part of the lesson—that Christ is not only the (step-)son of Joseph and son of Mary but truly also God—is conveyed when the patriarchs and prophets recognize Christ verbally, both welcoming him and calling him forth by reciting Scripture, and when Satan and Enfer must bow before the one they thought they had conquered. But there is a second stage, when the patriarchs and prophets themselves must learn the other part of the lesson Hell and Satan have already painfully confronted: that Christ is not only God but also a lowly man. As Christ leads them toward Heaven, the newly rescued souls encounter two anomalous figures and inquire, "Ki iestes vous ki ne fustes pas avoec nous en Infer, et vos estes ja corporelment en char et en os et en la glorie de paradis?" (Who are you who were not with us in Hell, and you are still embodied in flesh and bone and in the glory of Paradise?)[60] These mystery men turn out to be Enoch and Elijah, sent by

Christ to await the Second Coming; their very physicality conveys the ways in which the Resurrection has begun to change the terms in which life and death are understood, and the boundaries of what is possible.

Immediately afterward, the group meets a still more confusing figure, whose apparent incongruity confounds the saints. In the late twelfth- or early thirteenth-century verse translation by Chrestien, the encounter is presented as follows:

> Tant cum Enoc issi parla,
> Dismas i vint, sa croiz porta.
> Li seint demandent: "Ki es tu?
> Dunt venz? u vas? ke portes tu?
> Egardeure as de larun.
> De tun venir nus merveillun."
> Il respundi: "Vus dites veir.
> Léres fui jo, vus dites veir;
> Tuz mals e tuz larecins fis
> En terre tant cum jo fui vifs.
> Jo fui pris, li Judeu me pristrent
> E od Jesu en croiz me mistrent;
> Les miracles de la croiz vi
> E fermement en lui crei.
> J'entendi k'il fut Deus e pére
> E de tutes choses criére,
> E reis puissanz; a lui parlai,
> Sur la croiz merci lui criai:
> 'Sire, merci, mei remenbrez
> Quant en vostre regne vendrez.'
> Ma preiére tost entendi
> E dist a mei sue merci:
> 'Jo t'otrei oi ce jur vendras
> En parays, od mai serras.'"
> . . . .
> Quant li patriarche l'oirent
> E li prophete l'entendirent
> Ço ke li léres ad cunté
> A une voiz sunt escrié:
> "Beneiz seit Deus li tut puissanz,

Par ki tute rens est vivanz,
Pére de parmanableté
Ki sun pople ad revisité
E ad espiritelment mis
En la joie de parays."[61]

[While Enoch was saying this,
Dismas came there, carrying his cross.
The saints asked, "Who are you?
Where do you come from? where are you going? what are you
　　carrying?
You have the look of a thief.
We are astonished by your arrival."
He replied, "You speak the truth.
I was a thief, you are right;
I committed every possible wrong and theft
on earth while I was alive.
I was caught, the Jews took me
and put me on the cross with Jesus;
I saw the miracles of the Cross
and firmly believed in him.
I understood that he was God and father
and creator of all things,
and a powerful king; I spoke to him,
on the cross I begged his forgiveness:
'Lord, mercy, remember me
when you come into your kingdom.'
He heard my prayer at once
and gave me his pardon:
'I promise you, this day you will come
into Paradise, you will be with me.'"
. . . .
When the patriarchs heard this
and the prophets understood
what the thief had recounted,
with one voice they cried out:
"Blessed be God the all-powerful,
through whom everything lives,

Father of eternity
who has returned to his people
and put them spiritually
in the joy of Paradise."]

Chrestien's text makes the thief's appearance a literal interruption: he arrives as
Enoch is speaking. It then aptly conveys the perplexity of the saints, their difficulty in recognizing—even after the lesson in paradox that Christ's arrival in
Hell has just given them—that one with the appearance of a thief, the outward
signs of unworthiness, may yet be among the saved. In a sense, this is the moment when the full implications of Jesus' sacrifice, the reversals Christianity
will entail, take shape. The passage reinforces other key points of Christian
belief, notably in the thief's echo of the Creed, "J'entendi k'il fut Deus e pére /
E de tutes choses criére" (I understood that he was God and father, and creator
of all things), and in the reiteration, not quoted above, that Christ died on the
Cross for "les seinz Deu e ses amis" (the saints of God and his friends) who are
part of the "umaigne generation" (human lineage) descended from Adam.[62]

In all of this, Chrestien, like the prose translators, follows the Latin *Evangelium Nicodemi* quite closely and returns, as they do, to some of the key
terms and emphases of Christ's advent in Hell, especially the question of recognition.[63] The version of the narrative by André de Coutances mentioned
above spells out the implications of several of these moments in more detail.
André's account of Christ's arrival in Hell, almost alone in the tradition, more
or less eliminates his humbleness and smallness; instead the poet's language
consistently emphasizes Christ's power and victory, his godly rather than his
human nature. The lesson that that which is lowly can also be exalted is thus
deferred until the concluding discussion of the good thief, where the tensions
and contradictions inherent in Christian salvation emerge more visibly.

Meeting the thief, a "cheitif huens" (wretched man) whose cross "pareit
que mout li costout" (seemed to weigh upon him greatly), the saints are
bewildered.

"Qui es tu, va, qui çaienz vienz
O tel signe comme tu tienz?
Comment entras tu en ces portes,
Qui signe de laron aportes?
Par cest signe est certefiez
Qu'el monde fus crucefiez."[64]

["Who are you, now, who come in here
with such a sign as you have?
How did you enter into these gates,
you who are bearing the sign of a thief?
By this sign it is certain
that in the world you were crucified."]

The "qui es tu?" echoes the question asked by Hell of Jesus in other versions and marks, like that one, a misrecognition: here not so much of the figure himself but of the *sign* he carries with him.[65] The souls of the just have learned that the cross is a sign, but they have not yet learned how to read it. Their initial sense seems to be that the sign's new meaning applies only to Jesus, that only *his* Cross is redeemed, while the thief's remains a "signe de laron." The thief's role here is to help them understand the radical new dispensation that that sign actually institutes, whereby saviors and thieves, already linked by their unrecognizability and their sudden appearances in unexpected locations (God in Hell; the thief in Heaven) are made still more interchangeable by bearing the same sign.[66]

The thief himself continues the insistent references to the cross as a *signe*: "par mon pechié deservi / Qu'en cest signe fui estenduz / & por mon larrecin penduz" (for my sin I deserved to be stretched upon this sign and hanged for my thievery, 128, ll. 1796–98). The image of the thief "estenduz" on the cross once more recalls (as of course does the whole sequence) his kinship with Christ, and the passage sustains this link. The thief recounts that, unlike his fellow thief on Christ's left, he humbly begged for mercy ("Je criai merci umblement," 129, l. 1808)—a perfectly appropriate action that is, more surprisingly, mirrored a few lines later by Jesus: "When," the thief says, "we had escaped death, he gave me this sign that I bear on my back and said gently: 'Go,' he said, 'at once, with this sign that you are carrying'" ("Quant eschapé fumes de mort, / Cest signe que sor mon col port / Me balla & dist humblement: / 'Va t'en,' dist il, 'isnelement / O tot cest signe que tu portes,'" ll. 1819–23). Christ picks up, or rather turns out to be the originator of, the language of the cross-as-sign; more strikingly, he, like the thief, speaks "humblement"—a word that can certainly be translated as "gently" or "kindly" but that also answers the thief's humility with Christ's own, reminding the audience of the Incarnation as the ultimate instance of the saving power of humility and showing Christ assimilating himself to the thief just as the latter has conformed to him.

As the thief's exchange with Christ makes clear, the power of humility is available not only to Christ but, through the very Incarnation and Crucifixion themselves, to all who are willing to humble themselves. The good thief's account of his crime and his deserved punishment is followed by his introduction of the bad thief (known in the apocryphal tradition as Gestas), who "n'out creance ne foi" (had neither belief nor faith, 129, l. 1800). This phrase is echoed a few lines later, when Dismas specifies, "Je criai merci umblement / & dis *o creance & o foi*: / Sire, soviegne te de moi, / Quant tu en ton regne vendras" (I humbly begged for mercy and said with belief and faith: Lord, remember me when you come into your kingdom, ll. 1808–11, emphasis added). Jesus immediately mirrors this language as well, assuring Dismas of salvation and making it clear that "Gaaignié le t'a bone foi" (true faith has won this for you, l. 1817). The verbal repetitions and distinctions recall the image in the Holkham Bible, where size, posture, and color convey the ways in which the good thief is simultaneously like and unlike both Christ and the bad thief. Having both of them as part of the story, of course, retains the denigration of thieves even as it claims to surpass or trouble it and ensures that the good thief, as his designation suggests, will retain his association with a lowly role even as he becomes exalted.

The primary lesson of the good thief—that belief and true faith, coupled with or expressed as a willingness to acknowledge and repent one's wrongs, are the way to salvation—is of course thoroughly orthodox and time-honored. What is striking about his role in the *Évangile de Nicodème* tradition is, first, the way in which repetition and mirroring assimilate him to Jesus and distinguish him from the bad thief and, second, the emphasis placed on instruction: the thief has gained not only salvation itself but a thorough understanding of its workings, and he now passes that understanding along, becoming the teacher of the patriarchs and prophets. He even, like them, quotes Scripture and enters into the temporal recursion so characteristic of Christian history and liturgy by using events recounted in the Bible to claim the ongoing relevance of those events for the future. Indeed, this saint—the last and least of those who are the first to be saved, but also the first believing Christian to die—is himself the sign of what is to come, of the reversals of salvation; along with Christ, he stands at the very hinge of Christian history. As Arnold of Bonneval says, in the last words of his treatise on the *Septem verbis*, "those who were for a long time ashes have become teachers; and those who were buried have become masters."[67]

The thief also, strikingly, is a figure who offers hope not only to sinful Christians but even, Peter Comestor suggests, to Christ himself: in the *Historia scholastica*, Jesus' cry on the Cross, "Father, why have you forsaken me?" meant

not that the deity was separated from the humanity, but that because
the latter was so given over to trials by the Father he seemed abandoned, or said he was abandoned by the Father, since his Passion
then seemed almost useless, since there did not seem to be anyone in
the whole human race redeemed by it, except the thief who almost
alone believed in him [*nisi latro qui fere solus credebat in eum*].

The thief is "almost" alone, but not quite: "—except the blessed Virgin, whom
we also believe to have believed then."[68] The first sinner-saint and the Virgin
thus offer a thread of hope that links the Crucifixion and death of Jesus to the
Christian future in which many beyond the faithful thief will be saved. Like
the image Satan invokes of Jesus fearing death, this moment strongly connects
him to the human faithful through shared weakness.

The thief's association with both Jesus and Mary, and at the same time
with any Christian sinner, makes him a kind of shadow of Christ in his ability
to exemplify Christian paradox and to convey its teachings. In addition to
offering his own summation of the need for faith and repentance, he becomes
the occasion for the angel guarding the gates to offer a brief theological lesson
to the audience of the *Évangile*. Addressing the thief, the angel in André's version says,

> "Dismas, ci t'esta.
> Adan & ses fiuz viennent ci,
> De qui Deu a eu merci.
> Si entrera Adan tot ainz,
> Qui est père de toz les sainz;
> Après si i entreront tuit
> Quanqu'en avra e son conduit.
> Je ne te veil pas hors tenir
> Que ceenz ne puisses venir,
> Quer cel signe conois je bien;
> Mès un sol petit ci te tien.
> Se tu n'entres as premereins,
> D'entrer i soies tot certeins."[69]

> ["Dismas, stand here.
> Adam and his sons are coming here,
> on whom God has had mercy.

Adam will enter first of all,
as father of all the saints;
afterward everyone will enter there
whom he has brought with him.
I don't want to keep you out
so that you can't come in here,
for I know this sign well;
but stay here just a little while.
If you are not the very first to enter,
still you are quite certain to get in."]

This speech amounts almost to an apology for making Dismas wait; it also makes clear that the angel, at least, "knows this sign well" and that his delay in letting the thief enter reflects no doubt or misrecognition on his part. It may be the case that the last becomes first, but more important, this passage asserts, is the fact that there is enough for all, that last or first, least or greatest no longer matters; as in the parable of the vineyard (Matt. 20:1–16), all those who have received the mercy of God may enter. The angel is careful to point out that the patriarchs and prophets are equally recipients of that mercy; indeed, if one were to be strict about it, they have less right than the thief to enter a Christian Heaven.

Finally, this passage, like the tradition as a whole in its varied ways, shows the centrality of instruction and the ways in which the *Évangile* both teaches and plays with key themes and symbols of Christian belief. The use of "sign" and "cross" as *nearly* interchangeable terms in this passage is highlighted and clarified by the moments when *croiz* does appear. Within the thief's account, only Christ himself uses the word, when he says, "The angel who guards the entrance will take note of this sign and will let you proceed when he sees you holding the cross" ("Li angre qui l'entree garde / De cest signe se prendra garde / & te laira avant venir, / Quant la croiz te verra tenir," 129, ll. 1826–29). For Christ, the terms truly are interchangeable, even at this point in the story. Otherwise, however, only the narrator uses the word: when the thief first appears, "He carried a cross on his back" (Une croiz sor son col portout, 128, l. 1783). Once Dismas has told his tale,

& quant li douz sainz ce oirent
A Jhesum Crist graces rendirent,
Qui les pecheors ne revile

Ne lor penitance n'avile,
Mès volentiers les trait o sei,
Quant repentir les voit o fei.

[and when the gentle saints heard this,
they gave thanks to Jesus Christ,
who does not despise sinners
or look down on their penitence,
but willingly takes them with him
when he sees them repent faithfully.]
(130, ll. 1852–57)

Only at the end of the passage, when Dismas has explained his presence and the saints have reviewed the lesson they have just learned, does the poet—the inheritor of that lesson—again give the cross its proper name: "Then Dismas put his cross down and rested with the saints" ("Lors Dismas sa croiz jus posa / & o les sainz se reposa," ll. 1858–59). In other words, for the brand-new saints, the very first saved Christians, the cross is an untranslatable *signe*, which they cannot even name except to call it "sign": they know it means something, but they do not yet know what until the thief tells his tale, the saints rejoice in him, and the story of the Harrowing ends.

The *Descensus ad inferos* is a radical story in more than one way: it claims to look at the very roots of Christian salvation, its earliest mechanisms and results; it rehearses the scriptural history that foretells and surrounds that moment of salvation; and it performs the simultaneous acknowledgment and undermining of hierarchy so distinctive of Christian belief. At the end of the story it is not just Jesus Christ who "willingly takes with him" those who believe but also the thief himself—the first who can, by experience, teach salvation—and also, finally, the poet, who is both the recipient and the transmitter of this lesson.[70] As Catherine Sanok has observed, "Direct discourse allows for the collapse of contemporary and future audiences"; the thief and the poet here clearly instruct the readers or hearers of the *Évangile* as well as the saints and in doing so reinforce the basic point that the contemporary audience members, as much as the thief, are, if undoubtedly sinners, also potential saints.[71]

The repeated confrontations staged in the *Évangile* and especially in the *Descensus ad inferos*—the spat between Hell and Satan, the advent of Christ so great and so little, the mystery of Enoch and Elijah, dead but not dead, and

finally the puzzle of the thief in Heaven—function, in effect, as a primer of
basic Christian teaching that betrays how non-basic such teaching is, how it
inevitably touches on arcane, mysterious, and sometimes painful theological
issues.[72] It also, of course, offers comfort, the comfort not only of questions
answered (what *did* happen in those three days?) but of a salvation that does
not require theological knowledge, social position, or even a good life and that
insists on the ability of even the lowest to understand and convey the highest
lessons. As Erhard Dorn points out, the many sinner-saints of the Christian
tradition must have offered considerable reassurance to audiences all too
aware of their own sinfulness, and the good thief has a special role in this category.[73] While some other famous *sündige Heilige*, like Peter, Paul, and Mary
Magdalene, went on, despite their failings, to be figures of extraordinary spiritual merit and impact, the good thief—as his very designation suggests—is
defined entirely by the conjunction of sin and faith, and the moment of conversion that changes his own story and becomes part of the Christian narrative; he never lives a saintly life in the world.[74] His role has meaning, in Luke's
telling and the various retellings, through an alternating assimilation to, and
distinction from, the bad thief on the one hand and the patriarchs and prophets (and Jesus) on the other. While medieval theology may flirt with universal
salvation at times, the good thief stands for the idea that anyone *can* be saved
rather than that everyone *will* be. And in so doing he challenges those who
read or hear his story to make distinctions for themselves.

Few Are Saved? The Afterlife of the Good Thief

That the good thief's role in the Gospel made him part of the medieval Christian imagination well beyond his role in the *Evangelium Nicodemi* can be seen,
for example, in the work of Honorius Augustodunensis, whose *Elucidarium*,
as discussed in the previous chapters, became a basic textbook on Christian
doctrine for centuries after its composition in the first quarter of the twelfth
century. Two passages, here quoted from the work's most widely disseminated
French translation, give a clear sense of the role the thief could play in Christian instruction and pastoral care:

> Li deciples demande: Cil qui sont entrepris en aucun forfet, se ce est
> chose que il soient mené a torment, pueent il avoir aucune esper-
> ance de merci se il se repentent? Li mestres respont: Oil, mout

grant, car il i a tieus qui sont espurgié par icest tourment et si sont
sauvé ensement comme fu li lerres qui pendoit ou Nostre Seignor
en la croiz.

[The disciple asks: Can those who are caught in some misdeed, if it
is something that would condemn them to torments, have any hope
of mercy if they repent? The master responds: Yes, great hope, for
there are some who are purged through this torment and are saved,
just like the thief who hung with our Lord on the cross.]

Li deciples demande: Profite nous neant la peneance quant nous
sommes finé de cest siecle? Li mestres respont: Cil qui porloignent a
faire lor peneance jusque au jor de la mort, cil ne lessent pas le
pechié, ainz lessent li pechié eus, quar il ne vuelent pas que il soient
plus lor serf. Mes cil qui de tout le cuer se repentent en meisme la
mort, trouveront grans mercis, si comme fist li lerres quant il cria
merci. Et il est escrit que a quele heure que li pechierres se repente,
il sera faiz saus.[75]

[The disciple asks: Can penance do us any good when we are done
with this world? The master responds: Those who put off doing
penance until the day of death do not leave sin, but rather their sins
leave them, for they [the sins] do not want them [the sinners] to be
their slaves any longer. But those who repent with all their hearts
even at the hour of death will find great mercy, as did the thief
when he begged for mercy. And so it is written that in whatever
hour the sinner repents, he will be saved [Ezek. 33:12].]

The emphasis here is on the formal elements of confession, though out of
their usual order: satisfaction (the purgation the thief undergoes on the cross);
contrition (repenting with all one's heart); and confession (begging for mercy).
The thief became, indeed, closely identified with these key aspects of the sacrament of penance. As the *Glossa ordinaria* puts it, following Bede, "He had
no member free from torment, except heart and tongue, but all that he had
free, he offered. He believed in his heart, he confessed with his mouth."[76]

This strong association with penance made the thief a useful figure in didactic literature, especially as this sacrament became a more central focus of
lay instruction after the Fourth Lateran Council. The *Compileison*, a lengthy

and complex "series of treatises constituting a sort of handbook or manual of religious living" that includes a French translation of sections of the *Ancrene Riwle*, places him firmly in this context; he appears in the part of the work that deals with confession, and specifically in a chapter on the need to make confession with "ferme esperance de avoir pardon de tuz ses pecchez" (firm hope of pardon for all one's sins), avoiding the two pitfalls of despair and presumption.[77] After mentioning St. Peter's forgiveness by Christ, the text goes into some detail about the thief, as one whose example can serve as a bulwark against despair.

> [P]ensez ausint coment li laron sour la croiz, ki avoit vesqui tute sa vie malement en larcin e en totes autres desleautez, par une bele parole e une petite urette du jour tantost fu a lui acordez, e si en out gaigné de nostre seignur ke il averoit pardon e merci de tuz ses pecchez, e ke il en paradis serroit translatez oue les sauvez.[78]

> [Think also of how the thief on the cross, who had lived his whole life wickedly, in theft and in all kinds of other evil deeds, was reconciled with [Jesus] at once for one handsome speech in one brief moment of a day, and by this won from our Lord pardon and mercy for all his sins, and that he would be translated into Paradise with the saved.]

Here the focus is placed primarily on the thief's unlikeliness as a candidate for salvation, though the juxtaposition with St. Peter is a reminder, like the Harrowing, that even the virtuous can stand in dire need of forgiveness. At the same time, the passage echoes in its own way the emphasis on time so characteristic of the *Évangile*, though here the focus falls less on the conjunction of past, present, and future than on the "petite urette du jour," the single crucial instant that changes everything, the individual's own moment of judgment and decision. And of course any reader would already know that the thief's speech to Christ had indeed resulted in his "translation" to Heaven, his transformation into one of the saved, and thus must have represented true repentance.

In that repentance the thief has, as noted above, deployed the power of humility, which according to one preacher is even a power over God himself. As William of Waddington puts it in the *Manuel des pechiez* (c. 1260), again in a section on confession,

Pur ceo dist de confessiun
Seint Bernard li sages hom,
"O humilite de repentanz,
O esperance des confessanz,
Cum as mervillusement
Poer su Deu omnipotent!
Tu veins Deu par ta vertu
Qe par nul poer est vencu,
Le juge qe est si dreiturel,
Qe desur tute rien fet a duter.
L'empire vus trovez tres bien vaillant:
Mult est de tei la vertue grant
Qant pardun conquerez meintenant
Del empereur si pussant."[79]

[Therefore St. Bernard, the wise man,
said of confession,
"O humility of those who repent,
o hope of those who confess,
how wonderfully you have
power over all-powerful God!
You conquer, through your virtue,
God who is conquered by no power,
the judge who is so righteous,
who should be feared above all things.
You find a truly great authority:
how strong is your virtue
when now you win pardon
from so powerful an emperor."

The Latin source goes on to assert that the forgiveness of the prodigal son is even more astonishing than that of the good thief, since "Confession alone saved the thief on the cross; the mere will to confess saved [the prodigal]."[80] The good thief, by acknowledging his crimes and confessing his faith, fulfilled both of the standard criteria for effective confession, "humilite" and "esperance," but, intriguingly, the *Manuel* declines to mention him, perhaps finding his example too dangerous. Elsewhere, in a section on the need to confess willingly, not of necessity at the point of death—a context where the good thief is obviously a less-than-desirable model—the text perhaps pointedly incorporates the story of a different thief, Achor (the biblical Achan), who did *not* freely confess and so was executed after his confession was forced (Josh. 7:16–26).[81] William insists on the lesson: "Achor sunt trestuz cil hom / Qe confession funt de larun; / Qe iesqes point de al mort / Ne se confessant, il unt tort" (Every man who makes a thief's confession is Achor; those who do not confess until the point of death are wrong, *MP* EETS, 352–53, ll. 9687–90).

William of Waddington's avoidance of the good thief indirectly confirms the power of his story as well as the possible discomfort he could elicit, his ability to destabilize the delicate balance of hope and fear that medieval religious teaching tried to inculcate. Modern readings have sometimes overemphasized the negative side of this pairing, overlooking the emphasis on hope; as Alan Bernstein points out, however, in thirteenth-century Paris preachers who refer to Hell "nearly always continue to make the point that sinners can escape hell through the sacrament of penance," since sermons are intended as a goad to a particular behavior and aim "to inspire contrition and to encourage confession."[82] Brian Levy similarly notes, "From the beginning of the thirteenth century the aim of verse sermons shifts crucially, from merely inspiring dread of Hell to inculcating the need for repentance in order to escape the fires."[83] It is telling that William's *Manuel*, which tends toward the fear-inspiring side of the pastoral spectrum, is less welcoming of the good thief, with his potentially explosive deployment of paradox. By, in effect, assimilating himself to Christ, the exemplar of humility, the thief shows his understanding that humility is power, and it is his ability to embrace this paradoxical lesson that exalts him above the bad thief. It is not by his virtue—which is nonexistent—but by his understanding that he is saved. His understanding is theological—the human weakness of Jesus is at the same time the divine power of Christ—and pragmatic: displaying and claiming his own weakness will provide him a kind of power, will, in fact, enable him to compel God.

Catherine Rider discusses a thirteenth-century confession manual that shows how that compelling power extended also to the ecclesiastical hierarchy. Here the confessor is instructed that true contrition can suffice in the absence of every other requirement for salvation:

> And if confession and satisfaction and even baptism are lacking in adults, I say nevertheless that they are not to be held in contempt, but contrition in desire alone suffices, as is clear in the fortunate

thief who, on account of true contrition of heart, was worthy to hear the Lord saying, "This day you will be with me in Paradise."

[Et si desint confessio et satisfactio et etiam baptismus in adultis dico dummodo non habeantur contemptui, set in desiderio sufficit sola contritio ut patet in felici latrone qui pro vera cordis contritione audiri meruit a domino, dicente "Hodie mecum eris in paradiso."][84]

The thief's changed status can thus become the means by which others of equally limited spiritual claims escape the "contempt" that might otherwise come their way, not just theoretically but in the context of direct pastoral engagement. A preacher or confessor who recalled the story of the good thief was not only inculcating in his hearers the importance of true contrition and confession but also offering them an instance of reversal that undermined any monopolistic claims on teaching and judgment.

As in the *Évangile*, then, the uses of the thief in penitential contexts are available for manipulation; he is a figure of just punishment and merited escape, of disgrace and authority. His story of last-minute rescue is impeccably, indeed ostentatiously canonical, and it is his appearance in the Gospels that seems to drive most of his appearances as a figure of penance. At the same time, the currency of the *Évangile*, with its pervasive biblical references and extensions of the story, ensures that his eleventh-hour repentance and salvation are not left as an iconic moment (as they arguably are in the canonical Gospel account) but made part of a larger narrative of instruction, rereading, and interpretation that inculcates some of the most basic, but also most challenging, aspects of Christianity.[85] Even brief mentions of this story—that of the thief specifically or the *Descensus* more generally—thus had the potential to activate a far more complex knowledge of the faith than could the mere image of the thief on the cross and to convey to lay audiences the power of their own ability to learn and to repent.

We see this broader application of his story (as well as a reassertion of its biblical roots) in a thirteenth-century poem on the lives of Jesus and Mary, which begins,

Arestez vos ici un poi
Par .i. covent que je dirai:
Nostre seigneur deprierai

Pour ceus qui ce s'aresteront
Et ma parole escouteront,
Que Dieus leur face vrai pardon
Si con il fist celui larron
Qui a destre de lui pendi
Et mort et passion soufri.[86]

[Stop here a moment
and I will make you a deal:
I will pray to our Lord
for those who stop here
and listen to what I say
that God will grant them true pardon
just as he did for that thief
who hung on his right hand
and suffered death and passion.]

The thief's appearance here may be due to his presence in the story about to be told, that of Jesus' and Mary's earthly lives, but it also highlights the fact that, like the thief, the addressees of this "versified catechism" have the power to help themselves—to take note, as the thief did, of the wonders of God and to react appropriately.[87] The thief, who in the *Évangile de Nicodème* becomes the teacher of saints, is here recalled less on the basis of his contrition than as an exemplary learner who offers a model for others.

In this respect, the thief can be seen to provide an individual, personalized example of how one might be saved and of the distinctions and assimilations that required; in this respect, as well, he echoes Christ, as a figure whose concreteness helps convey an important doctrine in a way easy to grasp. Unlike Christ, however, whose lowliness can reach only so low given his sinless nature, the good thief—shadowed, implicitly or explicitly, by his companion the bad thief—can stand for the sinful believer even as he is able to address the patriarchs and prophets, giving his appeal a wide range. Like the figures within the *Évangile*, those who heard and received it must have been of quite varied spiritual status, and the text itself—apocryphal but asserting its canonicity; linked with "popular" drama but deeply indebted to learned culture—plays out the potential tensions between learned and lay. The story addresses them all on the basis not only of their shared need for mercy and grace but of their interest in the narrative of how God chooses and saves his own.

Here we might return briefly to the creedal context that is entwined with the history of the *Evangelium Nicodemi* and that, as we have seen, helps to originate—in its pairing of descent and ascent—the attention to status that plays out with such complexity in the stories of the good thief. Like those tales, literary reworkings of the Creed reflect the desires and demands of varied audiences whose curiosity about Christ's humanity does not seem to align neatly with any learned/unlearned or religious/lay dichotomy. In both the *Mirour de seinte eglyse* of St. Edmund of Abingdon (a translation of his Latin original, known as the *Speculum religiosorum*) and Pierre d'Abernon's *Lumere as lais*, the presentation and explication of the Creed show a central concern with how the audience might receive this foundational teaching and understand its own relation to that teaching, its place in the story of salvation.

The treatment of the Creed in the *Mirour de seinte eglyse* is particularly suggestive for thinking about audience. The work's twenty-three surviving manuscripts fall into two groups: the A version, in which there is a considerably longer section on the contemplation of God's divine nature, and the B version, which expands sections that treat the Creed, the commandments, and the sacraments. The text's editor, A. D. Wilshere, characterizes the A version as "religious" and the B as "lay," on the basis of these differences, but Nicholas Watson has rightly questioned the usefulness of such a designation and discussed the complexity of the work's audience.[88] The *Mirour* frequently accompanies other texts discussed in this book in manuscript, and in such vernacular didactic compilations the A and B versions are more or less equally represented, suggesting that there was no strict division between them according to audience. As Andrew Reeves notes, "Even with its contemplative, Victorine spirituality, the work is in fact remarkably similar to the sort of basic 'catechetical' program of instruction outlined in Grosseteste's statutes and Pecham's *Ignorantia sacerdotum*."[89]

The *Mirour*'s two versions of the section on the Creed show, in miniature, the same kinds of expansion that seem to have given rise to the Creed itself and to have produced and extended the *Descensus ad inferos*. The A version states, "Le tierz [article] est ke meyme cel Ihesu Deu e homme fu mort e enseveli, ni mie par nécessité mes pur nus rechater de sa pure volunté" (the third [article] is that this very Jesus, God and man, was dead and buried, not at all out of necessity but in order to redeem us purely of his own will), stressing redemption and the freedom of divine will.[90] The B version goes into considerably more detail:

Le tierce article si est; le Fiz la virgine Marie fu pené e crucifié, e en croyz mort soeffri, e en sepulture honestement fu mys. Ceste passion soeffri de son bon gree, e de sa bone volenté por nous reyndre e delivrer de l'enfernal chetiveté. A einfer sa alme descendi ove la deyté, e prist hors les almes k'aveient fet en leur vie sa volenté.[91]

[The third article is as follows: the Son of the Virgin Mary was tortured and crucified, and suffered death on the Cross, and was properly placed in the tomb. He suffered this Passion through his own good will, and out of his virtuous desire to save us and deliver us from hellish captivity. His soul descended to Hell with the Godhead, and took from there the souls that had done his will in their lives.]

The differences are substantial: "cel Ihesu Deu e homme" becomes "le Fiz la virgine Marie"; his suffering and torment on the Cross are added to the brief mention of his death; and, most significant for the present discussion, the *Descensus ad inferos* is included. The B version thus emphasizes the biblical-historical and "affective" aspects of this article, both of which became increasingly important in devotional texts and practices in the later Middle Ages. The reference to the Harrowing of Hell, like the other personalizing elements, increases the focus not only on the humanity of Jesus but on the role of those saved: "He suffered this Passion through his own good will . . . to save us and deliver us from hellish captivity. His soul descended to Hell . . . and took from there the souls that had done his will in their lives." The language of the B version associates the Harrowing of Hell with its implications for living Christians by emphasizing the adherence to God's will that leads to salvation.

If the French B version highlights the role of those hoping for salvation, the *Speculum religiosorum*, the putative Latin original of the text, instead places its focus on Jesus' recognition and claiming of the saved. This version, notably, offers more detail about Jesus' life than does the French A version, a reminder that interest in such detail was not limited to those who read in the vernacular and that a text's language does not always align in obvious ways with its choice of content. The *Speculum religiosorum* says,

The third article is the Son of God, who was also the son of the Virgin, who suffered, was crucified, died and was buried; and this of his own will and not unwillingly, for our redemption and liberation from death, that is from captivity in Hell. His soul, with his God-head, descended into Hell, and freed his people from Hell, restoring them to eternal life.[92]

[Tercius [articulum] est Filius Dei, qui et Virginis filius, passus est, crucifixus, mortuus et sepultus; et hoc spontaneus et non invitus, ad redempcionem et liberacionem nostram a morte, hoc est ab infer-nali captivitate. Cuius anima, cum sua deitate, descendit ad inferos, et ab inferis suos liberavit, quos eterne vite restituit.]

This version is closer to the Old French B version than to A, but its small differences from B are nevertheless instructive: instead of "those who had done [God's] will in their lives" the Latin text has simply "suos," "his own," emphasizing recognition and ultimate fate (*eterna vita*) rather than the ac-tions of the saved.[93] As the *Speculum religiosorum* and the French B version suggest, however, the added material in the text and its responsiveness to a desire for more detail and narrative power are not directed exclusively at lay readers. Even if these additions were originally scribal interpolations, as Wilshere suggests, they suggest that some Latin readers welcomed a fuller account of the nature of Christ and of his actions after the Passion.[94] Indeed, the *Mirour* elsewhere offers a reminder that earthly categories are of less im-portance than eternal ones when, in a discussion of the Pater Noster, it gives a list of earthly estates, ending with the pairs "les povres e les riches, les clers e les lays; e tous ceaus ki sunt destiné a la vye pardurable en chesqun' lignie, en chesqun ordre e en chesqun age" (the poor and the rich, the clerical and the lay; and all those who are destined to the life eternal, of every lineage, in every order and of every age).[95] The lesson of this part of the text is that just as all the heavenly hierarchies (angels, archangels, prophets, martyrs, confes-sors, virgins) do God's will in Heaven, so should all earthly ranks, pope to priest, king to poor man, do it on earth, if they hope to be saved; like many such estates accounts, this carefully accounts for hierarchies while simultane-ously offering a vision of inclusion: "en chesqun' lignie, en chesqun ordre e en chesqun age."

Pierre d'Abernon's *Lumere as lais* shares this interest in delineating, in varied ways, the identities of the saved (and thus, implicitly, the identities of his readers); he combines the French B text's attention to their actions with the Latin text's emphasis on Jesus' claiming of them. The disciple, noting that the master has clarified the nature of Jesus' suffering in the Passion, and the manner of and reason for it, asks that he now discuss its result (*issue*). The master replies,

> L'issue le profit esteit
> E le frut ke de ceo veneit.
> Dunt l'alme le duz Jhesu Crist
> Aprés sa passiun descendist
> En enfern pur deliverer
> Les suens ke le soleient amer.
> Ne delivera pas tutte gent
> For ses membres tut sulement
> K'avant l'aveient ben servi
> E aveient esperance en li,
> E ke sa venue desireient
> E crurent e i afeient,
> Kar grant siecle desiré esteit
> De la gent avant ke veneit.

> [The result was the benefit
> and the fruit that came from this.
> For the soul of the sweet Jesus Christ
> descended after his Passion
> into Hell, to deliver
> his people who loved him.
> He did not deliver all people,
> but only his members
> who before had served him well
> and had hope in him,
> and who desired his coming
> and believed and trusted in it,
> for he had long been desired
> by the people before he came.]
> (Pierre d'Abernon, *Lumere*, 1:160–61, ll. 5257–70)

Here the mention of those who had done God's will in their lives is expanded into an account that includes love, service, hope, desire, and belief—surely an implicit lesson for the audience—even as this passage, like the figure of the bad thief, insists also on those who will *not* be saved. This rendering picks up on central Christian ideas treated at length elsewhere in Pierre's text, reminding his audience of the lessons on love they have already been learning and that are necessary for their salvation, and on the importance of applying those lessons correctly in their own lives. This depiction of the Passion's effects also strongly recalls the expansion of the Creed constituted by the events of the *Gospel of Nicodemus*. Although the apocryphal Gospel is not specifically referred to, its influence is evident in Pierre's echo of the hope and longing, and the attention to temporality, so distinctively present in the *Évangile de Nicodème*.

Like the *Évangile*, with its depictions of the patriarchs and prophets as simultaneously text and body, vivifying their past words by speaking them in the (textual) present, the *Lumere* emphasizes temporal conjunctions to bring a historical representation to life. Pierre repeatedly evokes those rescued from Hell as being in the past but looking to the future: "avant l'aveient ben servi / E aveient esperance en li . . . sa venue desireient . . . grant siecle desiré esteit . . . avant ke veneit" (they had served him well before and had hope in him . . . they desired his coming . . . he was desired for a long time . . . before he came). The passage insists, through repetition and verbal echo, on past action and hope for the future; in doing so, it provides its audience with a promise that they too will be saved if their present actions, informed by the instruction they receive here, demonstrate their faith in what is to come. In a kind of inversion of the stories of death explored in the previous chapter, the recollection of the Passion, like the *Évangile de Nicodème* and its offshoots, asks audiences to look backward to those who looked forward, rather than forward to those looking back.

In the long history of accretions that eventually gives rise to the *Evangelium Nicodemi*—the evolution of baptismal formula into a Creed that elaborates on the nature of Christ; the addition to that Creed of the *Descensus ad inferos* that details the turn from descent to ascent; the elaboration of that account and its insertion into the apocryphal narrative of Christ's burial—we see an interaction of lay and clerical questions and responses, as Christians regardless of status considered the implications of Jesus' two natures, his death and Resurrection, and their own place in the story. The persistence of the good thief as an image of humility's power to save, of the need to understand Christ's two natures as a means to faith, and of the possibility of last-minute reprieve works powerfully to remind audiences that at the moment of death the last may become first, saints get their comeuppance, and the radical implications of Christian doctrine allow the last and least not only to enter Heaven but even to teach others the way. As we will see in the next chapter, the good thief becomes part of a lineage of sinner-saints who carry the message of reversal from apocryphal biblical literature into the realms of hagiography and even fabliau.

Chapter 4

Getting the Riffraff into Heaven: Jongleurs, Whores, Peasants, and Popular Eschatology

The *Évangile de Nicodème*, as the previous chapter argues, represents a process of questioning and response that created compelling narratives around key human moments of the canonical Gospels and particularly showcases the learning and dialogue—and awareness of the instability of earthly status—required by Christian belief. The influence of such Church teachings is clear in the broad manuscript diffusion of the *Evangelium Nicodemi* and its vernacular offspring but also in the echoes of the Descent and the Harrowing that appear in secular literature of various genres.[1] Here I take up the question of how earthly status inflects the moment of individual judgment in "popular" narratives that represent the salvation of despised individuals—peasants, whores, jongleurs—with a particular focus on a subgroup I call the eschatological fabliaux. Considerably less earnest than the doctrinal works discussed in earlier chapters, these Continental French texts nevertheless explore related questions and reflect the widespread dissemination of religious teaching about the moment of death encouraged by, but not limited to, sermonic discourses. If the self-aware teaching of doctrinal works and the various confrontations of the *Évangile de Nicodème* draw our attention to the interlaced creation and reception of religious instruction in the vernacular, the fabliaux take up the challenge posed at the end of the *Évangile* by beginning to retell the story of salvation in a fully vernacular mode. Indeed, these texts are the only ones I examine here that make no claim to be linguistic translations; instead, they perform a different kind of *translatio*, transferring Christian imagery and teaching into a new genre.

These "funny short stories in verse" choose to be funny on a topic whose humor was not always appreciated in the didactic literature of the time: eschatology, or more specifically individual eschatology—the fate of the soul at the point of death.[2] Such fabliaux' confounding of our expectations about the various Great Divides of medieval culture—between clerical and lay, the didactic and the entertaining, the sacred and the profane—is both salutary and, as it were, topical.[3] That is, their interest in the moment of death and its outcome, while it draws on various themes and images that appear also in clerical texts from papal decrees to popular sermons, does not just upend or mock the teachings of those works but implicitly poses them sharp questions, questions that coalesce around a crucial aspect of the idea of judgment: the ability to make distinctions, to sort and categorize. In thinking about the moment of an individual's death, these fabliaux comment not only on that moment's possible outcomes and implications but on the educational project that both referred to and, ideally, shaped the moment of judgment.

This chapter emphasizes jongleurs (*jogleors*), peasants (*vilains*), and whores (*putains*) for two reasons. First, their lowly status, whether moral or social, when put in an eternal context, picks up on and extends the pressing questions of Christian reversal already touched on in the story of the good thief: will the last *really* be first? And which "last" do we mean, precisely? Such questions comment in turn on the very process of lay spiritual instruction that was taking place at the time, asking, implicitly and sometimes explicitly, who should be doing the teaching. And second, jongleurs and peasants, at least, hold a privileged, if difficult, place in that process of instruction: jongleurs as the figures whose capacity to disseminate information and instruction was a thorny model for the clergy as they tried to do the same, and *vilains* as the limit case, so to speak, of the laity, the ultimate *illiterati* who could represent the spiritual status of the increasingly literate wealthy laity even as they embodied the antithesis of its worldly status.[4]

That all three of these groups represent, in different ways, what a modern reader might regard as abjection—that which "disturbs identity, system, order"—makes them particularly useful for an examination of questions about status in this very status-conscious period.[5] Indeed, their place as, in St. Paul's words, "the refuse of this world, the offscourings of all" (*purgamenta huius mundi . . . omnium peripsima*, 1 Cor. 4:13), could make them the vehicles of an impeccably Christian exercise in role reversal. Jongleurs, for instance, come in for scathing critique in clerical texts of this period. They are regarded not simply as objectionable but indeed as completely beyond the pale: the jongleur's "social uselessness (he is good for no one and nothing) is sufficient to justify his exclusion from the social body and the community of the faithful."[6] He is thus, not surprisingly, also excluded from the community of the saved. The *Lucidaires* based on Honorius Augustodunensis's *Elucidarium* presents an exchange between master and disciple on a variety of topics, including the hopes of salvation of various worldly estates, from the clergy on down through fools and infants. After inquiring as to the hopes of prelates, priests, other ministers of the Church, monks, knights, merchants, and artisans—for most of whom, particularly the secular estates, the outlook is fairly grim—the disciple asks about jongleurs. Here the answer is unequivocal. "Quele esperance pueent avoir li jugleour?" asks the disciple. "Nulle," replies the master. (What hope can the jongleurs have? None.) The rationale is soon given: in intention, they are ministers of the Devil (de toute lor entencion sont il minstre au deable); those who have scorned God, He will scorn (pour ce que il furent escharnisseur, si les escharnira Dieus).[7] Honorius's edict—from a work that, as we have seen, was translated into almost every European vernacular and had an extraordinarily extensive influence in the late Middle Ages—represents an early instance of the ever-growing supply of pronouncements on who goes to Heaven and suggests the dim ecclesiastical view of jongleurs.

Another, more famous example comes from the uncategorizable "chantefable" *Aucassin and Nicolette*, from the early thirteenth century. Warned that if he takes Nicolette as his mistress he will never go to Heaven, Aucassin replies,

En paradis qu'ai je à faire? Je n'i quier entrer, mais que j'aie Nicolete ma tresdouce amie que j'aim tant; c'en paradis ne vont fors tex gens con je vous dirai. Il i vont ci viel prestre et cil viel clop et cil manke qui tote jor et tote nuit cropent devant ces autex et en ces vies creutes, et cil a ces viés capes ereses et a ces viés tatereles vestues, qui sont nu et decauc et estrumelé, qui moeurent de faim et de soi et de froit et de mesaises; icil vont en paradis: aveuc ciax n'ai jou que faire. Mais en infer voil jou aler, car en infer vont li bel clerc, et li bel cevalier qui sont mort as tornois et as rices gueres, et li buen sergant et le franc home: aveuc ciax voil jou aler; et s'i vont les beles dames cortoises qui eles ont deus amis ou trois avoc leur barons, et s'i va li ors et le argens et li vairs et li gris, et si i vont herpeor et jogleor et li roi di siecle: avoc ciax voil jou aler, maisi que j'aie Nicolete ma tresdouce amie aveuc mi.[8]

[What would I want with Heaven? I don't want to enter there unless I could have Nicolette, my darling beloved whom I love so much; for the only people who go to Heaven are the kind I'll tell you about. Old priests go there, and the lame and the one-armed who crouch in front of altars and in old grottoes all day and night, and those dressed in old tattered cloaks and old rags, who are naked and shoeless and barefoot, who died of hunger and thirst and cold and diseases; those people go to Heaven: I have nothing to do with them. But I want to go to Hell, for the handsome clerks go to Hell, and the handsome knights who died in tournaments and in great wars, and the good men-at-arms and the noblemen: I want to go with them; and also the beautiful courtly ladies go there, who have two or three lovers as well as their husbands, and gold and silver and rich furs; and harpers and jongleurs and the kings of the world go there: I want to go with them, provided I might have my darling beloved Nicolette with me.]

The passage is in keeping with the work's overall topsy-turvy and parodic nature but also has echoes, as we will see, both in fabliaux and in the Marian miracles discussed in the next chapter. It manages, like many of those works, to poke fun at both the saved and the damned; the religious *escharnissement* implicitly directed at "li bel clerc . . . li bel cevalier . . . et . . . les beles dames cortoises" on their elegant way to Hell is paralleled by the social scorn heaped on the ratty hordes of the saved. Like Honorius, the anonymous creator of *Aucassin and Nicolette* thus has his hero dispatch jongleurs en masse to Hell, though here it is clear that they will have a great deal of high-class company. Indeed, Honorius has no very kind word to say about knights, either, since "il vivent de proie, et de rapine se vestent; et de ce si achatent possesions et richesces. Et pour ce si est Dieus iriés a eus" (they live by plunder, and clothe themselves through theft; and with this they buy possessions and riches. And God is angry with them for this).[9] Aucassin's parodic account, that is, has much the same bottom line as Honorius's severe pronouncements. At the same time, jongleurs' precarious and dependent social position can make them simultaneously outcast and universal in a way that we seldom see with knights: "Le jongleur, comme le *stultus*, le *simplex*, l'*ydiota*, manifeste l'abîme de péché qui sépare l'homme de Dieu," so that his salvation showcases both the necessity and the availability of grace, the all-important divine contribution to an individual's chance at eternal life.[10]

The divided but largely negative attitude toward peasants was in some ways similar to that shown to jongleurs, although the former's abjection derived primarily from courtly rather than clerical value systems. As *laboratores*, those who work, whose labor feeds the other orders of society, they were not subject to the accusations of uselessness that excised jongleurs from the social body. Honorius, for instance, gives them one of his few favorable assessments, declaring of *vilains*, "Une grant partie en i a des saus de ceus qui simplement vivent, car il pessent le pueple Nostre Seignor de leur grains sueurs et de leur travaus; quar il est escrit que cil qui manjuent le labor de lor mains qu'il sont beneuré" (There are a great number of the saved among those who live simply, for they feed the people of our Lord with their great sweat and their labors; for it is written that those who eat the labor of their hands will be blessed).[11] At the same time, by etymological accident the very name *vilain* takes on the "moral connotation of abjection" attached to the unrelated Old French *vil*, so that *vilain*, originally a neutral term for a countryman, can be used as a condemnation rather than simply a description.[12] Like jongleurs in clerical texts, *vilains* may be seen as outcasts of a kind; they are often depicted as demonic or bestial in ways that distance them from the rest of humanity—a tendency on display in both *Aucassin and Nicolette* and Chrétien de Troyes' *Yvain*.[13] We might note that Aucassin's catalogue of who goes to Heaven, who to Hell takes no account of peasants at all; for the most part they simply do not form part of the chivalric imagination except when needed for contrast.

The same might be said of whores with regard to the religious imagination: that is, their great function, like that of *vilains* in the courtly sphere, is to provide contrast. Since representations of prostitutes in medieval literature appear most extensively in the numerous *vitae* of harlot saints, however, the contrast here is contained within a single figure. Ruth Mazo Karras points out that the ultimate harlot saint, Mary Magdalene, was "probably the most popular saint (after the Virgin Mary) in all of medieval Europe," making it clear that the conjunction of exaltation and abjection held an enduring fascination in this as in other realms.[14] While prostitutes do not tend to get their own entry in estates lists—their fate being, presumably, too obvious to require mention—they have a role in some ways similar to that of jongleurs, in that they lure others to sin ("ministers of the Devil," as Honorius says of jongleurs) and in their association with excess.[15] They also have the potential, exemplified by Mary Magdalene, to embody both the most negative and the most positive qualities associated with women (carnality on the one hand; ardent religious devotion on the other), just as peasants and jongleurs can convey both worldliness and simplicity.

Despite the differences in their eternal fates according to various sche-
mata, peasants, whores, and jongleurs are often discussed in spatial terms or,
more precisely, in terms of social *place*. One of the most troubling features of
jongleurs, for those who wished to critique them, was their tendency to wander. This "perpetual errancy" confirmed their lack of a place in society, according to the churchmen: "they traversed all social classes, but belonged to
none."[16] They were thus placeless not only in terms of social representations,
such as the three orders or the categorizing of the world by social or professional estates, but also in terms of social rank and literal physical movement.
The emphasis on prostitutes as "common women" can have a similar effect of
social placelessness; a fourteenth-century French *mystère* has Mary Magdalene
declare, "I was never slow to sin, / but always ready, / Peasant, townsman,
clerk or priest!"[17] For peasants, the problem is the reverse: the very name
vilain, from medieval Latin *villanus*, implies a link to a place, and the image
of peasant laborers as the "feet" of the Church gives them a very definite place
in the imagined social body. But it also weighs them down, as it were, with the
burden of that place, and peasants who have the effrontery to leave their designated location in the social scheme are treated as moral and social transgres-
sors.[18] All three groups, that is, hint at uneasiness surrounding the idea of a
fixed social or moral location, the fear that efforts to keep people in their
places may not be sustainable.

The recurrent notion of a "proper place" becomes strikingly pertinent
when we turn to texts that deal with its ultimate manifestation, the place of
the soul after judgment. Jacques Le Goff famously argued that the gradual
emergence of the "third place" in the twelfth and thirteenth centuries was part
of a larger obsession with "middleness"—in this case, the *mediocriter boni* and
mediocriter mali, the not entirely good and not entirely bad of Augustine's
four-part scheme, who in the later period are collapsed into one large category
of *mediocres*, those "for which a recommendation . . . must be made" as to
their final assignment.[19] As Le Goff notes, "In order for Purgatory to be born,
the notion of 'intermediacy' had to take on some substance, had to become
'good to think [with]' for the men of the Middle Ages."[20] In light of this
strong association between social categorization, eternal fate, and Purgatory, it
is intriguing to note that Purgatory appears not at all in the fabliaux and other
texts discussed below. Their approach to status bypasses any mediating categories, any way of accommodating those in the middle—and this is perhaps
because they specifically and emphatically treat groups that, as noted, were
perceived as being not in the middle but at the extremes, the lowest of the low,

the offscourings of all. The way in which they present members of those
groups, however, serves not simply to challenge an existing categorization but
to question the very *process* of categorization—to ask the other characters in
the stories, and implicitly their audiences, but also a modern reader to think
again about how we decide who goes where, and to question our own distinctive status as experts—as *litterati*.[21]

Bad Company: Saints, Sinners, and Manuscript Contexts

The fabliaux I discuss below are by no means alone in offering a tricky juxtaposition of the profane and the eternal; two other examples can help sketch
out the problems of categorization and context that frame the fabliaux' comic
reversals. The first is a *dit* known as *Des Putains et des lecheors* (Whores and
Jongleurs) or *Des Trois commandemens* (The Three Commandments).[22] It recounts how, when God created the world, he established three classes: knights,
clerks, and laborers—the familiar "those who fight, those who pray, those who
work" triad of medieval European society—and assigned each its proper
sphere.[23] As God turns to go after completing this work, however, he is im-
portuned by a crowd of whores and jongleurs, who ask him to support them,
too, as he has done so much for others. At this point, God turns to St. Peter
(apparently the action takes place *sub specie aeternitatis*) and asks who these
people are, suggesting that even their creator finds them difficult to account
for. Peter tells him that they are "Une gens . . . forfaite, / Que vos avés autresi
faite / Com çaus qui de vos biens se fient" (a wicked people, whom you created just as you did those who trust in your goodness).[24] The conversation
both highlights Peter's foundational role in Christianity and points to the story's temporal incoherence, its simultaneous participation in two different moments of salvation history; it also may recall Peter's own famous role as a
sinner-saint, one who refused to recognize God.

After Peter's explanation, God goes back to the knights and clerks, com-
mending the jongleurs to the particular care of the former and the whores to
the latter. The remainder of the poem, which is almost half its length, is devoted to the observation that while the clerks have kept God's commandment
honorably, feeding, dressing, and sleeping with the whores, the knights have
fallen down badly on their part of the bargain, failing to reward or sustain the
jongleurs. The moral is clear: "Si cis fableaus dist voir, dont sont / De cest
commant li clerc sauvé / Et tuit li chevalier danné" (If this fabliau tells the

truth, then in light of this commandment clerks are saved, and all the knights are damned, ll. 84–86). This text's marked interest in social groups is sustained by the work that immediately follows it in Bern, Burgerbibliothek, MS 354, *L'Escommeniement au lecheor*, a mock "excommunication" of a broad and motley assortment of people, including "Vilain qui devient chevaliers, / Jugleor qui n'est mençongiers" (A peasant who becomes a knight, a jongleur who is not a liar, ll. 45–46) and "pute esposee / Se de lecheor n'est privee" (a whorish wife, if she is not intimate with a *lecheor*, ll. 201–2). On the other hand, the poem concludes, "J'escommeni toz tricheors, / Fors sol putains et lecheors: / Que Diex les mete a granz anors!" (I excommunicate all scoundrels, save only whores and *lecheors*: may God give them great honor, ll. 261–63). The text's editor notes that the exclusion of whores and jongleurs from excommunication is peculiar to this version—a "striking coincidence" at the very least, given its proximity to *Des Putains*, and one that reinforces the importance of the estates element here.[25]

Like didactic works, but in a comic vein, *Des Putains et des lecheors* thus conjoins questions of eternal status and the existing social hierarchy. In the thirteenth century the "three orders" model, while still a default option mentioned in many texts, was coming under considerable strain, due particularly to the ever-increasing expansion of the category of *laboratores*—that is, those who were neither clerks, monks, nor knights. The whores and jongleurs whose economic well-being is so central to this tale would, in the great scheme of things, seem to fall into this final category, though they complicate it by being laborers whose labor has no visible product and only dubious claims to social utility.[26] At the same time, they are here clearly depicted as having a place in the social order, however parasitic and belated, and one that, moreover, is explicitly guaranteed by God's "commandment." The tale thus demonstrates the widespread tendency to think simultaneously in terms of earthly status and eternal reward but shows that this tendency was by no means always a matter of either reinforcing or reversing hierarchies; the difficulty of fitting the *putains et lecheors* into the tripartite structure reveals that there is "excess baggage which cannot be contained in these categories, which are consequently revealed to be unstable."[27] *Des Putains* thus has it both ways, managing to claim a foundation in eternity for the existing "official" order of society while also mocking its inability to represent that society adequately.

In doing so, the *dit* has chosen its groups well; despite their reviled status, both jongleurs and *putains* were indisputably part of, and in reality not marginal to, medieval society.[28] *Des Putains et des lecheors*, which could equally have been written by a clerk or a jongleur, insofar as those categories can be reliably distinguished, takes advantage of the simultaneous ubiquity and (theoretical) exclusion of the two groups. By associating jongleurs with whores, it allows each group's negative associations to infect the other, and it places both of them outside the three central categories; at the same time, the whores and jongleurs are given a special dispensation from God as those deserving, like the poor, of support and linked by divine decree to the emphatically "canonical" categories of chivalry and clergy. The *dit* also asserts that the clerks' good treatment of the whores is being inscribed on their eternal account book; their "works" (*uevre*) in this regard will serve them well in Heaven.[29]

The setting and personages of *Des Putains et des lecheors*—various social orders, plus God and St. Peter, in a frame that happily intermingles eternal and contemporary elements—are ones that recur throughout the texts I will look at here. That texts deploying sacred personages for comic effect may have formed a recognizable group is intermittently suggested by manuscript context. All the fabliaux I consider here appear, as is typical of the genre, in manuscripts with wildly varied contents—manuscripts of the kind that used to be dubbed "miscellanies" but are lately more often seen as "anthologies." Although four manuscripts contain more than one of the texts discussed here, in two cases they are so far apart, and in manuscripts so large and varied, that nothing can be deduced about their relationship. In the other two cases, however, we find members of this group juxtaposed or in close quarters. Both instances involve the fabliau of *Le Vilain qui conquist paradis par plait* (The Peasant Who Argued His Way into Heaven) discussed below, which is the most widely attested of this group, appearing in five manuscripts, a large number for a fabliau. In the first, Paris, BnF fr. 19152, *Vilain qui conquist* immediately follows *S. Pierre et le jongleur*; Keith Busby has called them, in this context, "surely a matching pair" and noted the pervasive "moral and didactic concerns" of the manuscript, which seem to extend even to its fabliaux.[30] In Nottingham, University Library, MS Middleton L.M.6, *Vilain qui conquist* is separated from *Des Putains* only by Raoul de Houdenc's *Dit des eles* (a work on chivalric ideals, more commonly known as the *Roman des eles*). Interestingly, the outlier of the group is Rutebeuf's *Le Pet au vilain*, which appears only in the massive compilation Paris, BnF fr. 837, where it is many folios away from both *S. Pierre et le jongleur* and *Le Vilain qui conquist paradis par plait*. The tendency for Rutebeuf's works to travel together in an author-compendium within a larger manuscript may well have influenced their transmission; the more "detachable," often anonymous fabliaux are more likely to be found in company with one another.[31] On the other hand, Richard Trachsler has noted that Jehan Bodel's fabliau *Le Vilain de Bailluel*, which appears in a group of fabliaux also containing *Le Pet au vilain* in Chantilly, Musée Condé, MS 475, involves a peasant who believes himself to be dead (on the assertion of his adulterous wife) and thus gestures toward afterlife-vision narratives, suggesting a possible thematic connection.[32]

This manuscript proximity is of interest for two reasons. First, since in both the Paris and Nottingham manuscripts the pair of texts includes one about a peasant and one about a jongleur (or jongleurs), they suggest that the status questions raised by each group may have been seen as comparable. Second, in their joining of disparate realms—and perhaps especially in their use of St. Peter, who appears in three of these four texts—they challenge what might at first glance seem to be one of the greatest gaps between medieval genres, that which separates fabliaux from hagiography. The two genres usually travel together only in very large and varied collections, and indeed their codicological profiles, so to speak, are very different: while hagiography provides "[t]he clearest examples of manuscripts defined as genre collections," fabliaux are persistently miscellaneous, appearing almost exclusively in manuscripts with widely varied kinds of texts.[33] While within those manuscripts they often appear in pairs or small groups, it seems clear that one of the roles of fabliaux was to respond to or comment upon the other genres they accompanied.[34] It is now widely acknowledged that the fabliaux display considerable overlap and intertextual play with such genres as romance and epic, but perhaps partly for the codicological reasons noted here, as well as the apparent antipathy between the two genres, their links to hagiographical narratives have drawn less interest. In popular eschatology, however, the religious figures and doctrines that are the bread and butter of saints' lives are adopted into a very different milieu.[35] Simon Gaunt, while calling fabliaux and hagiography "[i]n many respects . . . worlds apart as genres," nevertheless makes them the subjects of consecutive chapters in his *Gender and Genre*, noting "their mobile view of gender as a construct and their clear sense of gender as a hierarchy"; that mobility and "mistrust of fixed hierarchies" are part of what connects the two genres' treatments of religious figures as well.[36]

In addition to shared themes and formal features that characterize both fabliau and hagiography, these categories have at least one known author in common, the "clerc-jongleur" Rutebeuf, whose extensive archive contains five tales usually characterized as fabliaux as well as two Marian miracles (including a play of Theophilus) and the lives of SS. Mary the Egyptian and Elizabeth of Hungary.[37] Indeed, a good number of the relatively few manuscripts that contain both fabliaux and saints' lives do so because they contain his collected works. Yet Rutebeuf, while perhaps unusual in making use of both genres, is by no means sui generis, as his predecessor Jehan Bodel confirms; both authors are picking up on certain resonances and concerns that characterize both hagiography and fabliau.[38] The saints, as portrayed in their medieval *vitae*, are quite capable of adopting an outspokenness that, while it cannot rival the most salacious fabliaux, does share their enjoyment of verbal wit; and like fabliaux, many saints' lives (particularly those of the martyrs) center around a struggle for primacy that features a dramatic reversal highlighted by linguistic skirmishes, and enter with considerable enthusiasm into the details of physical harm. Finally, there are instances where a saint—most commonly St. Martin—appears in a fabliau (as he also does in exempla), making it into a kind of parodic miracle tale where the recipient of the saint's magical aid ends up worse off than he started. In Bodel's late twelfth-century *Les Souhaiz que sainz Martins dona anvieus et coveitous* (The Wishes St. Martin Granted to Envious and Covetous), the envious man, granted a wish that he knows his covetous companion will double for himself, asks to have one eye put out so that his companion will lose both. The story, as Keith Busby notes, follows the "sacred parodies" of the *Usurer's Paternoster* and *Creed* in Bern, Burgerbibliothek, MS 354 (which also, as noted above, contains *Des Putains et des lecheors*); and it appears as an exemplum in Jacques de Vitry's *Sermones vulgares* in the early thirteenth century.[39]

Rutebeuf, writing later in the century, is a clear inheritor of narrative and manuscript traditions that could encompass, and play with, the shared elements of saints' lives and fabliaux—especially fabliaux that exploit the scenes and language of religious history and devotion. The energy gained from contrast is evident in his life of the harlot saint Mary the Egyptian, one of several insular and Continental *vitae* of this well-known figure.[40] The verbal wit that characterizes even Rutebeuf's most "serious" works is in evidence from the beginning, where the poet belabors the word *oevre*, "work":

Ne puet venir trop tart a euvre
Boenz oevriers qui sans laisseir euvre,
Car boenz ovriers, sachiez, regarde,
Quant il vient tart, se il se tarde.
Et lors n'i a ne plus ne mains,

Ainz met en euvre les .II. mainz,
Que il ataint toz les premiers:
C'est li droiz de toz boens ovriers.
D'une ovriere vos wel retraire . . .[41]

[A good worker who works without wearying
cannot start his work too late,
for the good worker, you may be sure,
when he arrives late, looks to see if he is behind.
And then there is nothing for it,
but he puts both hands to work
so that he catches up with all the leaders:
that's the right of all good workers.
I want to tell you about a working girl . . .]

One might be forgiven, in the first few lines, for thinking that the work referred to is the poet's own—perhaps especially in the case of Rutebeuf, whose "repentance" forms the subject of more than one of his poems and who is here writing a piece that might well be seen as a late start on good works after youthful indiscretions.[42] We soon discover, however, that the work in question is that of the whore, not the jongleur—but that she, too, eventually redeems herself. Having begun her conversion when miraculously blocked from entering a church, and gaining entry only through prayer to the Virgin, she ultimately finds, against the odds, a "porte overte" (open door, l. 13) in Heaven, echoing "ouvra" (worked) just above: her works open the door.

Throughout his account of her early sinful life, Rutebeuf plays with the idea of Mary's "calling" as a whore, semicomically portraying it as a vocation pursued with admirable energy and focus: "S'entencions fut toute pure / A plus ovreir de la luxure" (She had the purest intention of working harder at lasciviousness, ll. 111–12). Like jongleurs, Mary becomes an instrument of Satan, costing God many souls; like the jongleurs, too, she is "without bounds or measure" ("N'i avoit bone ne mesure," l. 48) and much given to "geuz" and white nights.[43] Ultimately, of course, she mends her ways and becomes a *meretrix Dei* with a very different calling but one that, like her first profession, benefits from her utter devotion to her work. Mary's bad qualities and low status, once recast by repentance, provide the energy that fuels her as a saint and make her an exemplary figure able to instruct others.

The poem is obsessed throughout with repentance and salvation; God is

frequently characterized as "He who rescued us from Hell," and the central
characters, Mary and the devout abbot Zozimas, declare their intention to live
a life that will make them worthy at the Last Judgment.[44] As Suzanne Nash
has pointed out, Rutebeuf's poem is characterized, "[m]ore than any other
version in the tradition . . .[,] by elements taken from the Church service:
prayer, incantation, litany, Scripture"; it also contains two passages that echo
the Credo—all of which showcase the tale's connections to basic Christian
education.[45] Though emphatic about these links, Rutebeuf is not alone in
making them. In version *T* of the legend, the Creed and Pater Noster play an
important role in the second meeting of Mary and Zozimas: after she has
crossed the river to reach him and they have kissed one another,

> Ele li quiert le Credo Dé
> Qu'il li die por l'amor Dé,
> Et il li dist molt belement
> Et le Patrenostre ensement;
> L[a] dame respont aprés lui,
> Molt s'entregardent ambedui.[46]

> [She asks him for the *Credo in Deum*,
> that he should tell her for the love of God,
> and he tells it to her very kindly
> and the Pater Noster as well;
> the lady repeats after him,
> they look at one another intently.]

In this appealingly dialogic encounter, Mary's request and response frame
Zozimas's speaking of the prayers and the passage ends on a moment of mutual regard. Mary is here cast as an idealized, elementary learner in a way that
highlights the legend's recurrent interest in status and teaching.

Rutebeuf approaches the pervasive theme of status by showcasing penitence as the quality that can reverse apparent hierarchies. Before he meets the
fledgling saint, Zozimas falls into spiritual pride, going so far as to boast, "N'a
il es desers qui me vaille: / Je sui li grains, il sont la paille" (There is no one in
the desert to equal me: I am the wheat, they are the chaff, ll. 569–70)—a characterization that, in this context, cannot but be ironic. He is rescued from his
inflated self-image by a divine visitation that sends him first to the desert

hermits and then to Mary herself, and he "becomes aware of his own sinful-ness by hearing Mary's confession," a neat inversion of the usual hierarchy between priest and penitent.[47] His subsequent interactions with her consist largely of humility contests, in which each participant emphasizes his or her unworthiness to bless the other. The poem thus plays out, and plays with, the status reversals that are intrinsic to Christian teaching and the efficacy of pen-itence in making the last first.

Interestingly, an anecdote surviving in numerous versions narrates a sta-tus reversal or challenge similar to that in the life of Mary the Egyptian but in which the role of the sinner saved by penitence, who subsequently offers a humbling model to a figure of more conventional piety, is played by a jon-gleur. Silvère Menegaldo gives a brief account: a hermit falls into spiritual pride as a result of his own excellence and has a vision in which he is told that a jongleur will be his fellow in Paradise. He is angry until he meets his future companion and hears about his life, which is still more holy than his own; he then repents and sees the jongleur precede him into Heaven.[48] A third version of the tale—deriving from the *Vitae Patrum* and included in the *Manuel des pechiez*—tells of a holy abbot who has a revelation, while praying, that he has yet to reach the spiritual perfection of two virtuous married women in a nearby town.[49] The parallel structures of the tales cast jongleurs, reformed harlots, and laywomen in a shared role that insists both on their perceived lowliness and on the exaltation it enables. Rutebeuf's poem follows a tradition that insists on the power of holy simplicity and, as it were, remedial faith, and meditates, in its own way, on how the work of whores and jongleurs can serve divine ends—most obviously by producing hagiography itself.

The association between *jouglerie, puterie,* and *clergie* is displayed explic-itly in another version of Mary the Egyptian's life, which survives in a Marian miracle collection that forms part of British Library, Royal MS 20.B.XIV, a codex composed primarily of doctrinal poetry including the *Mirour de seinte eglyse* and the *Manuel des pechiez*. Whereas Rutebeuf's version emphasizes Zozimas's pride in his learning, setting him up as "an 'intellectual' monk who has learned about sin and salvation 'par les enseignemenz'" in order to knock him down, and version *T* depicts Mary as a childlike learner, the account in the Royal MS follows and expands on its Latin source in approaching learned-ness from another angle.[50] The anonymous Anglo-French poet demonstrates Mary's miraculous virtue in part through her miraculous *clergie*. When she addresses Zozimas,

Sicum unke ne sout lettrure,
Ele li precha de l'escripture
Si ben de parfunde cleregie,
Cum ele ust leüe tute sa vie
De devinité en escole,
Tant fu clerigele sa parole.[51]

[though she never knew how to read,
she preached to him on Scripture
with deep learning, as well
as if she had been reading about divinity
in school all her life,
her speech was so clerical.]

If this version of the story avoids the question of Zozimas's spiritual pride, which is never mentioned, it nevertheless emphasizes a different approach to learnedness. The reversal enabled by Mary's conversion does not just give her moral status but allows her to inhabit the place of a clerk: her unconventional path has converged with that of the trained teacher, and like the good thief addressing the patriarchs and prophets, she uses the power of her own story to vault into a noble position in the spiritual hierarchy, to make her lowliness the grounds of her exaltation.

Remediable Outcasts and Fabliau Eschatology

The *Vie de sainte Marie l'Egypcienne* is linked to the stories of *vilains* and *jongleurs* both through its intense interest in status reversal and through the protagonist's own "vilainie" or "vilaine" status—which in this case is, of course, moral rather than social. After naming Mary, Rutebeuf comments, "Ainz n'oïstes parleir de fame / Qui tant fust a s'arme vilainne, / Nes Marie la Magdelainne" (You never heard tell of a woman so vile [or base] in soul, not even Mary Magdalene, ll. 20–22), and later makes reference to her "vilainne vie" (wicked life, l. 65). If Mary's baseness is entirely due to her behavior, however, that of the *vilain* presented in *Le Pet au vilain*—another of Rutebeuf's works, and the first of the eschatological fabliaux I consider here—has a much more complex relation to his own actions.

The beginning of *Le Pet au vilain* plays on the double meaning of "vilain," casting into relief the overlap or contamination that turned the term from a neutral social designation into an insult or an eternal death sentence. Like *Des Putains et des lecheors*, this narrative begins on a grand theological scale. Rutebeuf comments that Heaven is only for those who are charitable; those who have "no goodness, faith, or loyalty" will be excluded, since there is no "human compassion" in them. These are the "gent vilainne." Thus far it might seem that we are being asked to consider moral qualities. But immediately Rutebeuf exploits the ambiguity of "vilainne" to turn it into a social designation: "Ce di ge por la gent vilainne / C'onques n'amerent clerc ne prestre, / Si ne cuit pas que Dieux lor preste / En paradix ne leu ne place" (I am speaking of the base/wicked people [*gent vilainne*] who have never loved clerks or priests; I do not think that God will give them a place or situation in Paradise).[52] Given the treatment usually doled out to *vilains* in medieval French literature, one could hardly be surprised if they objected to clerks. In fact, though, Rutebeuf's assertion here—that peasants' dislike of the clergy will keep them out of Heaven—is so outrageous that it immediately undermines the very identification he plays on, of *vilainie* as a social status with *vilainie* as a moral status, and correspondingly calls to mind the considerable range of views on the standing of peasants, whether literary, earthly, or eternal. The contrast and alleged contest between peasants and clerks is made still more problematic when Rutebeuf goes on, in the lines that follow those quoted above, to assert that it will never please Jesus for a peasant to have lodging with Mary's son, since this "n'est raisons ne droiture: / Ce trovons nos en escriture" (is not reasonable or just, as we see in Scripture, ll. 15–16). This final appeal to the ultimate religious authority, and specifically the ultimate written authority, gives the game away. Scripture, obviously, tells us nothing of the sort; in fact, it tells us the opposite.[53] If the first Christian soul to enter Heaven is an undisputedly "base" one, that of a thief saved by last-minute repentance and faith, clearly social status is no guarantee of eternal status: the foundational lesson about who can be saved by the ability to apprehend Christ's two natures insists that such apprehension is emphatically available to even the lowliest.

By beginning his tale in this way, then, Rutebeuf frames it with an implicit critique of clerical uses of scriptural authority that shadows the coming tale just as the association of the "work" of poetic composition with that of wanton seduction shadows the *Vie de sainte Marie l'Egypcienne*. Like the figure of Zozimas in Mary's *vita*, the introduction to *Le Pet au vilain*, with its problematic use of Scripture, slyly implies that clerics (whose affinity with jongleurs and whores moves in and out of phase) are snobs unable to

appreciate the central tenets of the religion from which they draw their authority. That this is not accidental—that the peasant's fart has a deeper connection to both eschatology and social status as expressed through learning
than might at first appear—is suggested by Chaucer's reworking of a similar
motif in the *Summoner's Tale*, whose dénouement relies on a careful and
mathematically precise solution (described in the tale as "ars-metrike") of the
problem of how to divide a fart.[54] This solution to the problem, a problem
that is repeatedly, indeed obsessively, associated with the "cherl" or low-status
layman who presented it, demonstrates, in the view of the courtly audience,
that "subtiltee / And heigh wit made hym speken as he spak; / He nys no fool,
ne no demonyak."[55] Chaucer's tale is, among other things, a savage parody of
the misuse of learning by religious figures—in this case by a friar, a member of
a group also detested by Rutebeuf, though this is not at issue in *Le Pet au
vilain*.

Rutebeuf's tale is far less obviously concerned with clerical overreaching.
Instead, the story here goes that, just as peasants are forbidden to enter Heaven
because of their alleged hatred of the clergy, they are also barred from Hell—
for reasons about to be explained by the fabliau itself. A peasant on his deathbed is visited by a demon ready to collect his soul. The peasant, however, has
been eating large quantities of beef and garlic stew to sustain himself, and releases a fart so tremendous that the demon mistakes it for his soul and carries
it off in his sack. When he releases it in Hell, the stench is such that peasants
are forever banned from the infernal domain.[56] Since they are also closed out
of Heaven, Rutebeuf says, he does not know where they go; perhaps they sing
with the frogs, or possibly they go to "reduce their penance" in Cocuce, where
Audigier shits in his hat.[57] This concluding intertextual nod to the scatological
epic of *Audigier* reminds us that we are in the world of parody—a world
marked by clerical self-mockery, or at least clerical mockery of clerical literary
productions. The reception of *Audigier*, as Kathryn Gravdal remarks, "teaches
us something about the limits of critical language"; in *Le Pet au vilain*, which
seems almost impossible to discuss without falling into either pedantry or
puerility, or both, the joke is on the clerks—and on their modern scholarly
descendants. Yet while Rutebeuf's tale is clearly a parody, commenting more
on "literary traditions and conventions" than on the real world, its introduction of eschatological elements extends its implications, and its frame clearly
casts an eye toward issues beyond the literary.[58]

Le Pet au vilain essentially claims to be an origin story, a rationale for the
alleged fact that peasants have "ne leu ne place" (neither place nor situation, l.

11) in the afterlife, in a kind of refusal to imagine the very intermediate zone that Purgatory was coming to offer in this period. Rutebeuf's tale, like the others considered here, evades or overlooks a discussion of the "third place" as a theological locale, emphasizing instead the broader concern with status of which Purgatory was one expression. This may be a result of theological conservatism, not uncommon in "popular" (i.e., widely available) texts, including Honorius's *Elucidarium* and its translations, rather than any deliberate choice. What is striking is that the same impulse that made Purgatory so appealing—the impulse to account for the full range of human moral and social status—is still present here but manifests itself in comic terms. Rutebeuf's claim not to know where peasants end up serves to *dis*-locate the "third place" that could account for those who allegedly have no place in the existing scheme of things, possibly including poets; his wordplay associates him with the placeless spirit. He says of himself, "Rutebeuf ne seit entremetre / Ou hom puisse arme a vilain metre" (Rutebeuf doesn't know how to tackle [*entremetre*] where one should put the soul of a peasant, ll. 67–68); Rosanna Brusegan comments, "Rutebeuf does not know how to 'compose,' 'write,' on the third place situated between Paradise and Hell, except to wish to put (*mettre*) himself between (*entre*) these two realms."[59] Like the alternately vicious and virtuous "work" of Mary the Egyptian, the plight of the peasant soul evokes the ambivalent situation of the *clerc-jongleur* himself, denying him any comfortable distance from the eschatological issues at hand.

Similarly communal effects, as we have seen, arise from the individual judgments in *Des Putains et des lecheors*, where the despised classes entwine themselves with, and indeed shape, the eternal fate of others, and in *Le Pet au vilain*, whose main character unknowingly bars his entire social group from Hell as well as Heaven, leaving them placeless. Another fabliau, however, that of *Saint Pierre et le jongleur*, takes a more encouraging view of damnation, or salvation, by class. In this tale, an unusually pathetic jongleur, so addicted to dicing that he is often without clothes, an habitué of the tavern and the brothel, living a "fole vie" of perpetual play, finally meets his end and is carried off to Hell.[60] Once there, he is (rather rashly) left in charge by Satan while the devils go out hunting for souls. St. Peter appears and challenges him to a dice game, which is described in lengthy and loving detail. The jongleur bets damned souls as his stake, and his earthly luck holds: he loses them all (though not without accusations of cheating and a fistfight with Heaven's gatekeeper). Upon Satan's return, the fortunate wretch is banished from Hell forever and flees to Heaven, where Peter ushers him in the gate and then slams it on an enraged mass of demons. In response to this event, Satan bans jongleurs from Hell for all time, ensuring their salvation.

Having a jongleur who loses at dice be the literal saving grace of all the souls in Hell as well as of his own despised class would seem to suggest, beyond mere topsy-turvydom, a clever replaying of the various schemes and structures that decide who goes where.[61] The evocation of the Harrowing of Hell and the Crucifixion—the former by way of the "cleaning out" of Hell and the latter more associatively through dicing, which recalls the soldiers casting lots for Christ's garment—is moreover a reminder of some significant religious truths equally central to the *Évangile de Nicodème*: that no one is saved by his own merits; that the last shall be first.[62] The strong association between jongleurs and "the space of game and spectacle," moreover, means that this protagonist's dicing is not just a recognizable characteristic of his group (as other jongleur texts would confirm) but even one of its defining qualities, a reference to its social function of game, chance, frivolity, randomness, *inutilité*.[63] To have this very uselessness become supremely useful is the text's ultimate joke, a comic reassertion of the fundamentally important Christian promise that God is no respecter of persons and that earthly categories pale in the light of Judgment. Indeed, a fourteenth-century text, the *Ci nous dit*, goes even further, imagining Christ himself as the winner of the ultimate dice game. Following his account of the Crucifixion, the anonymous author notes the saving power of Christ's death and then observes, "Quant .II. honmes jeuent aus des, cil qui a gaaingnié meit sa main seur l'argent. Ainssi descendi li debonnaires Jesucriz en esperit en enfer querre sa gaaingne, quant il dit a Adam, Paiz soit a toy" (When two men play at dice, the one who has won puts his hand on the money. Just so did the gentle Jesus Christ descend in spirit into Hell to seek his winnings, when he said to Adam, Peace be with you).[64] Whether this account was influenced by the fabliau, or whether both derive from a tradition of metaphors for Christ's victory, there is no way to tell; but the reappearance of the dice game puts Christ, momentarily, alongside St. Peter and the jongleur in the despised role of the gambler, just as the emptying of Hell depicts the dicing jongleur as an accidental savior.

A similar pleasure in questioning assigned roles and challenging eternal boundaries is central to the final tale I consider here, *Le Vilain qui conquist paradis par plait*, which plays on the question of what can be known about salvation. It addresses a concern raised already in *Le Pet au vilain*, among many other texts: as Marie de France's late twelfth-century *Espurgatoire seint Patriz* puts it, "Plusurs coveitent a saver / des almes, ci nus dit pur veir, /

coment eles [e]issent des cors / e ou vont quant eles sunt hors" (Many people want to know about souls, as we are truly told, about how they leave the body and where they go when they are out). *Le Vilain qui conquist* rejects, however, Marie's claim, drawn from her Latin source, that "devom plus cremer e doter / ke enquerre ne demander" (we should rather fear and doubt than inquire or ask) about such matters and indeed constitutes a mocking endorsement of the idea that knowledge, especially when allied with its "popular" counterpart, "native wit" or *engin*, can save you.[65] Like *Le Pet au vilain*, *Le Vilain qui conquist* begins by setting up misleading expectations, calling itself a "mervellose aventure"—a characterization that suggests romance—and emphasizing that this is a story that "nos trovomes en escriture" (we find in scripture), allying it with a literary rather than an oral tradition and implicitly with high culture and *clergie*.[66] The next line, however, starts to give the game away, introducing the central character as a peasant (*vilain*), an improbable protagonist for a story of courtly adventure. This *vilain*'s soul, when no one comes to collect it at the point of death, follows St. Michael to Paradise, where St. Peter blocks it at the gates. St. Peter tells the peasant soul that no one can enter save by judgment, and that anyway, "Nos n'avons cure de vilain" (we don't care for peasants, l. 28); he drives the point home by suggesting that this particular soul is an überpeasant: "vilains n'a rien en cest estre; / Plus vilains de vos n'i puet estre" (this is no place for peasants, and nobody could be more of a peasant than you, ll. 29–30). Heaven, in other words, seems to share the courtly view of *vilains*.

It is at this point, however, that the story begins to make clear that the tale and its protagonist will challenge sacred territory not only in action but in words; the peasant intends to claim not just a spot in Heaven but a right to generic modes his culture would deny him. Unawed by the saint, the soul responds to his challenge by taking up and revising a literally foundational Christian metaphor: "Fait li ame, 'Beaus sire Piere, / Tostans fustes plus durs que piere!'" (The soul said, "Good sir Peter, you always were harder than rock!" ll. 31–32). This confounding statement is followed by a couplet that is intriguingly unstable in the manuscripts. The gist is that God was crazy to make Peter an apostle, but in the course of making this outrageous statement, the soul swears by, according to manuscript variation, the holy Pater Noster (i.e., God in the form of a prayer, MSS ACD); St. Thomas the apostle, soon to appear on the scene in this tale (MS B); or St. Peter himself (MS G).[67] The variety of holy names invoked here suggests that the copyists were responding to the *mise-en-abîme* produced by the spectacle of a soul swearing by the very figures he is addressing (or shortly to address) and whose instability or unacceptability as authoritative figures is the point of his oath—since Peter, the rock on which the Church is built, the peasant goes on to note, is also Peter who denied Christ three times. From this he draws his triumphant conclusion: "Ne devés pas les cles avoir: / Alés fors o les desloiaus. / Mais je sui prodom et loiaus; / S'i doi bien estre par droit conte" (You should not have the keys: go out there with the unbelievers. But I am a good man, and faithful; I should be here by true account, ll. 42–45).

The *vilain*'s claim to have the "true story," to be in Heaven by "droit conte"—a formulation that covers both reckoning and recounting—recalls Rutebeuf's assertion that it is not "raisons ne droiture" that peasants should enter Heaven and marks the tale's explicit entry into the matter of who gets to tell the tale. The allegation that Peter should not hold the keys to Heaven—which are, of course, the sign of priestly office—is a challenge to more than just Peter's role as gatekeeper. In this context, it emphasizes the peasant's claim to be the one with the straight story, the one who knows what the Church would teach him. The status reversal is reflected in Peter's adoption of the *vilain*'s language of recounting/retelling: he goes off to tell St. Thomas the "straight story" ("a conté a droiture," l. 49, echoing the *vilain*'s "droit conte") of his "mesaventure." Thomas, dispatched to deal with the intruder, invokes a hierarchy of the faithful, declaring to the soul that this is a place for martyrs and confessors, only to be accused of talking like a lawyer ("plus estes cois / Des responsaus que nus legistes," ll. 62–63) and, implicitly, behaving like one, too, when he took his oath that he wouldn't believe in the Resurrection until he touched Christ's wounds.[68] As with Peter, the *vilain* then asserts that it is not he but Thomas who is in the wrong place: "Çaiens ne devés vos pas ester, / Car faus fustes e mescreans!" (You should not be in here, for you were false and unbelieving! ll. 72–73). Discomfited, Thomas goes straight back to St. Peter and recounts his defeat.

At this point St. Paul steps in and goes to tackle the errant soul, who meanwhile is wandering around enjoying Paradise.[69] Like his predecessors, Paul inquires, "Who brought you here?" and adds, in an unwitting echo of the peasant's words to Thomas, "A peasant must not enter here" ("Çaiens ne doit vilains entrer," l. 83).[70] The implication that a peasant's soul should never even have set foot in Heaven, the sense of discrepancy or inappropriateness that he obviously arouses in his saintly opponents, recalls Rutebeuf's joke at the beginning of *Le Pet au vilain*; it is also not entirely unlike the tendency, now happily on the wane, to wonder what fabliaux are doing in manuscripts alongside their more seemly textual cousins. The peasant, like the fabliau, is treated like dirt in the "old" sense of "matter out of place."[71] Paul, however, raises a key question, one that echoes the stories of both the good thief and Mary the Egyptian: "Ou fesistes vos la deserte / Que la porte vos fu overte?" (When did you do anything that deserved having the door opened to you? ll. 85–86). Like the peasant's accusations of the saints, or the patriarchs' and prophets' misrecognition of the thief with his cross, the question highlights the fact that one cannot *deserve* to enter Heaven; everyone there, except God himself and Mary, is a sinner. Heaven, we might say, is precisely the place for dirt, for the lowest of the low, provided it recognizes itself as dirt.

The peasant is well ahead of the saints in this regard. His response to Paul's accusation of, in effect, generic vagrancy is very much to the point. Reminding the saint of his well-known stint as a persecutor of Christians, he remarks that St. Stephen, "Cui vos fesistes lapider" (whom you had stoned, l. 93), could attest to Paul's cruelty and adds, pointedly, "Bien sai vo vie raconter" (I know well how to tell your life).[72] The reference to Paul's life is also, of course, a reference to his *vita*—that is, to the hagiographic narrative of his life. The soul thus not only claims a certain kind of authoritative biblical knowledge (as of course he has also done with the other two saints) but explicitly brings it into play as, in effect, his ticket to Heaven. He should get in not only because he is morally better than Peter the denier, Thomas the doubter, and Paul the persecutor but because he can marshal their own stories against them and turn fabliau into counterhagiography.

He can do so, moreover, because the kind of cleverness that he represents, far from being anathema to Heaven, turns out to be fully compatible with it. When Paul slinks back to his companions and tells them the "mervelle" of his defeat (l. 110), the three decide to complain to God. St. Peter once more recounts the story, upon which God declares that he wants to hear this "novele" himself (l. 121). Here, the "news" in Heaven is not the good news of the Gospel (by now, one supposes, rather old news) but the apparently unprecedented irruption of a peasant soul. If unprecedented as a peasant, however, the *vilain* does have forebears; in addition to those discussed above, we might recall the figure of that other sinner-saint, David, as presented in the Old French *Eructavit*, a twelfth-century reimagining and adaptation of Psalm 44 that "spread through several regions of France in the thirteenth century if not before" and had at least one Anglo-French version.[73] In this poem composed for Marie de Champagne David is cast as a "humble, 'illiterate' layman" as well as a jongleur and gains entry to Heaven only after a debate with an angelic gatekeeper that ends with the definitive intervention of God in David's favor.[74] Like the

good thief, the jongleur-king serves to embody and perform modes of vernacular exegesis destined for a lay audience; the peasant of this fabliau could be
seen as both their descendant and their student. For his soul proves, in the
end, to be strikingly orthodox and pious, further undermining any strict division between fabliau and didactic literature, vernacular performance and Latinate doctrine.

Accused by God of a slew of linguistic sins against the apostles, the soul
maintains that his right to be in Heaven at least matches those of the problematic saints, and he turns suddenly from the battle of words to an account
of his deeds on earth, which apparently were exemplary: he gave alms, paid
his tithes, fed, clothed, and warmed the poor, avoided strife, and, finally, confessed on his deathbed and received absolution and communion (figured here,
given his interlocutor, as *vo cors*, "your body," l. 152). This is essentially a catalogue of ideal lay behavior according to Church doctrine, of precisely the kind
being promulgated to the laity in the thirteenth century; and its focus on the
corporal works of mercy recalls their biblical context, Matthew 25:34–40,
which casts these actions in the light of eternity and makes clear their link to
the all-important virtue of charity.[75] As the soul points out to God, "Qui ensi
muert, on nos sermone / Que Deus ses peccíés li pardone. / Vos savés bien se
j'ai voir dit!" (They tell us that whoever dies this way will have his sins forgiven by God; you know well if I have told the truth, ll. 153–55). In other
words, the virtuous peasant is not just a clever pleader but has the evidence on
his side: if the story is told right, he is the one who should be in Heaven; while
no one can truly *deserve* entry, he has done what was asked of him, and the
saints' scorn is baseless. The finishing touch is his observation that since he is
now in Paradise, he can't very well be thrown out, as God promised that anyone who entered should never leave: "Vos ne mentirés pas ja por moi!" (You
will never perjure yourself on my account, l. 161), he concludes modestly.[76] In
quoting God's word back to him, this conquering *vilain* may be thinking of
Revelation 3:12, "He that shall overcome [*qui vicerit*], I will make him a pillar
in the temple of my God; and he shall go out no more."[77] The clergy generally
looked with disfavor on attempts to quote Scripture by those allegedly un-
qualified to do so, but their desire to regulate reflects the power of scriptural
authority, its capacity to justify anyone able to cite it rightly and, indeed, to
make him into a pillar of the Church.[78]

God, on whose part the reader senses a kind of divine amusement, then
gives the judgment that has been referred to, but deferred, throughout the
poem and that now seems to have been predetermined for him by a combina-

tion of the peasant's actions and his own words. Addressing the soul as "peasant" in two manuscripts, but in the three others as "friend," he grants his plea,
crediting him with, in essence, a legal victory and adding, in two manuscripts,
"Tu as esté a bone escole" (You have been well schooled, B163 and D151).[79] In
the other three manuscripts, there is a striking couplet: "Bien ses avant metre
ta verbe! / Li vilains dist en son proverbe . . ." (You certainly know how to use
your words! The peasant says, in his proverb . . . , ll. 165–66). The editors end
God's speech with "metre ta verbe," splitting the couplet, and put a blank line
between this and "Li vilains dist," making that the beginning of the (predict-
ably problematic) "moral" of the story. The unity of the couplet, however, and
the lack of any such division in the manuscripts make the change of voice
much less certain in the original text; the voice of the author speaking a moral,
God speaking his decision, and the peasant speaking a proverb overlap and
intermingle. Such an appeal to proverbial knowledge is common in Old
French texts; as Nancy Freeman Regalado notes, "Proverbs are virtually the
only verbal unit or patterned grouping of words which appear in every literary
genre regardless of stylistic level or subject matter"—a capacity to wander that
echoes that of the fabliaux and of this peasant protagonist.[80] There is, moreover, a widely disseminated text titled, precisely, *Les Proverbes au vilain*, copies
of which appear in the two manuscripts that contain both *Le Vilain qui conquist* and *S. Pierre et le jongleur*.[81] For God (and/or the author) to turn to the
vilain's proverb (just as the *vilain* turned to Scripture) thus not only offers a
pleasing irony in this tale of competing discourses but also suggests that the
fabliau's sense of authoritative speech is as capacious and miscellaneous as that
offered by medieval manuscripts.[82]

When the proverb itself arrives, it puts the finishing touch on the tale's
ambivalence about authoritative dicta: only two of the five manuscripts present the same saying at this point, and the applicability of some of the proverbs
cited is difficult to grasp. The one appearing in manuscript C, however, stands
out: "meint hom est a letre mis / Qui n'estoit pas si bien apris" (many a man
has been taught his letters who was not so learned, ll. 157–58). This seems to
credit the peasant with "native wit" rather than book learning, and indeed the
kind of knowledge he deploys was the sort widely available through verbal
instruction, as his own "on nous sermone" (they tell us/preach to us, l. 153)
suggests; at the same time, the tale has made clear the extent and sophistica-
tion of his understanding of clerical teaching. The final word, however, is less
clearly laudatory of the peasant. Despite their momentary divergence, all five
manuscript versions recollect themselves in time to provide a consistent but

seemingly inapplicable moral: "Nurture always defeats nature, falsity hooks righteousness; wrong gains ground and right is hobbled; cleverness is worth more than strength" ("Noreture vaint mais nature, / Fausetés amorce droiture; / Tors va avant et drois a orce: / Mels valt engiens que ne fait force," ll. 169–72).[83] While the last words—"Mels valt engiens que ne fait force"—might seem applicable to our modern sense of the *vilain*'s victory, their context of falsity, unnaturalness, and wrong makes it difficult to take this as a straightforward celebration.[84] We might, however, read the fourth line as an implicit reply to the first three: *when* things are topsy-turvy and wrong is winning against right, *then* wit is worth more than force; or perhaps, *even though* wrong tends to win out, *engin* can even the scales.

To accept either of these readings casts the saints, or at least their expectations of peasants, in the role of wrongful "force"—a role for which, it must be said, their actions in the tale provide some basis. Pierre d'Abernon's *Lumere as lais* invokes similar terms in the course of a complaint against "Princes e prelaz" who lead their subjects astray: "les demeinent si estreit / Ke l'en ne seit k'est tort ne dreit, / Ke ore est dreit ke ja fu tort, / Kar dreit ad tuz jurs le plus fort— / Tut eit il tort e riche seit / E forcible, sun tort est dreit" (they oppress them so strongly that one does not know what is wrong or right, for now what was once wrong is right, for the strongest is always right—even if he is wrong, should he be rich and powerful, [then] his wrong is right).[85] Pierre's wordplay, though not identical in message to the proverbial (if cockeyed) wisdom of *Vilain qui conquist*, similarly acknowledges the ability of the powerful to claim rights even when they are in the wrong; the peasant's victory over the saints, then, is a reminder that no power, except perhaps the highest one, can claim to be immune to such abuses. Of course, all such attempts to pin down a fabliau moral can be seen as a failure to get the joke; like many such morals, this one seems in itself to be a kind of generic trick, a suggestion that trying to read the story "straight," to subordinate it to a didactic or moral reading, is, if not necessarily a mistaken enterprise, then one that will show the partialness, the inevitable point of view, that even the most ostensibly authoritative reading must incorporate.[86]

If the other examples considered here suggest that there was widespread interest, however ludic, in how classes of people might be categorized for all eternity, *Le Vilain qui conquist paradis par plait* goes furthest in questioning that drive toward classification from the perspective of those classified, depicting the latter as figures of considerable agency, fortified by knowledge. Both the tale itself and its peasant protagonist are steeped in Christian instruction—but in Christian instruction of very much the "popular" kind: the major aspects of saintly biography, the basic requirements of the faith, fundamental ecclesiastical images like the keys of Heaven and the rock of the Church. In other words, the knowledge the peasant deploys to such effect is exactly the kind of knowledge we might expect a well-instructed thirteenth-century peasant to have. That he uses it to rebuke and confound the very embodiments of clerical authority, the authors and actors of Scripture, reflects an awareness of the radical potential of the Christian message when it is taken seriously—or, more accurately, when it is taken in jest. Even God needs to be kept honest.

The popular eschatology of the peasants, whores, and jongleurs discussed here not only embodies, in comic form, the dissemination of religious teaching in the vernacular that marked the late twelfth and, especially, the thirteenth centuries but also shows the astuteness—the *engin*—with which that teaching could be shaped by and for nonclerical audiences. Modern gatekeepers, scholarly and otherwise, do well to note the challenge posed by these texts' deployment of holy simplicity and native wit. A distanced or condescending approach to fabliau, or popular hagiography, or their modes of knowledge is already accounted for and mocked by these texts, which offer a salutary reminder of the value—for saint and sinner, expert and neophyte alike—of the virtue of humility. The chapter that follows will explore another genre that is simultaneously indebted to and wary of clerical knowledge, the miracles of the Virgin whose suspicion of clerks has been repaid with interest in modern scholarship.

Chapter 5

Queen of the Rabble, Empress of Clerks: Learning Humility in Marian Miracles

While scholars often link the Virgin Mary, and especially her miracles, particularly with the "popular" side of medieval thought, the Virgin's extraordinary range of relevance—across social groups, generic registers, and levels of discourse—makes her an ideal figure for exploring the intersection and mutual informing of lay and clerical cultures, and recent scholarship has emphasized her importance to the project of lay edification that is the central focus of this book.[1] The growing importance in the twelfth and thirteenth centuries of Marian legends and prayers in the instruction of the laity, the many miracles that valorize holy simplicity and status reversal, and Mary's frequent intervention at the moment of death, as well as the manuscripts whose combinations of texts particularly highlight such themes, make Marian devotion a suitable end point for a discussion of the intersections of status, learning, and salvation.

Mary herself was, in the later Middle Ages, often associated with literacy through images of her mother, Anne, teaching her to read, and already in the eleventh and twelfth centuries in England there began to appear Hours of the Virgin, which were to become a crucially important element of late medieval lay education.[2] At the same time, her miracle stories have been seen as "especially prone to simplify moral issues and theological questions" in their effort to appeal to the full range of Christian believers, particularly the least educated among them.[3] Like exempla, however, Marian devotion clearly appealed to the theologically gifted as well as to the "least of the laity"; if her miracles can be seen as one of the most accessible and broadly disseminated modes of that devotion (along with prayers and rituals that the miracles themselves often promote), it does not necessarily follow that they fail to do justice to the fundamental theological teachings concerning God's mother. The miracles provide an intensely vivid account of Mary's relation to Christ and, by extension, the theology of the Incarnation, and do so while insisting that the heights of theological complexity are, in fact, immediately adjacent to, if not overlapping with, the most quotidian and homely of practices.[4] They thus investigate, as discussed further below, the productive instability of status that we see in many of the teaching texts explored in other chapters and provide, often in strikingly dramatic form, an image of the transformational conversion enabled by "basic" Christian learning and practice.

Setting the early thirteenth-century *Miracles de Nostre Dame* by the Benedictine monk Gautier de Coinci and a mid-thirteenth-century, anonymous Anglo-French collection preserved in British Library, Royal MS 20.B.XIV in the context of Marian devotion more broadly, this chapter addresses the substantial subsets of the miracles that feature deeply unlearned or seriously wicked protagonists whose devotion to Mary saves them from damnation, often at the last possible moment. By contrasting such figures with other characters—often clerics or devils—who fail to appreciate the power of devotion to Mary, such miracles repeatedly stage a reversal that can uncomfortably implicate not only figures in the tales but even their authors and readers. Those who would scoff at Marian miracles, that is, are already included and rebuked within the miracles themselves, which insist that even those barely embarked on basic learning have understood something crucially important: that it is the effort to learn and the love with which that learning is undertaken that count in the end—and that the end, while it may appear to be an upheaval or a sudden event, is in fact continuous in subtle ways with an ongoing, if unrecognized, process of preparation. In a sense, Marian miracles as a genre take on the role of their own despised protagonists: written off as simple, popular, unsophisticated, they are easily disregarded, or valued for qualities other than their theological teaching. But the miracles, like those protagonists, in fact have grasped, and take care to convey, the theological underpinnings of their own narratives of hope and rescue. Adulation of Mary is presented as representing and reinforcing an intuitive grasp not only of the significance of the Incarnation but of its promise that the last shall be first, that the lowest shall be highest, and, implicitly, that the tiniest fragment of Christian understanding contains within it the whole.

Mary's Reach: Universal Teaching and Impossible Beliefs

The two collections that form my primary focus here are one small part of a huge phenomenon, the growth of Marian devotion in the later Middle Ages. While the didactic verse compilations emphasized in earlier chapters are primarily English in origin (though with important Continental counterparts like the *Lucidaires* or the *Somme le Roi*), and the eschatological fabliaux are peculiar to Continental manuscripts, Marian legends have, like the *Évangile de Nicodème*, a cross-Channel and indeed pan-European dissemination. The earliest miracle collections were in Latin and were produced in England in the eleventh century; the earliest vernacular collection, from the twelfth century, is Anglo-Norman, and the vogue for producing such compilations quickly swept through the European vernaculars as well as attaining broad distribution in Latin.[5] Marian miracles are, in effect, as encompassing in their geographic distribution as in their famously capacious range of protagonists.[6]

Of the two collections considered here, the *Miracles de Nostre Dame* of Gautier de Coinci, composed around 1218–30, had by far the wider dissemination, surviving wholly or in part in some 114 manuscripts, fifty-nine of which (including most of the complete or "semicomplete" ones) date from the thirteenth century.[7] So vast a tradition means that the *Miracles'* manuscript contexts are quite varied, but there are some common threads worth noting even beyond the frequently appearing material that addresses the earthly life of the Virgin and of Jesus. As Michelle Bolduc has pointed out, Gautier's *Miracles* appear in several manuscripts also containing the Old French *Eructavit*, the versified account of Psalm 44 that stars the sinner-saint David; three of the four manuscripts containing both *Eructavit* and the *Miracles* are among the "most complete and most trustworthy in terms of transmission" and show, as Olivier Collet suggests, "a tendency to thematize their content."[8] Adrian Tudor, among others, has noted the co-occurrence of Gautier's *Miracles* with the roughly contemporaneous first *Vie des pères*, "a remarkable collection of pious tales and miracles" that shares some features with the doctrinal works discussed here, in some twenty-three manuscripts.[9] Gautier's miracles also appear at times alongside works like the *Miserere* and *Romans de carité* of the Renclus de Molliens discussed in Chapter 1, or in compilations like Paris, BnF, fr. 1807, a thirteenth-century manuscript that contains an independent example of the Marian miracle "The Tumbler of Our Lady" and a verse *Lucidaires*.[10]

The insular French collections—those of Adgar in the twelfth century, the anonymous thirteenth-century author whose compilation is considered here, and Everard of Gateley (writing also in the thirteenth century)—provide a striking contrast in terms of distribution, surviving in only one or two complete copies each. Even the few manuscripts that represent them, however, include instances where the miracles form part of the program of twelfth- and thirteenth-century translation that linked lay and clerical worlds.[11] Everard of Gateley's three miracles appear in Oxford, Bodleian Library, MS Rawlinson poetry 241, where they lie between *Le Dialogue de saint Julien*, which treats "popular theology about death and the future life," and some exempla from the *Manuel des pechiez*; the exempla, in turn, are followed by the *Mirour de seinte eglyse*. These are only some of the many texts in the manuscript that address the need to "amender / La laie gent & ensencer / Que ne sevent pas tut la escripture / Que assetz est grant & obscure, / Iceux qe ne entendunt de lettrure / Ne qe as t[e]les choses ne ount mys lour cure" (improve and teach laypeople, who do not know all of Scripture, which is quite large and difficult—those who do not understand writing and have not put their efforts into such things).[12] A similar spirit of lay instruction seems to have inspired the creation of British Library, Royal MS 20.B.XIV, discussed in Chapter 1, where the anonymous thirteenth-century Anglo-French miracles take their place in a doctrinal-devotional compilation that also includes the *Chasteau d'amour* (a French translation of Robert Grosseteste's Marian allegory), the *Mirour de seinte eglyse*, and the *Manuel des pechiez* among its nine texts. Other Marian material beyond miracles—prayers, poems of praise, legendary histories, and so forth—is a frequent component of many of the manuscripts that incorporate didactic works.[13]

Mary's frequent appearances in the massive devotional output of the later Middle Ages are one testament to her importance in the religious teaching of the period, but her importance to the pastoral outreach of the thirteenth century is conveyed by a still more basic fact: it was in this period that the salutation Ave Maria became a regular, if not always indispensable, part of the basic knowledge required of the laity.[14] The Pater Noster and Creed had held this role for centuries, but the Paris synodal statutes of the early twelfth century were the first legislative text to include the Ave Maria as a prayer everyone should know. These statutes declare, "Priests should continually exhort the people to say the Lord's Prayer and 'Credo in Deum' and the Salutation of the Blessed Virgin."[15] England followed closely, with Bishop Richard Poore's 1217–19 Statutes of Salisbury making the Ave part of basic teaching; these statutes "direct parish priests to call children together often for instruction in the Creed, the Lord's Prayer, and the Hail Mary, and to admonish parents to do likewise," a further reminder of how fundamental this teaching was.[16] By the mid-thirteenth century, a version of the widespread miracle "The Tumbler of Our Lady" can convey its protagonist's utter simplicity by noting, "ne savoit mot de chanson / Ne patrenostre ne lecon / Ne la credo ne le salu / Ne rienz qui fust a son salu" (he did not know a word of any song, nor the Pater Noster, nor the lesson, nor the Creed, nor the Ave Maria, nor anything that contributed to his salvation).[17] The implication is that the "salu" is now on a par with these other basic teachings, though as we might expect its importance is particularly emphasized in this Marian miracle by its final position and by the *rime riche* that equates the Salutation with salvation.

The addition of the Ave Maria to the set of basic prayers allowed for a threefold explication that corresponded to existing triads in Christian belief. Robert Grosseteste, author of the *Chasteau d'amour*, declares in his *Templum Domini* "that the Creed must be learned *ad fidem*, the Lord's Prayer *ad caritatem*, and the Hail Mary *ad spem*"; the association of the Virgin with hope is one that the Marian miracles exploit to the fullest.[18] It could also be linked with the desire to learn; Bernard of Clairvaux associated hope with the "proficientium," the "learners" or those in the middle of the process of acquiring wisdom, and Marian miracles embrace and repeatedly depict such not-yet-perfect protagonists as they progress, often haphazardly, toward a kind of wisdom, and in doing so instruct the audiences of their stories.[19] Pierre d'Abernon's *Lumere as lais* spells out the connection of hope and learning: "Esperance dune entendement / A ki bien creit e fermement, / Dunt en Sapience trovum escrit / Del sage humme ke la le dit: / 'Ki espeire en Deu seurement / De verité averad entendement'" (Hope gives understanding to one who believes well and firmly, concerning which we find written in [the Book of] Wisdom of the wise man who says there: "He who truly hopes in God will have understanding of the truth," 1:183–84 ll. 6031–36). Marian miracles, as exempla on the power of hope, repeatedly show that hope as leading, indeed, to greater understanding, just as the Marian prayers that became part of basic teaching might form the foundation of more extensive or deeper knowledge.

Marian devotion can, however, inform theological complexity as well as pointing toward it; despite the "popular" or "vulgar" associations the Marian miracles continue to have in some modern scholarship, the almost unlimited power and efficacy that underpin them are as evident in theological writing as in less elevated contexts. As Jaroslav Pelikan notes,

The author of the most influential theological treatise ever written about Christ as Mediator, *Why God Became Man*, Anselm of Canterbury at the end of the eleventh century, also wrote a treatise *On the Virginal Conception and on Original Sin*, as well as fervent prayers addressed to the Virgin as Mediatrix. As Anselm himself pointed out, the two treatises were closely connected, because consideration of Christ the Mediator provoked the question of "how it was that God assumed a man from the sinful mass of the human race without sin," which was also a question about Mary.[20]

Such questions could be approached by way of monastic and, later, scholastic theology, but they were also a crucial and repeated aspect of works that sought to arouse devotion to Mary: it was important not only that audiences love and revere the saint but that they know *why* they should, and considerable lyrical and narrative energy is expended in this effort. The repetitiveness of Marian miracles derives in large part from their considerable ingenuity in conveying, by varied means, certain fundamentally important Christian truths and attempting to inculcate them through such repetition-with-variation.[21] It is also important to recall that Marian miracles, though a distinctive subgroup of the texts and images that promoted the cult of God's mother, were of course integrated into a broader tradition that included liturgical practices (both public and private, as in Books of Hours) and prayers; there are a number of miracles that promote the saying of a particular prayer or prayers, or that aim to institute a liturgical event, such as the feast of the Nativity of the Virgin. Such overlap between forms of devotion can be seen in a series of historiated initials in one of the Psalms in the de Brailes Hours (c. 1240) that portray scenes from a miracle discussed below, "the priest of one mass," linking the biblical Psalm to the realm of Marian narrative.[22] The Virgin's utter centrality to the doctrine of the Incarnation, and thus to Christian belief in general, allows her miracles to range across genres and forms.

It also allows them to address theological issues of ultimate importance. The inherent complexity of the Incarnation and its intimate embrace of status reversal make it a plot point or subject for debate in many of the miracles, which thus stage the process of coming to believe or, in the case of the devils featured in a number of point-of-death miracles, wrongly refusing to believe something that is incredible and yet true. Marian miracles that portray the dispute over a soul (between angels and devils, Mary and devils, etc.) use dialogue to depict the countervailing forces that make salvation both always available and precarious of attainment. Miri Rubin has suggested that "Listeners must have been encouraged as the teaching on sins and repentance taught in churches was countered by Mary's miracles," but as we have seen the need to balance hope and fear is emphasized also in preaching and doctrinal literature; Marian literature is more a counterpart than a counterpoint to such teaching.[23] Like the works discussed in earlier chapters, it imagines teaching and learning in participatory, dialogic terms, inviting inquiry by way of paradox and reversal and giving ample attention and credit to those of limited understanding as they, like the more learned, grapple with the central mysteries of the faith.

In a miracle concerning a Saracen devoted to an image of the Virgin, but not to Christianity, the protagonist states clearly the difficulty of apprehending her role:

"Par foi," fait il, "ce fu merveille
Se li grans Diex qui tot cria
Por home tant s'umelia
Qu'hons terrïens volt devenir!
Mais ce ne poïst avenir
Par nule raison, ce me samble,
Qu'hons poïst estre et Diex ensamble.
Et d'autre part, s'il avenist
Que Diex por home hons devenist,
Ne voi je pas n'il ne puet estre
Que d'une virge peüst naistre."[24]

["In faith," he said, "it would be a marvel
if the great God who created everything
so humbled himself for humankind
that he wished to become an earthly man!
But this could not happen
in any reasonable way, it seems to me,
that he could be a man and God together.
And on the other hand, if it were to happen
that God became man for mankind,
I do not see how it could be
that he could be born of a virgin."]

He addresses head-on two major, interconnected points of the Christian faith, both of which center on apparently impossible conjunctions (God and man, virgin and mother). The miracle goes on to dramatize the process of coming to believe them: the image grows breasts that run with oil, converting the astonished Saracen. As Gautier de Coinci, the author of this version, says explicitly, the Saracen thus offers an example a fortiori of the behavior that can be expected of Christians and, especially, of the Christian clergy: if even a Saracen can so honor Mary, surely clerics can show more honor to the altar (ll. 89–95, 202–8). The lesson drawn is a moral one, but in the course of presenting it Gautier addresses the same issues that engaged theologians. He also engages directly—as do many Marian miracles—with the problem of doubt. A complaint already widespread in medieval accounts of miracles of the Virgin is the difficulty of believing in them, and their tellers often seem engaged in the attempt to "accommodat[e] cognitive habits to the maintenance of truths often repellent to natural dispositions," as Steven Justice puts it.[25] Marian miracles, that is, far from being a bizarre outgrowth of Christian belief, live at its very center, reiterating over and over the need for faith in things that seem impossible and the infinite possibilities opened by that faith.

The miracles also offer an outstanding example of another fundamental concept, the primacy of love in Christian teaching. The figures in miracles learn through their love for Mary and her love for them: love is instructive, love is corrective, love is what makes it possible to learn. As Rachel Fulton has noted, the growth in devotion to Christ and Mary in the high and late Middle Ages is "a story of the effort to identify empathetically with the God who so emptied himself as to become incarnate from a human woman and to die a humiliating death," a formulation that recalls Philippians 2:6 and, like the Saracen's musings, links Christ's self-humiliation to Mary's role in the Incarnation.[26] Such empathy could, as the works studied here demonstrate, spill over into the second part of the first commandment, to love your neighbor as yourself. The "mediatory" role of both Christ and Mary, their willingness to descend, corresponds with the emphasis on transmission, familiarity, and connection that characterizes many of the doctrinal texts examined here; Daniel O'Sullivan suggests, for example, that the quality of "familiar strangeness" foregrounded by Gautier de Coinci in his Marian lyrics belongs both to their subject, Mary, and to their mode, as a "new vernacular devotional poetics."[27]

Mary in particular embodied the duality of the mediatory role, as the person "through whom we ascend to him who descended through her to us."[28] As the anonymous author of the thirteenth-century Anglo-French miracles puts it,

> Tut sei jeo cheitif e dolerus,
> Une ren me fet si curagus;
> Tut seit ele reïne coroné,
> Si est ele de ma lignée,
> E de ma char e de mun sanc
> Est eshaucé en si halt banc;
> Tut passe ele tute creature,
> Ele n'ublist mie sa nature.
> Sa grant pité, sa grant franchise
> Nus met trestut en cel aprise
> Ke nus osum od lui parler
> Cum od un de nus et araisuner.[29]

> [Though I am a sad wretch,
> one thing makes me so bold [as to compose this book]:
> although she is a crowned queen,
> yet she is of my lineage,
> and from my flesh and my blood
> is exalted to so high a seat;
> though she surpasses every creature,
> she did not forget her nature.
> Her great compassion, her great nobility
> makes us thoroughly understand
> that we may dare to address her
> and speak with her as with one of us.]

The author here takes a theological point—Mary's humanness and the link it provides to Jesus—as the basis of his own humble confidence and thus models for his audience the identification with Mary that is essential, that enables one to trust in her when it is most difficult to do so and to pass that trust along to others "of us." The seemingly simple or naïve attention to Mary's physicality, the corporeality that the miracles so insist on, is at the same time the expression of a theological complexity—"high" and "low" conjoined.

Mary is, in a formula with a thousand variations, both the one who "surpasses every creature" and the one who, because she *is* after all a creature, is still "one of us."[30] It is in this light that the true force of Marian miracles in the teaching efforts of the twelfth and thirteenth centuries becomes visible. Like Christ himself, like the preachers who ascend and descend Jacob's ladder speaking with angels and then with men, the miracles reach from the height of Mary's sanctity to the depth of her corporeality and in doing so bring sanctity down to earth and exalt the corporeal. While this ascent/descent pairing is, as Anselm suggests, implicit in any devotion to Mary, the miracles' focus on an immensely wide range of protagonists and on the depths to which they can sink makes these texts, in a more focused way than Marian praise poetry, legendary history, or prayer, an imaginative embodiment of the saint's capacity to instruct, convert, and redeem the lowest of the low so that they can come face-to-face with the Most High.

In this regard Mary becomes, despite her uniqueness, part of a broader system of encouragement and instruction, and repeatedly appears alongside figures already familiar to us from previous chapters. In the twelfth-century *Miserere* of the Renclus de Molliens, for example, we see an interesting progression. The end of strophe 234 asserts that true repentance will bring pardon; in strophe 235, Mary Magdalene, Mary the Egyptian, Peter, and Paul are cited as reassuring instances of sinner-saints; in strophe 236, we are given the story of Theophilus in brief. This most famous of Marian miracles is followed, in strophes 237–53, by praise and then another miracle of the Virgin (the monk who sang too quietly).[31] The reassurance provided, that is, by the recollection that even egregious sinners can have a high place in Heaven slides into the reassurance that this lesson applies to those closer to hand than figures from the Gospels or the stories of the early hermits. And Mary is the vehicle of that reassurance, the one who extends the pardon to all who trust in her. At times the link is made more direct; the life of Mary the Egyptian appears, in the anonymous Anglo-French collection as elsewhere, as a Marian miracle, and in Gautier's miracle of the noblewoman who killed the child she had borne to her son, the pope encourages the penitent by reminding her of Peter, Mary Magdalene, and Mary the Egyptian.[32]

Pierre d'Abernon provides a further reminder of this alternative litany of sinner-saints that was available to comfort the sinful Christian, and again associates them with Mary. At the end of a chapter "On the value of hope" (*Del profit d'esperance*), Pierre recalls the humble sinners whose example is so important in the *Évangile de Nicodème* and the teaching about repentance and salvation that shapes both didactic texts and their imaginative progeny like the *Vilain qui conquist paradis par plait*. He translates from St. Bernard at some length:

"Sire Deu, n'aviez en despit
Le larun k'en vus s'afia
K'en la croiz merci te cria,
Ne la peccheresce plurante
Sur tei, la Maudeleine orante,
Ne le Caneneu preant,
Ne celi al tounu seaunt,
Ne cele ke [de] avutire fu encusee
Dunt ele en deust estre lapidee,
Ne seint Pere ke te niot,
Ne seint Pol ke te pursiwot,
Ne ces ke te mistrent en la croiz
Pur ki preastes plurant des oiz."[33]

["Lord God, you did not despise
the thief who trusted in you,
who asked you for mercy on the cross,
nor the sinner weeping
over you, the praying Magdalene,
nor the pleading Canaanite,
nor him who sat in the custom house,
nor her who was accused of adultery
for which she was to be stoned,
nor St. Peter who denied you,
nor St. Paul who persecuted you,
nor those who put you on the Cross,
for whom you prayed with tears in your eyes."]

Pierre's quotation forms part of a discussion of hope that extends to 455 lines, considerably more than the account of the four cardinal virtues and faith put together. The quoted passage concludes a chapter on four things that help sustain faith: God's mercy; the sinner's penance; Christ's Passion and the Redemption; and the goodness or humility (*debonerté*) of God, "Ke n'ad nul humme en despit" (who despises no man, l. 6125). It is immediately followed by a chapter on the fifth and, it seems, most important thing that sustains hope: "la duce Marie / Ki sun fiz pur nus tuz jurs prie" (the gentle Mary, who continually prays to her Son for us, ll. 6145–46). This chapter on Mary, which takes up precisely half of the entire discussion on hope, continues to rely heavily on Bernard, with assistance from Augustine, to convey the power of Mary's intercession, its universality, and the hope it provides to sinners; indeed, the chapter's rubric reads, "Ke nostre Dame est nostre esperance" (That our Lady is our hope).[34]

Like the presence of the anonymous Anglo-French collection among the didactic texts of Royal 20.B.XIV, or the Marian prayers and praise poems that appear in many devotional miscellanies, the Renclus's and Pierre's linking of the sinner-saints and Mary as mediatrix brings Marian narrative fully into the ambit of the vernacular transmission of doctrine and the project of universal education. In doing so, it demonstrates the continuities and exchanges, rather than the contrasts, between different cultural forms, different genres, different learners and teachers. High and low, lettered and unlearned, are all in need of the hope that Mary offers and learn from one another in the course of coming to understand fully the extent of her power.

Status and Learning in Gautier de Coinci

If Mary's link to the sinner-saints is a reminder of her disregard for, or rather her ability to transform, earthly status, this willingness to cross boundaries is conveyed also by her miracles' ostentatious catholicity of address. Marian collections of any scope depict protagonists from across social, professional, and moral spectra, attending to such distinctions in a way that both preserves and transcends them. In a Latin collection discussed by Evelyn Wilson, BnF lat. 12593, this range is self-consciously addressed; the prologue indicates the compiler's intention of bringing together miracles "performed 'in different times and in diverse places, upon diverse persons of either sex, of different age, and of different condition and status; whatever is to be found in the books of the saints or scattered about in the writings of the faithful,'" and, Wilson notes, "he groups the legends according to the social status of the individuals about whom they are told."[35] In most collections, however—including both Gautier's and the Anglo-French ones—the various social and professional groups are disseminated more or less at random throughout the collection, which might present (to take one sequence from the anonymous thirteenth-century collection) miracles featuring a beggar; a thief; a wicked monk; an unfortunate pilgrim; a simple-minded chaplain; two aristocratic brothers, one of whom is a cardinal; a worldly and avaricious peasant; a sinful prior; a clergeon who becomes a bishop; and a young monk.[36] At other points, nuns, aristocratic ladies, illicit mistresses, abbesses, and empresses are the focus of Mary's love and attention.

While few miracle collections are organized by status, they nevertheless tend to include a wide range of social categories. In written form, then, they had the potential to function as haphazard *ad status* collections, assuring any sinful reader not only that there was someone like him who had been helped by the Virgin but that he had company from across the social spectrum—an assurance that might, of course, be unsettling as often as it was reassuring. Mary is thus a universal saint not only in terms of region but in terms of type of sinner; she becomes the saint of each status, the saint who can adapt to the particularities of any situation, any sinner, and then bring that individual into the idealized whole of the Church.[37] As Gautier puts it, near the end of a miracle where Mary has repeatedly saved a thief from his punishment, "Quant un larron reconfortas, / As tiens donné tost confort as" (When you comfort a thief, you have quickly given comfort to all your people, I Mir 30, ll. 123–24). The echo of the thief on the cross is surely not accidental; like him, Gautier's nameless thief, worthless except in his devotion to Mary, yet manifests thereby the faith that saves him and makes him an example for all "her people."

While Mary's universality is evident across the spectrum of Marian works, nowhere is it so insistently important as in the miracles. But as narratives, often expanded into the vernacular from briefer Latin versions, the miracles have tellers who mediate the stories to an audience just as Mary mediates heavenly grace to her devotees.[38] We saw above, in the self-deprecating account of the anonymous Anglo-French compiler, that the presenter of the miracles may well—and very often does—present himself as one of the sinful wretches dependent on the Virgin's help, thus linking him to his audience; the "we" that William of Waddington invokes in the *Manuel des pechiez* is much in evidence here. At the same time, the tales' attention to status, especially when that status involves learning, can implicitly draw a contrast between the teller and his protagonists.

The potential disjunction between a transcendence of earthly status and its rearticulation through the emphatic learnedness of a translator is evident throughout Gautier de Coinci's *Miracles de Nostre Dame*. Whereas authors like Robert of Gretham or Pierre d'Abernon acknowledge the gap between their own learnedness and that of their audiences, their proximity, real or imagined, to specific interlocutors of whom they think highly eases to some degree the strain of the status differential between teacher and student. Gautier, a nobly born monk, does not filter his teaching through this sense of close connection to an admired listener. On the one hand, he makes an emphatic appeal to a universal audience of devotees, in which he includes himself: "Saluons la, toutes et tuit, / Devotement et jor et nuit. / Saluons la, grant et petit, / Se nos volons que por nos prit. / Saluons la, et clerc et lai," he writes in one miracle (Let us all, women and men, devoutly greet her both day and night. Let us, great and small, greet her, if we wish her to pray for us. Let us, both clerk and lay, greet her, I Mir 29, ll. 229–33). The repetition reinforces the point; distinctions of gender, of status, of learnedness are subsumed into a greater "we." The fact that "clerc et lai" concludes this listing, however, gives it a particular emphasis and reminds us of the potential disparity between Gautier and his audience. "Trouvère de nostre dame" he may be, but he is also indubitably a *clerc*, and as a monk is within the inner circle, so to speak, of *clergie*; he is also from a high-status background, and such addressees as are named specifically—his "particular friends," in a phrase echoing Pierre d'Abernon—are either nobles or professed religious and thus in some way or another already like himself.[39]

As a result, Gautier's miracles offer a rich opportunity to explore the confrontation between high and low status in both courtly and clerical terms. While Gautier upholds, as any proponent of Mary must, the value of simple faith and the irrelevance of earthly status, the gap between his own considerable learnedness and aristocratic sympathies and the lowly protagonists he represents sometimes leads to a presentation in which his own allegiances are not entirely clear. On the surface, conflict is avoided; many of Gautier's miracles of holy simplicity focus approvingly on the power of unlearned devotion—though "unlearned" in these miracles is a relative term, since in fact the miracles present characters who have learned only one thing, but have learned that thing very, very well. At the same time, promoting the most basic kinds of repetition—the adherence to a single mass or a single prayer—in language whose *annominatio*, repetition-with-variation, is its most distinctive formal feature creates an implicit contrast between the mode of the teller and the mode of the protagonist.[40] If repetition is to be valorized, Gautier seems to suggest, he can do repetition more beautifully than anyone.

This is not to imply, however, that Gautier deliberately undermines such characters; indeed, he is at pains to praise their assiduity. Their learning is often presented in terms that recall the kind of repeated, ingrained knowledge that, as noted in the Introduction, Foucault saw as central to accounts of classical ethics. In I Mir 14, which belongs to the category "the priest of one mass," Gautier introduces his protagonist:

Mais bien vos puis de lui tant dire
Qu'il ne savoit chanter ne lire
En romancier, chartre ne brief,
Ne ne savoit longue ne brief.
Une messe sanz plus savoit,
Salve sancta parens, qu'avoit
Aprise d'enfance et d'usage.[41]

[But I can tell you this much about him,
that he did not know how to sing or read,
in a French book, a charter or a letter;
he didn't know a thing.
He knew only one mass,
Salve sancta parens,
which he had learned in childhood and by repetition.]
(ll. 5–11)

He sings it in and out of Lent, at Pentecost and Christmas, for the living and for the dead. The idea of a text learned in childhood and often repeated comes up again in I Mir 38.[42] Here, a virtuous and generous rich man whom the Devil has tried unsuccessfully to tempt is eventually freed of his adversary by a bishop who makes the Devil reveal himself. When the Devil says that his power has been limited by "Ne sai quel prïere en latin, / Qu'il rote et dit chascun matin" (some prayer in Latin that he chants and says every morning, ll. 289–90), the bishop inquires further. The rich man replies,

Biau sire,
Par verité vois puis bien dire
Que j'onques letres ne connui,
Mais il est voirs, quant enfez fui,
C'une orison par us apris
Que chascun joor a dire empris
Une foïe a tot le mains,
A genolz et a jointes mains,
Devant l'ymage Nostre Dame.[43]

[Good sir,
I can certainly tell you in truth

that I never knew my letters,
but it is true that, when I was a child,
I learned a prayer by repetition
that I undertook to say
at least once each day,
on my knees and with hands joined,
before the image of our Lady.]
(315–23)

In both instances, that is, a prayer learned in childhood and through "us" or "usage" proves to be immensely powerful. As Foucault notes, "the essential element [in a 'conversion to the self'] is . . . exercise, practice, and training; *askesis* rather than knowledge," and this is precisely the kind of "conversion" or turning-toward that Marian miracles emphatically validate. The saying of the same prayer "chascun joor," the habitual bowing or kneeling to an image, the repetition of a single mass in every situation both instill and display salvific understanding; these learners are learning something that they already know and yet must always continue to practice.[44]

Another miracle on a similar theme, I Mir 23, demonstrates further the spectrum of learnedness.[45] Gautier presents it, again, as a miracle of holy simplicity:

Un brief myracle mout aoinne
Conter vos veil d'un symple moine.
Symples estoit et symplement
Servoit Dieu et devotement.
N'iert pas telz clers com sainz Ansiaumes.
Sa miserele et ses set saumes
Et ce qu'apris avoit d'enfance
Disoit par mout bone creance
Selonc sa symple entencïon.

[I want to tell you a short, very suitable miracle
about a simple monk.
He was simple, and simply
and devoutly served God.
He was not as learned as St. Anselm.
He said his *Miserere* and his seven Psalms

and what he had learned in childhood
with true belief,
according to his simple understanding.]
(ll. 1–9)

Gautier's fondness for repetitive wordplay is, as noted above, one of his most distinctive features as a poet; most of the miracles end with several lines playing on versions of a particular word or sound. Here, however, his repetition of "symple(s)," like the monk's prayer, involves no variation (apart from the addition of -ment in one case). It does not, that is, form part of a poetic pattern but seems intended to establish through mimicry the utter simplicity of the monk's almost childlike faith—"apris d'enfance" making another appearance. The monk nevertheless shows himself somewhat more ingenious than the priest of one mass: distraught that he does not know any prayer that would properly commemorate Mary, he devises a mnemonic out of five Psalms beginning with the letters MARIA.[46] When he dies, five fresh red roses are found in his mouth. The prayer thus created effectively conjoins two forms of protoliteracy: the knowledge of the alphabet—of letters, rather than literature—and the knowledge of memorized texts, in this case, the Psalms that were among the texts most broadly familiar to any Christian audience and becoming ever more available by way of the psalter.[47] Gautier pointedly says that the monk "N'i quist autre phylosophye" (sought no other philosophy, l. 25) and recommends to "toz lettrés" (all the learned) that they say these Psalms once a day, kneeling before "l'image a la pucele / Qui alaita de sa mamele / Et norri son fil et son pere" (the image of the maiden who fed and nursed at her breast her son and her father, ll. 57–59), a practice that would not only assimilate them to this emphatically "simple" monk but would also precisely imitate the actions of the rich man in I Mir 38. That figure's prayer, too, is held up as an example: "A toz lettrés conseil et lo / Qu'il l'aüsent et qu'il l'aprengent" (I advise and recommend to all learned people that they use it and that they learn it, ll. 338–39). Even St. Anselm, Gautier implies, with all his learning, gets no greater reward than the simple devout.

The closing advice to the "lettrés" in the miracle of the simple monk represents a subtler challenge than those depicted in the narratives of the priest of one mass (who is rebuked and dismissed by his bishop for his ignorance, before being reinstated at Mary's command) or the rich man tested by the Devil; it implies, without quite stating it, that in one respect at least these holy simpletons outshine Gautier's learned audience. This implicit confrontation between the lettered and the simple is also echoed, as noted above, in the very singleness, the lack of variation, in the monk's prayer, which—like that of the pious layman and the priest of one mass—distinguishes him from his chronicler. In this context, it is striking that the two miracles of simple churchmen, the priest of one mass and the monk who devised the MARIA prayer, are among the shortest in the entire collection; the former runs to 94 lines, the latter to a mere 68.[48] The tale of the rich man, though told at more typical length (346 lines), concludes quite abruptly: Gautier's miracles consistently end with a kind of sermon, a "queue," that points out what lessons and behaviors the miracle teaches, but while these are often quite long and usually include Gautier's characteristic wordplay, the conclusion of this story barely outlasts the naming of the prayer and involves no *annominatio*.[49] While the miracles of the simple priest and monk do include some wordplay, their sermonic conclusions are brief, in keeping with their overall brevity. Perhaps a lengthy and verbally elaborate disquisition on a tale that emphasizes the virtues of simplicity seemed to invite comparisons not entirely to the poet's advantage.

The critique of learnedness that remains latent in these miracles of holy simplicity and repetition comes out more explicitly, however, in a later series of three narratives, II Mir 19–21.[50] The most notable of these for my purposes is II Mir 20, "D'un Vilain," to which I return below, but the tales that bracket it also present, in different ways, the thorny problem of how to value earthly learning in light of eternity. The first is the famous tale of the wrongful judge Étienne and his seemingly holy brother Perron; the latter dies, and the former follows him soon afterward.[51] At judgment, Étienne is condemned by SS. Lawrence and Agnes, whose churches he had despoiled, but he is saved when St. Pri (i.e., St. Préject), to whom he was devoted, appeals to Mary. While this last-minute rescue is being arranged, however, he has been taken down to Hell, where he sees his brother, to his surprise. Perron explains that he was avaricious and is paying the price but can be saved if the pope and cardinals will say mass for him; this thus becomes a purgatorial-journey-and-intercession miracle of the kind extensively studied by Jacques Le Goff. Gautier does not emphasize this aspect of the story, however. Instead, he opens the tale with the observation that those "qui la lettre n'entendent" (who do not understand writing) can hear miracles and come to believe in and fear God, while those who misuse their talents will have to answer for it at judgment, and concludes with a long rebuke of those who put their learnedness to bad ends, largely on the Pauline theme "la scïence de cest mont / Musardie est lasus amont" (the knowledge of this world is foolishness there above, ll. 445–46). Or, as Gautier puts it with more detail,

> Diex palera si fort latin
> Qu'il en seront tout esgaré.
> Tout leur *ergo*, tout leur *quare*,
> Leur fallaces, leur argument
> Vaillant la keue d'un jument
> Ne leur vauront en la presence
> De Dieu, qui est fonz de scïence.

> [God will speak such strong Latin
> that they will be completely at a loss.
> All their *ergo* and *quare*,
> their tricks, their arguments,
> will not be worth a mare's tail,
> nor will they help them in the presence
> of God, who is the fount of knowledge.]
> (ll. 432–38)

Like the story of the master whose student visits him from Hell and who subsequently goes to study "the logic that does not fear the 'therefore' of death" (discussed in Chapter 2), this miracle highlights the insufficiency of learnedness—and indeed, specifically of Latin—in the face of death. The unexpected fate of Perron also introduces the theme of the "judger judged," further insisting on the ultimate uselessness of worldly status.

If the story of Perron and Étienne primarily rebukes lawyers, judges, and others who use their learning to gain earthly power, then II Mir 21, separated from it only by the tale of the peasant yet to be discussed, strikes closer to Gautier's home territory.[52] Here, in one of the many stories that convey the Virgin's particular fondness for jongleurs, we are told of a talented minstrel devoted to singing the Virgin's praise who, on pilgrimage to Rocamadour, performs for her in the church and then requests a candle from the altar as payment.[53] Her image bends down to give it to him, but a cranky monk, suspicious and resentful of the performer's "enchantments," takes the candle from him and returns it to its place. The same thing happens twice more, to the great edification (and, one suspects, enjoyment) of the spectators. While this is not strictly a member of the long-lived "Tumbler of Our Lady" miracles, like them (and like "The Priest of One Mass") it depicts a figure of high religious standing as wrongly dismissive or disdainful of holy simplicity.[54] In this case, the conflict between the high-status figure and the simple one embraces Gautier's two primary self-identifications—as a monk and as a trouvère of Nôtre Dame—and he comes down fully on the side of the jongleur, distancing himself from his profession and embracing his avocation.[55] The concluding remarks address religious who need wine to sing or do not turn their hearts to it as the jongleur (and of course Gautier himself) did. In this case, that is, Gautier finesses the ambivalence that holy simplicity can create in the clergy by including another figure with whom he can identify, allowing the trouvère to outshine the monk.

By contrast, the disdain that can be evoked by lowly protagonists is on spectacular display in II Mir 20, titled simply "D'un Vilain," which, like the story of Étienne and Perron, conjoins the themes of death and instruction.[56] A greedy peasant who ignores most feast days, is obsessed with gain, and encroaches on his neighbors' lands nevertheless does not work on Saturday, in honor of the Virgin; willingly hears Sunday mass; and has done his limited best to learn and recite the Ave Maria. He also, despite being "as stiff as a stool," bows to images of the Virgin wherever he finds them and gives to the poor when asked in her name.[57] His lack of learning is carefully established:

Norris n'estoit pas en couvent,
Car ne cuit pas, par un apostre,
Qu'il seüst nes sa patrenostre;
Mais il avoit tant esploytié
Ne sai le tiers ou la moytié
Savoit du salu Nostre Dame,
Que li avoit apris sa fame.

[He was not raised in a convent,
for I do not believe, by any apostle,
that he knew even his Pater Noster;
but he had worked hard enough
to know, perhaps, a third or a half
of the salutation to Our Lady [i.e., the Ave Maria],
which his wife had taught him.]
(ll. 40–46)

The peasant's ignorance outshines that of most other protagonists of holy simplicity miracles; he is devoid of even the most basic learning, apart from scraps
of the Ave Maria, making him a radical example of the efficacy of Marian devotion without any other support. His fate also makes it clear that the mere
will or intention to honor Mary is sufficient, since despite his labors he can
only learn "a third or a half" of the salutation.[58]

Both the peasant's low status and his lack of learning become an issue when
he is taken ill and dies and the devils come for his soul—only to be challenged,
to their surprise, by a band of angels on the same errand. The devils' first argument shows the conflation of social and moral status that we saw in Rutebeuf's
Pet au vilain: "Se robeürs, vilainz, larons / Metez ou ciel, . . . / Dont est la Dieu
parole fable" (If you put robbers, peasants, and thieves in Heaven . . . then
God's word is a fable, ll. 72–74), they say, pointing out the peasant's general lack
of virtue while at the same time implying that this is simply characteristic of a
vilain. Further, they ask, "Enne porront mout dolant estre / Chevalier, dames,
clerc et prestre, / Qui en enfer vont a grans torbes, / Se cis vilainz, qui put les
torbes, / Qui ne seut onques bu or ba, / Em paradys lassus s'en va?" (Won't
knights, ladies, clerks and priests, who go to Hell in great crowds, be very dis-
tressed if this peasant, who pollutes the earth, who doesn't know a thing, goes
up to Paradise? ll. 81–86).[59] They go on to call him "bestiaus . . . plus que beste"
(more beastly than a beast, l. 89) and a "vilainz bobelinz champestre" (stupid
rustic peasant, l. 94), both insults Gautier favors for this particular status.[60]

The angels, however, are sure of their ground and give an answer that is
striking in its absoluteness: "Vos savez bien," they say, "qu'il n'avint onques /
Ne n'avenra ja a nul fuer / Que nus qui bien amast de cuer / La douce mere au
roy celestre / Dampnez ne perdus peüst estre" (You know well that it never
happened nor will it ever happen by any means that anyone who truly loved
in his heart the sweet mother of the heavenly king could be damned or lost, ll.
104–8). They point out, further, that the peasant was repentant on his deathbed and called repeatedly on Mary. The devils make a pettish reply about
Mary's excessive generosity to those who show her any devotion, noting again
that the peasant did not know even his Pater Noster, but the angels insist that
with the salutation always on his lips he must be saved. This leads the devils to
offer a mocking critique of the peasant's way of saying the salutation:

"Quant cis vilainz aprez ses buez
Huchié avoit: 'Hez!' ou 'Hari!'
Lors si disoit: 'Ave Mari,'

He! com plaisant salu ci a!
Quant il avoit dit *gracia*,
Ainz qu'il venist a *plena do*,
Dis fois disout ou: 'Hez!' ou: 'Ho!'
N'onques ne seut li vilainz bus
Outre le *mulieribus*
N'ainc, bien le puet jurer uns abbes,
A droit n'en dit quatre sillabes."

["When this peasant had shouted after his oxen,
'Giddy-up!' or 'Get on!'
then he would say 'Hail Mary'—
what a lovely salutation *that* is!
When he had said 'full of,'
before he got to 'grace God,'
twice he'd have said 'Giddy-up!' or 'Whoa!'
Nor did this stupid peasant ever know
anything beyond 'among women,'
nor ever—an abbot could swear to it—
did he get four syllables of it right."][61]
(ll. 152–62)

As in the case of the monk with the MARIA prayer, or the lawyers whose *quare* and *ergo* will not help them, Gautier here demonstrates his own maca-ronic virtuosity, juggling and rhyming Latin words with vernacular ones in a way that assumes an audience capable of getting the joke—though in doing so, of course, they would be laughing with the devils.

By displaying his learning and poetic skill through the demonic voices of the text, Gautier creates a problematic conjunction and an implicit identifica-tion that shadows the rest of the tale. The angels point out to the devils, in an emphatic defense of intention over ability,

Diex est tant doz, bien le savez,
Qu'il ne prent garde a nezun fuer
Fors a l'entencïon dou cuer.
Diex ausi tost sanz nul delai
Comme le clerc entent le lai.
Li lais ne fait mie a gaber

Pour ce s'il ne seit sillaber:
Puis qu'a bien pense et a bien tent,
Comment qu'il die, Diex l'entent.

[God is so good, you know it well,
that he does not care at all about anything
but the intention of the heart.
God hears the layman as quickly
as the clerk, without delay.
The layman should not be mocked
because he does not know his syllables:
provided that he thinks of and holds to the good,
however he may say it, God will understand.]
(ll. 166–74)

The devils, tellingly, immediately respond that this is a wonder, since God might not listen to someone who "rote et verseille" all day, that is, a monk; the angels validate this observation, saying that a clerk or priest who "toute jor saumoye et lit" (sings Psalms and reads all day) but has a wicked heart will be ignored by God. By contrast, "Diex entent luez, c'est la some, / La symple fame et le symple home / Qui tout son cuer souslieve es cielz / Et dit: 'Merci, biaus sire Diex'" (God soon hears, to sum it up, the simple woman and the simple man who raise their whole hearts to Heaven and say, "Mercy, good Lord God," ll. 187–90). As Abelard said of the Creed, "No slowness of wit or weak intelligence can be offered as an excuse, for these things [i.e., the words of the Creed] are so little that there is no one, however dull and ignorant (*hebes et barbara*) he may be, who cannot say this, and speak all the words; so great, that if anyone could fully grasp their meaning, it would be believed sufficient for his eternal salvation."[62] The story of the *vilain* goes this one better: not even the Creed or the Pater Noster, but even a halting and incomplete version of the Ave, or a simple "God, have mercy," is enough.

This still does not persuade the devils to give way, however, and they continue to get in their digs at the peasant, returning to the issue of his social status:

Il n'i a el,
Toz jors tient Diex ceste riote:
Un vilain symple, un ydiote

Aimme assez mielz, c'en est la some,
Qu'un soutil clerc ne c'un sage home.
Ces folz agrestes, ces senglers,
Ces vilains a ces durs sollers
Aimme assez mielz que roys ne dus.
Plus mainne Diex ou ciel lassus
De vilains a blanches chappetes,
De veves fames, de vielletes,
De mesiaus, de tors, de croçus,
De contrefais et de boçus
Qu'il ne face de bele gent.
Li fort, li preu, li bel, li gent,
Les beles dames de grant pris
Qui traïnant vont vair et gris,
Roy, roÿnes, duc et contessez
En enfer viennent a granz pressez,
Mais ou ciel vont pres tout affait
Tort et boçu et contrefait.
Ou ciel va toute la ringaille:
Le grain avons et Diex la paille.

[There is no way out of it,
God always holds to this foolishness:
to sum it up, he loves a simple peasant,
an idiot, better than
a subtle clerk or a wise man.
This foolish rustic, this wild boar,
this peasant with his wooden shoes
he loves far better than a king or duke.
God leads to Heaven above
more peasants with white cloaks,
widows and old women,
lepers, cripples, the lame,
the deformed, and hunchbacks,
than he does beautiful people.
The strong, the worthy, the beautiful, the noble,
the lovely ladies of great worth
who go along trailing fancy furs,

kings, queens, dukes and countesses
come to Hell in great crowds,
but nearly all the cripples and the hunchbacks
and the misshapen go to Heaven.
All the riffraff go to Heaven;
we have the grain and God the chaff.]
(ll. 198–220)

The theme and its implied critique are familiar; we might be reminded here of
Aucassin's speech about how all the best people go to Hell.[63] Gautier gets great
mileage, however, out of the status reversals inherent in Christianity by having
them presented in the devils' voice: having God's embrace of the lowest of the
low depicted as ludicrous foolishness further associates him with the "ringaille" he so loves and further demonstrates the devils' complete incomprehension of the heavenly system of value. Again, that system does not simply
mean valuing the riffraff over those of high status; it involves assessing the
"entencion" and inner worth of each individual, as the angels have just noted
with regard to priests and clerics. The broad-brush characterization of groups
practiced by Honorius Augustodunensis and many after him is nevertheless
tempting, and the angels respond to the devils that "Les povres genz qui nïent
n'ont / Symple et devot et humele sont" (poor people who have nothing are
simple and devout and humble, ll. 237–38), a declaration as unpersuasive as
the devils' outright rejection of the "ringaille."[64]

    After further disputation along the same lines, the devils eventually give
up the fight, but their 170 lines of resistance to the angels (who speak some 86
lines in reply), culminating in a 60-line rant, give the sense that this debate
itself, and especially the devils' part in it, is at least as important as the account
of the peasant himself, which occupies the first 64 lines of the miracle. To
some extent this points, again, to the value of the hostile witness; the devils'
uncomprehending rage at God's affection for the riffraff, Mary's immense
power, and the usefulness of a garbled prayer put these lessons across in a
lively and effective way. The dispute dramatizes the balance between hope and
fear, using dialogue as a way to depict the competing forces that make salvation both accessible and difficult to achieve. At the same time, the form of this
lesson—its use of demonic voices and the space it gives to the reassertion of
earthly ideas about status—demonstrates the tension created by a learned poet's attempt to exalt his own antithesis.[65]

    The excursus that follows the miracle showcases this less kindly reading, and in doing so focuses our attention more closely on the potentially thorny relationship between the learned translator and his simple protagonist, suggesting that Gautier himself had some ambivalence about just how salvageable the riffraff really are. In the story of Étienne and Perron, Gautier had concluded by rebuking those who, like Étienne, misuse their learning; in the story of the jongleur's candle, he lambastes monks who show less devotion than the lay hero of his tale. Here, however, having established, by way of angelic speech, the worth of "povres genz" and devout peasants, he uses his conclusion to emphasize their many failings. Reino Hakamies suggests that by expanding on the details of the peasant's devotion to Mary, Gautier creates "the necessary contrast between the peasant of the miracle and those of whom he speaks in his sermon," but the sweeping condemnation of peasants that Gautier issues and its similarity at points to that of the demons make the relationship between miracle and "sermon" a more ambivalent one than this acknowledges.[66] "[M]aufé sont vilain de vile" (Town peasants are cursed, l. 346), Gautier begins, adding that they are "si fol et si rude / Que bestial sont comme bestes" (so foolish and crude that they are as bestial as beasts, ll. 354–55). The latter accusation echoes that launched some lines earlier by the devils and seems directed more at peasants' learning and manners than at their morals.

Gautier does offer a critique of peasants' alleged disrespect for God and the Church: "Diex touz les confont, / Les fox vilains, les fox agrestes / Qui ne welent garder les festes, / Honnourer Dieu, clerc ne provoire" (God confound them all, the foolish peasants, the foolish rustics who do not wish to respect feast days, [or] honor God, cleric or priest, ll. 374–77). As its concluding words suggest, however, this complaint ends up having less to do with peasants' irreligious attitudes than with what we might call status panic on Gautier's part: he asserts that many a peasant would punch or slap him and that "Pluiseurs vilains clers heent trop / Ausi com Esaü Jacob" (Many peasants hate clerics excessively, just as Esau did Jacob, ll. 391–92).[67] Such allegations, with their suggestion of an uncomfortable closeness between peasants and clerics, recall the satirical poem *Les .xxiij. manieres de vilains*, which, after cataloging types of *vilains*, shifts into a scatological and scathing litany of curses against them that repeatedly asserts that they "heent clergie[,] . . . n'aiment clers ne chapelains" (hate learning/the clergy, do not love clerks or chaplains) and so forth.[68] Here, as in that poem, Gautier ends up more or less ventriloquizing an imagined opponent, reporting that just the other day "uns vilains ors" (a dirty peasant, l. 396) had expressed to him a wish, conveyed in indirect speech, that there were only one priest in the world, suspended in an old basket in the

clouds, where he could sing with the cranes—a fate that perhaps echoes Rutebeuf's consignment of peasants to "sing with the frogs" in *Le Pet au vilain*,
discussed in the previous chapter. The peasant, according to Gautier, added
that if he had five hundred or a thousand children he would not let one of
them become a priest, and would consider it better than a hundred marks for
there to be no "clerks, psalters, or books" ("Mis i vauroit avoir cent livres /
Qu'il ne fust clers, sautiers ne livres," ll. 415–16). After a few more insults,
Gautier recounts, the peasant concluded by giving the underlying and most
important reason for his hatred of clerks: he wouldn't trust a tonsured ass
around his wife or his daughter.[69] Gautier responds to this final accusation
rather unconvincingly, saying,

> . . . ne sont mie toutes voires
> Les paroles que cil en dïent
> Qui volentiers des clers mesdïent.
> Peu les aimment et mains les croient;
> Et loins et pres trop les mescroyent.
> Ne sai se c'est de voires faites
> Vilain cuident que braies traites
> Aient adez clerc et provoire,
> Mais ceste chose n'est pas voire
> Ne par est pas, je n'en dout mie,
> Li leuz si grans com on le crie.
> Vilain cuident bien, par saint Pierre,
> De fust doient estre ou de pierre
> Tuit cil qui ont corone es testes.

> [. . . by no means all the things
> they [peasants] say about clerks,
> whom they gladly slander, are true.
> They love them little and trust them less;
> near or far, they mistrust them all too much.
> I don't know if it is on account of actual deeds
> that peasants believe that clerks and priests
> have loose britches,
> but this thing is not true
> and I have no doubt the wolf
> is not as large as he is claimed to be.

Peasants truly believe, by St. Peter,
that all those with a tonsure on their heads
should be made of wood or stone.][70]
(ll. 438–51)

As a defense of clerks, this is distinctly underwhelming, apparently providing excuses for their behavior rather than an actual denial. The idea that clerks, being only human (rather than wood or stone), should not be so harshly rebuked for falling into temptation is scarcely a ringing endorsement of clerical virtue.

Gautier soon returns to the (rather querulous) attack, however, saying that rustics always hate clerks, are more vicious and faithless than dogs, more traitorous than Ganelon, and deserving of all ills, because "Peu ont creance et foy petit" (They have little belief and small faith, l. 471). Since the miracle to which this diatribe is attached has shown the opposite, Gautier seems to be wandering somewhat from the point and, again, sailing rather close to the position of the devils or the attitudes expressed even by saints in the eschatological fabliaux, whereby peasants, merely by virtue of being peasants, cannot possibly be imagined as potential inhabitants of Heaven. He concludes by claiming that peasants' various misfortunes—which are described in some detail—are due to their lack of respect for the Church and its ministers and their failure to tithe properly.[71] They have such tough hides and such stupid brains that no good can enter them; they are so wicked and foul that preachers, clerks, and priests cannot pound any worth into them. Gautier himself, he says in a prolonged *annominatio* on various forms of "batre," gives it up as a bad job. Only in the final lines does he soften his position, hoping that God, who chastises and strikes his own to beat down their vices, will give such a beating "to them and us" that "we" will experience the delights of Heaven. The overall effect is to present clerics and peasants as implacable (if intimately related) adversaries, despite the fact that, as the devils have suggested, peasants' devotion to the Ave might seem to assimilate them: babbling the prayer, "Tout welent estre clerc et prestre" (they all want to be clerks and priests, l. 277), the devils sneer. Here the very engagement with *clergie*—however limited, however partial—that animates the learners of all the works discussed in this book is implicitly validated through its condemnation by demons.

It is troubling, then, that in this story's lengthy *queue*, Gautier clearly sides with clerks in an imagined face-off with peasants, since doing so inevitably affiliates him with the devils who scorn the peasant for both his lowly status and his limited learning. Even more troublingly, this conclusion betrays a sense of clerks' uncomfortable proximity and vulnerability to peasants. If indeed a garbled Ave Maria is enough to get you into Heaven, what becomes of clerical privilege, the clerks' command of the tools and language of higher learning? If clerics cannot be trusted around peasants' wives and daughters, what becomes of their exalted and angelic role? The miracles of the rich man, the simple priest and monk, and Étienne and Perron leave Gautier with some stable ground on which to stand, a perspective from which he feels able to critique, but "D'un Vilain" pushes the lesson of holy simplicity so far that even its author cannot quite embrace the status confusion it requires. Peasants' role as Esau to the clerics' Jacob, Gautier's ability to ventriloquize both devils who share his scorn and peasants who pay it back with interest, and the clergy's apparent inability to fulfill their side of the teaching contract by knocking some good into their recalcitrant audiences: all of these cast a discomforting light on the conjunction of cleric and peasant, learned and unlearned. If the didactic works with which we began negotiate their status issues, in part, by way of the different kinds of cultural capital held by a noble lay reader and her or his clerical teacher, Gautier's Marian miracles show how difficult it can be for the clerical teacher to embrace fully those miracles' own insistence on the transcendent, and instructive, power of holy simplicity when that quality is embodied by a figure who is the antithesis of the clerk.

Sinners and Teachers in the Anonymous Anglo-French Miracles

While Gautier pays lip service, then, to the value of even the most basic learning, the relative brevity of such tales in his collection and the miracle of the *vilain* make it clear that his sympathetic identification with such simple souls is limited. Gautier's self-presentation, as well as his lyrics and the illumination of his manuscripts, make him the storyteller, Marian devotee, and holy trouvère par excellence; above all, the sermonic addresses that conclude many of his miracles put him in the role of the preacher, critiquing faults while attempting to remain above the fray—though his miracles, as noted above, make this exalted position difficult to sustain at points and direct our attention to the ways in which the miracles' protagonists and audiences might challenge the author's clerical privilege. Writing slightly later, probably around the mid-thirteenth century, the anonymous compiler of the Anglo-French miracles that appear in British Library, Royal MS 20.B.XIV evades this problem by directing attention toward those protagonists and audiences, and away from himself. His textual persona is far less insistent than Gautier's, so that his claim to be one among the faithful in need of Mary's assistance—a claim shared by virtually every reteller of miracles—is here borne out by a lack of self-presentation or verbal pyrotechnics. Like Pierre d'Abernon or Robert of Gretham, he situates himself primarily as a translator, rather than a poet, and in his narratives it is the figures in the tales who take center stage, often becoming the primary storytellers; the compiler acts more as their transmitter than in any privileged role as commentator or judge.

As noted above, this compiler credits his own temerity in compiling the miracles to his trust in his kinship with Mary, and says in his Prologue that he composes his text "Pur mei et altres solacer" (to comfort myself and others), a formulation that recalls Robert of Gretham's embrace of humility in his *Miroir*, where he similarly claims that he writes "pur mei e altres amender" (to reform myself and others).[72] If Gautier's all-encompassing call to audiences focuses on his text's universality, that of the anonymous compiler, like Robert's or Pierre's remarks in their prologues, emphasizes the personal nature of his undertaking and the common ground he shares with his audience and with the audiences and tellers in the tales. His sympathy for and assimilation to his lowly protagonists are evident in his versions of miracles also told by Gautier. The tale of the "priest of one mass" (XXIII) as told in this collection, for example, is generally similar to Gautier's but heightens the virtue and pathos of the good, simple priest, here called a chaplain. The narrative recounts, "Mult fu de bone e seinte vie, / Mes ne sout gueres de clergie; / Une messe chantout chescun jur / De nostre dame par grant amur" (He was of very good and holy life, but he hardly had any learning; every day he sang one mass, that of our Lady, out of great love, 103, ll. 5–8). When he is denounced to the bishop, his lack of "clergie" is reemphasized and, in fact, his very status as a cleric is questioned: "a l'eveske fu encusé, / Ke li chapelein fu lai en fin, / Ne saveit gueres mot de latin" (it was alleged to the bishop that the chaplain was in fact a layman; he knew hardly a word of Latin, 103–4, ll. 18–20). The bishop's rebuke, by comparison with that in Gautier, is elaborated; three separate times he refuses mercy to the chaplain, who pleads piteously. Most strikingly, at the bishop's instruction that he return to school to learn more prayers/masses, the priest balks: "'Sire,' fet il, 'entre altres enfanz / Un homme ke est de karante anz, / Ke ad perdu vue & oïe, / Semblereit ore grant briconie / Ke fuse ore remis a lettre, / Ne me saveroi, sirre, entremettre'" ("Lord," he said, "it would seem a great folly that now a man who is forty years old, who has lost his sight and hearing, should at this point be put back to learn his letters among other children, nor would I know, lord, how to undertake it," 104–5, ll. 53–58). The detail suggests an awareness of, and even sympathy for, the chaplain's position that is, of course, ratified by the miracle itself. While Gautier, that is, conveys the basic message of the worth of simple devotion, the Anglo-French compiler imaginatively enters into the situation in ways that increase our engagement with the protagonist, our sense of him as an individual, and our awareness of the difficulties of learning as well as its rewards.

In the tale of the peasant devoted to Mary (XXV), too, the Anglo-French compiler tilts the story in ways that emphasize less the peasant's irredeemable rusticity than his consistent effort and its just reward. In this version, the peasant's death is characterized as "nostre commun destin" (our common destiny, 113, l. 20), making him a more universal figure than he is in Gautier's telling, and the devils who come to take him seem to want him as a companion (the word "compaignie" is often repeated in this narrative), unlike those in Gautier who disdain him as much as the author himself does. The angels, who win the argument considerably faster in this instance—providing the devils, therefore, with less room in which to mock the peasant's limitations—stake their claim on the devils' self-evident lack of "dreiture" and "reisun" (a pairing repeated in ll. 56 and 71): since the peasant served Mary "always, day by day" (tuz jurs de jur en jur, 114, l. 57) and "honored her as much as he could and saluted her as best he could" (onura atant ke il pout / E la salua al mels ke il pout, ll. 59–60), obviously he is hers. The emphasis on his fundamental righteousness recalls that in *Le Vilain qui conquist paradis par plait*, where "droit" is so important in the story, and the shortcomings of his devotion are not detailed or caricatured here as they are in Gautier; instead his steadfastness is presented as a straightforward justification for Mary's intervention.

In the end, the peasant is led "[d]evant la seinte duce face / De nostre dame ke l'ad salve" (before the sweet, holy face of our Lady who saved him, 115, ll. 84–85) in a moment of confrontation that echoes the "face-to-face" repeatedly evoked in texts focused on death. It refocuses our attention on this specific protagonist while also substituting a moment of mercy for that of judgment.[73] The miracle concludes, like the others in this collection, with a prayer that, like the mention of "our common destiny," assimilates the audience to the protagonist: may God pardon "nos folies, / Nos pecchez & nos vileinies, / Ke ne seum a chef de tur / Dampnez pur nostre grant folur" (our follies, our sins and our wrongs, so that in the end we may not be damned for our great wickedness, ll. 91–94). This use of "vileinies" makes it a moral rather than a social marker, one that applies not to the social category of *vilains* but to anyone who behaves wrongly. Whereas Gautier's devils and his concluding sermon try to depict peasants as a class apart, and one with a particularly vexed relationship to the clergy, for the Anglo-French compiler they are one social group among others, no more or less easily incorporated into the generalized audience of Marian miracles than any other.

Another miracle about a peasant (XLIX) makes even clearer the fluidity of status, its ability to shift in light of the situation. Here, a peasant riding through the woods at night passes a little chapel and is accosted by a beautiful maiden, who greets him kindly, addresses him as "Prodome," and asks that he come speak to her lady. When he comes before Mary—who is of course the lady in question—she tells him to have the chaplain in charge of the chapel rebuild it to please her, demonstrating in detail how the building should take place. When the *vilein* carries his message, however, a lady friend of the chaplain's mocks the idea that this "deble vilein" (feeble peasant, 215, l. 108, though perhaps with a pun on "devilish") could ever have seen Mary; she is promptly punished with a broken leg, upon which the chaplain "comensa le overaine / Par le vilein ke l'enseigne" (began the work according to the peasant's instruction, 216, ll. 137–38). The *vilein* himself becomes a master mason through his vision. In spite of his rusticity, that is, he plays the roles of "prodome," messenger, and builder, instructing the priest not only in the rebuilding of the chapel but in a truer appreciation of the insignificance of earthly status. He also plays a role we see throughout the Anglo-French collection, one that extends the lesson taught to the chaplain: as the messenger for Mary, the recounter of her instructions, he becomes a figure for the messenger who translates these stories, the translator himself.[74]

This depiction of a teller within the tale who echoes the teller outside is repeated in many miracles; while such events certainly appear also in Gautier, they are more consistently highlighted in the second Anglo-French compilation. The effect derives both from the greater simplicity and directness of the translation, which emphasizes the narrative itself rather than the poet's skill at elaboration, and through the repetition of key words or phrases both within and across various miracles. Thus, for example, the compiler's self-characterization as one who tells his stories "pur mei et altres solacer" is echoed later in his reference to Hugh of Cluny, source of one of his stories (XXII), who "solleit bon cuntes conter / Pur sei & altre solacer" (was accustomed to tell good stories to comfort himself and others, 98, ll. 11–12), confirming the community of tellers he comes from and the tendency of those tellers to cast themselves also as audiences, as those "reassured" by the narratives. And if the tellers are also audiences, they share both roles with figures in the stories themselves: this compiler's desire to show others telling their stories is one of his most characteristic moves as an author and echoes his claim in the prologue to be just "one of us."

As presented here, these retellings are distinguished both by their completeness and by their insistence on the power of stories to reverse shame by revealing it. The focus on completeness is striking: in tale after tale, a character tells, often "de chef en chef," his or her story, repeating in miniature the events the story has just recounted and putting the audience within the story in the same position as the audience outside it. Such moments are, of course, not unique to Marian miracles, but here the events retold tend to have a consistent form, in which a rescued sinner relates his or her own fall and redemption to a wide audience. In a number of cases, this is highlighted by the rhyme, with the teller specifically characterizing shame (*hunte*) as the kernel of the story (*cunte*). In miracle XIV, a nun who abandons her abbey, where Mary takes her place until she repents, returns "Vers la mesun cunter sun cunte, / Od grant vergoin, od mult grant hunte" (to the house to tell her story, with great embarrassment and shame, 70, ll. 124–25). In another instance, the lecherous sacristan of miracle XVI dies in a state of sin but is returned to life by Mary. He goes to his brethren and "tut lur conta sun conte / De sa folie & de sa hunte" (told them the whole story of his wickedness and his shame, ll. 123–24); here the full sequence of events is re-reported in brief.

The theme is particularly pronounced in the story of a pregnant abbess (XIII). This proud, harsh lady becomes pregnant (by unspecified means; the focus here is on the result, not the cause, of her sin) and confides in one sister, her prioress, who promptly tells the tale so widely that it reaches the ears of the bishop. The abbess is accused and summoned to face the results of her "huntage," but before this takes place Mary spirits the infant away, so that the abbess appears to be innocent. The angry bishop "Ardre voleit & mettre a hunte / Ke avant li cunterent le cunte" (wanted to burn and put to shame those who had told him the story before, 66, ll. 165–66). When the abbess sees this, she repents and "De tut en tut cunté li ad / Coment la merci Deu li savad / De la folie & de sa hunte, / De tut en tut conta sun cunte" (told [the bishop] from start to finish how God's mercy saved her from folly and from her shame; she told him her story from start to finish, ll. 173–76). The concealment and ill-natured report that have constituted the story thus far become, with a rushing sense of release—"de tut en tut cunté li ad . . . De tut en tut conta sun cunte"—a source of rescue in themselves, saving the accusers as the abbess herself has been saved. And so may we all be saved, the narrator concludes: just as Mary "delivered" this sinner, so may she protect us in this life "De pec-ché, hunte & vileinie" (from sin and shame and wrongdoing, 67, l. 206) and may we join her after our death. The abbess herself is already preserved from her accusers when she confesses, but the story is not complete until she has made the lesson visible to others and passed along the mercy that has been shown to her. As the compiler says elsewhere, "Seignurs, mult funt a entendre / Cuntes dunt homm poet ben aprendre; / Si tuz nel funt, alkuns le frunt, / Ke par ceste conte amendé serrunt" (Lords, one should pay attention to stories from which one can learn; if not everyone does so, some will, at least, who will be reformed by this story, 195, ll. 1–4). The verb *amender* is one repeatedly used of figures sent back from judgment to repair their wicked lives in hopes of a better outcome later; the miracles give their listeners the chance to get it right the first time.

The pairing of *conte* and *honte* in these stories evokes confession, but here of course the confession is a public one, made for instructive rather than self-reforming purposes; the teller has already been miraculously reformed, has undergone a conversion and in some cases a rebirth. Like the *Évangile de Nicodème* tradition, these retold stories make (former) sinners into teachers and co-opt the audience as guarantors and, ultimately, retellers themselves. The epilogue to the collection prays that Mary will give special help to "tuz iceuz noméement / Ke unt escoté tant bonement / E tuz icels ke le escrit lir-runt / E as altres puis le dirrunt" (all those who have listened well, and all those who have read the work and have then told it to others, 254, ll. 23–26)—and, of course, to the translator himself. He remains nameless to the end, not a figure set apart from those to whom and of whom he speaks but part of a "compainie" united by its inevitable sinfulness but also by its trust in Mary and the solace it takes in hearing and telling her stories, for the improvement of self and others.[75] If Gautier's lively, combative miracles thrive—like the es-chatological fabliaux—on opposition, dispute, and hierarchy, even as they claim ultimate unity, those of the Anglo-French compiler embrace instead the model of assimilation between teacher and learner that we see in works like the *Lumere as lais* and the *Miroir*.

Death and Temporality

The Anglo-French compiler's interest in the process of telling, which links him both to his characters and to his audience, echoes and sometimes accompanies the similar conjunction whereby—as in the exempla told by Honorius Augustodunensis—the audience is invited to imagine and experience the death of another as a way to prepare for their own. In both cases, the miracles ask for simultaneous attention to past (the events of the story; the audience's own past actions); present (the hearing or reading of the story; the audience's current spiritual state); and future (the potential retelling of the story; the hearer's future behavior and ultimate fate). The connection between past action, present learning, and future fate that the miracles emphasize is one they share with other texts considered in this book, and as with those stories, the conjunction of times is also expressed as one of process and event, of the continual or repeated and the transformational and unexpected—of teaching and death.

Such a conjunction is precisely what Michel Foucault suggests characterizes conversion: prepared for by the kind of repeated practice depicted in many miracles, it also "requires a single, sudden, both historical and metahistorical event" that involves "a transition from one type of being to another, from death to life, from mortality to immortality" and, finally, "renunciation of oneself, dying to oneself, and being reborn in a different self and a new form."[76] All of these features of Christian conversion are, as we have seen, made strikingly concrete and evident in Marian miracles. The repeated activity, *us* or *usage*, the sustained devotion to Mary that characterizes nearly all the miracles and makes possible the moment of conversion is, in effect, the only grounds for salvation in many cases. The "historical and metahistorical event" of death and judgment, where a sinner's *askesis* and the moment of death make possible a complete transition, echoes the many turning points in Christian history, perhaps above all Christ's Descent into Hell and re-ascent to earth and Heaven.

The *Évangile de Nicodème*, as I argued in Chapter 3, dramatizes the moment in Christian history when past and future fold together: the prophecies are fulfilled, the gates of Hell and Heaven are opened, the Descent reaches its nadir and becomes ascent. Marian miracles replay the story of the good thief, the sinner saved at the last minute, from another angle, emphasizing less the unique event than the superimposition of the timeless on the quotidian. In these narratives, so pervasively that it is almost difficult to notice, literal *every-day* repetition—"tuz jurs de jur en jur," as the anonymous Anglo-French collection puts it, "every day, from day to day"—forms a chain that eventually links to eternity. The many miracles that insist on this repetitive practice reinforce the link between present behavior and future events, even as they show how easy it is for such *usage* to be undervalued—by the devils, certainly, but implicitly also by any living Christian who fails to follow this simple path to Heaven.

Both the power of repetition and its connection to the extraordinary are evident in miracles that emphatically recall biblical events. In Gautier's I Mir 29, the story of a devout nun who rushed her prayers, Mary says to her of the Ave,

> Suer, cis salus m'est si tres biaus
> Que toz jors m'est fres et novialz.
> Qui de bon cuer le me pronunce
> Tout ausi grant joie m'anunce
> Con fist Gabriel, li archangles,
> Quant me dist qui li rois des angeles
> S'aomberroit en mes sains flans.
> Fres et novialz m'est en toz tanz.
> Quant vient a *Dominus tecum*,
> Tant m'est sades et de doz non
> Qu'il m'est avis qu'en mon saint ventre
> Sains Esperis de rechief entre.
> Au cuer en ai si tres grant joie
> Qu'il m'est avis qu'enchainte soie
> Si com je fui quant mes doz pere
> Daigna de moi faire sa mere.[77]

[Sister, I find this salutation so very beautiful
that it is always fresh and new to me.
Whoever speaks it to me with good heart
announces to me joy as great
as did Gabriel, the archangel,
when he told me that the king of angels
would conceal himself in my holy sides.
It is always fresh and new to me.
When it comes to *Dominus tecum*,

it is so pleasant and sweetly named
that it seems to me that the Holy Spirit
enters once more into my holy womb.
I have such great joy in my heart from it
that it seems to me that I am pregnant
just as I was when my dear father
deigned to make me his mother.
(ll. 75–90)

The linking of the individual Christian's actions in the present to the biblical past is, of course, a "primary function of liturgy" and a familiar aspect of the prayers that grew out of it.[78] Here, Mary implicitly addresses the potentially problematic elements of a repetitive practice—the way in which it may become less compelling through familiarity—by insisting that the salutation is always "fresh and new" to her and implicitly should be so to the one who speaks it. She also points to the way that speaking the Ave casts the speaker in the role of Gabriel and in effect re-performs the Incarnation. The prayer thus sutures past event to present practice and at the same time brings that biblical past vividly to life by way of Mary and her affectionate, though admonishing, appearance to her devotee.[79]

Mary's interventions may also be linked, though usually less directly, to another biblical past, that of the Harrowing of Hell; but the very nature of that narrative links them to the future as well as the past. Gautier's I Mir 42 tells the tale of a lecherous monk—one, of course, with a great devotion to Mary—who drowns as he is trying to get home from a visit to his *amie*.[80] He dies without confession and seemingly damns himself beyond help, though his soul as it exits the body laments and calls on Mary. When the devils come to claim him, the angels appear to contest their right, explicitly invoking the Harrowing:

"Ele est nostre," li angele dïent,
"Car en la crois dou sacré sanc
Qui degouta de son saint flanc
Li rois dou ciel la rachata.
De la prison d'enfer jeta
Et deslia de vos lïens
Diex par sa mort crestïens."

["[His soul] is ours," the angels say,
"for on the Cross, with the holy blood
that ran from his blessed side,
the King of Heaven redeemed it.
From the prison of Hell God,
through his death, cast out Christians
and freed them from your bonds."]
(ll. 90–96)

The syntax of the original here foregrounds the historical events—Jesus'
bloody death on the Cross, the Harrowing of Hell—that constitute the Redemption; the upshot of those actions (redemption and freedom from the
Devil) follows, but our attention is initially focused on the process by which
they are achieved. Like Mary's detailed recollection of the Annunciation in I
Mir 29, the angels' assertion links the contemporary individual to the biblical
(in this case, the apocryphal biblical) past.

The case, however, as elsewhere in Gautier, does not go unchallenged.
Here the grounds for challenge are not those of social status, as in the miracle
of the *vilain* discussed above, but those of mere justice: "'Seignor angele,' font
li dyable, / 'Diex en la crois, ce n'est pas fable, / Rescost de mort toz ses amis, /
Mais cist estoit ses anemis, / Car il metoit toute sa cure / En lecherie et en luxure,'" ("Lords, angels," the devils say, "it is no lie that God on the Cross rescued all his friends from death, but this one was his enemy, because he put all
his care into lechery and lust," ll. 97–102). This allows the author of miracles to
address directly the discomfort with Mary's apparent lack of discretion as to
whom she saves and to explore what, precisely, is the relation between the salvific actions of Christ and Mary in the past and their effect on present sinners.
Using the devils to express doubt over whether devotion to Mary outweighs a
lifetime of sin or an unconfessed death, the miracles are careful to insist on the
righteousness of Mary's and Christ's interventions. Gautier repeatedly refers to
Christ as "le roi qui ne mente" (the king who does not lie) and has him, in
some particularly difficult cases, insist that he cannot "desdire" his own dictum
that, for example, only souls without sin can enter Heaven; we can hear, in
such conversations, echoes of the theological labor that also undergirds such
works as Robert Grosseteste's *Chasteau d'amour*, with its careful accounting for
justice and righteousness as well as mercy and peace.[81] In a Marian context the
crucial message, as both figures within the tales and Gautier himself repeatedly

emphasize, is that true and unrestrained faith in Mary's goodness and power is inevitably efficacious. Gautier seems untroubled by the implications of this view; more than once, he hints at the potentially universal salvation available through Mary. In a miracle about a monk who is without redeeming qualities except his devotion to St. Peter (who eventually persuades Mary to resuscitate him so he can do penance), Gautier asserts near the end, "N'est nus chaitis tant aterrés / Ne tant lachiés ne tant serrés / En ordure n'en vilonie, / Se d'entier cuer la sert et prie, / Qu'ele nel giet fors de pechié" (There is no wretch so fallen, so entwined or entrapped by filth or villainy that if he serves her and prays to her with his whole heart she will not cast him out of sin, ll. 201–5), and a few lines later he adds, "Se nos volons, toz nos vaurra / En paradys mener et metre" (If we wish it, she will be able to lead and put us all in Paradise, ll. 210–11).[82] In the miracle of the pilgrim of St. James that immediately follows this one, Mary similarly allows a damned soul to return to its body and make amends; the Devil says bitterly, "Ne demoroit en enfer ame, / Je cuit, se Diex la voloit croire" (Not a single soul would remain in Hell, I don't think, if God wanted to believe her, ll. 124–25).[83] The logic here seems designed to point toward the *possibility* of universal salvation—not, in this case, achieved mystically, as some later Middle English texts seem to imply, or through the comic inversion of the eschatological fabliaux but attained through individual human will and intention.[84]

The mutuality of this promise, the requirement of help from both sides, reflects the mutuality of Mary's, and Christ's, relationship to humankind and the history of the Incarnation. If only every sinner would put true and heartfelt faith in Mary, Hell could be emptied out, and this is not only her promise but indeed her function: she became the source of Christ's human flesh *because* he wanted to rescue sinners from Hell. Gautier is here repeating a lesson allegedly authorized by Augustine; as Pierre d'Abernon translates it, "entre vus e nus alliance / Grant i trues e covenance, / Ke ceo ke vus estes estes pur nus, / E ceo ke nus sumes sumes par vus!" (between us and you [Mary] I find great alliance and affinity, for what you are, you are for us, and what we are, we are through you, *Lumere,* 1:189, ll. 6221–24).[85] As in William of Waddington's recasting of Augustine, the beauty of the Latin parallel is intensified by the internal and end rhymes of the French verse, with *nus* chiastically linked to, and thus enclosed by, *vus.* Pierre goes on to make reference to the *felix culpa* motif that forms the theological basis for this depiction of Mary. The sinning human, in effect, gives rise to the need for, and thus the existence of, the means of his salvation: she—and Christ—exist for him as the sinner must exist for her. As Pierre puts it in his own voice, "par seint Austin, cest honur / N'eust pas eue sanz peccheur" (according to St. Augustine, without the sinners, she would not have had this honor, ll. 6249–50). Like many of Gautier's formulations that might, in the miracle context, seem extreme, the theological point itself is impeccably orthodox and grounded in authority. So is the tropological upshot, which is that sinners must complete their part of this process: as Mary says to the devils in the drowned-monk miracle (I Mir 42), "Et ce dist Diex et l'Escriture / Qu'en quelconque eure gemira / Li pechierres que sauz sera" (God and Scripture say that in whatever hour the sinner groans [i.e., repents] he will be saved, ll. 322–24). This verse (Ezek. 33:12), which Honorius Augustodunensis had associated with the good thief, is a reminder that whatever Mary's power, she cannot act to help the sinner if the sinner does not act to help himself.

This principle can, however, be stretched to its limit, as we see in one final miracle. Gautier's I Mir 28 tells the story of a knight who, like the *vilain* discussed above, has no good quality except his devotion to Mary; again like the peasant, he loves Mary but shows no honor to God.[86] In view of this, however, Jesus softens the knight's heart, to such good effect that he soon makes a wise man of the fool ("tost fait d'un fol sage"): the knight forms the sincere intention of founding and joining a monastery. He dies, however, before he can do more than survey the land he intends to use, and there follows the familiar contest between angels and devils over his soul. The devils insist, "Saus ne puet estre telz roberres / Se Diex ne vielt estre menterres" (Such a plunderer cannot be saved unless God wants to be a liar, ll. 113–14), and demand that the case be heard by the "roi qui ne mente." An angel goes to get the verdict and returns in triumph, saying that the devils would certainly have won if Mary had not stepped in. He reports her argument: that Jesus became man in her to save sinners. Jesus concurs with this, repeating it in his turn.[87] When Jesus decides in Mary's favor, the devils lament that all estates would be in Hell if it were not for God's mother: "De clers, de moignes, de nonains, / De chevaliers et de vilains / Fust enfers plains dusqu'a la geule / S'ele ne fust trestoute seule" (Hell would be full to the brim with clerks, monks, nuns, knights, and peasants, if only it weren't for her alone, ll. 187–90). The imagined heaping together of various estates in Hell and their (implied) actual heaping together in Heaven are, of course, replicated in the miracle collection itself, where knights and monks, empresses, peasants, and clerks, all saved by Mary, inhabit the same manuscript pages.

Once again, then, an apparently hopeless case is decided in Mary's favor through an insistence that the strict reading of the devils' rights is fundamentally mistaken: in choosing her for his mother, God in effect declared his intention to redeem sinners and draw them to himself. As the living conduit of his loving desire for mankind, she reminds him over and over of the ultimate truth about the Incarnation, so that in the end the king who cannot lie cannot deny her.[88] If the salutation to Mary has the power even to empty Hell (as the miracle of the *vilain* discussed earlier also asserts), it can do so only if put in "usage": any idiot who can babble the Ave can help re-perform the Harrowing, not because Mary is wantonly merciful but because devotion to the Ave signals a fundamental understanding that Mary is worthy of honor; and theologically Mary is worthy of honor only because she is the mother of God. Orthodox teaching *must* either jettison prayer to Mary—as of course happens in the Reformation—or account for it theologically, by accepting the transitive property of love.[89] Here as elsewhere, the miracles engage with, and put into narrative practice, the foundational teachings of Christianity. It is no coincidence that Grosseteste's *Chasteau d'amour*, which over its brief span covers the essentials of the Trinity, the Redemption, and most of the other indispensable doctrines, makes Mary's body its titular image; she is also, notably, the only figure whom the author directly addresses.

The *Chasteau's* opening argument between mercy and justice, one that is so often replayed in Marian miracles, appears in the anonymous Anglo-French collection in a version that does not simply adopt the terms of this debate but attempts to convey a particular understanding of them. When the devils, trying to claim the soul of a sacristan who drowns while out on a lustful escapade (xvi), make an appeal to "dreiture," righteousness (81, l. 71), Mary picks up their language, inviting them to take the case to "Jhesu Crist, ke nus tuz veit, / Il nus face juger le *dreit*; / Si trovez plus *dreiturel* de lui, / Seürement vus tenez a celui" (Jesus Christ, who sees us all: he will judge the right for us; if you find anyone more righteous than he, by all means hold to him, 82, ll. 91–94, emphasis added).[90] Righteousness takes a turn, however, when "Dampnedeu pur sa duce mere, / Ke *a bon dreit* deit aver chere, / Comanda ke l'alme fu remenée / Al cors" (God, for his sweet mother, whom by rights he should hold dear, commanded that the soul be taken back to the body, ll. 97–100, emphasis added). Righteousness is not violated; it is simply that the devils' idea of righteousness is limited. Jesus' love for his mother is a higher or truer "right." Miracle XXI, the monk of St. Peter, expresses the idea slightly differently; here Jesus asserts (in response to Mary's request that he help the soul),

Ma bele mere, n'est pas *dreit*
Ke vers vus escondit i eit,
Mes cist par *dreit* jugement
Dust estre liveré a dampnement
Cum cil ke trop est peccheür;
Jeo grant pur la vostre amur
Ke l'alme pus repeirer
Al cors & pus sei amender.[91]

[My dear mother, it is not right
that this should be denied you,
but this man, by righteous judgment,
should be delivered to damnation
as one who has been too much a sinner;
I grant, for your love,
that the soul can return
to its body and then reform itself.]

Technically both "rights" have been preserved, reconciled through God's ability to undo the finality of death, but the devils—and the story itself—clearly view this as a victory for Mary's right of love over the devils' right of judgment. Her willingness to deal with the dividedness of her devotees, their simultaneous love of her and submersion in sin, enables the "true work of justice" by working with human nature as it is "rather than opposing to it a sharp or rigid conception of good and evil."[92] This flexibility not only works to the advantage of the faithful; the miracles imply that it also, if rightly understood, offers a deeper and more nuanced knowledge of salvation history.

That history is based in transformation, in the translation of Word into flesh, and engaging with it fully has the power not only to save people but to remake them. In the case of the knight who died before fulfilling his vow (I Mir 28), Jesus responds to Mary's intercession in striking form: as a sign of the knight's forgiveness and in recognition of his intention—an intention "counted as a deed," as the miracle's rubric puts it, thus preserving the claims of righteousness—God sends him a monk's hood to wear. The action initiates the wicked knight into the social group of which Gautier himself is a member and resonates with a pattern Kathryn A. Duys has noted, wherein miraculous gifts of clothing help establish Gautier's composite authorial persona as monk and minstrel.[93] That persona derives both from intention and from (musical) performance and reminds us that while the miracle of this knight—like so many other Marian miracles—emphasizes intention, it does not in fact do away entirely with action. Like other protagonists, the knight already has a virtuous *habitus*: "En lonc tanz ne se departi / Ne ne remut de cest usage" (over a long period he did not stray or shift from this practice, ll. 52–53) of honoring Mary. Despite his apparent lack of spiritual worth, it is in fact this virtue, this "set of practices cultivated systematically with the goal of habituation," that makes him eligible, with Mary's help, for a posthumous monk's cowl: the change of life and status is granted by miracle, but that miracle itself responds to an existing *habitus*.[94] Gautier's central message, of course, is that this is a habit for his audience, too, to learn; both the history of the Incarnation and the ultimate future of death resolve themselves into a present moment by offering this text, like others we have seen, as a mirror. Near the end of the knight's story, Gautier exclaims, "He! Diex, quel myreor ci a / A pecheür qui bien se myre. / Mout a dur cuer qui ne souspire / Qui ce myracle oit reciter" (Ah! God, what a mirror is here for any sinner who looks at himself well. He has a hard heart indeed who does not sigh when he hears this miracle recited, ll. 206–9). Since Gautier himself, in his monk's hood and minstrel's mantle, is figuratively reciting it at this very moment—an image the manuscripts replicate, as Duys has shown—the "mirror" is before the audience; if they too manifest a pious intention, honoring Mary in practice or in song, they too can, indeed *will*, be saved: it is only right.

Just as the devils' claim that Mary scandalously overturns Jesus' righteous judgment is carefully answered in the miracles, then, the suggestion that she saves the undeserving is shown to be incorrect, and both claims fail because they undervalue, or misunderstand, the love that binds both devotee and Christ to Mary, their mediatrix. Worthless though they may appear in the eyes of the devils (and of many of those on earth, the knight's story notes), Mary's sinful devotees have in fact done the one thing that can save them; their continual practice both manifests and constitutes their love and faith, demonstrating that they have learned what is most important. As Norman Tanner and Sethina Watson note, "practice itself was a form of learning and it was in this sense that Bonaventure could speak of the faithful learning through 'the usage and custom of the church . . . and by means of its solemnities and priestly activities.'"[95] The Marian miracles in effect extend such "learning" to private devotions and prayers, which thus become an expression of understanding as well as love. If the debates between devils and angels or the affectionate conversations between Christ and Mary that enliven the miracles echo the theological accounts of figures like Anselm and Grosseteste, the homely, inept, partial efforts of the faithful show themselves, too, to be part of a system of teaching whose first lesson is love: "De rien ne t'estuet penser / Fors Deus e tun proeme amer," Christ says to his "brother" humankind in the *Chasteau d'amour* (You need think of nothing but loving God and your neighbor).[96] Like the mirror held up by Robert of Gretham's sermons or Edmund of Abingdon's treatise on contemplation, Marian miracles are teaching texts that put an affectionate, familiar face on the mysteries of Christian doctrine so that their addressees may see both that doctrine and themselves more truly. Deploying their own versions of the conflict, lively interaction, and reversals that characterize the informal teaching of the thirteenth century, they endeavor by means of translation to create likeness, a common ground of knowledge and practice between the devout audience, the saved sinners in the miracles, and the teacher who brings them together and in doing so, he hopes, saves himself.

Afterword

The preceding chapters have considered what twelfth- and, especially, thirteenth-century French teaching texts, insular and Continental, can help us see about the self-understanding of medieval teachers and learners, but I hope they have also suggested some implications for modern participants in those categories. If the intense exchange between master and disciple in instructional dialogues implies and indeed performs the potential for mutual assimilation, the reversals of the *Évangile de Nicodème* and the eschatological fabliaux are a lively reminder that students make their own uses of what they are taught, and can sometimes teach their teachers. The Marian miracles, finally, make the ever-present potential for status reversal one of their central themes and, in their tendency to alienate scholarly sensibilities, implicate us in an unfinished debate over the interaction between learned and unlearned approaches to such crucial issues as education, status, and salvation (or, as we might call it, success).

For all their intermittent playfulness and enjoyment of reversal, these texts, in their original situations, nevertheless focus on something that all concerned could surely agree was of universal interest and importance: the fate of the soul at the moment of death. I have tried, however, to show that their ways of envisioning that moment, while they may draw on the techniques of "terrifying the audience" sometimes imagined as the heart of medieval religion, give at least as much attention to the earthly relationships, decisions, and actions that prepare for it and to the hope these can provide. The "innovations in the daily life of the faithful" created by the reforming Church of the eleventh to thirteenth centuries may have contributed to the power of the papacy, but this does not have to mean that "the formation of a persecuting society" is the only lens through which we can understand them.[1] If we consider, so to speak, the frontlines of orthodox Christian instruction from the perspective of its purveyors and its recipients (groups with fluid boundaries, as noted above), we can see both an intense investment in and a lively intellectual engagement with the judgment of the individual, in both senses: these works aim to cultivate the individual's judgment—his or her discretion, discernment, self-knowledge—so that the judgment of the individual on the point of death can have the desired outcome. Marian miracles take this claim to its furthest extent, insisting that anyone who has attempted seriously, however ineptly, to engage in Christian devotion has in doing so indicated a foundational understanding of the tenets of the faith that "spiritually ambitious" self-formation may build on but does not leave behind.[2] In their emphasis on reversal at the point of death, moreover, the miracles, like other instructive texts, insist on the limits of earthly hierarchies and valuations, including the valuation of learning.

These texts, taken as a tradition, work collectively and sometimes in overlapping ways to think through the implications for teacher and student of bringing clerical forms and knowledges to new audiences. In doing so they provide us with a rich context for thinking about the intensely interpersonal and imaginative doctrinal encounters of many later texts that grapple with the same essential questions. The baffled dreamer of the Middle English *Pearl*, with his confusion about how his beloved child can be a queen; the frustrated Will of *Piers Plowman*, trying to figure out what really is *basic* to Christian teaching; even Christine de Pizan, reworking religious and didactic dialogues to fashion an instructive persona capable of engaging with the full range of earthly and heavenly topics: all are responding to a long and deep history of informal instruction that the texts considered here exemplify. Engaging with theology, the Bible, sermons, and the confessional, but working alongside them or in their interstices, these works insist that we think about teaching in action, in process, and in embodied forms.

The relationality of these texts—the assumption, and often the depiction, of dialogue or instructive encounter that is so important in all of them—is ultimately what drew me to them. The works and genres considered here have all, in their own ways, been at times marginal or neglected: apocryphal, unoriginal, basely "popular" or scurrilous, even just plain dull, they have drawn various kinds of scorn. Ultimately, however, they express the linking of love and knowledge: the love of knowledge itself but also, and more important, the conjunction of love and knowledge that ideally constitutes teaching and learning, whether medieval or modern. As these texts assert over and over, the crucial virtue for a Christian is humility, and the power of humility derives from Christ's willing humbling of himself and assimilation to humankind, the ultimate expression of love. One who has grasped both this idea and its counterpart—that God, like the teacher, desires that humankind in turn should assimilate itself to the divine, through love and knowledge—has learned the lesson that leads to all others. Even in comic or gleefully combative treatments of this theme, like that in *Le Vilain qui conquist paradis par plait*, the message is implicit: through teaching and learning, the student and the teacher become like one another, the peasant quoting God as God quotes the peasant in return. In the end, like the master and disciple, intensely engaged in the mutual assimilation required for teaching to be effective, they occupy the same heavenly space. And if the space of Heaven is one that modern scholarship can consider only at a certain remove, the scene of instruction is one where, despite our distance, we can continue to engage, as students and as teachers, with our medieval counterparts.

Notes

PREFACE

1. See, for example, Joachim Bumke, "The Adoption of French Aristocratic Culture in Germany," in his *Courtly Culture: Literature and Society in the High Middle Ages* (Woodstock, N.Y.: Overlook Press, 2000).

2. Anglo-Norman remains the name of the main scholarly society in the field and thus the preferred title term for invaluable reference works such as Ian Short, *Manual of Anglo-Norman*, 2nd ed. (Oxford: Anglo-Norman Text Society, 2013) and Ruth J. Dean and Maureen B. M. Boulton, *Anglo-Norman Literature: A Guide to Texts and Manuscripts* (London: ANTS, 1999). On "French of England," see the foundational article by Nicholas Watson and Jocelyn Wogan-Browne, "The French of England: The *Compileison, Ancrene Wisse*, and the Idea of Anglo-Norman," *Cultural Traffic in the Medieval Romance World: Journal of Romance Studies* 4.3, special issue, ed. Simon Gaunt and Julian Weiss (Winter 2004): 35–58—where, notably, insular French is placed in a broader Romance context—as well as Jocelyn Wogan-Browne et al., eds., *Language and Culture in Medieval Britain: The French of England, c. 1100–c. 1500* (York: York Medieval Press, 2009). Ardis Butterfield, *The Familiar Enemy: Chaucer, Language, and Nation in the Hundred Years War* (Oxford: Oxford University Press, 2009), working primarily on a later period, prefers "Anglo-French" and "insular French."

3. Christopher Cannon, *The Grounds of English Literature* (Oxford: Oxford University Press, 2004). As Elizabeth Robertson points out, however, in a generally very positive review of the book, the "isolation" of the Middle English works Cannon explores might look less complete if one took more account of both the Latin and French works surrounding them and the prevailing cultural "commitment to Christianity": "*The Grounds of English Literature* by Christopher Cannon," *Journal of English and Germanic Philology* 106.4 (2007): 531–34, at 532, 534.

4. Watson and Wogan-Browne, "French of England," 41–42.

5. Katherine C. Little, *Confession and Resistance: Defining the Self in Late Medieval England* (Notre Dame, Ind.: University of Notre Dame Press, 2006), 50. Other examples include Fiona Somerset, *Clerical Discourse and Lay Audience in Late Medieval England* (Cambridge: Cambridge University Press, 1998); Nicole R. Rice, *Lay Piety and Religious Discipline in Middle English Literature* (Cambridge: Cambridge University Press, 2008); and Katharine Breen, *Imagining an English Reading Public, 1150–1400* (Cambridge: Cambridge University Press, 2010).

6. Somerset, *Clerical Discourse*, 4. See Watson and Wogan-Browne, "French of England," and Nicholas Watson, "Lollardy: The Anglo-Norman Heresy?" in *Language and Culture in Medieval Britain*, ed. Wogan-Browne et al., 334–46, for recent critiques of a Middle English–centric account of the aftermath of Lateran IV.

7. Vincent Gillespie, "*Doctrina* and *Predicacio*: The Design and Function of Some Pastoral Manuals," *Leeds Studies in English* 9 (1980): 36–50, at 45, 37.

8. Breen, *Imagining*, 11; though see Watson, "Lollardy," 337, for a different view.

9. M. B. Parkes, "The Literacy of the Laity," in *The Medieval World*, ed. David Daiches and Anthony Thorlby (London: Aldus Books, 1973), 555–77, at 557.

10. Watson, "Lollardy," 336.

11. Butterfield, *Familiar Enemy*, xxii. See further her remarks about the "doubleness" of the story of both French and English in this period, xxiii–xxvii.

12. The quoted phrase is from Breen, *Imagining*, 11.

13. See the discussion of "high" and "low" languages in R. A. Lodge, "Language Attitudes and Linguistic Norms in France and England in the Thirteenth Century," in *Thirteenth Century England IV: Proceedings of the Newcastle-upon-Tyne Conference 1991*, ed. P. R. Coss and S. D. Lloyd (Woodbridge, Suffolk: Boydell Press, 1992), 73–83, and Susan Crane, "Social Aspects of Bilingualism in the Thirteenth Century," in *Thirteenth Century England VI*, ed. Michael Prestwich, R. H. Britnell, and Robin Frame (Woodbridge, Suffolk: Boydell Press, 1997), 103–15, especially 105–7. On the status of French in England more generally, see Ian Short, "Patrons and Polyglots: French Literature in Twelfth-Century England," in *Anglo-Norman Studies XIV*, ed. Marjorie Chibnall (Woodbridge, Suffolk: Boydell Press, 1992), 229–49; Elizabeth Salter, "Culture and Literature in Earlier Thirteenth-Century England: National and International," in *England and International: Studies in the Literature, Art, and Patronage of Medieval England*, ed. Derek Pearsall and Nicolette Zeeman (Cambridge: Cambridge University Press, 1988), 29–74, esp. 32–35; and William Rothwell, "The Role of French in Thirteenth-Century England," *Bulletin of the John Rylands University Library of Manchester* 58 (1976): 445–66.

14. Gilles Deleuze and Félix Guattari, *A Thousand Plateaus: Capitalism and Schizophrenia*, trans. Brian Massumi (Minneapolis: University of Minnesota Press, 1987), 23, 25.

15. Catherine Rider, "Lay Religion and Pastoral Care in Thirteenth Century England: The Evidence of a Group of Short Confession Manuals," *Journal of Medieval History* 36 (2010): 327–40, at 328.

16. Dorothy L. Owen, *Piers Plowman: A Comparison with Some Earlier and Contemporary French Allegories* (London: University of London Press, 1912).

17. William Langland, *The Vision of Piers Plowman: A Complete Edition of the B-Text*, ed. A. V. C. Schmidt (London: J. M. Dent, 1987).

18. Robert of Gretham, *Miroir*.

19. On the thirteenth-century Bible, see Clive R. Sneddon, "The *Old French Bible*: The First Complete Vernacular Bible in Western Europe," in *The Practice of the Bible in the Middle Ages: Production, Reception, and Performance in Western Christianity*, ed. Susan Boynton and Diane J. Reilly (New York: Columbia University Press, 2011), 296–314. Leonard Boyle argued that the famous attack of Innocent III on the people of Metz was directed far more at the specter of lay preaching than at Scriptures in the vernacular: "Innocent III and Vernacular Versions of Scripture," in *The Bible in the Medieval World: Essays in Memory of Beryl Smalley*, ed. Katherine Walsh and Diana Wood (Oxford: Basil Blackwell for the Ecclesiastical History Society, 1985), 97–107; while Margriet Hoogvliet has recently suggested that modern scholarship tends (still) to overemphasize resistance to lay reading of the Bible and overlook counterevidence: "Encouraging Lay People to Read the Bible in the French Vernaculars: New Groups of Readers and Textual Communities," *Church History and Religious Culture* 93 (2013): 239–74.

20. See Rita Felski, "After Suspicion," *Profession* (2009): 28–35.

INTRODUCTION

1. *MP* Roxburghe, 373, ll. 10502–6; *MP* EETS, 374, ll. 8801–4.

2. The importance of right belief (orthodoxia), not just right *practice* (orthopraxis), in Christianity is part of what leads both to the teaching imperative of Lateran IV and to its potentially explosive implications; as Jean-Charles Payen pointed out a number of years ago, "les oeuvres françaises traitant de la confession élargiront volontiers leurs perspectives jusqu'à rappeler non seulement ce qu'il est indispensable que sache le fidèle pour la bonne conduite de sa vie morale, mais aussi les points essentiels de la doctrine chrétienne en général": *Le Motif du repentir dans la littérature française médiévale (des origines à 1230)* (Geneva: Droz, 1968), 561. The present study in many ways complements Aden Kumler's *Translating Truth: Ambitious Images and Religious Knowledge in Late Medieval England and France* (New Haven, Conn.: Yale University Press, 2011), which explores the transmission of religious doctrine in the same period and area with a focus on the use of images in illuminated manuscripts for noble patrons.

3. The enormous project of translation into French in the late Middle Ages is magisterially surveyed in the collaborative collection *Translations médiévales: Cinq siècles de traductions en français au Moyen Âge (XIe–XVe siècles). Étude et Répertoire*, 3 vols., dir. Claudio Galderisi (Turnhout: Brepols, 2011). Nicholas Watson has noted the "radical potential latent in pastoral theology's pedagogical programme" in the context of Middle English mysticism and argued for the importance of Anglo-French works in the later rise of Lollardy: "The Middle English Mystics," in *The Cambridge History of Medieval English Literature*, ed. David Wallace (Cambridge: Cambridge University Press, 1999), 539–65, at 549–50, and "Lollardy."

4. An essay by Marjorie Curry Woods and Rita Copeland, "Classroom and Confession," in *The Cambridge History of Medieval English Literature*, ed. David Wallace (Cambridge: Cambridge University Press, 1999), 376–406, explores the double meaning of *disciplina* as "the regulation of knowledge and the regulation of the self" (377), and Rice, *Lay Piety and Religious Discipline*, considers discipline in a similar vein in later texts; see especially x–xi and her chapter titled "Dialogic Form and Clerical Understanding," 47–80.

5. Augustine, Sermon 169, in *Sermones de Scripturis*, PL 38:23–994, ch. 11, col. 923. Pierre d'Abernon, who translates the same teaching, renders it differently, remaining characteristically close to the form of the Latin: "seint Austin dit ensement / De ceste chose acordaument, / Ke dit: 'Ki sanz tei te cria / Sanz tei dreiturel ne te fra'" (Pierre d'Abernon, *Lumere*, 1:166, ll. 5451–54).

6. Adrian Armstrong, Sarah Kay, et al., *Knowing Poetry: Verse in Medieval France from the "Rose" to the "Rhétoriqueurs"* (Ithaca, N.Y.: Cornell University Press, 2011), 4.

7. Pierre d'Abernon, *Lumere*, 1:166, ll. 5449–50.

8. Augustine was, however, a true model for the kind of teaching we see in the thirteenth-century vernacular works; as John C. Cavadini notes, his *Sermones ad populum* consistently invoke the image of himself and his hearers as *condiscipuli* engaged in a "joint venture of inquiry," even if later preachers did not always retain this aspect of his thought. Cavadini, "Simplifying Augustine," in *Educating People of Faith: Exploring the History of Jewish and Christian Communities*, ed. John Van Engen (Grand Rapids, Mich.: William B. Eerdmans, 2004), 63–84, at 77.

9. On anchorites as "mediatory" teachers, see Anneke Mulder-Bakker, *Lives of the Anchoresses: The Rise of the Urban Recluse in Medieval Europe* (Philadelphia: University of Pennsylvania Press, 2005); on the friars, see David L. d'Avray, *The Preaching of the Friars: Sermons Diffused from Paris Before 1300* (Oxford: Oxford University Press, 1985). The known authors of the main didactic works I examine do not include any friars; these works are affiliated instead with the

(archi)episcopate (Maurice de Sully, Robert Grosseteste, Edmund of Abingdon, William of Waddington), the Augustinian canons (Edmund of Abingdon; possibly Pierre d'Abernon and Robert of Gretham), or household chaplains/confessors (Adam de Perseigne, Robert of Gretham, Frère Laurent). The recluse Barthélemy de Molliens wrote two influential works discussed below, while practically anyone might compose Marian miracles, from the *clerc-jongleur* Rutebeuf to the Benedictine monk Gautier de Coinci.

10. Caroline Walker Bynum, *Jesus as Mother: Studies in the Spirituality of the High Middle Ages* (Berkeley and Los Angeles: University of California Press, 1984), 22. On the Patarenes, see Brian Stock, *The Implications of Literacy: Written Language and Models of Interpretation in the Eleventh and Twelfth Centuries* (Princeton, N.J.: Princeton University Press, 1983), 151–240. Suzanne LaVere, "From Contemplation to Action: The Role of the Active Life in the *Glossa ordinaria* on the Song of Songs," *Speculum* 82.1 (January 2007): 54–69, discusses a relatively early example (before 1135) of the shift toward an idea of the apostolic life that centered on preaching (67–68).

11. C. Stephen Jaeger, *The Envy of Angels: Cathedral Schools and Social Ideals in Medieval Europe, 950–1200* (Philadelphia: University of Pennsylvania Press, 1994), 4 and passim. Among the figures Jaeger considers, Honorius Augustodunensis and Hugh of St. Victor are particularly important for the works I address here. See also the collection *Teaching and Learning in Northern Europe, 1000–1200*, ed. Sally N. Vaughan and Jay Rubenstein (Turnhout: Brepols, 2006), which, like Jaeger's book and the present one, emphasizes the central role of personal interaction in teaching.

12. As Ronald J. Stansbury puts it, "the reforms of Lateran IV . . . did not simply appear *ex nihilo* from this council or the mind of Pope Innocent III" but were part of a larger movement stretching back to the late eleventh century (Introduction to *A Companion to Pastoral Care in the Late Middle Ages (1200–1500)*, ed. Ronald J. Stansbury [Leiden: Brill, 2010], 1–6, at 2). On the pastoral project reflected in and furthered by the canons of the Fourth Lateran Council, see Franco Morenzoni, *Des Écoles aux paroisses: Thomas de Chobham et la promotion de la prédication au début du XIIIe siècle* (Paris: Institut d'Études Augustiniennes, 1995); Leonard E. Boyle, "The Fourth Lateran Council and Manuals of Popular Theology," in *The Popular Literature of Medieval England*, ed. Thomas Heffernan (Knoxville: University of Tennessee Press, 1985), 30–43; and Yves Lefèvre, ed., *L'Elucidarium et les Lucidaires: Contribution, par l'histoire d'un texte, à l'histoire des croyances religieuses en France au moyen âge* (Paris: E. de Boccard, 1954). On an earlier period in France, see also Pierre Riché, *Écoles et enseignement dans le Haut Moyen Âge, fin du Ve siècle–milieu du XIe siècle* (Paris: Picard, 1989), 314–34.

13. Odette Pontal, *Les Statuts synodales*, Typologie des sources du moyen âge occidental 11 (Turnhout: Brepols, 1975), 44–45; she also notes two slightly earlier sets of English canons (not statutes) as being the first to introduce teaching on the sacraments into ecclesiastical law (44). The richness of the English synodal sources in this period is often noted, but Pierre Michaud-Quantin observes that they are not unique: "the most remarkable [records], or at least the best explored in the current state of research, are those of the French dioceses, particularly north of the Loire, and the English dioceses": "Les Méthodes de la pastorale du XIIIe au XVe siècle," in *Methoden in Wissenschaft und Kunst des Mittelalters*, ed. Albert Zimmermann with the assistance of Rudolf Hoffmann (Berlin: Walter de Gruyter, 1970), 76–91, at 80. See also Roy M. Haines, "Education in English Ecclesiastical Legislation of the Later Middle Ages," in *Councils and Assemblies*, ed. G. J. Cuming and Derek Baker, Studies in Church History 7 (Cambridge: Cambridge University Press, 1971), 161–75.

14. Payen, *Motif du repentir*, 563; he suggests that there may be less-known Continental French works of this type still to be found (note 29), but his own examples, as this suggests, are

primarily Anglo-French (see 558–60), the thirteenth-century exceptions being Jean de Journy's *Dîme de pénitence* and Frère Laurent's *Somme le Roi*, both from the last quarter of the century. See also E. J. Arnould, *Le "Manuel des péchés": Étude de littérature religieuse anglo-normande (XIIIme siècle)* (Paris: Librairie E. Droz, 1940), on the "rapports constants entre Oxford et Paris" that informed works of this type (33).

15. Kumler, *Translating Truth*, 9; see also Short, *Manual of Anglo-Norman*, 32. On the cross-Channel (and beyond) transmission of French religious instruction, see Morenzoni, *Des Écoles aux paroisses*, and Hoogvliet, "Encouraging Lay People to Read the Bible in the French Vernaculars."

16. On this broader transmission of learning, see, for example (in addition to Galderisi, *Translations médiévales*, note 3 above), Charles F. Briggs, "Teaching Philosophy at School and Court: Vulgarization and Translation," in *The Vulgar Tongue: Medieval and Postmedieval Vernacularity*, ed. Fiona Somerset and Nicholas Watson (University Park: Pennsylvania State University Press, 2003), 99–111; David F. Hult, "Poetry and the Translation of Knowledge in Jean de Meun," in *Poetry, Knowledge and Community in Late Medieval France*, ed. Rebecca Dixon and Finn E. Sinclair (Cambridge: D. S. Brewer, 2008), 19–41; and Bernard Ribémont, *"De natura rerum": Études des encyclopédies médiévales* (Orléans: Paradigme, 1995). Different areas of knowledge overlap; the *Image du monde*, a translation (or collection of translations) of Honorius Augustodunensis's *Imago mundi*, which in itself combines science, geography, meteorology, and astronomy, frequently appears in encyclopedic compilation manuscripts alongside sermons, devotional works, romances, and other varied texts. See Armstrong and Kay, *Knowing Poetry*, 101–34, on the *Image du monde* and other versified encyclopedias, including several works discussed here.

17. On "the effective storage of verse in the memory and its ready retrieval and redeployment as quotation" as part of "what makes poetry propitious to conveying knowledge and to establishing communities," see Rebecca Dixon, "Knowing Poetry, Knowing Communities," in *Poetry, Knowledge and Community in Late Medieval France*, ed. Rebecca Dixon and Finn E. Sinclair with Adrian Armstrong, Sylvia Huot, and Sarah Kay (Cambridge: D. S. Brewer, 2008), 215–24, at 216, 215. G. H. Russell, "Vernacular Instruction of the Laity in the Later Middle Ages in England," *Journal of Religious History* 2.2 (1962): 98–119, calls verse "the natural medium for this kind of vernacular didactic literature" (102).

18. Paris, BnF fr. 12581, f. 359va. This text is a variant of the one described at http://www .arlima.net/ad/dialogue_du_pere_et_du_fils.html, and I use this title for the whole tradition; see Dean and Boulton, *Anglo-Norman Literature*, items 632–34 for Anglo-French versions.

19. Étienne de Fougères, *Livre des manières*, ed. R. Anthony Lodge (Geneva: Droz, 1979), ll. 385–400.

20. As Frédéric Gros points out, Michel Foucault's work on early Christian monastic communities discusses how "an obligation to tell the truth about oneself was established, structured by the theme of an other . . . and death" (Michel Foucault, *Hermeneutics of the Subject: Lectures at the Collège de France, 1981–1982*, ed. Frédéric Gros, trans. Graham Burchell [New York: Palgrave Macmillan, 2004], 510); see further discussion of Foucault's late work below. Also relevant here is the work of Emmanuel Levinas, whose ideas of the "encounter with another" as foundational to self-consciousness and of dialogue as offering "a chance for . . . love and resemblance in love" could be seen as models for the religious teacher (*Of God Who Comes to Mind*, trans. Bettina Bergo [Stanford, Calif.: Stanford University Press, 1998], 146, 147).

21. Little, *Confession and Resistance*, 5. See also Kumler, *Translating Truth*, 3.

22. As Joseph Goering aptly notes, "During the centuries that followed [the Fourth Lateran Council], this internal forum [of confession] would become the training ground for the

Christian conscience and a school where both clergy and laity would learn the Church's canon law." Goering, "The Internal Forum and the Literature of Penance and Confession," *Traditio* 59 (2004): 175–227, at 178.

23. See Alan E. Bernstein, "The Invocation of Hell in Thirteenth-Century Paris," in *Supplementum Festivum: Studies in Honor of Paul Oskar Kristeller*, ed. James Hankins, John Monfasani, and Frederick Purnell Jr. (Binghamton, N.Y.: Medieval and Renaissance Texts and Studies, 1987), 13–54; Jacques Le Goff, *The Birth of Purgatory*, trans. Arthur Goldhammer (Chicago: University of Chicago Press, 1984); and Virginia Brilliant, "Envisaging the Particular Judgment in Late-Medieval Italy," *Speculum* 84.2 (April 2009): 314–46. As Eileen Gardiner notes, the otherworld journeys so popular in medieval Christian culture generally claim to represent "the religious experience of an individual" (Gardiner, ed., *Visions of Heaven and Hell Before Dante* [New York: Italica Press, 1989], xxii).

24. Jean Delumeau, *Sin and Fear: The Emergence of a Western Guilt Culture, 13th–18th Centuries*, trans. Eric Nicholson (New York: Palgrave Macmillan, 1990).

25. Catherine Brown notes this difference between English "doctrine" and Latin "doctrina" and argues that to study medieval teaching in only its nominal rather than its verbal implication is to shortchange our understanding of medieval didactic texts: *Contrary Things: Exegesis, Dialectic, and the Poetics of Didacticism* (Stanford, Calif.: Stanford University Press, 1998), 9.

26. Guy Lobrichon makes a similar suggestion about the rise of biblical paraphrases in French in the twelfth century, seeing them as one expression of the increased permeability of lay and clerical worlds: "Un Nouveau genre pour un public novice: La paraphrase biblique dans l'espace romane du XIIe siècle," in *The Church and Vernacular Literature in Medieval France*, ed. Dorothea Kullmann (Toronto: Pontifical Institute of Mediaeval Studies, 2009), 87–108. On the development of the idea of the *mediocriter boni* from Augustine's *non valde boni* and *non valde mali*, see Le Goff, *Birth of Purgatory*, 220–25.

27. Eamon Duffy, *The Stripping of the Altars: Traditional Religion in England, c. 1400–c. 1580* (New Haven, Conn.: Yale University Press, 1992), 62.

28. Kumler, *Translating Truth*, demonstrates this for elites, but the point is not limited to those able to afford luxury manuscripts. On requirements for Christian belief, see Norman Tanner and Sethina Watson, "Least of the Laity: The Minimum Requirements for a Medieval Christian," *Journal of Medieval History* 32 (2006): 395–423, and Rider, "Lay Religion and Pastoral Care in Thirteenth Century England," 335.

29. M. T. Clanchy, *From Memory to Written Record: England, 1066–1307* (Oxford: Blackwell, 1993), 238. On Valdes, see Brian Stock, "History, Literature, and Medieval Textuality," *Yale French Studies* 70 (1986): 7–17; on the preachers, see Bernstein, "Invocation of Hell."

30. R. E. Latham, ed., *Revised Medieval Latin Word-List from British and Irish Sources, with Supplement* (London: Oxford University Press for the British Academy, 1980), entry "clericus" (91).

31. Ad Putter, "Knights and Clerics at the Court of Champagne: Chrétien de Troyes's Romances in Context," in *Medieval Knighthood V: Papers from the Sixth Strawberry Hill Conference, 1994*, ed. Stephen Church and Ruth Harvey (Woodbridge, Suffolk: Boydell Press, 1995), 243–66; Jean Dunbabin, "From Clerk to Knight: Changing Orders," in *The Ideals and Practice of Medieval Knighthood II: Papers from the Third Strawberry Hill Conference*, ed. Christopher Harper-Bill and Ruth Harvey (Woodbridge, Suffolk: Boydell Press, 1988), 26–39; Carla Casagrande and Silvana Vecchio, "Clercs et jongleurs dans la société médiévale (XIIe et XIIIe siècles)," *Annales* 34.5 (1979): 913–28; Jeanne-Marie Boivin, "Les Paradoxes des *clerici regis*: L'exemple, à la cour d'Henri II Plantagenêt, de Giraud de Barri," in *Le Clerc au moyen âge*, Senefiance 37 (Aix-en-Provence: Centre Universitaire d'Études et de Recherches Médiévales d'Aix, 1995), 47–61.

32. The trope was not a new one; Giles Constable notes in the sixth to eighth centuries the increasing tendency to present saints as having "modest or middling origins": *Three Studies in Medieval Religious and Social Thought: The Interpretation of Mary and Martha, The Ideal of the Imitation of Christ, The Orders of Society* (Cambridge: Cambridge University Press, 1995), 347.

33. Alastair Minnis, *Fallible Authors: Chaucer's Pardoner and Wife of Bath* (Philadelphia: University of Pennsylvania Press, 2008), 420n5. See also Gary Macy, "The 'Invention' of Clergy and Laity in the Twelfth Century," in *A Sacramental Life: A Festschrift Honoring Bernard Cooke*, ed. Michael Horace Barnes and William P. Roberts (Milwaukee, Wis.: Marquette University Press, 2003), 117–35, esp. 132–33. Fiona Somerset explores these terms in considering the concept of "lewed clergie" (*Clerical Discourse*, 13); see also her remarks on the miraculous infusion of *clergie* (16).

34. On "common culture," see Richard Kieckhefer, "The Specific Rationality of Medieval Magic," *American Historical Review* 99 (1994): 813–36, at 833. Neil Cartlidge makes a similar point in a different context: "The Composition and Social Context of Oxford, Jesus College, MS 29 (II) and London, British Library, MS Cotton Caligula A.IX," *Medium Aevum* 66 (1997): 250–69, at 262.

35. The quoted phrase comes from John Frankis, "The Social Context of Vernacular Writing in Thirteenth Century England: The Evidence of the Manuscripts," in *Rethinking the South English Legendaries*, ed. Heather Blurton and Jocelyn Wogan-Browne (Manchester: Manchester University Press, 2011), 66–83, at 76. See also Alan Bernstein's point about the internal complexity of, and overlap between, "clergy" and "laity" ("Invocation of Hell," 13–14 and note 39).

36. Alexandra Barratt discusses the varied manuscript contexts and audiences of many of the Anglo-French works considered here in "Spiritual Writings and Religious Instruction," in *The Cambridge History of the Book in Britain, Vol. 2: 1100–1400*, ed. Nigel Morgan and Rodney M. Thomson (Cambridge: Cambridge University Press, 2008), 340–66; see also the astute remarks about not prejudging audience in Jocelyn Wogan-Browne, "How to Marry Your Wife with Chastity, Honour, and *Fin' Amor* in Thirteenth-Century England," in *Thirteenth Century England IX: Proceedings of the Durham Conference 2001*, ed. Michael Prestwich, Richard Britnell, and Robin Frame (Woodbridge, Suffolk: Boydell Press, 2003), 131–50.

37. The quotation is from Clanchy, *From Memory to Written Record*, 241; see also Parkes, "The Literacy of the Laity," 559–60, and C. S. Watkins, "Sin, Penance and Purgatory in the Anglo-Norman Realm: The Evidence of Visions and Ghost Stories," *Past and Present* 175.1 (2002): 3–33, at 6–7. Jean Dunbabin, while questioning whether peasant priests were numerous, acknowledges that England seems to have offered more opportunities than other areas for even very poor parish clergy to attend university: "Jacques Le Goff and the Intellectuals," in *The Work of Jacques Le Goff and the Challenges of Medieval History*, ed. Miri Rubin (Woodbridge, Suffolk: Boydell Press, 1997), 157–67, at 163.

38. On the "axiomatic" nature of the association of *laicus* and *illiteratus*, and the "discrepancy between theory and practice," see Clanchy, *From Memory to Written Record*, 226–30; for instances of churchmen fiercely upholding what Clanchy calls "fantasies" (226), see Ruedi Imbach, *Laien in der Philosophie des Mittelalters: Hinweise und Anregungen zu einem vernachlässigten Thema* (Amsterdam: B. R. Grüner, 1989), 21–26. Nicholas Orme notes the spreading of literacy "from a few of the lay aristocracy to most of the order between about the middle of the twelfth century and the middle of the thirteenth": *From Childhood to Chivalry: The Education of the English Kings and Aristocracy, 1066–1530* (London: Methuen, 1984), 143–44; see also Elisabeth Schulze-Busacker, "Littérature didactique à l'usage des laïcs aux XIIe et XIIIe siècles," in *Le Petit peuple dans l'Occident médiéval: Terminologies, perceptions, réalités*, ed. Pierre Boglioni, Robert

Delort, and Claude Gauvard (Paris: Publications de la Sorbonne, 2002), 633–45, on the broadening of audience in Continental and insular French alike.

39. See Kathryn Gravdal, *Vilain and Courtois: Transgressive Parody in French Literature of the Twelfth and Thirteenth Centuries* (Lincoln: University of Nebraska Press, 1989), 12–19.

40. Paul Freedman, *Images of the Medieval Peasant* (Stanford, Calif.: Stanford University Press, 1999), 204–35, demonstrates the prevalence of negative views of the peasantry but also acknowledges the countervailing positive characterizations. For an example of "rustical[is] stultiti[a]" as preferable, in monks, to "curiali[s] faceti[a]," see Jaeger, *Envy of Angels*, 211 (and accompanying note, 445).

41. Jocelyn Wogan-Browne, "'Cest livre liseez . . . chescun jour': Women and Reading c. 1230–c. 1430," in *Language and Culture in Medieval Britain*, ed. Wogan-Brown et al., 239–53, at 243, 244. See also the discussion of this image in Kumler, *Translating Truth*, 76–80.

42. Stock, *Implications of Literacy*, 27. He remarks further that *idiota*, in particular, "harboured within its range of meaning the idea of blessed simplicity which was clearly exposed in two biblical texts," Acts 4:13 and 1 Corinthians 14:16 (29). The idea that the early spread of Christianity was due particularly to the "lower orders" was recognized in the Middle Ages; for one example, see Constable, *Three Studies*, 355.

43. Freedman, *Images of the Medieval Peasant*, 219.

44. In Honorius Augustodunensis's *Speculum ecclesiae*, PL 172:807–1108, in fact, the category of *agricolae* is represented by a married couple; see the discussion in Chapter 2.

45. Jocelyn Wogan-Browne, "Women's Formal and Informal Traditions of Biblical Knowledge in Anglo-Norman England," in *Saints, Scholars, and Politicians: Gender as a Tool in Medieval Studies*, ed. Mathilde van Dijk and Renée Nip, Medieval Church Studies 15 (Turnhout: Brepols, 2005), 85–109, at 100.

46. Somerset, *Clerical Discourse*, 14. See also Cavadini, "Simplifying Augustine," who points out that the *Sermones ad populum* do not avoid difficult topics but that Augustine instead "styles his sermons as acts of inquiry, as instances of seeking understanding of Scripture" in a way that makes the "school" of Scripture accessible to a wide audience (72–73).

47. Kumler, *Translating Truth*, makes a powerful case for the "transformative" effect of "the visual translation of religious truth" in deluxe manuscripts of many of the works considered here (240); I suggest that the texts' language performs a similar function.

48. On the overlap between "confessional literature—handbooks for priests and doctrinal and moral guides for laity" like those considered here and "pedagogical texts and classroom practices" still primarily aimed at clerical training, see Woods and Copeland, "Classroom and Confession"; the quoted phrases appear on pp. 377 and 376. On education for aristocratic women, see 378–79.

49. I do not mean to suggest that texts like Marian miracles, otherworld journeys, or even fabliaux necessarily had lay authors or exclusively lay audiences—this is clearly not the case—though some of these were (as most famously in the case of Rutebeuf) composed by *clercs-jongleurs*, a group lying on the border between cleric and non-cleric. My point here is simply that works of this kind generally imagine at least a mixed lay-clerical audience, if not primarily a lay one, and that they can thus be seen as participating in the reception of such ideas, their reworkings for a non-clerical audience. See Evelyn Birge Vitz, *Orality and Performance in Early French Romance* (Cambridge: D. S. Brewer, 1999), on the collaboration of clerics and jongleurs in the production of vernacular literature.

50. Foucault, *Hermeneutics of the Subject*, 332. Although Foucault himself draws a sharp line between "philosophical" and "Christian" *askesis*, many of the authors and concepts impor-

tant to his characterization of the former—particularly Seneca and Cicero, as well as the maxim "Gnosce te ipsum"—are influential in twelfth-century Christian thought, especially among those strongly interested in teaching. See Franklin T. Harkins, *Reading and the Work of Restoration: History and Scripture in the Work of Hugh of St. Victor* (Toronto: Pontifical Institute of Mediaeval Studies, 2009), 120–25, and Jaeger, *Envy of Angels*, where the importance of Cicero, in particular, is emphasized throughout.

51. Boyle, "Manuals of Popular Theology," 35.

52. Foucault, *Hermeneutics of the Subject*, 332. On teaching as building, see Claire M. Waters, "The Labor of *Aedificatio* and the Business of Preaching," *Viator* 38 (2007): 167–89.

53. Foucault, *Hermeneutics of the Subject*, 322, 323, 325. We are very close here, though Foucault does not use the term, to the *habitus* studied by Breen, *Imagining*, and, of course, by Pierre Bourdieu. The internalized, incorporated knowledge of which Foucault speaks is also characteristic of monastic *meditatio*, which involved learning "with one's whole being"—body, memory, intelligence, and will; Jean Leclercq, *The Love of Learning and the Desire for God: A Study of Monastic Culture*, trans. Catharine Misrahi (New York: Fordham University Press, 1982), 17.

54. There is an important difference here from the *Manuel*'s Middle English offspring, *Handlyng Synne*, where it is sin itself that is handled, rather than the book.

55. C. A. Robson, *Maurice of Sully and the Medieval Vernacular Homily* (Oxford: Basil Blackwell, 1952), 178, ll. 51–62. Compare the similar image from a penitential text edited by Tony Hunt, which urges the penitent to confess if "la professiun ke vus uverastes sollempnement en l'abit de religiun u de virginité u de viduité n'avez mie sous les meins gardé" (you have not kept hold of [lit. "kept under your hands"] the profession you made solemnly in the habit of religion or virginity or widowhood). Tony Hunt, ed., *"Cher alme": Texts of Anglo-Norman Piety*, trans. Jane Bliss (Tempe: Arizona Center for Medieval and Renaissance Studies, 2010), 306.

56. Pierre d'Abernon, *Lumere*, 2:20, ll. 7721–24. Hesketh notes that Pierre's uses of this expression are the only ones that appear in the *Anglo-Norman Dictionary* and proposes the reading used here or the alternative "God . . . will not be there when he reaches for Him" (3:127).

57. See Katherine Zieman, *Singing the New Song: Literacy and Liturgy in Late Medieval England* (Philadelphia: University of Pennsylvania Press, 2008), 36–37, 42–43. The Psalms were, of course, a foundational element of Christian education in the Middle Ages; see Lobrichon, "Nouveau genre," on their consistent presence in aristocratic education in France from at least the ninth century (92).

58. The work of Hugh of St. Victor is an important twelfth-century background for this approach; as Franklin T. Harkins puts it, in Hugh's theology, "The fallen and dis-ordered human being begins to be re-ordered and restored to the image of God by engaging in a detailed program of ordered reading" (*Reading and the Work of Restoration*, 10). See also the discussion in Duncan Robertson, *Lectio Divina: The Medieval Experience of Reading* (Collegeville, Minn.: Liturgical Press, 2011), 212–24.

59. Michel de Certeau, *The Practice of Everyday Life*, trans. Steven Rendall (Berkeley: University of California Press, 1984), 166. See also Nicholas Watson's remarks on empathy and learning in "Desire for the Past," *Studies in the Age of Chaucer* 21 (1999): 59–97.

60. De Certeau, *Practice of Everyday Life*, 176.

61. The quoted phrase belongs to Michel Zink, whose approach to these works I share, attempting "à accepter lucidement d'être vraiment dupe," the condition, as he suggests, of reading any literature. Michel Zink, *Poésie et conversion au moyen âge* (Paris: Presses Universitaires de France, 2003), 5, 4.

CHAPTER I

1. Hans Robert Jauss, *Question and Answer: Forms of Dialogic Understanding*, ed. and trans. Michael Hays (Minneapolis: University of Minnesota Press, 1989), 51–94, especially 74–78. The inherent unruliness of dialogue is explored in Nancy Mason Bradbury, "Rival Wisdom in the Latin *Dialogue of Solomon and Marcolf*," *Speculum* 83.2 (2008): 331–65, and Peter Dronke, "Peter of Blois and Poetry at the Court of Henry II," *Mediaeval Studies* 28 (1976): 185–235, particularly the last section on dialogue, debate, and *sic et non*.

2. Sarah Kay, *The Place of Thought: The Complexity of One in Late Medieval Didactic Poetry* (Philadelphia: University of Pennsylvania Press, 2007), xi. See also Christopher Baswell, "Talking Back to the Text: Marginal Voices in Medieval Secular Literature," in *The Uses of Manuscripts in Literary Studies: Essays in Memory of Judson Boyce Allen*, ed. Charlotte Cook Morse, Penelope Reed Doob, and Marjorie Curry Woods (Kalamazoo: Western Michigan University, Medieval Institute Publications, 1992), 121–55, at 124–26, on the instability of dialogue as an authoritative form.

3. Seth Lerer, *Boethius and Dialogue: Literary Method in "The Consolation of Philosophy"* (Princeton, N.J.: Princeton University Press, 1985), 32; on the "progressively inward" movement of "educated pursuits" in the sixth century, see p. 19.

4. Mary Carruthers, *The Craft of Thought: Meditation, Rhetoric, and the Making of Images, 400–1200* (Cambridge: Cambridge University Press, 2000), 199.

5. Thanks to the digitization initiative at the Bibliothèque nationale de France, the images can now be seen at http://gallica.bnf.fr/ark:/12148/btv1b53000323h/f703.image.r=12581.langFR and http://gallica.bnf.fr/ark:/12148/btv1b53000323h/f831.image.r=12581.langFR.

6. For an instance of the master-disciple image in a copy of the *Lumere as lais*, see Kumler, *Translating Truth*, 100 (fig. 26); here the image appears in the course of the text rather than at its head. She also discusses the images that accompany *Le Dialogue du père et du fils* and *Mirour de seinte eglyse* in Paris, BnF fr. 13342; particularly striking in this instance, as Kumler notes, is the fact that despite the different forms of the two texts the images are, again, very similar (153–56, figs. 53 and 54).

7. This is the first and, according to Yves Lefèvre, the "most important" of the several French translations of the *Elucidarium*; Lefèvre, *L'Elucidarium et les Lucidaires*, 272.

8. For this scribe, not only the translation of Honorius's text and the *Dialogue du père et du fils* but also a third text on the Holy Land are all connected; not until the conclusion of the "terre de promission" text does he write, "Explicit Lucidarius" (f. 368ᵛ).

9. BnF fr. 12581, f. 344ʳ. A somewhat different version of the text, with translation, can be found in Hunt, *"Cher alme,"* 24–69, with the title *Dialogue of Father and Son* (Dean and Boulton, *Anglo-Norman Literature*, item 633). I discuss this version further below.

10. Ernstpeter Ruhe, "Pour fair la lumière as lais?: Mittelalterliche Handbücher des Glaubenswissens und ihr Publikum," in *Wissensorganisierende und wissensvermittelnde Literatur im Mittelalter: Perspektiven ihrer Erforschung*, ed. Norbert Richard Wolf (Wiesbaden: Ludwig Reichert Verlag, 1987), 46–56, at 52. On the emergence of dialogue as a "ruminative practice of questions and answers" that teaches "a deeper understanding of faith," and its move out of a monastic setting, see Alex J. Novikoff, *The Medieval Culture of Disputation: Pedagogy, Practice, and Performance* (Philadelphia: University of Pennsylvania Press, 2013), especially 34–105; the quoted phrases come from p. 225.

11. Kumler, *Translating Truth*, 46.

12. The quotation comes from Rice, *Lay Piety and Religious Discipline*, 51.

13. Important exceptions to this neglect include, in addition to Kumler, *Translating Truth*, and Hunt, *"Cher alme,"* recent work by Jocelyn Wogan-Browne and Nicholas Watson as well as Matthew Sullivan's investigations of the *Manuel des pechiez*. Also valuable is the work of a group of German scholars on the *Elucidarium* and its vernacular offspring: Monika Türk, *"Lucidaire de grant sapientie": Untersuchung und Edition der altfranzösischen Übersetzung 1 des "Elucidarium" von Honorius Augustodunensis* (Tübingen: Max Niemeyer Verlag, 2000); Ernstpeter Ruhe, ed., *Elucidarium und Lucidaires: Zur Rezeption des Werks von Honorius Augustodunensis in der Romania und in England* (Wiesbaden: Ludwig Reichert Verlag, 1993); and Ruhe, "Pour faire la lumière as lais?" From an earlier generation, the work of Lefèvre, *L'Elucidarium et les Lucidaires*, and Arnould, *Le "Manuel des péchés,"* remains foundational, as do the many manuscript investigations of the indefatigable Paul Meyer.

14. Prologues are added, for example, to the *Petit sermon* (London, British Library, Cotton MS Domitian A.xi., f. 89ra; see the discussion below) and *Mirour de seinte eglyse* (London, British Library, Royal MS 20.B.XIV, f. 53^r); in Oxford, Bodleian Library, MS Bodley 399, exempla from the *Manuel des pechiez* are imported to the *Lumere as lais*, while in Pembroke College, Cambridge, MS 258, four exempla from the *Manuel* follow passages excerpted from the *Mirour de seinte eglyse*; and the *Manuel* itself acquires a book devoted to Mary that postdates its original composition (Matthew Sullivan, "A Brief Textual History of the *Manuel des Péchés*," *Neuphilologische Mitteilungen* 93 [1992]: 337–46).

15. For examples, see the discussion in *Mirour de seinte eglyse (St. Edmund of Abingdon's "Speculum Ecclesiae")*, ed. A. D. Wilshere (London: ANTS, 1982), xx, or Tony Hunt's account of the alterations made to a French text on the Pater Noster to update its addressee to a new audience in *"Cher alme,"* 75–77.

16. Numbers of surviving manuscripts are taken from the invaluable handbook by Ruth J. Dean with the assistance of Maureen Boulton, *Anglo-Norman Literature*. Here I count all manuscript appearances, including fragments and extracts, but not manuscripts now lost. The works listed here are items 635, 629, 618, 243, 602, 628, 601, 559, and 636 in Dean and Boulton.

17. Oxford, Bodleian Library, MS Laud miscellaneous 471, f. 94^v. On the development and role of prologues, including this one, see Geneviève Hasenohr, "Les Prologues des textes de dévotion en langue française (XIIIe–XVe siècles): Formes et fonctions," in *Les Prologues médiévaux*, ed. Jacqueline Hamesse (Turnhout: Brepols, 2000), 593–638; she remarks on the "conditions de production—à demande individuelle, réponse individuelle" (618) that make these works so diverse.

18. Pierre d'Abernon, *Lumere*, 1:19, ll. 688–92.

19. See here Jean-Claude Schmitt, "Au XIIIe siècle, une parole nouvelle," in *Histoire vécue du peuple chrétien*, ed. Jean Delumeau, 2 vols. (Toulouse: Privat, 1979), 1:257–79.

20. Lefèvre, *L'Elucidarium et les Lucidaires*, 333. Valerie Flint also comments on the text's theological "crudity" and its very wide distribution: "The 'Elucidarius' of Honorius Augustodunensis and the Reform in Late Eleventh-Century England," *Revue bénédictine* 85 (1975): 178–89, at 178–79; see also Türk, *"Lucidaire de grant sapientie,"* and Ruhe, *Elucidarium und Lucidaires*, as well as the research project directed by Sarah James and Huw Grange, "Spreading the Light: Mapping the Vernacular *Elucidarium* in Medieval England" (project website http://www.kent.ac.uk/mems/research/Elucidarium-1.html).

21. "Hic fac finem si velis. Si autem tempus permittit, adde haec": Honorius Augustodunensis, *Speculum ecclesiae*, PL 172:807A–1108A, at col. 819A; on the audience's potential cold and tiredness, see col. 817B.

22. "Ad omnes sermones debes primum versum Latina lingua p[r]onunciare, dein patria lingua explanare" (*Speculum ecclesiae*, PL 172:829B).

23. The phrase "inferior ac seculari vicinior" comes from *Quod monachis liceat predicare*; I take the quotation from Valerie I. J. Flint, "The Chronology of the Works of Honorius Augustodunensis," in *Ideas in the Medieval West: Texts and Their Contexts* (London: Variorum Reprints, 1988), item VII, 238 (reprinted from *Revue bénédictine* 82 [1972]: 215–42). On the "rhetoric of reform" in the eleventh century, which had lasting influence, see Kathleen G. Cushing, *Reform and the Papacy in the Eleventh Century: Spirituality and Social Change* (Manchester: Manchester University Press, 2005), 111–38.

24. Flint, "Chronology of the Works of Honorius," 227, 232.

25. *Speculum ecclesiae*, PL 172:815.

26. *Speculum ecclesiae*, PL 172:827.

27. *Speculum ecclesiae*, PL 172:861.

28. The nineteenth-century editor of the *Romans de carité* consulted twenty-five complete manuscripts of the poem: *"Li Romans de Carité" et "Miserere" du Renclus de Moiliens, poèmes de la fin du XIIe siècle*, ed. A.-G. van Hamel (Paris: F. Vieweg, 1885; repr., Geneva: Slatkine, 1974), 1:xxxvi. The Archives de littérature du moyen âge lists thirty-two manuscripts (including fragments): http://www.arlima.net/qt/reclus_de_molliens.html. There is no more recent edition.

29. *Romans de Carité*, ed. van Hamel, strophe 60, ll. 1–4 (1:33).

30. Quotation from strophe 69, ll. 11–12 (1:37); see also strophes 70–71 (1:38).

31. See Cushing, *Reform and the Papacy*, especially chapters 5–7; also R. N. Swanson, "Angels Incarnate: Clergy and Masculinity from Gregorian Reform to Reformation," in *Masculinity in Medieval Europe*, ed. D. M. Hadley (London: Longman, 1999), 160–77.

32. Thomas was a student of Peter the Chanter at Paris and imbibed the pastoral spirit of the Chanter's circle; see the discussions in Morenzoni, *Des Écoles aux paroisses*, especially 13–24, 67–95, and John W. Baldwin, *Masters, Preachers, and Merchants: The Social Views of Peter the Chanter and His Circle* (Princeton, N.J.: Princeton University Press, 1970), esp. 1:34–36, 107–16.

33. The distinction between clergy and laity is strongly emphasized, for example, in the *Manuel des pechiez*, which asserts that "religius" (later equated with "clers") are "plus pres de Dee" and that "Les clers qe sunt bien lettré / Sevent quant cheent en peché, / Pur ceo, de euz tesrai de gree, / Qe vers moi ne seient coroucé. / Mes, tant lur di certeinement, / Plus blamés serrunt qe autre gent, / Si il pechent au[si] sovent / Cum fet celi qe rien n'entent": *MP* Roxburghe, 5, ll. 96, 99, 101–8; *MP* EETS, 5, ll. 96, 99, 101–8. As we will see below, however, other vernacular works of the late thirteenth century trouble this strict division.

34. Emphasis added. "Debet enim predicator esse quasi liber et speculum subditorum ut in operibus prelati quasi in libro legant, et in speculo videant quid sibi faciendum est . . . fratres imitatores mei estote sicut et ego Christi": Thomas of Chobham, *Summa de arte praedicandi*, ed. Franco Morenzoni, Corpus Christianorum Series Latina 82 (Turnhout: Brepols, 1988), 24, quoting 1 Cor. 2:1.

35. This is, of course, reminiscent of the influential notion of "textual communities" proposed by Stock, *Implications of Literacy*, but allows for a more individualized conception of such reading.

36. In offering his patron direct access to Scripture (allowing for the demands of verse translation), Robert is part of a larger trend, visible in Maurice de Sully's French sermons but also in the wave of Bible translations into French in this period. See particularly Hoogvliet, "Encouraging Lay People to Read the Bible in the French Vernaculars," which argues that such translation was by no means limited to the aristocracy.

37. Aline was the wife of Alan de la Zouche, the probable patron of the *Corset*, a theological work also written by a chaplain called Robert—likely this same author. The evidence is

persuasively set out in K. V. Sinclair, "The Anglo-Norman Patrons of Robert the Chaplain and Robert of Greatham," *Forum for Modern Language Studies* 6 (1996): 193–208; see also the discussion of the *Corset* in Wogan-Browne, "How to Marry Your Wife."

38. Robert of Gretham, *Miroir*, ll. 469–72. Further citations from this edition are given in the text. Mary Carruthers notes a similar moment in Richard of Fournival's roughly contemporary *Bestiaires d'amours*; see *The Book of Memory: A Study of Memory in Medieval Culture* (Cambridge: Cambridge University Press, 1990), 223–24.

39. The quoted phrase is Aden Kumler's, from her discussion of a manuscript containing the *Chasteau d'amour* (Princeton University Library, Taylor MS 1), where there is an image of the work's author, Robert Grosseteste—already deceased at the time of its copying—holding the end of a scroll that is also held by Baroness Joan Tateshall, the manuscript's patron. As Kumler notes, "The image represents a moment of pastoral dialogue, a dialogue that would have been enacted by Joan and her book as she mouthed Grosseteste's words and gazed at his image. In this way the initial's representational fiction makes possible an imagined pastoral encounter and Grosseteste's ministry is granted new life and efficacy" (*Translating Truth*, 45). On this manuscript, see also Adelaide Bennett, "A Book Designed for a Noblewoman: An Illustrated *Manuel des Péchés* of the Thirteenth Century," in *Medieval Book Production: Assessing the Evidence*, ed. Linda L. Brownrigg (Los Altos, Calif.: Anderson-Lovelace, 1990), 163–81, at 173.

40. Herbert Grabes, *The Mutable Glass: Mirror-Imagery in Titles and Texts of the Middle Ages and English Renaissance*, trans. Gordon Collier (Cambridge: Cambridge University Press, 1982), points out that *Speculum* is one of the earliest, and by far the most widespread, "metaphorical" book titles (19), and he notes that whenever it threatened to become a dead letter "writers would endeavour to re-establish or intensify the figurative power of the metaphor by taking it up again in the prefatory material or in the text itself" (21). Robert's text, however, seems to bear the distinction of being the earliest original composition with the title *Miroir* (see Grabes, *The Mutable Glass*, 248); the translation of Edmund of Abingdon's *Speculum religiosorum* as the *Mirour de seinte eglyse* is probably somewhat earlier. Grabes compares Robert's extensive explication with that provided in the twelfth-century *Speculum virginum*, which also addresses an audience (of nuns) possibly less familiar with the metaphor (49).

41. *Étude sur "Le Miroir ou les Évangiles des domnées" de Robert de Gretham, suivie d'extraits inédits*, ed. Marion Y. H. Aitken (Paris: Honoré Champion, 1922) 116, ll. 11536–41. Portions of the *Miroir* not yet edited by Duncan and Connolly are cited from this text.

42. *Étude sur "Le Miroir,"* ed. Aitken, 123–24, ll. 15651–56.

43. Jocelyn Wogan-Browne, "Time to Read: Pastoral Care, Vernacular Access and the Case of Angier of St. Frideswide," in *Texts and Traditions of Medieval Pastoral Care: Essays in Honour of Bella Millett*, ed. Cate Gunn and Catherine Innes-Parker (Woodbridge, Suffolk: York Medieval Press, 2009), 62–77, at 68. On the canons' teaching mission, see Caroline Walker Bynum, *"Docere verbo et exemplo": An Aspect of Twelfth-Century Spirituality* (Missoula, Mont.: Scholars Press, 1979); on literary influence, see Jean-Pascal Pouzet, "Augustinian Canons and Their Insular French Books in Medieval England: Towards an Assessment," in *Language and Culture in Medieval Britain*, ed. Wogan-Browne et al., 266–77.

44. Morgan Powell, "Translating Scripture for *Ma dame de Champagne*: The Old French 'Paraphrase' of Psalm 44 (*Eructavit*)," in *The Vernacular Spirit: Essays on Medieval Religious Literature*, ed. Renate Blumenfeld-Kosinski, Duncan Robertson, and Nancy Bradley Warren (New York: Palgrave, 2002), 83–103, at 83; *Eructavit: An Old French Metrical Paraphrase of Psalm XLIV*, ed. T. Atkinson Jenkins (Dresden: Gedruckt für Gesellschaft für romanische Literatur, 1909), xx, n. 1.

45. The complaint is a familiar one; Pierre d'Abernon similarly chastises those "seculers" who "le siecle eiment e unt en us / Ne pount en lur quer truver / Delit de oir ne de saver / Quant de Deu tuche la matire / Par parler ou chanter ou par lire, / Mes si la matire est de folie, / La mettent entent e[n] l'oie" (Pierre d'Abernon, *Lumere*, 1:14, ll. 493–500).

46. I have slightly modified the punctuation of the Old French. On the role of intention in accounting for a work's authorship, see Zink, *Poésie et conversion au moyen âge*, 155–59, 226n2.

47. On the "interweaving" of social and Latinate authority in works for aristocratic patrons, see Wogan-Browne, "'Cest livre liseez . . . chescun jour,'" 250. M. Dominica Legge long ago pointed out that "patronage cut across natural [*sic*] barriers and confused categories": *Anglo-Norman in the Cloisters: The Influence of the Orders upon Anglo-Norman Literature* (Edinburgh: Edinburgh University Press, 1950), 119.

48. John W. Coakley has worked extensively on such collaborations; see, for example, his book *Women, Men, and Spiritual Power: Female Saints and Their Male Collaborators* (New York: Columbia University Press, 2006). The chapter on Jacques de Vitry and Marie d'Oignies is particularly relevant both in time and for its engagement with lay spirituality. The mutual necessity of student and teacher echoes and in a sense extends Emmanuel Levinas's sense of the subject as called into being by the Other; Ann Chinnery, "Encountering the Philosopher as Teacher: The Pedagogical Postures of Emmanuel Levinas," *Teaching and Teacher Education* 26 (2010): 1704–9, makes it clear how resonant Levinas's pedagogy and philosophy are with the approaches of the medieval teachers addressed here.

49. Phyllis B. Roberts, "Master Stephen Langton Preaches to the People and Clergy: Sermon Texts from Twelfth-Century Paris," *Traditio* 36 (1980): 237–68, at 242, 243.

50. Nicholas Watson, "Conceptions of the Word: The Mother Tongue and the Incarnation of God," *New Medieval Literatures* 1 (1997): 85–124; on current theological debates concerning kenosis and Augustine's influence on the concept, see Stephen Pardue, "Kenosis and Its Discontents: Towards an Augustinian Account of Divine Humility," *Scottish Journal of Theology* 65.3 (August 2012): 271–88. For an example (from a medieval German context) of how self-emptying can lead to reversal in teaching, see Sara S. Poor, "Women Teaching Men in the Medieval Devotional Imagination," in *Women, Men, and Religious Life in Germany, 1100–1500*, ed. Fiona J. Griffiths and Julie Hotchin (Turnhout: Brepols, 2014), 339–65, especially 343–48.

51. See Margaret F. Nims, "*Translatio*: 'Difficult Statement' in Medieval Poetic Theory," *University of Toronto Quarterly* 43 (1974): 215–30; the quoted phrase is Carolyn Dinshaw's in response to Nims's work: *Chaucer's Sexual Poetics* (Madison: University of Wisconsin Press, 1989), 140.

52. The quoted phrase is from Pierre d'Abernon, *Lumere*, discussed further below (1:143, ll. 4679, 4686).

53. The author of the *Roman des romans* makes a similar comparison, saying of himself, "Jeo nel comense [the *Roman*] par nule presumpcie, / Ne par fiance de ma bone clergie, / Car petit [sai] & sui de fole vie / E li men sen ne suffit mie; / Mes jeo sai ben, ne pus unkes doter, / Ki cil ki fet les langes muer / E fist l'asnesce a Balaam parler / Poet fole langage a ben dire turner" (London, British Library, Royal MS 20.B.XIV, f. 96).

54. Chinnery, "Encountering the Philosopher as Teacher," 1707; as she notes just above, "For a *maître à penser* in this sense, there is always something more to be learned from a text, something to be taken from the questions and challenges posed by students"—a concept formally enshrined in dialogue texts, where such questions give rise to the master's discourse.

55. Hunt, *"Cher alme,"* 48.

56. On the infantilizing of the laity in some medieval discourses, see Rita Copeland,

Pedagogy, Intellectuals, and Dissent in the Later Middle Ages: Lollardy and Ideas of Learning (Cambridge: Cambridge University Press, 2004), 23–24.

57. The Middle English translation spells this out more clearly: "Þe litel ben þe lewed folk . . . Hii ben litel, bot nouȝt in God, ac in lowe obedience to her suverainnes ac for to have heiȝe mede in þe blis of hevene" (Robert of Gretham, *Miroir*, ll. 6–9).

58. *Étude sur "Le Miroir,"* ed. Aitken, 118, ll. 11632–35. The passage in the *Pastoralet* similarly puts humility in the context of Christian history: "Nostre Sires trova humilité pur nostre redempcion. Li enemis qi fust fait avant qe toutes choises furent faites, voist qe l'en le veïst eslevé sour toutes choses. Nostre Sire se deigna faire petit en toutes choses" (Gregory the Great, *Le Pastoralet: Traduction médiévale française de la "Regula pastoralis,"* ed. Martine Pagan [Paris: Champion, 2007], 324, 326).

59. Duncan Robertson, "The Experience of Reading: Bernard of Clairvaux, *Sermons on the Song of Songs*, I," *Religion and Literature* 19.1 (Spring 1987): 1–20, at 4.

60. As Powell says with regard to the *Eructavit*, "The staging of the poem as personal instruction to Marie [de Champagne] from her spiritual advisor did not exclude other audiences from avid interest in the text" ("Translating Scripture," 96); he also notes the prevalence of female patron figures in "early vernacular [French] adaptations of scripture" (97). Robert's text survives in six substantial (though not always complete) versions and a further four fragments or excerpts (Dean and Boulton, *Anglo-Norman Literature*, item 589); the *Miserere* survives, in whole or in part, in some thirty manuscripts, usually accompanying the *Romans de carité* (see *Romans de Carité*, ed. van Hamel, vii–xxxvi).

61. Addressing Aline, Robert writes, "vus ai fait cest escrit / U vus purrez lire a delit. . . . Quant de lire vus prendra cure / Traez avant cest escripture" (I have made you this book where you can read at your pleasure. . . . When you wish to read, take out this book, ll. 63–64, 69–70).

62. Thomas of Chobham, *Summa de arte praedicandi*, 75.

63. Pierre uses this name in the *Secré de secrez:* "Mes ore priez, pur Deu amur, / En ceste fin pur le translatur / De cest livre, ke Piere ad nun / K'estreit est de ces de Abernun" (quoted in Pierre d'Abernon, *Lumere*, 3:2). Hesketh says that Pierre here "claims affinity with" the d'Abernon family, but the sense of this passage would seem rather to be that he claims descent from them. Alexandra Barratt discusses the likely readership of the *Lumere* in "Spiritual Writings and Religious Instruction," 352. The verse translation of the *Evangelium Nicodemi* by the Norman poet André de Coutances, discussed in Chapter 3, similarly dedicates itself to "ma dame & ma cosine," "la dame de Tribehou," again pointing to the varied roles that teacher and student might occupy for one another (Gaston Paris and Alphonse Bos, eds., *Trois versions rimées de l'Évangile de Nicodème, par Chrétien, André de Coutances et un anonyme* [Paris: Didot, 1885], 76, ll. 115, 109).

64. "Et ut labor meus non solum presenti proficiat aetati, disputata curavi stylo transmittere posteritati" (Honorius Augustodunensis, *Elucidarium sive Dialogus de summa totius Christianae theologiae*, PL 172:1109). On Honorius and dialogue, see Novikoff, *Medieval Culture of Disputation*, 56–60.

65. See particularly Wogan-Browne, "Time to Read."

66. Brown, *Contrary Things*, 10.

67. For these rubrics, see http://www.arlima.net/ad/dialogue_du_pere_et_du_fils.html. The quotation is from Paris, BnF, nouvelle acquisition française 4338, f. 42^v (second quarter of the fourteenth century). The same rubric appears in two later fourteenth-century manuscripts, Avignon, Bibliothèque municipale, MS 344, f. 1^r, and Paris, BnF fr. 1136, f. 33^r, and apparently the need continued, since a fifteenth-century translation of the *Elucidarium* into French (Lefèvre's Translation IV) similarly adds a prologue explaining the format: "Cest livre fist un

maistre par la priere de ses disciples. Sy est appellé cest livre Elucidaires, car maintes obscures choses y reluisent. Et parlent en cest livre .ii. personnes, c'est assavoir le maistre et le disciple. Le disciple demande et le maistre enseigne. Et la où il y a .D. senefie que ly disciples demande, et la où il y a .M. senefie que ly maistres respont" (London, British Library, Royal MS 19.C.XI, f. 114).

68. This comfort in combining instruction and pleasure is of course not novel in medieval literature; see Glending Olson, *Literature as Recreation in the Later Middle Ages* (Ithaca, N.Y.: Cornell University Press, 1982), especially 19–38, though Olson notes that he has "tended to avoid discussing instances where pleasure appears as part of a work meant primarily for instruction" (11), as is clearly the case here.

69. Stephen Justice, "Did the Middle Ages Believe in Their Miracles?" *Representations* 103.1 (Summer 2008): 1–29, at 13.

70. The quoted phrase derives from Aquinas's definition of thought: "Thought gives rise to a certain investigation: we say 'to think' [*cogitare*] as though 'to knock together' [*coagitare*], that is to discuss [*discutere*], and to bring together one thing with another" (my translation; text cited in Justice, "Did the Middle Ages Believe in Their Miracles," 26n50).

71. "Salomon . . . quasi tumultuantis turbae suscepit sensum . . . quasi tot in se personas diversorum suscipit . . . eosque ad unam sententiam revocat"; Gregory to Peter: "In hac re amplius venerari debes, in qua morem egregii praedicatoris imitaris" (*Dialogorum Libri IV*, PL 77:324, 235). The English translations are from Gregory the Great, *Dialogues*, trans. Odo John Zimmerman, Fathers of the Church 39 (New York: Fathers of the Church, 1959), 193, 196.

72. See here Christopher Baswell's apt comments on "that point where Latin moves into the vernacular, a move which allows for an even greater variance and absorption of marginal voices" in a text: "Talking Back to the Text," 144.

73. Hesketh notes that the general/special or genus/species distinction derives from scholastic habits of "classification and subdivision" visible throughout the text (Pierre d'Abernon, *Lumere*, 3:69).

74. Kumler, *Translating Truth*, 97. Images from the manuscript can be seen in her figs. 24–26. See also Lucy Freeman Sandler, "The *Lumere as lais* and Its Readers: Pictorial Evidence from British Library MS Royal 15.D.II.," in *Thresholds of Medieval Visual Culture*, ed. Elina Gertsman and Jill Stevenson (Woodbridge, Suffolk: Boydell Press, 2012), 73–94.

75. Short, "Patrons and Polyglots," 231. On the appeal of French works of doctrine for the clergy, see, for example, Dean and Boulton, *Anglo-Norman Literature*, 345, and M. Dominica Legge, "The 'Lumiere as Lais': A Postscript," *Modern Language Review* 46 (1951): 191–95, at 194, as well as Ruhe, "Pour faire la lumière as lais?" 48–49.

76. Jeffrey Kittay and Wlad Godzich, *The Emergence of Prose: An Essay in Prosaics* (Minneapolis: University of Minnesota Press, 1987), argue that writing down the vernacular inevitably assimilates it to Latin, given the latter's frequent use as almost a synonym of "lettrure."

77. See Geoff Rector, "An Illustrious Vernacular: The Psalter *en romanz* in Twelfth-Century England," in *Language and Culture in Medieval Britain*, ed. Wogan-Browne et al., 198–206, on the "dynamic (not hierarchy) among languages" in twelfth-century England and the "simultaneously ancillary and fraternal relation" of *romanz* to Latin, one that recalls the shifting relationship between clerical teacher and lay learner (200).

78. Text and translation from Hunt, *"Cher alme,"* 78, 79; I have modified the punctuation of the translation slightly. The author's identity and the date are not entirely certain, but I follow Hunt's account (71–73).

79. London, British Library, Cotton Domitian A.xi., f. 89ra. This is the first sentence of the prologue; its somewhat breathless and tangled syntax may imply a relatively untrained writer.

The "ke seit" of the first sentence is only awkwardly translatable: "the thing that be what a man can do in this life that is most pleasing to God."

80. Examples of the importance of order could be multiplied; Pierre also, for instance, organizes all the work's varied "intentions" (*fins*) under one overarching one: "La fin est dit veraiment / Deus meimes principaument, / Kar fin est [e] perfecciun / De ceo k'en cest livre entendum. / Autre fins nepurquant i unt, / Mes a cette tuttes ordinez sunt" (Pierre d'Abernon, *Lumere*, 1:18, ll. 639–44).

81. "Orthodoxus est recte credens, et ut credit recte vivens" (*Etymologies* 7.14.5).

82. Bernard McGinn, *The Growth of Mysticism: Gregory the Great Through the Twelfth Century (The Presence of God: A History of Western Christian Mysticism, Vol. 2)* (New York: Crossroad, 1994), 155. See also Harkins, *Reading and the Work of Restoration*, particularly his section titled "Restoration by Reading: Re-ordering Humankind's Knowing and Loving," 112–36.

83. I have quoted only part of the passage, which refers, interestingly, to the *fallen* angels; presumably, however, the good angels have knowledge at least as great and, like the fallen angels, "n'unt d'estudie mestier" (l. 1360).

84. A lengthy discussion of sinning through ignorance later in the text notes that those who are trying to learn more ("icés numeement / Ki de saver unt grant talent / E se entremettent sur tute rien / De saver k'est mal e k'est bien," 1:106, ll. 3369–72), the implicit audience of the *Lumere* itself, are less blameworthy in their ignorance. Those, on the other hand, who avoid going to sermons, or sleep through them, or who "Le precheur regardent apertement / Dreit en miliu le visage" but "ja au departir ne sunt plus sage" (1:107, ll. 3420–22)—descriptions that may ring a bell with any teacher—are showing themselves not to be God's people, since they do not wish to hear his words (ll. 3397–3406).

85. Pierre d'Abernon, *Lumere*, 3:11; the specific scholastic modes Hesketh cites are the work's "encyclopaedism, its division into books, distinctions, chapters and smaller enumerated sub-paragraphs, its almost unconscious introduction of Aristotelian causes, its formally constructed arguments and its invocation of named authorities." Matthias Hessenauer builds an admittedly "circumstantial" case, however, for Pierre's reliance on the example set by Robert Grosseteste: "The Impact of Grosseteste's Pastoral Care on Vernacular Religious Literature: *La Lumière as Lais* by Pierre de Peckham," in *Robert Grosseteste: New Perspectives on His Thought and Scholarship*, ed. James McEvoy (Turnhout: Brepols; Steenbrugis: In Abbatia S. Petri, 1995), 377–91. Hessenauer emphasizes Grosseteste's and Pierre's shared focus on pastoral care, though he sees the *Lumere* as being directed to a clerical audience.

86. The lines in brackets appear in only one manuscript, albeit an "outstanding" one: Pierre d'Abernon, *Lumere*, 3:30.

87. Pierre d'Abernon, *Lumere*, 3:71. Hesketh points out that while vernacular treatments of Boethius frequently omitted this material, Jean de Meun would soon treat it extensively in the *Roman de la rose* (3:72).

88. The term "contemplation" had already entered French well before this, notably in Edmund of Abingdon's *Mirour de seinte eglyse*; the work survives in two redactions, one of which drastically reduces the discussion of contemplation, possibly because it was deemed a potentially dangerous realm for the laity to enter. See *Mirour de seinte eglyse*, ed. Wilshere, xi.

89. There is a similar moment later, when the master, having discussed the order of priests, apologizes for having "described in French what it would be better to say in Latin," only to have the disciple immediately note that thanks to the master, anyone who does not know Latin will be heartened, "Pus k'en franceis as demustré / Ceo k'en latin li fu celé" (because you have made known in French that which would have been hidden from him in Latin); the disciple adds that

he will pray to God to reward the master's labor, since anyone who attends to this lesson will benefit by it (Pierre d'Abernon, *Lumere*, 2:122, ll. 11283–96). The remarks may be directed toward priests who can read only in the vernacular, but as the master's self-criticism suggests, putting them in French makes them available to lay readers as well.

90. The widely popular text *De disciplina scolarium* insists on a continuity between the roles of disciple and master: "[Q]ui non novit se subici, non noscet se magistrari. Miserum autem est eum magistrum fieri, qui numquam novit se discipulum esse." Pseudo-Boethius, *De disciplina scolarium*, ed. Olga Weijers (Leiden: Brill, 1976), 99. I am grateful to Andrea Denny-Brown for drawing my attention to this text.

91. Jean-Claude Schmitt, "Du Bon usage du 'Credo,'" in *Faire croire: Modalités de la diffusion et de la réception des messages religieux du XIIe au XVe siècle*, Collection de l'École française de Rome 51 (Rome: École française de Rome, 1981), 337–61, at 343.

92. See, for example, Book I, ch. 11 ("Ou meint Deus"): "La le veient par grant delit / Les angles e chescun eslit" (Pierre d'Abernon, *Lumere*, 1:25, ll. 849–50); Book 6, ch. 91 ("Une recapitulacion dé joies avant dites"): "Deu, si li plest, nus doin[t] sa grace / K'ove li le veum face a face!" (2:193, ll. 13735–36).

CHAPTER 2

1. Quoted in Le Goff, *The Birth of Purgatory*, 224.

2. Oxford, Bodleian Library, MS Laud miscellaneous 471, f. 121ᵛ. The story is originally told of, and the inset verse attributed to, the twelfth-century cleric Serlo of Wilton, author of a famous book of proverbs; see Marcel Schwob, *La Légende de Serlon de Wilton* (Paris: Édition de la Vogue, 1899). The meaning "embroidered with letters" for "litteratus" is dated to 1204 and 1295 in Latham, *Revised Medieval Latin Word-List*, entry "litter/a."

3. On punitive teaching, see Bruce W. Holsinger, *Music, Body, and Desire in Medieval Culture: From Hildegard of Bingen to Chaucer* (Stanford, Calif.: Stanford University Press, 2001), 259–92, and Jody Enders, "Rhetoric, Coercion, and the Memory of Violence," in *Criticism and Dissent in the Middle Ages*, ed. Rita Copeland (Cambridge: Cambridge University Press, 1996), 24–55.

4. Jane Gilbert, *Living Death in Medieval French and English Literature* (Cambridge: Cambridge University Press, 2011), 4. Gilbert examines the role of death in texts with primarily "secular concerns," but I argue that even in religious works on death damnation need not be considered the central element of the picture.

5. Jean Delumeau's *Sin and Fear: The Emergence of a Western Guilt Culture, 13th–18th Centuries* (New York: Palgrave Macmillan, 1990), as its title partly suggests, more or less takes up where this book leaves off, in the late thirteenth to early fourteenth centuries; and the rise of the famous *artes moriendi* is, despite its earlier roots, distinctively a late medieval phenomenon. At the same time, of course, death continued to be available as an "imaginative tool" for living; see Amy Appleford, *Learning to Die in London, 1380–1540* (Philadelphia: University of Pennsylvania Press, 2014).

6. Neil Cartlidge, "Sir Orfeo in the Otherworld: Courting Chaos?" *Studies in the Age of Chaucer* 26 (2004): 195–226, at 219–20.

7. See the account in Bennett, "A Book Designed for a Noblewoman."

8. *MP* Roxburghe, 72, ll. 2627, 2637, 2643; *MP* EETS, 79–80, ll. 2654, 2663, 2669; further citations are by line number in the text.

9. On the bonds between living and dead that the doctrine of Purgatory claims and exploits, and on the use of exempla in that context, see Le Goff, *Birth of Purgatory*, especially 11–12, 293–316.

10. D. D. R. Owen, *The Vision of Hell: Infernal Journeys in Medieval French Literature* (Edinburgh: Scottish Academic Press, 1970), 113.

11. Gilbert, *Living Death*, 2.

12. This moment came to be hotly disputed in the fourteenth century; there was disagreement over the exact point (before or after the Last Judgment) at which the blessed would see God face-to-face in the *visio Dei*. Caroline Walker Bynum offers a brief, clear account of the controversy in *The Resurrection of the Body in Western Christianity, 200–1366* (New York: Columbia University Press, 1995), 283–85.

13. G. R. Evans, *Bernard of Clairvaux* (New York: Oxford University Press, 2000), 115.

14. Bernard of Clairvaux, *Epistola 191, Ad Innocentium ex persona domini archiepiscopi Remensis, et al.*, PL 182:357B–358B, at col. 357B–C.

15. Bernard of Clairvaux, *Epistola 337, Ad Innocentium pontificem, in persona Franciae episcoporum*, PL 182:540B–542D, at col. 540C; Brilliant, "Envisaging the Particular Judgment in Late-Medieval Italy," 316.

16. John R. Sommerfeldt, *Bernard of Clairvaux on the Life of the Mind* (New York and Mahwah, NJ: The Newman Press, 2004), 125 (a quotation from a letter to Stephen of Palestrina, PL 182:537A); for the complaint about looking face-to-face, see *Epistola 192, ad Magistrum Guidonem de Castello*, PL 182:358–59, at 358C.

17. See D. E. Luscombe, *The School of Peter Abelard: The Influence of Abelard's Thought in the Early Scholastic Period* (Cambridge: Cambridge University Press, 1969), 5–6, on Abelard's popularity as a teacher and particularly on the influence of his students (and other disputants) on his writings.

18. Luscombe, *School of Peter Abelard*, 14–59; see esp. 19.

19. On the importance of earthly and heavenly community in Bernard's sermons for this feast, see Anna Harrison, " 'If one member glories . . .': Community Between the Living and the Saintly Dead in Bernard of Clairvaux's Sermons for the Feast of All Saints," in *History in the Comic Mode: Essays in Honor of Caroline Walker Bynum*, ed. Rachel Fulton and Bruce Holsinger (New York: Columbia University Press, 2007), 25–35, 299–302.

20. Bernard of Clairvaux, *In festo omnium sanctorum sermo I*, PL 183:453B–462C, at 455C.

21. On this dual impulse in preaching, see Waters, *Angels and Earthly Creatures*, 57–72.

22. Odette Pontal, ed., *Les Statuts synodaux français du XIIIe siècle, I: Les statuts de Paris et le Synodal de l'Ouest* (Paris: Bibliothèque Nationale, 1971), 94, c. 73. The sinner-saints are discussed further in the chapters that follow.

23. Abelard's interest in the role of intention in sin is a case in point, having both speculative and practical implications; Luscombe, *School of Peter Abelard*, notes some later discussions of confession and penance that show traces of Abelard's ideas (100, 168–70, 218–19).

24. Abelard as quoted by Bernard: *Contra quaedam capitula errorum Abaelardi Epistola CXC seu Tractatus ad Innocentium II pontificem*, PL 182:1055C. On Abelard as *vulgarisateur*, see Robson, *Maurice of Sully*, 6; he suggests, further, that "perhaps [Abelard's] most permanent achievement (for which the credit must indeed be shared with Honorius of Autun and others) lay in the spreading of Augustinian concepts previously grasped by the few" (6).

25. Bernard of Clairvaux, *Epistola 188, Ad episcopos et cardinales curiae, de eodem*, PL 182:351A–353D, at col. 353C.

26. Evans, *Bernard of Clairvaux*, 120. One of Abelard's followers mocks what he sees as a

similar divergence in Bernard's teaching, suggesting that it veers between the "rustic" and "unintelligible impossibility" (Luscombe, *School of Peter Abelard*, 39).

27. George L. Hamilton, "The Gilded Leaden Cloaks of the Hypocrites (Inferno XXIII, 58–66)," *Romanic Review* 12 (1921): 335–52, at 348, demonstrates the tale's wide currency. The versions listed above are printed or excerpted in Anton E. Schönbach, "Studien zur Erzählungsliteratur des Mittelalters. Erster Theil: Der Reuner Relationen," in *Sitzungsberichte der Philosophisch-Historischen Classe der Kaiserlichen Akademie der Wissenschaften* 139 (Vienna: Carl Gerold's Sohn, 1898), 13–15, 27, 31–32, 33–34, 35, respectively.

28. The story appears in Hélinand of Froidmont, *Chronicon*, PL 212:771C–1082C, at cols. 984C–985B.

29. Watkins, "Sin, Penance and Purgatory," 22. Watkins points out the care many such narratives take to establish their historicity, and their appearance in chronicles as well as "more explicitly didactic collections" (6; see also 11).

30. Schönbach, "Studien zur Erzählungsliteratur des Mittelalters," 31–32.

31. Elizabeth Allen, *False Fables and Exemplary Truth in Later Middle English Literature* (New York: Palgrave Macmillan, 2005), 2 and passim.

32. Honorius, *Elucidarium*, col. 1134B.

33. Honorius, *Speculum ecclesiae*, cols. 862C, 862D. Further citations are by column number in the text.

34. The mnemonic function of the exemplum is explicitly noted, in each case, by a rhyming phrase: "Ne autem vento oblivionis haec a memoria vestra tollantur, vinculo hujus exempli fixa teneantur" (*Speculum ecclesiae*, col. 863D); "Ne hoc a pectore vestro evanescat, per enarrationem hujus exempli memoriae coalescat" (864C), and so forth.

35. The only sermon that lacks an exemplum is the last one, "Ad conjugatos"; here Honorius provides instead an extensive account of specific practices appropriate to the married, and the sermon is the longest in the collection. The address "Ad divites" does not have its own exemplum, but the immediately following sermon "Ad pauperes" concludes with an exemplum that contrasts the death of a pauper with that of a rich man and thus applies to both groups; see below.

36. Virginia Brilliant offers a list of "six distinct but related visual conventions or iconographic types" by which the particular judgment is represented in medieval art (with an emphasis on, but not limited to, late medieval Italy); the first two are "the angelic transport of the soul heavenward" (as in the case of the priest in Honorius's exemplum) and "the struggle between angels and devils for possession of a soul" ("Envisaging the Particular Judgment in Late-Medieval Italy," 317, 324). The latter, she points out, is considerably more common in northern Europe than in Italy; see also Chapter 5.

37. A somewhat similar story is told in the *Manuel des pechiez* of Abbot Macarius, who, upon asking "Ki en ciel sun pier serreit," is informed that he has yet to equal in holiness two laywomen in the next town who have obediently given up their desire to live a religious life and never quarrel with their husbands: *MP* EETS, 69–71, ll. 2421–94, *MP* Roxburghe, 62–65, ll. 2395–2468. Chapters 3 and 4 consider other examples of such unexpected saints and the lessons they offer to the holy figures who meet them.

38. On preachers as sowers of the Word, see the parable of the sower and its explication, Mark 4:3–20. Preachers are imagined as the feet of the Church because of Isaiah 52:7 and Romans 10:15, farmers for the reason Honorius himself cites here, that they support the Church by feeding it: "Vos quoque, fratres et socii mei, qui agrum colitis, pedes Ecclesiae estis, quia eam pascendo portatis" (*Speculum ecclesiae*, col. 866A). Farmers also get a relatively gentle treatment in the *Elucidarium*, where they are one of the few groups of whom anything good is said.

39. The Anglo-French *Dialogue du père et du fils* recounts a similarly structured story: a hermit's servant, in town on an errand, sees a rich man being carried to his grave with honor and returns to the hermitage to find his master devoured by wild beasts. He decides to return to his life in the world, since God does not reward those who serve him, but a voice from Heaven quickly sets him straight. The story is immediately followed by that of Dives and Lazarus. Hunt, *"Cher alme,"* 52.

40. Hugh of St. Victor, *De tribus maximis circumstantiis gestorum*, ed. William M. Green, *Speculum* 18 (1943): 484–93, at 491, quoted in Michelle Bolduc, *The Medieval Poetics of Contraries* (Gainesville: University Press of Florida, 2006), 50.

41. LaVere, "From Contemplation to Action," 64. The Gloss she discusses is earlier than 1135 and thus contemporary with Bernard and Abelard; there is not a neat progression here but a gradual shift whereby material that had been discussed primarily among professed religious moved into a wider sphere, often by way of the schools (as in LaVere's example).

42. See Baldwin, *Masters, Preachers, and Merchants*, 1:107–16.

43. Cited in ibid., 1:113. See also Roberts, "Master Stephen Langton," 237–68.

44. Thomas of Chobham, *Summa de arte praedicandi*, 137. From c. 1115 until the late sixteenth century *subditus* commonly has the ecclesiastical meaning "member of the flock": Latham, *Revised Medieval Latin Word-List*, entry "subdit/io."

45. Waters, *Angels and Earthly Creatures*, 60–61.

46. Robert W. Ackerman, *"The Debate of the Body and the Soul* and Parochial Christianity," *Speculum* 37.4 (1962): 541–65, at 542; the essay investigates the transformations of tone and emphasis that attend translation into English from Latin in the early fourteenth-century *Desputisoun bitwen þe Bodi and þe Soule*, touching on a number of the issues discussed here. Michel-André Bossy considers the status implications of such dialogues (focusing primarily on Latin examples) in "Medieval Debates of Body and Soul," *Comparative Literature* 28.2 (1976): 144–63.

47. London, British Library, Arundel MS 288, for example, contains the *Manuel des pechiez*; a work on Purgatory attributed to Robert Grosseteste; a sermon on the Passion; the *Petit sermon*; and the *Mirour de seinte eglyse*. An Anglo-French "Desputeison de l'alme et du corps" (attributed in some manuscripts to the fourteenth-century Franciscan Nicholas Bozon) occurs among some other texts added at the end in a different hand. In Oxford, Bodleian Library, MS Selden supra 74, a miscellany, this same "Disputeison" appears (again in a different hand) before part of a chapter table for the *Lumere as lais*; later in the manuscript there is a copy of the *Mirour de seinte eglyse*. Another body-and-soul debate poem, which begins "Un Samedi par nuit" (see Dean and Boulton, *Anglo-Norman Literature*, item 692), survives in both insular and Continental French versions; one of the latter appears in the massive compilation Paris, Bibliothèque de l'Arsenal, MS 3516 immediately before a verse *Lucidaires* by Gilbert de Cambres.

48. Peter Brown, *The Cult of the Saints: Its Rise and Function in Latin Christianity* (Chicago: University of Chicago Press, 1981). While the social contexts are very different, Brown's remarks on the shortcomings of "our own learned tradition" in dealing with "popular religion" remain relevant for many of the texts under study here (12–13).

49. Honorius, *Elucidarium*, col. 1153B.

50. Roberts, "Master Stephen Langton," 266.

51. "Verbum propositum exemplo vulgari claudere volo propter simplices": Roberts, "Master Stephen Langton," 268.

52. Constable, *Three Studies*, 354, quoting from Bernard of Clairvaux, *Sermo I in festo S. Andreae* (PL 183:503D–509A, at 506C–D). On the *non valde boni/mali*, a categorization to which I will return later in this chapter, see Le Goff, *Birth of Purgatory*, 220–25.

53. Constable, *Three Studies*, 354.

54. *Étude sur "Le Miroir,"* ed. Aitken, ll. 17485–88.

55. On "kynde knowynge," see Langland, *Vision of Piers Plowman*, Passus I.138–47. It is not the least of the poem's cosmic jokes that repeated face-to-face, dialogic teaching of the kind imagined in so many didactic works generally proves frustrating and mystifying rather than illuminating for Will.

56. Thomas of Chobham, *Summa de arte praedicandi*, 50.

57. The quotation is from Thomas of Chobham: "in die mortis . . . tunc est cuilibet suus dies judicii" (*Summa de arte praedicandi*, 49–50).

58. *MP* Roxburghe, 424, ll. 824–29. This material does not appear in the EETS edition, having no counterpart in *Handlyng Synne*.

59. Only a saint, it seems, is likely to recognize this lesson before death: William of Waddington also recounts a story of St. John the Almsgiver in which the saint repeatedly donates to the same beggar (who keeps appearing in different disguises). When asked about his extreme generosity, John replies, "ceo est Deu, par aventure, / Ki me vient esprover / Si almoine dune sanz reprover" (*MP* Roxburghe, 215, ll. 5602–4; *MP* EETS, 221, ll. 5644–46).

60. *MP* Roxburghe, 425, note l-l. The variant is from London, British Library, Harley MS 4657; Furnivall, the editor, uses Harley 273 as his base text.

61. I have not been able to trace this couplet, which may of course be William's own invention, but the use of fragments of secular lyric in preaching is not at all uncommon; see Siegfried Wenzel, *Preachers, Poets, and the Early English Lyric* (Princeton, N.J.: Princeton University Press, 1986) for a discussion of (primarily) Middle English examples.

62. The consonance between this final book and its subject is echoed in a passage that discusses the sixth (and final) age of the world, linking it both to the six ages of human life and to the six days of creation; Pierre d'Abernon, *Lumere*, 1:136, ll. 4420–96. In this passage both Christ and humankind play the role of "derein" or "fin."

63. Pierre d'Abernon, *Lumere*, 2:146–52, ll. 12101–304. These exempla are among the most famous and widely disseminated treatments of Purgatory; see Hesketh's note to l. 12101, 3:162. As he points out, two of the exempla appear also in the *Manuel des pechiez* (*MP* EETS, 341–42, ll. 7791–7836 and 321–23, ll. 7521–70; *MP* Roxburghe, 339–41, ll. 7739–84 and 319–20, ll. 7473–7520).

64. On Sicily's infernal reputation, see Le Goff, *Birth of Purgatory*, 201–8, discussing this passage from Gregory.

65. Le Goff discusses the evolution of the concept of *mediocriter boni*, a modification of Augustine's more distinct *non valde boni* and *non valde mali*, in the late twelfth and thirteenth centuries; Pierre sometimes uses this threefold model, elsewhere a four-part schema that more closely recalls Augustine (see below). Le Goff, *Birth of Purgatory*, 220–25.

66. As noted early in this chapter, Raoul Ardent considered it impossible to make such distinctions; Pierre, however, seems confident of the possibility, perhaps because of the greater concreteness and sense of certainty conveyed by the pervasive recounting of stories about the afterlife in the intervening period.

67. Speaking of the "mauveis meinement," who are in need of relief from their sufferings, the master urges particular consideration of one's family and friends: "Pur ceo chescun ke pere e mere ust / Morz de ceo penser mut dust, / U autre ami ke ben amast, / Bien sereit si a dreit pensast" (Pierre d'Abernon, *Lumere*, 2:163, ll. 12695–8).

CHAPTER 3

1. John Parker, *The Aesthetics of Antichrist: From Christian Drama to Christopher Marlowe* (Ithaca, N.Y.: Cornell University Press, 2007), 139.

2. On the "popular" Bible, see James H. Morey, "Peter Comestor, Biblical Paraphrase, and the Medieval Popular Bible," *Speculum* 68.1 (1993): 6–35. The fundamental importance of the Creed from an early date—it was often a required accompaniment to baptism—is demonstrated in Jean Longère, "Enseignement du 'Credo,'" *Sacris erudiri* 32 (1991): 309–42.

3. Andrew Reeves, "Teaching the Creed and Articles of Faith in England: 1215–1281," in *A Companion to Pastoral Care in the Late Middle Ages (1200–1500)*, ed. Ronald J. Stansbury (Leiden: Brill, 2010), 41–72, at 44; the point is further emphasized at 45–46. Catherine Rider points out the relatively ambitious instruction offered by some thirteenth-century confession manuals in "Lay Religion and Pastoral Care."

4. For recent overviews, see Hoogvliet, "Encouraging Lay People to Read the Bible in the French Vernaculars," and Sneddon, "The *Old French Bible*."

5. Morey, "Peter Comestor," 25. Recent work has emphasized the variety of avenues to biblical knowledge; see, for example, Margriet Hoogvliet, "The Medieval Vernacular Bible in French as a Flexible Text: Selective and Discontinuous Reading Practices," in *Form and Function in the Late Medieval Bible*, ed. Eyal Poleg and Laura Light (Leiden: Brill, 2013), 283–306; Wogan-Browne, "Women's Formal and Informal Traditions"; and Eyal Poleg, "'A Ladder Set Up on Earth': The Bible in Medieval Sermons," in *The Practice of the Bible in the Middle Ages: Production, Reception, and Performance in Western Christianity*, ed. Susan Boynton and Diane J. Reilly (New York: Columbia University Press, 2011), 205–27.

6. Lobrichon, "Nouveau genre," 90.

7. Baldwin, *Masters, Preachers, and Merchants*, 1:12. On the *Historia scholastica*, "l'enseignement du plus en vogue parmi les maîtres," see Lobrichon, "Nouveau genre," 100.

8. Sneddon, "The *Old French Bible*," 299. On French translations of instructive material of various kinds, see Armstrong et al., *Knowing Poetry*, and Galderisi, *Translations médiévales*.

9. The list of manuscripts that contain this prose version can be found at http://jonas.irht. cnrs.fr/oeuvre/1870. A substantial number of these also contain parts of Maurice de Sully's sermons; for an abbreviated account of the conjunction of these two texts, see Robson, *Maurice of Sully*, 73.

10. Richard O'Gorman points out that the three "metrical" versions of the *Évangile* "are all associated in one way or another either with Normandy or with Anglo-Norman England," but if one includes the prose tradition the French tradition is as strongly Continental as it is insular: "The *Gospel of Nicodemus* in the Vernacular Literature of Medieval France," in *Medieval Gospel of Nicodemus*, ed. Izydorczyk, 103–31, at 105.

11. Powell, "Translating Scripture."

12. The thieves' placement—one on the right of Jesus, one on the left—is specified in Luke 23:33; as François Bovon notes, this placement recalls Matthew 25:31–46, the parable of the sheep and the goats (also discussed in Chapter 2): *Luke 3: A Commentary on the Gospel of Luke 19:28–24:53*, ed. Helmut Koester, trans. James Crouch (Minneapolis: Fortress Press, 2012), 306.

13. In doing so, Luke creates a problem: how can the two jeering thieves of Matthew and Mark be reconciled with the distinctly different figures he presents? Bede attempts to resolve this by suggesting that the plural used in the other gospels should be understood as a singular, offering the supposed parallel, "What is more commonly the case, for example, than that someone might say, 'And peasants insult me,' even if (only) one were insulting?" As so often, the *rustici* get

a bad rap from the *clerici*; see the following chapter. Bede, *In Lucae evangelium expositio*, PL 92:301D–634D, col. 618C.

14. High-quality images of the entire manuscript are available on the British Library's website: http://www.bl.uk/manuscripts/Viewer.aspx?ref=add_ms_47682_fs001r. For an edited version of the text, see F. P. Pickering, ed., *The Anglo-Norman Text of the "Holkham Bible Picture Book,"* ANTS 23 (Oxford: Basil Blackwell for the ANTS, 1971). Pickering emphasizes the work's debt to authoritative written sources (the *Historia scholastica* of Peter Comestor, Gospel harmonies) as well as to "popular religious literature" (xvi).

15. *Ci nous dit: Recueil d'exemples moraux*, ed. Gérard Blangez (Paris: Société des Anciens Textes Français, 1979, 1986), 1:80, ch. 63, italics in edition.

16. In the full Crucifixion scene on f. 32^r, the body as well as the head of the bad thief is given this gray-black color, further differentiating him from the good thief.

17. Bede, *In Lucae evangelium expositio*, PL 92:301D–634D, at col. 601C–D.

18. Bede, *In Lucae evangelium expositio*, PL 92:618D–619A. Parts of this passage appear in the *Glossa ordinaria in Evangelium secundum Lucam*, PL 114:348B–C.

19. Bovon, *Luke 3*, 310.

20. See Sister John Vianney McCulloch, "A Study of Arnold of Bonneval († 1157) with a Translation and Critique of the *Tractatus de septem verbis Domini in cruce*" (M.A. thesis, Catholic University of America, 1963), 14–15; and André Wilmart, "Le Grand poème bonaventurien sur les sept paroles du Christ en Croix," *Revue bénédictine* 47 (1937): 235–78, at 263–64.

21. McCulloch, "Study of Arnold of Bonneval," 32–33; Arnold of Bonneval, *Tractatus de septem verbis Domini in cruce*, PL 189:1677B–1726B, at cols. 1678D–1679A. I use McCulloch's translation with occasional minor emendations.

22. Arnold of Bonneval, *Tractatus de septem verbis*, PL 189:1689B.

23. Arnold of Bonneval, *Tractatus de septem verbis*, PL 189:1689D–1690A.

24. Steven Justice, "Eucharistic Miracle and Eucharistic Doubt," *Journal of Medieval and Early Modern Studies* 42.2 (2012): 307–32; he discusses the conjunction of Incarnation and Eucharist on p. 323.

25. Owen, *Vision of Hell*, gives an overview of the various accounts (95–96). Other biblical "sources" sometimes noted are Matthew 27:51–53 and 2 Timothy 1:10, and Jacques Le Goff also points to Matthew 12:40, Acts 2:31, and Romans 10:6–7 as origins for the *Descensus ad inferos*. Le Goff, *The Birth of Purgatory*, 44.

26. Owen, *Vision of Hell*, 102. As Alvin Ford observes of the apocryphal gospels generally, "ces écrits eurent pour but principal l'avancement de la Foi en élucidant des obscurités antérieures, par exemple, les lacunes des évangiles canoniques" (*L'Évangile de Nicodème: Les versions courtes en ancien français et en prose*, ed. Alvin E. Ford [Geneva: Droz, 1973], 13).

27. Brian Murdoch, *The Apocryphal Adam and Eve in Medieval Europe: Vernacular Translations and Adaptations of the "Vita Adae et Evae"* (Oxford: Oxford University Press, 2009), 12. Miri Rubin makes a similar point about accounts of the Virgin Mary's life; see Rubin, *Mother of God: A History of the Virgin Mary* (London: Allen Lane, 2009), 3.

28. Zbigniew Izydorczyk, "The Unfamiliar *Evangelium Nicodemi*," *Manuscripta* 33 (1989), 177.

29. "passus sub Pontio Pilato, crucifixus, mortuus et sepultus, descendit ad inferna[;] tertia die resurrexit a mortuis." This is the version Liuwe H. Westra calls T, the "textus receptus" that is the basis for the vernacular versions of the Creed; see Westra, *The Apostles' Creed: Origins, History, and Some Early Commentaries* (Turnhout: Brepols, 2002), 21.

30. See Westra: "This addition [i.e., the reference to the Descent into Hell], which is

already found in the late fourth-century form of the Creed about which Rufinus informs us, was apparently adopted from Northern Italy by a number of other churches, though in different formulations" (*Apostles' Creed*, 237); further discussion in his ch. 3 and appendix. Jaroslav Pelikan and Valerie A. Hotchkiss, eds., *Creeds and Confessions of Faith in the Christian Tradition, Vol. I: Early, Eastern, and Medieval* (New Haven, Conn.: Yale University Press, 2003) take Rufinus's account, which mentions the *Descensus*, to be a reliable indicator of the "baptismal creed of the Church of Rome," which they date to the second century (681). Notably, however, the "nearly identical text" that appears in a Greek letter from Marcellus, bishop of Ancyra, dating from 340, does not mention the *Descensus*, suggesting its variable inclusion (681, 682).

31. *Évangile*, ed. Ford, 14. Both the "Lateran Creed" of 1215 and Innocent III's version of the Creed include "descendit ad inferna/inferos": see, respectively, Norman Tanner, ed., *Decrees of the Ecumenical Councils* (London: Sheed and Ward; Washington, D.C.: Georgetown University Press, 1990), 1:230, and Innocent III, *De sacro altaris mysterio libri sex,* PL 217:773B–916A, at col. 828A. Peter Abelard also includes it in his *Expositio Symboli quod dicitur Apostolorum*, PL 178:617D–30A.

32. In addition to Le Goff, *Birth of Purgatory*, and Owen, *Vision of Hell*, see Eileen Gardiner, ed., *Visions of Heaven and Hell Before Dante* (New York: Italica Press, 1989) and Watkins, "Sin, Penance and Purgatory."

33. Kenosis has in recent years been a subject of vigorous theological debate; for a summary of that debate, and a response that takes an Augustinian approach, see Pardue, "Kenosis and Its Discontents."

34. Peter Lombard, *In Epistolam ad Ephesios*, PL 192:169B–222C, at cols. 200A–B.

35. Pelikan and Hotchkiss, *Creeds and Confessions*, 113; Leo I, *Epistola ad Flavianum episcopum Constantinopolitanum adversus haeresim Eutychianam*, PL 62:503A–508B.

36. Pelikan and Hotchkiss, *Creeds and Confessions*, 114, 115; Leo I, *Epistola ad Flavianum episcopum*, PL 62:503A–B.

37. Pelikan and Hotchkiss, *Creeds and Confessions*, 116; Leo I, *Epistola ad Flavianum episcopum*, PL 62:504B–C.

38. Pelikan and Hotchkiss, *Creeds and Confessions*, 117–18; Leo I, *Epistola ad Flavianum episcopum*, PL 62:505B–C.

39. Pelikan and Hotchkiss, *Creeds and Confessions*, 116; Leo I, *Epistola ad Flavianum episcopum*, PL 62:505A.

40. On the history of interpretations of the Descent into Hell (or the Harrowing of Hell, as it is more often called in English) in Christian antiquity and the Middle Ages, see Josef Kroll, *Gott und Hölle: Der Mythos vom Descensuskampfe* (Darmstadt: Wissenschaftliche Buchgesellschaft, 1963), 1–182; he particularly emphasizes its dramatic and dialogic elements. C. W. Marx, *The Devil's Rights and the Redemption in the Literature of Medieval England* (Cambridge: D. S. Brewer, 1995), explores the Harrowing as one element in the contest over the theological issue of the Devil's "right" to humanity; see 47–58.

41. Westra, *Apostles' Creed*, 48, 47. See also Pelikan and Hotchkiss, *Creeds and Confessions*, which argues that early proclamation/preaching (i.e., kerygma) and baptismal formulae preserved and disseminated the earliest forms of the Creed: kerygma, 10–11; baptism, 11–15; catechetical instruction, 19–21.

42. Nims, "*Translatio*," 220.

43. *Évangile*, ed. Ford, 14–15; see also the discussions of vernacular versions in Zbigniew Izydorczyk, ed., *The Medieval Gospel of Nicodemus: Texts, Intertexts, and Contexts in Western Europe* (Tempe, Ariz.: Medieval and Renaissance Texts and Studies, 1997). For an exploration of

how the early narrative of the Harrowing might have developed, see Allen Cabaniss, "The Harrowing of Hell, Psalm 24, and Pliny the Younger: A Note," *Vigiliae Christianae* 7.1 (1953): 65–74. Parker, *Aesthetics of Antichrist*, 169–77, discusses the *Evangelium*'s problematic early history and its enormous later influence, particularly in religious drama.

44. Counting versions of the *Évangile* precisely is rather difficult, since all are translations and some are versions or recombinations of earlier translations, but Alvin Ford distinguishes five branches of the prose tradition: short versions A (ten manuscripts) and B (twenty-three manuscripts), the various long versions (fourteen manuscripts), a "heteroclite" version that combines elements from the short and long versions (one manuscript), and two paraphrases (one unique, the other in three manuscripts; in these the *Descensus* section is quite brief). See *Évangile*, ed. Ford, 21–27; I have made additions and modifications to the list based on O'Gorman, "*Gospel of Nicodemus* in the Vernacular Literature of Medieval France." There are also three versions in verse, those of Chrestien, André de Coutances, and an anonymous poet; these are edited in Paris and Bos, *Trois versions rimées,* and discussed by O'Gorman (103–6).

45. "Istum novimus Joseph fabri filium de Maria et dicit se esse filium Dei et regem": *The Gospel of Nicodemus: Gesta Salvatoris,* ed. H. C. Kim (Toronto: Pontifical Institute of Mediaeval Studies, 1973), 13.

46. References to the raising of Lazarus—cited by Enfer and Satan as they try to decide whom they are dealing with—are another such cross-temporal marker, one particularly emphasized in dramatic performance. V. A. Kolve notes the episode's references forward to the Resurrection and the Last Judgment in the Middle English cycle plays (*The Play Called Corpus Christi* [Stanford, Calif.: Stanford University Press, 1966], 79–81), and Mark C. Pilkington points out the role of Lazarus's resurrection in the action of the Harrowing of Hell plays: "The Raising of Lazarus: A Prefiguring Agent to the Harrowing of Hell," *Medium Aevum* 44 (1975): 51–53.

47. Version B, from *Évangile*, ed. Ford, 93; I have modified the punctuation. The corresponding passage from version A can be found on p. 52; it does not contain any Latin.

48. The twelfth-century *Jeu d'Adam* provides a relevant example; while the prophets represented there are not the same as those presented in the *Évangile*, their role as the righteous confined to Hell is similar and anticipates the need for the Harrowing. David Bevington, *Medieval Drama* (Boston: Houghton Mifflin, 1975), 113–21.

49. Robert of Gretham, *Miroir*; Hoogvliet, "Medieval Vernacular Bible," 302.

50. This promise to Seth, though ultimately part of the widespread *Vita Adae et Evae* tradition, appears first in the *Evangelium Nicodemi* (Murdoch, *Apocryphal Adam and Eve*, 15–16).

51. This is an inversion of the Monophysite controversy, where the claim was that Jesus was (only) God and not truly a man; see the discussion of Pope Leo and Eutyches above.

52. Both quotations from *Évangile*, ed. Ford, 94.

53. *Évangile*, ed. Ford, 95; Ps. 24:7. On Psalm 24 and the Harrowing, see Cabaniss, "Harrowing of Hell." The texts invoked here, "Tristis est anima mea" and "Tollite portas," are part of the liturgy; the latter, for the first Sunday in Advent, thus associates the Harrowing of Hell with the Incarnation. I am grateful to Susan Boynton for noting this connection. On the "deception" account of the Incarnation, see the discussions in Marx, *Devil's Rights and the Redemption*, and Parker, *Aesthetics of Antichrist*, 169–77.

54. *Évangile*, ed. Ford, 95.

55. Paris and Bos, *Trois versions rimées*, 54, ll. 1729, 1733. The French "forme de serf" translates the Latin's "in forma servi" (*Gospel of Nicodemus*, ed. Kim, 42), which in turn echoes Philippians 2:7, "formam servi accipiens." Peter Abelard makes a similar point about the simultaneous greatness and smallness of the Apostles' Creed itself: "Nullus autem de stoliditate

sensus, vel tenuitate ingenii causetur, quia haec tam parva sunt, ut nemo tam hebes et barbarus sit, qui hoc dicere, et verbis omnibus enuntiare non possit, tam magna, ut qui horum scientiam pleniter capere potuerit, sufficere sibi credatur ad salutem perpetuam." Abelard, *Expositio Symboli*, PL 178:618.

56. See, for example, Innocent III, *De sacro altaris mysterio*: "Sed qui in sepulcro secundum carnem quievit, secundum animam descendit ad inferos" (PL 217:906B), or Edmund of Abingdon's *Mirour de seinte eglyse* (discussed below).

57. Marx, *Devil's Rights and the Redemption*, 56.

58. Justice, "Eucharistic Miracle and Eucharistic Doubt," 310, 311.

59. Paris and Bos, *Trois versions rimées*, 112, ll. 1285–91.

60. *Évangile*, ed. Ford, Tradition B, 97.

61. Paris and Bos, *Trois versions rimées*, 61–62, 63, ll. 1957–80, 2005–14.

62. Paris and Bos, *Trois versions rimées*, 62, ll. 2003, 2001.

63. Cabaniss, "Harrowing of Hell," points out that in some early texts Psalm 24's "Tollite portas" is read as an appeal to the gates of Heaven, not Hell, to let Christ enter, "since Christ, still bearing the marks of crucifixion, was not immediately recognizable to the guardians of the celestial gates" (73n28)—a moment echoed in the misrecognition of the thief in the *Evangelium Nicodemi*.

64. Paris and Bos, *Trois versions rimées*, 128, ll. 1787–92; further references in text.

65. On the Cross as "a powerful and yet ironic sign" for Augustine (and his medieval inheritors), see Pardue, "Kenosis and Its Discontents," 280, 281, where he quotes Augustine's characterization of its role: "'[Christ] was glorified by that which was made low; he raised up the lowly by that to which, when he was made low, he descended.'" The slightly dizzying language here effectively captures the Cross's paradoxical role.

66. See Parker, *Aesthetics of Antichrist*, 163–66, on saviors and thieves.

67. McCulloch, "A Study of Arnold of Bonneval," 74, but I have modified the translation: "et qui diu fuerant cineres, fiunt doctores; et qui sepulti, magistri" (Arnold of Bonneval, *Tractatus de septem verbis*, PL 189:1726B).

68. Peter Comestor, *Historia scholastica*, PL 198:1632B–C.

69. Paris and Bos, *Trois versions rimées*, 130, ll. 1835–47; further citations in text.

70. This suspicion of the powerful and learned is visible in the beginning of the story also, where Annas and Caiaphas seek to persuade Pilate that the sun has disappeared as the result of an eclipse (which they carefully explain in scientific terms; see Paris and Bos, *Trois versions rimées*, 78, ll. 157–70) and later urge him to guard the tomb so that the "nonsavant" (80, l. 219) will not be fooled into believing that Jesus has risen when in fact his disciples have stolen him away.

71. Catherine Sanok, *Her Life Historical: Exemplarity and Female Saints' Lives in Late Medieval England* (Philadelphia: University of Pennsylvania Press, 2007), 107. Morgan Powell points out a similar effect in the Old French *Eructavit*, which depicts King David as a jongleur who goes to sing at the wedding of the King and Queen of Heaven and is blocked by the heavenly gatekeeper: "through the staging of David's performance within the poem, his song functions as a play-within-the-play, and forces the recognition that what happens in it is also happening here, now, in the performance as received" (Powell, "Translating Scripture," 87).

72. Thus, Enoch and Elijah form one of the *Ioca monachorum*, riddling catechetical questions ("Who died but was not born? —Adam. Who was born but did not die? —Enoch and Elijah"); the question of primacy in Heaven and who deserves entry is famously taken up in the Middle English *Pearl*; and the most difficult of these, how someone could be "a god and yet a man," as a Middle English lyric puts it, and what the implications of that might be, occupies

essentially every theological or doctrinal author of the entire Middle Ages. There is nothing in Christian belief as readily available or deeply mysterious as the Incarnation, as Satan's questions demonstrate.

73. Erhard Dorn, *Der sündige Heilige in der Legende des Mittelalters* (Munich: Wilhelm Fink, 1967), 9. See also the discussion of the good thief, 105–7, where he notes, "Both in preaching and in legend St. Dismas stands out as one of the great unmistakable examples of the penitent and pardoned sinner" (107).

74. See Breen, *Imagining*, 38–39.

75. Both quotations are from Türk, *"Lucidaire de grant sapientie,"* 334–35, II.83; 340–41, II.95.

76. *Glossa ordinaria*, PL 114:348B.

77. *The French Text of the "Ancrene Riwle," Edited from Trinity College Cambridge MS. R.14.7*, ed. W. H. Trethewey, EETS o.s. 240 (London: Oxford University Press for the EETS, 1958), ix, 92. For further discussion of the *Compileison*, see Watson and Wogan-Browne, "The French of England."

78. *French Text of the "Ancrene Riwle,"* ed. Trethewey, 95–96; I have slightly modified the transcription.

79. *MP* Roxburghe, 375, ll. 10567–80, a section that does not appear in the EETS edition; I have modified the punctuation. The quotation is not actually from St. Bernard but from one of his students, Guerric, abbot of Igny (d. 1157), in his *Sermo II, Sabbato hebdomadae Quadragesimae, De parabola filii prodigi*, PL 185:96C–100A, at col. 96C–D.

80. Guerric of Igny, *Sermo II*, PL 185:96D.

81. *MP* EETS, 351, ll. 9619–86; *MP* Roxburghe, 350–51, ll. 9655–9721.

82. Bernstein, "The Invocation of Hell," 44.

83. Brian J. Levy, *Nine Verse Sermons by Nicholas Bozon: The Art of an Anglo-Norman Poet and Preacher* (Oxford: Society for the Study of Mediaeval Languages and Literature, 1981), 13–14.

84. Rider, "Lay Religion and Pastoral Care," 334n54.

85. While Crucifixion images and the *Évangile de Nicodème* made the two thieves widely recognizable figures, they appear in only two of the thirty-two creedal prayers from (mostly secular) twelfth- and thirteenth-century French works discussed in Sr. Mary Pierre Koch, *An Analysis of the Long Prayers in Old French Literature with Special Reference to the "Biblical-Creed-Narrative" Prayers* (Washington, D.C.: Catholic University of America Press, 1940), 149.

86. Quoted in Jean Bonnard, *Les Traductions de la Bible en vers français au moyen âge* (1884; Geneva: Slatkine Reprints, 1967), 227. The poem survives in four manuscripts, according to Bonnard.

87. The quoted phrase is that of Carol Symes, *A Common Stage: Theater and Public Life in Medieval Arras* (Ithaca, N.Y.: Cornell University Press, 2007), 166.

88. *Mirour*, ed. Wilshere, xi; Nicholas Watson, "Middle English Versions and Audiences of Edmund of Abingdon's *Speculum religiosorum*," in *Texts and Traditions of Medieval Pastoral Care: Essays in Honour of Bella Millett*, ed. Kate Gunn and Catherine Innes-Parker, York Medieval Publications (Cambridge: Boydell and Brewer, 2009), 115–31, especially 122.

89. Reeves, "Teaching the Creed," 66, 67; see also Watson, "Versions and Audiences," 120–21. The renewed attention to the "literal sense" and to historical understanding of the Bible is a Victorine contribution to the spirituality of the twelfth and thirteenth centuries whose influence is felt in many of the texts under discussion here. See Beryl Smalley, *The Study of the Bible in the Middle Ages* (Notre Dame, Ind.: University of Notre Dame Press, 1978), 89, 196, 214.

90. *Mirour*, ed. Wilshere, 36, 13.8–10.

91. Ibid., 37, 13.11–16.

92. Edmund of Abingdon, *"Speculum religiosorum" and "Speculum ecclesie,"* ed. Helen P. Forshaw, Auctores Britannici Medii Aevi 3 (London: Oxford University Press for the British Academy, 1973), 62.

93. A similar attention to recognition characterizes one of the discussions in the *Lucidaires*. The master says, "just as the dove chooses the pure grains, so God chooses his elect, who are beneath all kinds of people and even thieves [*ses eslis qui sont desouz toutes manieres de gens et encore de larons*]; for he knows well who they are for whom he poured out his blood": Martha Kleinhans, *"Lucidaire vault tant a dire comme donnant lumiere": Untersuchung und Edition der Prosaversionen 2, 4 und 5 des "Elucidarium"* (Tübingen: Niemeyer, 1993), 480.

94. *Mirour*, ed. Wilshere, xv–xvi.

95. *Mirour*, ed. Wilshere, 53, 17.109–17.

CHAPTER 4

1. The most famous such echo appears in *Le Chevalier de la charrette* by Chrétien de Troyes, in which the nameless hero (later identified as Lancelot) enters an otherworld from which no one returns and proves to be a prophesied savior who is able to free its prisoners: *Le Chevalier de la charrette, ou Le Roman de Lancelot*, ed. Charles Mela (Paris: Librairie Générale Française, 1992), ll. 1882–936.

2. "Les fabliaux sont des contes à rire en vers" is Joseph Bédier's often-quoted definition of this notoriously slippery genre: *Les Fabliaux: Études de littérature populaire et d'histoire littéraire du moyen âge*, 2nd rev. ed. (Paris: Émile Bouillon, 1895), 30.

3. Keith Busby has argued persuasively for fabliau's "central position in the corpus of medieval French literature," a centrality that makes it unsurprising that the genre would take on pressing theological questions among the many others it addresses: *Codex and Context: Reading Old French Verse Narrative in Manuscript* (Amsterdam: Rodopi, 2002), 1:439 and the full discussion, 1:437–63. See also Barbara Newman, *Medieval Crossover: Reading the Secular Against the Sacred* (Philadelphia: University of Pennsylvania Press, 2013), 167–222, for further demonstration that "no person, text, or practice in medieval culture was deemed so holy as to lie beyond the bounds of parody" (174).

4. On the similarities between clerics (especially as preachers) and jongleurs, see Casagrande and Vecchio, "Clercs et jongleurs," 920. The authors characterize jongleurs as the "expression limite du monde profane" (917) but also as competitors with the clergy in a more direct sense—for patronage or alms—and as cautionary examples for clerics inclined to histrionic behavior (915, 916). On the overlapping associations between laity, illiteracy, and rusticity, see the Introduction.

5. Julia Kristeva, *Powers of Horror: An Essay on Abjection*, trans. Leon S. Rudiez (New York: Columbia University Press, 1982), 4. On status, see, e.g., D. E. Luscombe, "Conceptions of Hierarchy Before the Thirteenth Century," in *Soziale Ordnungen im Selbstverständnis des Mittelalters*, ed. Albert Zimmerman (Berlin: Walter de Gruyter, 1979), 1:1–19, and Giles Constable, "The Structure of Medieval Society According to the Dictatores of the Twelfth Century," in *Law, Church and Society: Essays in Honor of Stephan Kuttner*, ed. K. Pennington and R. Somerville (Philadelphia: University of Pennsylvania Press, 1977), 252–67.

6. Casagrande and Vecchio, "Clercs et jongleurs," 914. On views of jongleurs in the period, see also Edmond Faral, *Les Jongleurs en France au moyen âge* (Paris: Champion, 1910); John W. Baldwin, "The Image of the Jongleur in Northern France Around 1200," *Speculum* 72.3 (1997):

635–63; and most recently Silvère Menegaldo, *Le Jongleur dans la littérature narrative des XIIe et XIIIe siècles: Du personnage au masque* (Paris: Champion, 2005). Both Menegaldo and Baldwin nuance the clerical rejection of jongleurs, noting that they formed part of the great ecclesiastical households as well as secular ones.

7. Türk, *"Lucidaire de grant sapientie,"* 321, II.58.

8. *Aucassin et Nicolette: Chantefable du XIIIe siècle,* ed. Mario Roques (Paris: Champion, 1965), 6, VI.24–39.

9. Türk, *"Lucidaire de grant sapientie,"* 319, II.54.

10. Casagrande and Vecchio, "Clercs et jongleurs," 917.

11. Türk, *"Lucidaire de grant sapientie,"* 322, II.61. On the recognized importance of peasant labor, see Freedman, *Images of the Medieval Peasant,* 15–39.

12. Gravdal, *Vilain and Courtois,* 12.

13. Micheline de Combarieu du Grès, "Image et représentation du *vilain* dans les chansons de geste (et dans quelques autres textes médiévaux)," in *Exclus et systèmes d'exclusion dans la littérature et la civilisation médiévales* (Aix-en-Provence: Édition C.U.E.R.M.A., 1978), 7–26, at 15.

14. Ruth Mazo Karras, "Holy Harlots: Prostitute Saints in Medieval Legend," *Journal of the History of Sexuality* 1.1 (1990): 3–32, at 4. Duncan Robertson discusses the "revolutionary reversal" that the salvation of such figures represents: *The Medieval Saints' Lives: Spiritual Renewal and Old French Literature* (Lexington, Ky.: French Forum, 1995), 95.

15. Karras notes the prostitute's responsibility for her customers' sins: "Holy Harlots," 11–12. Brunetto Latini defines jongleurs through their association with excess: "celui ki se desmesure est apelés jougleour et menestrier" (quoted in Willem Noomen, ed., *Le Jongleur par lui-même: Choix de dits et de fabliaux* [Louvain: Peeters, 2003], 5).

16. Casagrande and Vecchio, "Clercs et jongleurs," 914.

17. Quoted in Karras, "Holy Harlots," 22; she emphasizes the importance of commonness and "indiscriminate sexuality" in the medieval depictions of these saints throughout (5; see also 10, 25).

18. See Latham, *Revised Medieval Latin Word-List,* entry "villa" (512–13).

19. Le Goff, *Birth of Purgatory,* 233. See also Gravdal's remark that "[i]n twelfth- and thirteenth-century French literature, one of the chief preoccupations of written texts is the coding and interpretation of the social order" (*Vilain and Courtois,* 1–2), as well as the remarks on categorization and its discontents throughout her introduction (1–19).

20. Le Goff, *Birth of Purgatory,* 7. See also his "Trades and Professions as Represented in Medieval Confessors' Manuals," in *Time, Work, and Culture in the Middle Ages,* trans. Arthur Goldhammer (Chicago: University of Chicago Press, 1980), 107–21, especially 115–17.

21. Compare also the discussion of the fabliaux' original audiences, particularly Jean Rychner, *Contribution à l'étude des fabliaux,* 2 vols. (Geneva: Droz, 1960), and "Les Fabliaux: Genre, styles, publics," in *La Littérature narrative d'imagination: Des genres littéraires aux techniques d'expression* (Paris: Presses Universitaires de France, 1961), 41–52.

22. The first title appears in Bern, Burgerbibliothek, MS 354 (ff. 42^r–43^r), the second in Nottingham, University Library, MS Middleton L.M.6 (ff. 349^v–350^r). The latter, formerly neglected, has now been edited several times; see Richard Straub, *"Des Putains et des lecheors*: La version oubliée du manuscrit G," *Vox romanica* 52 (1993): 164–79; Philippe Ménard, "Une nouvelle version du dit *Des Putains et des lecheors,"* *Zeitschrift für romanische Philologie* 113 (1997): 30–38, and Noomen, *Jongleur par lui-même,* 188–92, which I use here. While "lecheors" can be an insult of wide-ranging meaning, a designation of jongleurs as "lechierres" is not uncommon (see Noomen, *Jongleur par lui-même,* 5–6; but also Ménard, "Nouvelle version," 38n64).

23. The *Bible* of Hugues de Berzé similarly locates the three orders at a crucial moment in sacred history. Having given a brief account of the Passion and Resurrection, Hugues writes, "Quant il nous ot d'enfer rescous, / S'ordena trois ordres de nous," these being the familiar "provoires," "chevaliers," and "laboreours." Hugues de Berzé, *La "Bible" au seigneur de Berzé*, ed. Félix Lecoy (Paris: Droz, 1938), ll. 179–80.

24. *Des Putains et des lecheors*, in Noomen, *Jongleur par lui-même*, 190, ll. 31–33.

25. Daron Burrows, ed. and trans., *Two Old French Satires on the Power of the Keys: "L'Escommeniement au lecheor" and "Le Pardon de foutre"* (London: Modern Humanities Research Association and Maney Publishing, 2005), 19.

26. On the expansion of "those who work," see Le Goff, "Trades and Professions," and Maria Corti, "Structures idéologiques et structures sémiotiques dans les *sermones ad status* du XIIIe siècle," in *Archéologie du signe*, ed. Lucie Brind'Amour and Eugene Vance (Toronto: Pontifical Institute of Mediaeval Studies, 1982), 145–63.

27. Simon Gaunt, *Gender and Genre in Medieval French Literature* (Cambridge: Cambridge University Press, 1995), 238.

28. On jongleurs as a group "bien ancrée dans la société médiévale," see Noomen, *Jongleur par lui-même*, 6, and Baldwin, "Image of the Jongleur"; on prostitution in medieval France and Languedoc, see Jacques Rossiaud, *Medieval Prostitution*, trans. Lydia G. Cochrane (New York: Blackwell, 1988), and Leah Lydia Otis, *Prostitution in Medieval Society: The History of an Urban Institution in Languedoc* (Chicago: University of Chicago Press, 1985), especially 15–24 on the "acceptance" of prostitution in the twelfth and thirteenth centuries. Jacques Le Goff remarks, however, that while the list of " 'impure' or 'dishonest' trades . . . began to shrink in the thirteenth century," certain categories still earned "[o]pprobrium and exclusion," including jongleurs, prostitutes, and usurers: Le Goff, "Introduction: Medieval Man," in *Medieval Callings*, ed. Jacques Le Goff, trans. Lydia G. Cochrane (Chicago: University of Chicago Press, 1987), 25.

29. The clerks are "large et obedient, / As putains l'uevre le tesmogne": Noomen, *Jongleur par lui-même*, 192, ll. 76–77.

30. Busby, *Codex and Context*, 1:452.

31. See Wagih Azzam, "Un recueil dans le recueil: Rutebeuf dans le manuscrit BnF f. fr. 837," in *Mouvances et jointures: Du manuscrit au texte médiéval*, ed. Milena Mikhaïlova (Orléans: Paradigme, 2005), 193–201.

32. Richard Trachsler, "Uncourtly Texts in Courtly Books: Musings on MS Chantilly, Musée Condé 475," in *Courtly Arts and the Art of Courtliness*, ed. Keith Busby and Christopher Kleinhenz (Cambridge: D. S. Brewer, 2006), 679–92, at 689–90.

33. The quotation is from Busby, *Codex and Context*, 1:464; on hagiography and fabliau, see also Pamela Gehrke, *Saints and Scribes: Medieval Hagiography in Its Manuscript Context*, Modern Philology vol. 126 (Berkeley: University of California Press, 1993), 6.

34. Busby speaks of fabliaux' "function as the wider intertext of Old French literature" (*Codex and Context*, 1:463); see also Gaunt, *Gender and Genre*, 235, on the "dialectic" the fabliaux create with other genres.

35. J. Morawski, "Mélanges de littérature pieuse: Les miracles de Notre-Dame en vers français," *Romania* 61 (1935): 145–209, notes a related but inverse phenomenon, Marian miracles' borrowings from the fabliaux, and points to the religious figures and themes of *Vilain qui conquist paradis* and *S. Pierre et le jongleur*. See also Brian J. Levy, "*Or escoutez une merveille!* Parallel Paths: Gautier de Coinci and the Fabliaux," in *Gautier de Coinci*, ed. Krause and Stones, 331–43.

36. Gaunt, *Gender and Genre*, 233, 235.

37. Noomen, *Jongleur par lui-même*, 1. For the texts of these tales, see Rutebeuf, *Oeuvres complètes*, ed. and trans. Michel Zink (Paris: Classiques Garnier, 2005).

38. On Bodel, author of the *Jeu de saint Nicholas* as well as a number of early fabliaux, see Symes, *A Common Stage*, 37–43.

39. See Busby, *Codex and Context*, 1:444; Thomas Frederick Crane, *The Exempla or Illustrative Stories from the Sermones Vulgares of Jacques de Vitry* (1890; reprint, New York: Burt Franklin, 1971), 81–82.

40. Peter F. Dembowski, *La Vie de sainte Marie l'Égyptienne: Versions en ancien et en moyen français* (Geneva: Droz, 1977), collects all the Old and Middle French versions except for that of Rutebeuf and a version that appears in *Renart le contrefait*; he discusses the legend's origins and its dissemination in French (13–24).

41. Rutebeuf, *Vie de sainte Marie l'Egypcienne*, in *Oeuvres complètes*, ed. Zink, 456, ll. 1–9. Further citations are given parenthetically in the text. Rutebeuf's enthusiasm for *annominatio* is often linked to that of Gautier de Coinci in his *Miracles de Nostre Dame*; see Chapter 5. Gautier de Coinci, *Les Miracles de Nostre Dame*, ed. V. Frédéric Koenig, 4 vols., Textes littéraires français 64, 95, 131, 176 (Geneva: Droz, 1955–70).

42. Suzanne Nash, "Rutebeuf's Contribution to the Saint Mary the Egyptian Legend," *French Review* 44.4 (1971): 695–705, suggests that the "good workers" in question are also all sinners (since she sees this couplet as a "reassuring reminder of God's mercy," 699); see also Karl D. Uitti, "The Clerkly Narrator Figure in Old French Hagiography and Romance," *Medioevo romanzo* 2.3 (1975): 394–408, at 403–8.

43. Although the Old French spelling is unusual, I follow here Michel Zink's translation of "bone" as "borne," meaning "boundary, limit": Rutebeuf, *Vie de sainte Marie*, in *Oeuvres complètes*, ed. Zink, 459, l. 48.

44. See, e.g., ll. 269–72, 293–94, 404, 1052, 1068 for "He who rescued us from Hell" and ll. 224–28, 346–48, 1073–76 on the Last Judgment.

45. Nash, "Rutebeuf's Contribution," 697, 700. The echoes of the Creed come in Mary's address to the Virgin (Rutebeuf, *Vie de sainte Marie*, in *Oeuvres complètes*, ed. Zink, 470, ll. 261–71) and in one of Zozimas's responses to Mary (514–16, ll. 1052–76), which refers to Christ as, among other things, "cil . . . qui d'enfer brisa la porte" (ll. 1067–68), recalling the *Descensus ad inferos*.

46. Dembowski, *Marie l'Égyptienne*, 58, ll. 1183–88.

47. Nash, "Rutebeuf's Contribution," 701.

48. Menegaldo, *Jongleur dans la littérature narrative*, 449. See also L. Karl, "La Légende de l'ermite et le jongleur," *Revue des langues romanes* 63 (1925): 111–41, and Brian J. Levy, "L'Ironie des métiers, ou le récit chiasmatique: À propos du conte pieux *De l'Ermite et du jongleur*," *Reinardus* 5 (1992): 85–107.

49. *MP* EETS, 69–71, ll. 2421–94, *MP* Roxburghe, 62–65, ll. 2395–2468. A German tradition in which, similarly, "the master/teacher or confessor enters into dialogue with an unlearned laywoman and eventually becomes her disciple" (and which invokes Mary of Egypt) is explored in Poor, "Women Teaching Men," 345.

50. Nash, "Rutebeuf's Contribution," 700.

51. Hilding Kjellman, ed., *La Deuxième collection anglo-normande des miracles de la Sainte Vierge et son original latin* (Paris: Champion; Uppsala: Akademiska Bokhandeln, 1922), 57, ll. 294–99. The Latin says simply that Zozimas "audivit . . . divinae scripturae, cum illiterata esset, noticiam" (49).

52. Rutebeuf, *Le Pet au vilain*, in *Oeuvres complètes*, ed. Zink, 64–69, ll. 8–11. Further

citations are given parenthetically in the text. Compare the mocking *vilain-clerc* hostility depicted in *Les .xxiij. manieres de vilains*: Edmond Faral, ed., "*Des Vilains* ou *Des .xxii. manieries* [sic] *de vilains*," *Romania* 48.2 (1922): 243–64.

53. Scripture was often, indeed, used specifically to designate true speech as against "fable"; see the examples cited in *The Songe d'Enfer of Raoul de Houdenc*, ed. Madeline Timmel Mihm (Tübingen: Niemeyer, 1984), 12, all deriving from early thirteenth-century French verse narratives. A bogus appeal to Scripture to support the truth of a fabliau could thus be seen as a kind of in-joke.

54. On the interplay between learning and social status, see Imbach, *Laien in der Philosophie des Mittelalters*, 22–23. Julia Kristeva notes, in another context, the conjunction of scatology and eschatology: "These bodily fluids, this defilement, this shit are what life withstands, hardly and with difficulty, on the part of death. There, I am at the border of my condition as a living being" (*Powers of Horror*, 3, quoted in Gravdal, *Vilain and Courtois*, 77). Gravdal sees this as an expression of a "specifically modern perspective," but the recurrence of farting in medieval accounts of the moment of death suggests that for premodern people, too, the "border" of one's "condition as a living being" could be expressed in terms both scatological and eschatological.

55. Geoffrey Chaucer, *Canterbury Tales*, in *The Riverside Chaucer*, gen. ed. Larry D. Benson (Boston: Houghton Mifflin, 1987), III.2290–92. On the "cherl" emphasis in the tale, see Linda Georgianna, "Lords, Churls, and Friars: The Return to Social Order in the *Summoner's Tale*," in *Rebels and Rivals: The Contestive Spirit in "The Canterbury Tales,"* ed. Susanna Greer Fein, David Raybin, and Peter C. Braeger (Kalamazoo: Western Michigan University, Medieval Institute Publications, 1991), 149–72.

56. The motif of the "mistaken" entrant to Hell appears also in some otherworld vision narratives, where, however, both the intended prey and the one who ends up in Hell are people. See Owen, *Vision of Hell*, 12, 13.

57. On the significance and origins of Cocuce, see Rosanna Brusegan, "Cocuce: La troisième voie de Rutebeuf dans *Le Pet au vilain*," in *Plaist vos oïr bone cançon vallant? Mélanges offerts à François Suard*, ed. Dominique Boutet, Marie-Madeleine Castellani, Françoise Ferrand, and Aimé Petit (Villeneuve d'Ascq: Université Charles-de-Gaulle–Lille 3, 1999), 133–40. Gravdal characterizes Cocuce as a "scatological purgatory" that, despite its "low" qualities, was clearly designed for, and appreciated by, a "middling" audience, neither religious nor peasant (*Vilain and Courtois*, 75, 74–80).

58. The quoted phrases are from Gravdal, *Vilain and Courtois*, 68, 6. On the cleft stick in which Rutebeuf's joke leaves scholars, see Gaunt, *Gender and Genre*, 239.

59. Brusegan, "Cocuce," 135, 136.

60. Text in Noomen, *Jongleur par lui-même*, 154–84.

61. Nicholas Watson, "Visions of Inclusion: Universal Salvation and Vernacular Theology in Pre-Reformation England," *Journal of Medieval and Early Modern Studies* 27 (1997): 145–87, notes the potential of the Harrowing of Hell to imply universal salvation: Christ's victory over death can only be fully expressed "by depriving Satan of all souls" (149), as also happens in this fabliau.

62. The tale's own interest in clothing, and the broader, self-reflexive use of clothing in fabliaux more generally, as demonstrated by Howard Bloch, makes this possible reference more likely; see R. Howard Bloch, *The Scandal of the Fabliaux* (Chicago: University of Chicago Press, 1986), 22–58.

63. Casagrande and Vecchio, "Clercs et jongleurs," 913. The *Escommeniement au lecheor* declaims, "J'escommeni jeu de hasart, / Car il est tant de male part, / Qu'il nos essile toz e art"

(Burrows, ed. and trans., *Two Old French Satires*, 64, ll. 156–58)—quite the reverse of what happens in *S. Pierre et le jongleur*, of course, where dicing saves one from the flames rather than exiling one to them.

64. *Ci nous dit*, ed. Blangez, 1:81–82, ll. 1653–56, emphasis added. André de Coutances, in his versified *Évangile de Nicodème*, has Christ refer to the Harrowing as having "gaaigné" souls; a poem found in Lambeth Palace Library, MS 522 goes a step further, casting him as a thief—though one who only steals what is already his: "Mun cors fu en terre mis, / Ma alme descendi a mes amis / Deske en enfern ke dunc robay / Kant tuz les miens hors menay" (f. 82ᵛ).

65. Quotations are from Marie de France, *L'Espurgatoire seint Patriz*, ed. and trans. Yolande de Pontfarcy (Louvain and Paris: Peeters, 1995), 82, ll. 93–96, 99–100; I have modified the punctuation.

66. I use here Willem Noomen and Nico van den Boogard, eds., *Nouveau recueil complet des fabliaux* [*NRCF*] (Assen: Van Gorcum, 1983–98), vol. 5, which includes diplomatic transcriptions of all five manuscript versions, as well as an edited version. I draw on both the critical edition and the five manuscript versions, MSS A, B, C, D, and G, since it is the totality of manuscript versions that conveys the kinds of images and lessons this story might present, even if no given version, of course, contained them all. Quotations without manuscript siglum are from the critical text; the phrases quoted are from ll. 2, 1 (*NRCF*, 5:34).

67. See the diplomatic texts, *NRCF*, 5:12–13; the line in question is A31, B33, C35, D33, G33. The editors note Picard or Walloon features of some MSS and Burgundian aspects of another; concerning a similarly variable line (invoking either St. Alain, St. Germain, or St. Guilain) they observe, "la variation dans les noms des saints invoqués au vers A25/BGD27/C29 . . . suggère que le fabliau a beaucoup voyagé" (*NRCF*, 5:5).

68. Compare here the exemplum of the lawyer debating on his deathbed whether he should receive communion and dying in a state of mortal sin before he can decide (*judicare*)—an implicit critique of worldly learning, like the story of the student returned from Hell discussed in Chapter 2. See Crane, *Exempla*, 15.

69. Peter, Thomas, and Paul are standard members of the category of sinner-saints; see Dorn, *Der sündige Heilige*.

70. All the manuscripts have the initial question, "qui vos conduist?" but only MS G includes the (repetitive) remark about peasants' unwelcomeness in Heaven.

71. Mary Douglas, *Purity and Danger: An Analysis of the Concepts of Pollution and Taboo* (London: Routledge, 1966), 36; see also her point that "dirt is essentially disorder" (2). Michel Zink observes that fabliaux, which are in many respects an inherently disorderly genre, are found all over the place—in collections of fables, exempla repositories, etc. This suggests a different way of thinking about their generic "place": lacking a place of their own, they can migrate into other realms, like the peasants cast out of both Heaven and Hell in *Le Pet au vilain*. Michel Zink, *Medieval French Literature: An Introduction*, trans. Jeff Rider, Medieval and Renaissance Texts and Studies vol. 110 (Binghamton, N.Y.: Center for Medieval and Early Renaissance Studies, SUNY-Binghamton, 1995), 84.

72. This is the reading in A80, C92, D88; MSS B and G, and the critical text (which tends to follow G), have *recorder* instead of *raconter*.

73. Powell, "Translating Scripture," 96.

74. Ibid., 96. For the moment of David's entry, see Jenkins, *Eructavit*, ll. 291–302. For another instructive encounter at a gate, see Poor, "Women Teaching Men," 344–45.

75. This passage from the Gospel of Matthew is discussed in Chapter 2. Noomen and van

den Boogard date *Le Vilain qui conquist* to the first half of the thirteenth century based on its rigorous observation of declensions (*NRCF*, 5:5).

76. In another romance echo, the Middle English *Sir Orfeo* has the title character make a similar argument to the Fairy King who has stolen his wife, saying that though Orfeo and Heurodis may be an ill-matched couple, "Yete were it a wele fouler thing / To here a lesing of thi mouthe: / So, Sir, as ye seyd nouthe / What ich wold aski haue y schold, / & nedes thou most thi word hold"; Orfeo has entered the fairy kingdom and gained this promise in the guise of a harper—that is, in effect, of a jongleur (A. J. Bliss, ed., *Sir Orfeo* [Oxford: Oxford University Press, 1966], Auchinleck text ll. 464–68; I have slightly modified the spelling). See also the references to "le roi qui ne mente" in the Marian miracles discussed in the following chapter.

77. The Vulgate reads, "qui vicerit faciam illum columnam in templo Dei mei et foras non egredietur amplius." Noomen and van den Boogard suggest as a parallel John 10:28, "And I give them life everlasting; and they shall not perish for ever, and no man shall pluck them out of my hand" (*NRCF*, 5:381).

78. The early thirteenth century saw the rise of more than one heresy (most notably the Waldenses) whose characteristic problematics included a desire to read Scripture in the vernacular. See Peter Biller and Anne Hudson, eds., *Heresy and Literacy, 1000–1530* (Cambridge: Cambridge University Press, 1994), especially the essays by Moore, Gurevich, Patschovsky, and Brenon. Margriet Hoogvliet argues, however, that modern scholars may have overstated the "severe tensions" surrounding the idea of the laity reading vernacular Bibles by ignoring contrary evidence: "Encouraging Lay People to Read the Bible in the French Vernaculars," 254.

79. Elizabeth Kinne, "Rhetorical Reasoning, Authority, and the Impossible Interlocutor in *Le Vilain qui conquist paradis par plait*," in *The Old French Fabliaux: Essays on Comedy and Context*, ed. Kristin L. Burr, John F. Moran, and Norris J. Lacy (Jefferson, N.C.: McFarland, 2007), 55–68, points out the echoes of scholastic disputation as well as legal language in the text. The range of terms related to speech in this section of the fabliau is dazzling; there is a great deal of overlap among the versions, but between them they make use, in the course of roughly thirty-five lines, of *laidengier, blastengier, avillie[r], ranpote[r], mesaasme[r], jugement, renier, confesser, sermoner, pardoner, contredit, desdire, parole, otroier, mentir, desresnier,* and *pledier.*

80. Nancy Freeman Regalado, *Poetic Patterns in Rutebeuf: A Study in Noncourtly Poetic Modes of the Thirteenth Century* (New Haven, Conn.: Yale University Press, 1970), 253.

81. There is also a unique Anglo-French version of this text in Oxford Digby 86; see *Facsimile of Oxford, Bodleian Library, MS Digby 86*, introd. Judith Tschann and M. B. Parkes (Oxford: Oxford University Press for the EETS, 1996), ff. 143^r–149^v. A similar work, "Li Respit del curteis e del vilain," casts the *vilain*'s proverbs as part of a back-and-forth between interlocutors reminiscent of *Salomon and Marcoul*; on the latter text's faceoff between "peasant cleverness" and "medieval learned culture," see Bradbury, "Rival Wisdom," 340.

82. As Sarah Westphal notes, "the vast majority of [medieval] manuscripts have a miscellaneous character that defies the concept of genre as a principle of identity and separation," much as the peasant soul defies the attempts at classification proposed by his interlocutors: *Textual Poetics of German Manuscripts, 1300–1500* (Columbia, S.C.: Camden House, 1993), 9.

83. All five manuscripts end with a version of the final couplet; MSS B, C, and G also contain the preceding one. MS A makes "Tort va avant" the proverb that the *vilain* speaks, while D has, before the final couplet, "Engiens a fauxee droiture / Fauxers a veincue nature" (ll. 157–58). Noomen and van den Boogard wrestle with this pile-up of proverbs (*NRCF*, 5:382–83), and I draw on their tentative translation here.

84. On the complex evolution of Latin *ingenium* to Old French *engin*, and their range of meanings, see Robert Hanning, *The Individual in Twelfth-Century Romance* (New Haven, Conn.: Yale University Press, 1977), 105–38, and Alcuin Blamires, "Women and Creative Intelligence in Medieval Thought," in *Voices in Dialogue: Reading Women in the Middle Ages*, ed. Linda Olson and Kathryn Kerby-Fulton (Notre Dame, Ind.: University of Notre Dame Press, 2005), 213–30.

85. Pierre d'Abernon, *Lumere*, 2:109, ll. 10833–38.

86. See Christopher Young's apt remarks about the consistent failure of morals in German *maere*: "At the End of the Tale: Didacticism, Ideology and the Medieval German *Maere*," in *Mittelhochdeutsche Novellistik im europäischen Kontext. Beiheft zur Zeitschrift für deutsche Philologie*, ed. Mark Chinca, Timo Reuvekamp-Felber, and Christopher Young (Berlin: Erich Schmidt Verlag, 2006), 24–47.

CHAPTER 5

1. On Marian miracles' instructive aims, see, for example, Pierre Kunstmann, "Le Clerc de Notre-Dame: La littérature de miracle en langue vulgaire, traduction et création," in *The Church and Vernacular Literature in Medieval France*, ed. Dorothea Kullmann (Toronto: Pontifical Institute of Mediaeval Studies, 2009), 124–36; Michelle Bolduc, "Gautier de Coinci and the Translation of Exegesis," *Neophilologus* 93 (2009): 377–92. On the tendency to emphasize the "popular" nature of Marian literature, see Adrienne Williams Boyarin, *Miracles of the Virgin in Medieval England: Law and Jewishness in Marian Legends* (Cambridge: D. S. Brewer, 2010), 7.

2. On Books of Hours, see E. S. Dewick, ed., *Facsimiles of Horae de Beata Maria Virgine from English Manuscripts of the Eleventh Century* (London: Henry Bradshaw Society, 1902), and Claire Donovan, "The Mise-en-Page of Early Books of Hours in England," in *Medieval Book Production: Assessing the Evidence*, ed. Linda L. Brownrigg (Los Altos, Calif.: Anderson-Lovelace, 1990), 147–61. Donovan notes the rise of "personal religious books" in the thirteenth century as one aspect of the "developing importance of the laity in the Church" (151), though "abbreviated psalters arranged for private use had become a staple in both monastic and lay devotions" well before this, with examples stretching back at least to Charlemagne's time, as Rachel Fulton notes: *From Judgment to Passion: Devotion to Christ and the Virgin Mary, 800–1200* (New York: Columbia University Press, 2002), 148.

3. Sherry Reames, "Mary, Sanctity, and Prayers to Saints: Chaucer and Late-Medieval Piety," in *Chaucer and Religion*, ed. Helen Phillips (Cambridge: D. S. Brewer, 2010), 81–96, at 96.

4. As Rachel Fulton points out, "There was nothing obvious, or banal, for Honorius [Augustodunensis] and his contemporaries about Mary's role in the Incarnation. Rather, it was a living (and quite sore) point of theological and devotional debate," particularly with contemporary Jews (*From Judgment to Passion*, 284). The Marian miracles, though not directly engaged in such debates, retain the trace of them in their insistence on "champion[ing] the idea that God might deign to become human, and to do so—literally—*through* a woman" (284).

5. On the genre's early history, see R. W. Southern, "The English Origins of 'Miracles of the Virgin,'" *Medieval and Renaissance Studies* 4 (1958): 176–216, and the helpful brief account in Boyarin, *Miracles of the Virgin*, 1–7.

6. The breadth, depth, and historical extent of Marian devotion are hard to overstate, though of course it is a tradition with great internal variation. For an introduction, see (in addition to Fulton, *From Judgment to Passion*) Jaroslav Pelikan, *Mary Through the Centuries: Her Place in the History of Culture* (New Haven, Conn.: Yale University Press, 1998); Hilda Graef, *Mary: A*

History of Doctrine and Devotion, 2 vols. (London: Sheed and Ward, 1963); Miri Rubin, *Emotion and Devotion: The Meaning of Mary in Medieval Religious Cultures* (Budapest: Central European University Press, 2009) and her *Mother of God*.

7. On the dating of Gautier's work, see Gautier de Coinci, *Les Miracles de Nostre Dame*, 1:xxv–xxx. For a full list of manuscripts that builds on the work of Arlette P. Ducrot-Granderye, see Kathryn A. Duys, assisted by Kathy M. Krause and Alison Stones, "Gautier de Coinci's *Miracles de Nostre Dame*: Manuscript List," in *Gautier de Coinci*, ed. Krause and Stones, 345–66. They note, "A complete database of Gautier manuscripts is in preparation" (358n9).

8. Bolduc, "Gautier de Coinci," 390–91; Olivier Collet, "L'Œuvre en contexte: La place de Gautier de Coinci dans les recueils cycliques des *Miracles de Nostre Dame*," in *Gautier de Coinci*, ed. Krause and Stones, 26.

9. Adrian P. Tudor, *Tales of Vice and Virtue: The First Old French "Vie des Pères"* (Amsterdam: Rodopi, 2005), 15; he discusses most of the manuscript conjunctions in "Telling the Same Tale? Gautier de Coinci's *Miracles de Nostre Dame* and the First *Vie des Pères*," in *Gautier de Coinci*, ed. Krause and Stones, 305–6. A few more instances appear in Duys, "Manuscript List."

10. Collet identifies the manuscripts containing the works of the Renclus as Paris, Bibliothèque de l'Arsénal, 3517–18 and 3527 and Paris, BnF, fr. 23111 ("Œuvre en contexte," 24).

11. For a brief account of the two Anglo-French collections, see Dean and Boulton, *Anglo-Norman Literature*, items 558 and 559; a fuller account is available in Adgar, *Le Gracial*, ed. Pierre Kunstmann (Ottawa: Éditions de l'Université d'Ottawa, 1982), *Adgar's Marienlegenden nach der Londoner Handschrift Egerton 612* (Heilbronn: Gebr. Henninger, 1886), and Kjellmann, *Deuxième collection anglo-normande des miracles*.

12. This quotation, which appears on f. 131, is part of a text unique to this MS on the beginning and end of the world; see Dean and Boulton, *Anglo-Norman Literature*, item 606. The description of the *Dialogue* is from Dean and Boulton's entry on that text, item 628.

13. The *Chasteau d'amour* often accompanies works like the *Manuel des pechiez* (e.g., British Library, Harley MS 3860, Princeton University Library, Taylor MS 1) or the *Mirour de seinte eglyse* (e.g., Cambridge, Fitzwilliam Museum, McClean MS 123 [the Nuneaton Book] or British Library, Harley MS 1121, where a brief Anglo-French *Life of the Virgin* is sandwiched between the *Mirour* and the *Chasteau*). Lambeth Palace Library, MS 522 opens with the *Chasteau*, followed by the *Mirour*, and a few folios later by a verse *Évangile de Nicodème* (Dean and Boulton, *Anglo-Norman Literature*, item 501); the lengthy remainder of the manuscript contains more than twenty Marian prayers and petitions (see Dean and Boulton, *Anglo-Norman Literature*, items 740, 752, 760, 772–73, etc.—some of them repeated within the manuscript itself). See the discussion in Barratt, "Spiritual Writings and Religious Instruction," 351.

14. See Chapter 3 on the *Descensus ad inferos* section of the Creed, which similarly became a more established part of Church doctrine in this period. Although I will refer to it as such for the sake of simplicity, the Ave Maria is in this period not strictly a prayer, hence its designation as "salutatio" (in Latin) or "salu" (in French): it draws on the greetings of Gabriel and Elizabeth to Mary but does not, as a prayer would, request anything of her. The concluding section, "ora pro nobis peccatoribus nunc et in hora mortis" (pray for us sinners now and in the hour of our death), is certainly consonant with the Marian miracles' frequent focus on the point of death but only later became part of a formal prayer promulgated by the Church.

15. "Exhortentur populum semper presbyteri ad dicendam dominicam orationem et 'Credo in Deum' et 'Salutationem Beate Virginis'": Pontal, *Les Statuts synodaux français du XIIIe siècle*, 74, c. 62; quoted in Longère, "Enseignement du 'Credo,'" 316n24. The Paris statutes are at least partly the work of Eudes de Sully, bishop of Paris, 1196–1208 (the successor of Maurice de

Sully, though they do not seem to have been closely related); they also include an injunction on the proper performance of the Hours of the Virgin (Pontal, *Statuts synodaux*, 60, c. 25).

16. For Poore's instruction, see *Councils and Synods, with Other Documents Relating to the English Church, II: A.D. 1205–1313. Part I: 1205–1265*, ed. F. M. Powicke and C. R. Cheney (Oxford: Clarendon Press, 1964), 61, ch. 5; the quotation is from Haines, "Education in English Ecclesiastical Legislation," 172.

17. Paris, BnF fr. 1807, f. 142ʳ.

18. Haines, "Education in English Ecclesiastical Legislation," 172.

19. "Unde et triplicem hic licet considerare gradum; incipientium, proficientium, perfectorum. Initium enim sapientiae, timor Domini (Eccli. I, 16); medium, spes; charitas, plenitudo" (Bernard of Clairvaux, *In festo S. Andreae sermo I*, PL 183:503D–509A, at col. 506C–D); I owe the reference to Constable, *Three Studies*, 354.

20. Pelikan, *Mary Through the Centuries*, 129–30.

21. As Adrienne Williams Boyarin notes, "exemplary literature . . . is as sensitive and susceptible to its contexts as it is obstinately present and predictable. The status of Miracles of the Virgin as exemplary means not banality and repetition but rather mutability and flexibility that can absorb and expose shifting social and religious contexts" (*Miracles of the Virgin*, 11).

22. One image from the de Brailes Hours is reproduced in Donovan, "Mise-en-Page of Early Books of Hours," 148, fig. 1; all three can now be seen on the British Library website, http://www.bl.uk/manuscripts/FullDisplay.aspx?ref=Add_MS_49999, where they appear on ff. 44ᵛ, 45ᵛ, and 46ᵛ. Each is accompanied by a small notation in French at the bottom of the page briefly indicating the context. On the kind of reading that such inset images might promote, see Sylvia Huot, "Polytextual Reading: The Meditative Reading of Real and Metaphorical Books," in *Orality and Literacy in the Middle Ages: Essays on a Conjunction and Its Consequences in Honour of D. H. Green*, ed. Mark Chinca and Christopher Young (Turnhout: Brepols, 2005), 201–22.

23. Rubin, *Mother of God*, 233; on hope and fear, see, for example, Thomas of Chobham, in Chapter 2, and the discussion of Pierre d'Abernon's *Lumere* below.

24. Gautier de Coinci, *Miracles de Nostre Dame*, ed. Koenig, 3:24, I Mir 32 ll. 34–44.

25. Justice, "Did the Middle Ages Believe in Their Miracles?" 10.

26. Fulton, *From Judgment to Passion*, 3.

27. Daniel E. O'Sullivan, *Marian Devotion in Thirteenth-Century French Lyric* (Toronto: University of Toronto Press, 2005), 11.

28. Quoted in Pelikan, *Mary Through the Centuries*, 131.

29. Kjellman, *La Deuxième collection anglo-normande des miracles*, 6, ll. 65–76.

30. This human connection—which Gautier emphasizes more than once by using "humain" as an approving adjective (humane, kind)—is a slightly different one than the question of Mary's exemplarity for women discussed by Marina Warner, *Alone of All Her Sex: The Myth and Cult of the Virgin Mary* (New York: Vintage, 1983). If as a woman Mary redeems the female sex while arguably making it harder to admire any other woman, as mother of God and his link to humanness she is genuinely *like* those she helps.

31. The introduction to this miracle stresses the use of reason and the need to learn from the story, calling it "doctrinable" (strophe 238, l. 11). *"Romans de Carité,"* ed. van Hamel.

32. An earlier Anglo-French collection also presents Mary the Egyptian's life as part of a collection of Marian miracles, an association that presumably relies on the penitent's prayers to Mary from the earliest legends. See Dembowski, *Marie l'Égyptienne*, 18, 14. For Gautier's miracle of the incestuous mother, see *Miracles de Nostre Dame*, ed. Koenig, vol. 2, I Mir 18, ll. 463–75.

33. Pierre d'Abernon, *Lumere*, 1:186, ll. 6130–42. He is translating Bernard's *Sermo XXII in*

Cantica Canticorum, "De quatuor unguentis sponsi," PL 183:878A–884A, at col. 881C. The image of Christ praying with tears in his eyes is Pierre's addition.

34. Pierre d'Abernon, *Lumere*, 1:187.

35. Evelyn Faye Wilson, *The "Stella maris" of John of Garland, Edited, Together with a Study of Certain Collections of Mary Legends Made in Northern France in the Twelfth and Thirteenth Centuries* (Cambridge, Mass.: Wellesley College and the Mediaeval Academy of America, 1946), 16, 20; she quotes BnF fonds latin 12593, ff. 118–19: "diversis temporibus, diversis locis, et diversis personis utriusque sexus, diverse etatis, diverse conditionis et ordinis . . . que in sanctorum libris vel quoruncumque fidelium litteris dispersa reperimus."

36. These are miracles 19–28 in Kjellman, *Deuxième collection anglo-normande des miracles.*

37. This might be said to some degree of many "universal" saints, but the sheer number of works devoted to Mary and their internal extent and variety make it more emphatically and visibly part of her appeal. Other saints are patrons of particular subgroups of society; only Mary is mother of all.

38. Such expansion is most visible in Gautier's *Miracles de Nostre Dame*, but the demands of rhyme and the affective touches supplied by the compiler of the Anglo-French collection mean that in most cases his miracles are somewhat longer than their Latin counterparts.

39. Gérard Gros, " 'Por ses myracles biau rimer . . .': Étude sur le projet hagiographique de Gautier de Coinci," *Revue des sciences humaines* 251 (July–September 1998): 73–87, at 78–81; for the reference to "especïaus amies" (specifically, two countesses), see Gautier de Coinci, *Miracles de Nostre Dame*, ed. Koenig, 4:436, Epilogue l. 128.

40. On *annominatio*, see particularly Tony Hunt, *Miraculous Rhymes: The Writing of Gautier de Coinci* (Cambridge: D. S. Brewer, 2007), 37–47, 123–60.

41. For the sake of brevity, I use Koenig's numerical designations in the text, giving titles in footnotes. This is "De un Provoire qui toz jors chantoit *Salve*, la messe de Nostre Dame," in Gautier de Coinci, *Miracles de Nostre Dame*, ed. Koenig, 2:105–8. The phrase "ne savoir longue ne brief" is glossed by Olivier Collet, *Glossaire et index critiques des oeuvres d'attribution certaine de Gautier de Coinci (Vie de sainte Cristine et Miracles de Nostre Dame)* (Geneva: Librairie Droz, 2000), as "ne rien savoir, être ignare" (442); he links it with "ne savoir bu ne ba," which appears in the miracle of the peasant who tried to learn the Ave Maria (II Mir 20) discussed below.

42. "De l'Orison Nostre Dame," in Gautier de Coinci, *Miracles de Nostre Dame*, ed. Koenig, 3:107–20.

43. The prayer in question is "O beata et intemerata," a twelfth-century prayer associated in the manuscripts with Anselm of Canterbury; see Laurel Broughton, "The Rose, the Blessed Virgin Undefiled: Incarnational Piety in Gautier's *Miracles de Nostre Dame*," in *Gautier de Coinci*, ed. Krause and Stones, 281–99, at 296, and, on the prayer's history, André Wilmart, *Auteurs spirituels et textes dévots du moyen âge latin* (Paris: Études Augustiniennes, 1971), 474–504.

44. Foucault, *Hermeneutics of the Subject*, 210.

45. "D'un Moigne en cui bouche on trouva cinc roses nouveles," in Gautier de Coinci, *Miracles de Nostre Dame*, ed. Koenig, 2:224–26.

46. The Psalms are, as Gautier specifies, Magnificat (Ps. 33:4, with echoes in other Psalms; see also Luke 1:46), Ad Dominum (Ps. 119:1), Retribue servo tuo (Ps. 118:17), Inconvertendo (Ps. 125:1), and Ad te levavi (Ps. 122:1).

47. Broughton notes, "All these psalms can be found in the Divine Office and four of them occur in the Little Office of the Virgin, well established by Gautier's time" ("The Rose, the Blessed Virgin Undefiled," 293n34).

48. Only II Mir 14, at 56 lines ("Comment li horsfevres fu renluminez," *Miracles de Nostre Dame*, 4:73–76), and I Mir 13, at 92 lines ("De la Tavlete en coi l'ymage de la mere Dieu estoit painte," *Miracles de Nostre Dame*, 2:101–4), are comparably brief; many miracles run to several hundred lines.

49. Hunt discusses the *queue* as a "structural unit" that forms part of each tale (*Miraculous Rhymes*, 29–37) and notes Gautier's explanation that he defers these remarks to the end to avoid interrupting his story (29–30, quoting II Mir 28, 232–42).

50. Here as elsewhere I use Koenig's edition, but two of these, the miracle of the *vilain* and the miracle of the jongleur's candle at Rocamadour, have been edited by Reino Hakamies, *Deux miracles de Gautier de Coinci: D'un Vilain qui fut sauvé pour ce qu'il ne faisoit uevre le samedi et Du Cierge que Nostre Dame de Rochemadour envoia seur la viele au jougleour qui vïeloit et chantoit devant s'ymage* (Helsinki: Suomalaisen Tiedeakatemia, 1958). He includes the Latin miracles from which these derive and some helpful notes on the texts.

51. "De Deus freres, Perron et Estene," in Gautier de Coinci, *Miracles de Nostre Dame*, ed. Koenig, 4:134–53. The story appears also in Kjellmann, *Deuxième collection anglo-normande des miracles*, 106–12, and in Robert of Gretham, *Miroir*, where the offended saint is Cecilia (108–10, ll. 3356–3427). Robert attributes the story to Gregory, but despite the wealth of such afterlife narratives in the *Dialogues* this one does not appear there.

52. This is "Dou cierge qui descendi au jougleour," in Gautier de Coinci, *Miracles de Nostre Dame*, ed. Koenig, 4:175–89.

53. On the Virgin and jongleurs, see Carol Symes, "The Lordship of Jongleurs," in *The Experience of Power in Medieval Europe, 950–1350*, ed. Robert F. Berkhofer III, Alan Cooper, and Adam J. Kosto (Aldershot, Hamps.: Ashgate, 2005), 237–52, and "The Confraternity of Jongleurs and the Cult of the Virgin: Vernacular Devotion and Documentation in Medieval Arras," in *The Church and Vernacular Literature in Medieval France*, ed. Dorothea Kullmann (Toronto: Pontifical Institute of Mediaeval Studies, 2009), 176–97.

54. On the "jongleur de Nôtre Dame" tradition, see Jan M. Ziolkowski, "Juggling the Middle Ages: The Reception of *Our Lady's Tumbler* and *Le Jongleur de Notre Dame*," *Memory and Medievalism*, special issue of *Studies in Medievalism* 15 (2006): 157–97.

55. Anna Drzewicka discusses Gautier's kinship with his protagonist in "La Vièle du coeur: Une métaphore musicale de Gautier de Coinci," in *"Contez me tout": Mélanges de langue et de littérature médiévales offerts à Herman Braet*, ed. Catherine Bel, Pascale Dumont, and Frank Willaert (Louvain: Peeters, 2006), 175–89.

56. See Gautier de Coinci, *Miracles de Nostre Dame*, ed. Koenig, 4:154–74.

57. This catalogue is a considerable expansion on the Latin source's account of his devotion: "Sanctam DEI Genitricem saepius in mente habebat, & plerumque eam . . . , sicut sciebat, devote salutabat" (Hakamies, *Deux miracles*, 5).

58. This detail was important enough to form the title of the miracle in MS S (Paris, BnF nouvelle acquisition française 24541), which calls it "Du Vilain qui a grant poinne savoit la moitié de son *Ave Maria*" (Gautier de Coinci, *Miracles de Nostre Dame*, ed. Koenig, 4:154).

59. Reino Hakamies, "Deux addenda au vocabulaire de Gautier de Coinci: 'ne bu ne ba' – 'haistaus,'" *Neuphilologische Mitteilungen* 57 (1956): 220–24.

60. The devils use "bobelins" again later in this miracle to describe the *vilain* (l. 263); see also, for example, I Mir 42, where the Devil refers to peasants as "bobelins champestres" (l. 120), and I Mir 32, where Gautier *in propria persona* speaks of a "vilains bobelins champestre" (l. 214).

61. The wordplay in Gautier's text makes an exact translation impossible; I have tried to reproduce the effects as best I can.

62. Peter Abelard, *Expositio Symboli*, PL 178:617–30, col. 618.

63. See Chapter 4 for both Aucassin and the similarly twisted use of "grain" and "paille" by the monk Zozimas in Rutebeuf's *Vie de S. Marie l'Egyptienne*.

64. The devils' evocation of a range of figures characterized by bodily ability, age, gender, and so on, and linked to the "ydiotes" peasant, becomes, simply, "povres genz," a useful indicator of what that shorthand term can mean. Compare Fiona Somerset's point, regarding the late fourteenth-century *Dialogue Between a Lord and a Clerk*, that "the poor, the stupid, the old, and those without leisure—the whole of the lay population, it seems—all belong to the potential audience [the Lord] projects for an English translation": "'As just as is a squyre': The Politics of 'Lewed Translacion' in Chaucer's Summoner's Tale," *Studies in the Age of Chaucer* 21 (1999): 187–207, at 196.

65. Here I diverge from Jasmina Foehr-Janssens, whose intriguing account of the divided self in Gautier's miracles touches on many of the issues discussed here. She emphasizes Gautier's pleasure in "diabolising" the "rigorous condemnations of a rigid superego" and notes his identification with the despised figure of the jongleur; while it is certainly true that Gautier diabolizes the voice of those who despise the simple and humble, he also takes a great deal of enjoyment in mimicking it, and as noted below his commentary *in propria persona* makes it more difficult to separate him from this "rigid superego." Foehr-Janssens, "Histoire poétique du péché: De quelques figures littéraires de la faute dans les *Miracles de Nostre Dame* de Gautier de Coinci," in *Gautier de Coinci*, ed. Krause and Stones, 215–26, at 226.

66. Hakamies, *Deux miracles de Gautier de Coinci,* 7.

67. This fascinating comparison both "twins" peasants and clerks and suggests the divinely favored status of the latter—as well as, perhaps, their craftiness; though, given the context, it is probably Esau's foolishness in selling his birthright that Gautier has in mind. I am grateful to Adrienne Williams Boyarin for her comments on this passage.

68. See Faral, "*Des Vilains*," 260, ll. 29, 34.

69. The expression here, "Que s'uns asnes avoit corone, / Se le mesquerroit il, par s'ame, / Ou de sa fille ou de sa fame" (ll. 428–30), recalls the expression "Rex illiteratus est (quasi) asinus coronatus," first recorded in writing in the twelfth century (in works by William of Malmesbury and John of Salisbury, among others) and forming part of the history of debates about lay literacy. The context and, of course, the type of crown in question are different.

70. At this point and elsewhere, one might object that Gautier is depicting peasants' animus against secular rather than regular clergy, but the opening reference to peasants' potential physical attacks on him, as well as the later reference to "clerks, psalters, and books," suggest that he is opposing peasants as a group to the world of *clergie*—that is, both learning and the clergy—rather than to any particular subgroup. In any case, Gautier was certainly a *clerc* as well as a monk, and though there is no record of it the likelihood is that he was ordained a priest; see Gautier de Coinci, *Miracles de Nostre Dame*, ed. Koenig, 1:xxii.

71. Erhard Lommatzsch reads this catalogue as evidence of Gautier's sympathy for "the poor, thorny life of the peasant" but acknowledges that he ultimately gives "a cooler, priestly assessment" in seeing the peasant's sad lot as a just punishment (*Gautier de Coincy als Satiriker* [Halle: Max Niemeyer, 1913], 71). I am less inclined than Lommatzsch to credit Gautier with a coolly distanced perspective here, given the *ad hominem* energy of the rest of the "sermon."

72. Kjellmann, *Deuxième collection anglo-normande des miracles*, 6, l. 50; Robert of Gretham, *Miroir*, l. 444. Further citations from Kjellman's edition in this section are given by page and line number in the text.

73. Gautier simply reports that "the angels carried the soul to Heaven at our Lady's

pleasure," ll. 331–32; the protagonist himself has largely faded from view in the course of the long argument between angels and devils.

74. Compare here Morgan Powell's account of how the performance within the text blurs into the performance of it in the Old French *Eructavit*: "Translating Scripture," 94–96.

75. See miracle XXXIV: "Seignurs, ne me blamez mie / Si jeo vus conte par compainie / Petiz contes pur vus dedure" (Kjellmann, *Deuxième collection anglo-normande des miracles*, 146, ll. 1–3).

76. Foucault, *Hermeneutics of the Subject*, 211.

77. "De la Nonain a cui Nostre Dame abreja ses salus," in Gautier de Coinci, *Miracles de Nostre Dame*, ed. Koenig, 2:276. Mary tells the nun to say fewer Aves, but more carefully.

78. Fulton, *From Judgment to Passion*, 268.

79. As Duncan Robertson observes of the twelfth-century life of St. Mary the Egyptian (the version known as *T*), "The *Ave Maria* is fitted into French octosyllable and rhyme, and located in the space and time of the story; that story, conversely, acquires by the same device a contemporary timeless pertinence to the reader" (*Medieval Saints' Lives*, 112). Some Marian miracles perform the slightly different task of connecting Marian devotion to the liturgy or other ecclesiastical forms by recounting an origin legend for a particular feast: see, for example, Kjellman, *Deuxième collection anglo-normande des miracles*, miracles VII (feast of Mary's Nativity), X (saying of Compline), and XL (feast of Mary's Conception). The miracles having to do with the efficacy of particular prayers (like "O beata et intemerata") are another version of this theme.

80. "D'un Moigne qui fu ou fleuve," in Gautier de Coinci, *Miracles de Nostre Dame*, ed. Koenig, 3:165–90.

81. The *Chasteau d'amour*, as noted in earlier chapters, frequently accompanies many of the works discussed here. For the opening debate between the four daughters of God, and its resolution by Christ, see *Le Château d'Amour de Robert Grosseteste, evêque de Lincoln*, ed. J. Murray (Paris: Champion, 1918), ll. 217–456.

82. I Mir 24, "Dou Moigne que Nostre Dame resuscita," in Gautier de Coinci, *Miracles de Nostre Dame*, ed. Koenig, 2:235.

83. I Mir 25, "De Celui qui se tua par l'amonestement dou dyable," in Gautier de Coinci, *Miracles de Nostre Dame*, ed. Koenig, 2:241.

84. See Watson, "Visions of Inclusion."

85. Pierre d'Abernon, *Lumere*, 1:189. The lovely translation "affinity" for "covenance" is Hesketh's suggestion in his Glossary (3:181). The Latin version of the passage appears in late medieval manuscripts with an attribution to Augustine, but this seems to be one of many cases where his name was borrowed to provide authority; I have not found corresponding material in his works.

86. I Mir 28, "Dou Chevalier a cui la volenté fu contee por fait," in Gautier de Coinci, *Miracles de Nostre Dame*, ed. Koenig, 2:261–72.

87. Mary to Jesus: "Biaus tres doz fius, soviegne toi / Que char et sanc presis en moi / Por rachater les pecheürs" (ll. 141–43). Jesus to Mary: "Por pecheürs a moi ratraire / Volz je de vos ma mere faire" (ll. 159–60). The underlying idea here is scriptural; as the angel tells Joseph in a dream, Mary will have a son and "ipse enim salvum faciet populum suum a peccatis eorum" (Matt. 1:21).

88. For a suggestive reading that demonstrates the persistence of this theme in Marian miracles, see Boyarin, *Miracles of the Virgin*, 101–2.

89. Hilda Graef sums up the ongoing resistance to what she sees as the extremes of Marian devotion: "Now, it is one thing to surround Mary with such tokens of love and respect, but quite

another to say that God obeys her, that we can appeal from God's tribunal to hers, that she rules over the kingdom of mercy while leaving to her Son only that of justice, and similar things which, as Newman says, 'can only be explained by being explained away' " (*Mary: A History of Doctrine and Devotion*, 1:xviii). In medieval miracles, these are not "one thing . . . and quite another"; they are aspects of the same thing.

90. Miracle XVI, "Du Moine qui se noya et qui fut ressuscité par la Sainte Vierge," in Kjellman, *Deuxième collection anglo-normande des miracles*, 79–83; cf. Gautier's I Mir 42, "D'un Moigne qui fu au fleuve."

91. Kjellman, *Deuxième collection anglo-normande des miracles*, 96, ll. 85–92.

92. Foehr-Janssens, "Histoire poétique du péché," 224.

93. Kathryn A. Duys, "Minstrel's Mantle and Monk's Hood: The Authorial Persona of Gautier de Coinci in his Poetry and Illuminations," in *Gautier de Coinci*, ed. Krause and Stones, 37–63, especially 45–49.

94. The quotation is from Justice, "Did the Middle Ages Believe in Their Miracles?" 14. The term *habitus* could be used to refer to a potential but not yet activated good intention; Alister E. McGrath notes that Alan of Lille, in the late twelfth century, speaks of *virtutes in habitu* as existing "quando homo per illas potentias quamdam habet habilitatem, et pronitatem ad utendum eis, si tempus exigerit" (quoted in *"Iustitia Dei": A History of the Christian Doctrine of Justification*, 3rd ed. [Cambridge: Cambridge University Press, 2005], 120n276). See also the discussion of *habitus* in Breen, *Imagining*, 43–79.

95. Tanner and Watson, "Least of the Laity," 403.

96. *Le Château d'Amour de Robert Grosseteste*, ed. Murray, ll. 951–52.

AFTERWORD

1. R. I. Moore, *The Formation of a Persecuting Society: Power and Deviance in Western Europe, 950–1250* (Oxford: Blackwell, 1990), 71.

2. On spiritual ambition, see Rice, *Lay Piety and Religious Discipline*, and Kumler, *Translating Truth*.

Bibliography

MANUSCRIPTS AND FACSIMILES

Avignon, Bibliothèque municipale, MS 344.
Bern, Burgerbibliothek, MS 354.
Cambridge, Emmanuel College, MS 106.
Cambridge, Fitzwilliam Museum, McClean MS 123.
Cambridge, Pembroke College, MS 258.
Cambridge, St. John's College, MS F.30.
Cambridge, University Library, MS Gg.I.1.
Chantilly, Musée Condé, MS 475.
Facsimile of Oxford, Bodleian Library, MS Digby 86. Introd. Judith Tschann and M. B. Parkes.
    Oxford: Oxford University Press for the EETS, 1996.
London, British Library, Additional MS 47682.
London, British Library, Arundel MS 288.
London, British Library, Cotton MS Domitian A.xi.
London, British Library, Egerton MS 2781.
London, British Library, Harley MS 1121.
London, British Library, Harley MS 3860.
London, British Library, Royal MS 15.D.II.
London, British Library, Royal MS 16.E.IX.
London, British Library, Royal MS 19.C.XI.
London, British Library, Royal MS 20.B.XIV.
London, Lambeth Palace Library, MS 209.
London, Lambeth Palace Library, MS 522.
New Haven, Yale University, Beinecke Library, MS 492.
Nottingham, University Library, MS Middleton L.M.6.
Oxford, Bodleian Library, MS Bodley 399.
Oxford, Bodleian Library, MS Laud miscellaneous 471.
Oxford, Bodleian Library, MS Rawlinson poetry 241.
Oxford, Bodleian Library, MS Selden supra 74.
Paris, Bibliothèque de l'Arsenal, MS 3516.
Paris, BnF fr. 187.
Paris, BnF fr. 837.
Paris, BnF fr. 1136.
Paris, BnF fr. 1807.
Paris, BnF fr. 12581.

Paris, BnF fr. 19152.

Paris, Bibliothèque nationale de France, nouvelle acquisition française 4338.

Paris, Bibliothèque nationale de France, nouvelle acquisition française 10034.

Princeton, Princeton University Library, Taylor MS 1.

PRINTED EDITIONS

Abelard, Peter. *Expositio Symboli quod dicitur Apostolorum*. PL 178:617D–30A.

Adgar. *Le Gracial*. Ed. Pierre Kunstmann. Ottawa: Éditions de l'Université d'Ottawa, 1982.

Adgar's Marienlegenden nach der Londoner Handschrift Egerton 612. Ed. Carl Neuhaus. Heilbronn: Gebr. Henninger, 1886.

Arnold of Bonneval. *Tractatus de septem verbis Domini in cruce*. PL 189:1677B–1726B.

[Arnold of Bonneval.] McCulloch, Sister John Vianney. "A Study of Arnold of Bonneval († 1157) with a Translation and Critique of the *Tractatus de septem verbis Domini in cruce*." M.A. thesis, Catholic University of America, 1963.

Aucassin et Nicolette: Chantefable du XIIIe siècle. Ed. Mario Roques. Paris: Champion, 1965.

Augustine. *Sermones de Scripturis*. PL 38:23–994.

[Barthélemy, Renclus de Molliens]. *"Li Romans de Carité" et "Miserere" du Renclus de Moiliens, poèmes de la fin du XIIe siècle*. Ed. A.-G. van Hamel. 2 vols. Paris: F. Vieweg, 1885; repr., Geneva: Slatkine, 1974.

Bede. *In Lucae evangelium expositio*. PL 92:301D–634D.

Bernard of Clairvaux. *Contra quaedam capitula errorum Abaelardi Epistola CXC seu Tractatus ad Innocentium II pontificem*. PL 182:1053D–1072D.

———. *Epistolae*. PL 182:68C–662A.

———. *In Cantica Canticorum sermo I*. PL 183:878A–884A.

———. *In festo omnium sanctorum sermo I*. PL 183:453B–462C.

———. *In festo S. Andreae sermo I*. PL 183:503D–509A.

Biblia sacra iuxta Vulgatam versionem. Ed. Robert Weber with B. Fischer, I. Gribomont, H. F. D. Sparks, and W. Thiele. 4th ed. prepared by Roger Gryson. Stuttgart: Deutsche Bibelgesellschaft, 1994.

Bliss, A. J., ed. *Sir Orfeo*. Oxford: Oxford University Press, 1966.

Pseudo-Boethius. *De disciplina scolarium*. Ed. Olga Weijers. Leiden: Brill, 1976.

Burrows, Daron, ed. and trans. *Two Old French Satires on the Power of the Keys: "L'Escommeniement au lecheor" and "Le Pardon de foutre."* London: Modern Humanities Research Association and Maney Publishing, 2005.

Chaucer, Geoffrey. *The Canterbury Tales*. In *The Riverside Chaucer*. Gen. ed. Larry D. Benson. Boston: Houghton Mifflin, 1987.

Chrétien de Troyes. *Le Chevalier de la charrette, ou Le Roman de Lancelot*. Ed. Charles Mela. Paris: Librairie Générale Française, 1992.

Ci nous dit: Recueil d'exemples moraux. Ed. Gérard Blangez. 2 vols. Paris: Société des Anciens Textes Français, 1979, 1986.

Councils and Synods, with Other Documents Relating to the English Church, II: A.D. 1205–1313. Part I: 1205–1265. Ed. F. M. Powicke and C. R. Cheney. Oxford: Clarendon Press, 1964.

Crane, Thomas Frederick. *The Exempla or Illustrative Stories from the Sermones Vulgares of Jacques de Vitry*. 1890; New York: Burt Franklin, 1971.

Dembowski, Peter F. *La Vie de sainte Marie l'Égyptienne: Versions en ancien et en moyen français.* Geneva: Droz, 1977.

Dewick, E. S., ed. *Facsimiles of Horae de Beata Maria Virgine from English Manuscripts of the Eleventh Century.* London: Henry Bradshaw Society, 1902.

[Edmund of Abingdon.] *Mirour de seinte eglyse (St. Edmund of Abingdon's "Speculum Ecclesiae").* Ed. A. D. Wilshere. London: ANTS, 1982.

Edmund of Abingdon. *"Speculum religiosorum" and "Speculum ecclesie."* Ed. Helen P. Forshaw. Auctores Britannici Medii Aevi 3. London: Oxford University Press for the British Academy, 1973.

Étienne de Fougères. *Livre des manières.* Ed. R. Anthony Lodge. Geneva: Droz, 1979.

L'Évangile de Nicodème: Les versions courtes en ancien français et en prose. Ed. Alvin E. Ford. Geneva: Droz, 1973.

Faral, Edmond, ed. *"Des Vilains ou Des .xxii. manieries [sic] de vilains."* Romania 48.2 (1922): 243–64.

The French Text of the "Ancrene Riwle," Edited from Trinity College Cambridge MS. R.14.7. Ed. W. H. Trethewey. EETS o.s. 240. London: Oxford University Press for the EETS, 1958.

Gautier de Coinci. *Les Miracles de Nostre Dame.* Ed. V. Frédéric Koenig. 4 vols. Textes littéraires français 64, 95, 131, 176. Geneva: Droz, 1955–70.

Glossa ordinaria in Evangelium secundum Lucam. PL 114:243C–356A.

The Gospel of Nicodemus: Gesta Salvatoris. Ed. H. C. Kim. Toronto: Pontifical Institute of Mediaeval Studies, 1973.

Gregory the Great, Pope. *Li Dialoge Gregoire lo Pape: Altfranzösische Uebersetzung des XII. Jahrhunderts der Dialogen des Papstes Gregor, mit dem lateinischen Original . . . / Les Dialogues du pape Grégoire traduits en français du XIIe siècle accompagnés du texte latin . . . Vol. I: Text.* Ed. Wendelin Foerster. Amsterdam: Rodopi, 1965.

———. *Dialogorum Libri IV.* PL 77:149–430.

———. *Dialogues.* Trans. Odo John Zimmerman. Fathers of the Church 39. New York: Fathers of the Church, 1959.

[———.] *Le Pastoralet: Traduction médiévale française de la "Regula pastoralis."* Ed. Martine Pagan. Paris: Champion, 2007.

[Grosseteste, Robert.] *Le Château d'Amour de Robert Grosseteste, evêque de Lincoln.* Ed. J. Murray. Paris: Champion, 1918.

Guerric of Igny. *Sermo II, Sabbato hebdomadae Quadragesimae, De parabola filii prodigi.* PL 185:96C–100A.

Hakamies, Reino. "Deux addenda au vocabulaire de Gautier de Coinci: 'ne bu ne ba'— 'haistaus.'" Neuphilologische Mitteilungen 57 (1956): 220–24.

Hakamies, Reino, ed. *Deux miracles de Gautier de Coinci: "D'un Vilain qui fut sauvé pour ce qu'il ne faisoit uevre le samedi" et "Du Cierge que Nostre Dame de Rochemadour envoia seur la viele au jougleour qui vïeloit et chantoit devant s'ymage."* Helsinki: Suomalaisen Tiedeakatemia, 1958.

Hélinand de Froidmont. *Chronicon.* PL 212:771C–1082C.

———. *Les Vers de la Mort: Poème du XIIe siècle.* Trans. Michel Boyer and Monique Santucci. Traductions des classiques français du moyen âge 32. Paris: Champion, 1983.

———. *The Verses on Death of Hélinand of Froidmont: Les Vers de la mort.* Ed. and trans. Jenny Lind Porter. Introd. William D. Paden. Kalamazoo, Mich.: Cistercian Publications, 1999.

Honorius Augustodunensis. *Elucidarium sive Dialogus de summa totius Christianae theologiae.* PL 172:1109A–1176D.

————. *Speculum ecclesiae*. PL 172:807A–1108A.

Hugh of St. Victor. *The Didascalicon of Hugh of St. Victor: A Medieval Guide to the Arts*. Trans.
Jerome Taylor. New York: Columbia University Press, 1991.

Hugues de Berzé. *La "Bible" au seigneur de Berzé*. Ed. Félix Lecoy. Paris: Droz, 1938.

Hunt, Tony, ed. *"Cher alme": Texts of Anglo-Norman Piety*. Trans. Jane Bliss. Introd. Henrietta
Leyser. Tempe: Arizona Center for Medieval and Renaissance Studies, 2010.

Innocent III, Pope. *De sacro altaris mysterio libri sex*. PL 217:773B–916A.

Jenkins, T. Atkinson, ed. *Eructavit: An Old French Metrical Paraphrase of Psalm XLIV*. Dresden:
Gedruckt für Gesellschaft für romanische Literatur, 1909.

Kjellman, Hilding, ed. *La Deuxième collection anglo-normande des miracles de la Sainte Vierge et
son original latin*. Paris: Champion; Uppsala: Akademiska Bokhandeln, 1922.

Kleinhans, Martha, ed. *"Lucidaire vault tant a dire comme donnant lumiere": Untersuchung und
Edition der Prosaversionen 2, 4 und 5 des "Elucidarium."* Tübingen: Niemeyer, 1993.

Langland, William. *The Vision of Piers Plowman: A Complete Edition of the B-Text*. Ed. A. V. C.
Schmidt. London: J. M. Dent, 1987.

Legge, M. Dominica. "The Anglo-Norman Sermon of Thomas of Hales." *Modern Language Review* 30.2 (1935): 212–18.

Leo I. *Epistola ad Flavianum episcopum Constantinopolitanum adversus haeresim Eutychianam*. PL
62:503A–508B.

Levy, Brian J. *Nine Verse Sermons by Nicholas Bozon: The Art of an Anglo-Norman Poet and
Preacher*. Oxford: Society for the Study of Mediaeval Languages and Literature, 1981.

Marie de France. *L'Espurgatoire seint Patriz*. Ed. and trans. Yolande de Pontfarcy. Louvain:
Peeters, 1995.

Noomen, Willem, ed. *Le Jongleur par lui-même: Choix de dits et de fabliaux*. Louvain: Peeters,
2003.

Noomen, Willem, and Nico van den Boogard, eds. *Nouveau recueil complet des fabliaux*. 10 vols.
Assen: Van Gorcum, 1983–98.

Paris, Gaston, and Alphonse Bos, eds. *Trois versions rimées de l'Évangile de Nicodème, par Chrétien, André de Coutances et un anonyme*. Paris: Didot, 1885.

Peter Comestor. *Historia scholastica*. PL 198:1053–1722A.

Peter Lombard. *In Epistolam ad Ephesios*. PL 192:169B–222C.

Petit plet. Ed. Brian S. Merrilees. ANTS 20. Oxford: Blackwell for the ANTS, 1970.

Pickering, F. P., ed. *The Anglo-Norman Text of the "Holkham Bible Picture Book."* ANTS 23. Oxford: Basil Blackwell for the ANTS, 1971.

[Pierre d'Abernon.] *"Le Secré de secrez" by Pierre d'Abernun of Fetcham from the Unique Manuscript B.N. f. fr. 25407*. Ed. Oliver A. Beckerlegge. Oxford: Basil Blackwell for the ANTS,
1944. Repr., New York: Johnson Reprint Corporation, 1967.

Pontal, Odette, ed. *Les Statuts synodaux français du XIIIe siècle, I: Les statuts de Paris et le Synodal
de l'Ouest*. Paris: Bibliothèque Nationale, 1971.

[Raoul de Houdenc.] *The Songe d'Enfer of Raoul de Houdenc*. Ed. Madeline Timmel Mihm.
Tübingen: Niemeyer, 1984.

Rauf de Linham. *Kalender*. Ed. Tony Hunt. London: ANTS, 1983.

Rhys, Olwen, ed. *An Anglo-Norman Rhymed Apocalypse with Commentary*. Introd. Sir John Fox.
ANTS 6. Oxford: Basil Blackwell for the ANTS, 1946.

[Robert of Gretham.] *Étude sur "Le Miroir ou les Évangiles des domnées" de Robert de Gretham,
suivie d'extraits inédits*. Ed. Marion Y. H. Aitken. Paris: Honoré Champion, 1922.

Robson, C. A. *Maurice of Sully and the Medieval Vernacular Homily*. Oxford: Basil Blackwell, 1952.

Rutebeuf. *Oeuvres complètes*. Ed. and trans. Michel Zink. Paris: Classiques Garnier, 2005.

Thomas of Chobham. *Summa de arte praedicandi*. Ed. Franco Morenzoni. Corpus Christianorum Series Latina 82. Turnhout: Brepols, 1988.

Türk, Monika, ed. *"Lucidaire de grant sapientie": Untersuchung und Edition der altfranzösischen Übersetzung 1 des "Elucidarium" von Honorius Augustodunensis*. Tübingen: Max Niemeyer Verlag, 2000.

CRITICAL STUDIES

Ackerman, Robert W. "*The Debate of the Body and the Soul* and Parochial Christianity." *Speculum* 37.4 (1962): 541–65.

Allen, Elizabeth. *False Fables and Exemplary Truth in Later Middle English Literature*. New York: Palgrave Macmillan, 2005.

Appleford, Amy. *Learning to Die in London, 1380–1540*. Philadelphia: University of Pennsylvania Press, 2014.

Armstrong, Adrian, and Sarah Kay, with the participation of Rebecca Dixon, Miranda Griffin, Sylvia Huot, Francesca Nicholson, and Finn Sinclair. *Knowing Poetry: Verse in Medieval France from the "Rose" to the "Rhétoriqueurs."* Ithaca, N.Y.: Cornell University Press, 2011.

Arnould, E. J. *Le "Manuel des péchés": Étude de littérature religieuse anglo-normande (XIIIme siècle)*. Paris: Librairie E. Droz, 1940.

d'Avray, David L. *The Preaching of the Friars: Sermons Diffused from Paris Before 1300*. Oxford: Oxford University Press, 1985.

Azzam, Wagih. "Un Recueil dans le recueil: Rutebeuf dans le manuscrit BnF f. fr. 837." In *Mouvances et jointures: Du manuscrit au texte médiéval*, ed. Milena Mikhaïlova. Orléans: Paradigme, 2005. 193–201.

Baldwin, John W. "The Image of the Jongleur in Northern France Around 1200." *Speculum* 72.3 (1997): 635–63.

———. *Masters, Preachers, and Merchants: The Social Views of Peter the Chanter and His Circle*. 2 vols. Princeton, N.J.: Princeton University Press, 1970.

Barratt, Alexandra. "Spiritual Writings and Religious Instruction." In *The Cambridge History of the Book in Britain, Vol. 2: 1100–1400*, ed. Nigel Morgan and Rodney M. Thomson. Cambridge: Cambridge University Press, 2008. 340–66.

Baswell, Christopher. "Talking Back to the Text: Marginal Voices in Medieval Secular Literature." In *The Uses of Manuscripts in Literary Studies: Essays in Memory of Judson Boyce Allen*, ed. Charlotte Cook Morse, Penelope Reed Doob, and Marjorie Curry Woods. Kalamazoo: Western Michigan University, Medieval Institute Publications, 1992. 121–55.

Batany, Jean. "Quelques effets burlesques dans le 'Livre des Manières.'" In *Risus mediaevalis: Laughter in Medieval Literature and Art*, ed. Herman Braet, Guido Latré, and Werner Verbeke. Mediaevalia Lovaniensia series I, Studia XXX. Leuven: Leuven University Press, 2003. 119–28.

———. "Le Vocabulaire des catégories sociales chez quelques moralistes français vers 1200." In *Ordres et classes: Colloque d'histoire sociale Saint-Cloud 24–25 mai 1967*, ed. D. Roche and C. E. Labrousse. Congrès et Colloques 12. Paris: Mouton, 1973. 59–72.

Bédier, Joseph. *Les Fabliaux: Études de littérature populaire et d'histoire littéraire du moyen âge*. 2nd rev. ed. Paris: Émile Bouillon, 1895.

Bennett, Adelaide. "A Book Designed for a Noblewoman: An Illustrated *Manuel des Péchés* of the Thirteenth Century." In *Medieval Book Production: Assessing the Evidence*, ed. Linda L. Brownrigg. Los Altos, Calif.: Anderson-Lovelace, 1990. 163–81.

Bernstein, Alan E. *The Formation of Hell: Death and Retribution in the Ancient and Early Christian Worlds*. Ithaca, N.Y.: Cornell University Press, 1993.

———. "The Invocation of Hell in Thirteenth-Century Paris." In *Supplementum Festivum: Studies in Honor of Paul Oskar Kristeller*, ed. James Hankins, John Monfasani, and Frederick Purnell Jr. Binghamton, N.Y.: Medieval and Renaissance Texts and Studies, 1987. 13–54.

Bevington, David. *Medieval Drama*. Boston: Houghton Mifflin, 1975.

Biller, Peter, and Anne Hudson, eds. *Heresy and Literacy, 1000–1530*. Cambridge: Cambridge University Press, 1994.

Blamires, Alcuin. "Women and Creative Intelligence in Medieval Thought." In *Voices in Dialogue: Reading Women in the Middle Ages*, ed. Linda Olson and Kathryn Kerby-Fulton. Notre Dame, Ind.: University of Notre Dame Press, 2005. 213–30.

Bloch, R. Howard. *The Scandal of the Fabliaux*. Chicago: University of Chicago Press, 1986.

Boivin, Jeanne-Marie. "Les Paradoxes des *clerici regis*: L'exemple, à la cour d'Henri II Plantegenêt, de Giraud de Barri." In *Le Clerc au moyen âge*. Senefiance 37. Aix-en-Provence: Centre Universitaire d'Études et de Recherches Médiévales d'Aix, 1995. 45–61.

Bolduc, Michelle. "Gautier de Coinci and the Translation of Exegesis." *Neophilologus* 93 (2009): 377–92.

———. *The Medieval Poetics of Contraries*. Gainesville: University Press of Florida, 2006.

Bonnard, Jean. *Les Traductions de la Bible en vers français au moyen âge*. 1884; Geneva: Slatkine Reprints, 1967.

Bossy, Michel-André. "Medieval Debates of Body and Soul." *Comparative Literature* 28.2 (1976): 144–63.

Bovon, François. *Luke 3: A Commentary on the Gospel of Luke 19:28–24:53*. Ed. Helmut Koester. Trans. James Crouch. Minneapolis: Fortress Press, 2012.

Boyarin, Adrienne Williams. *Miracles of the Virgin in Medieval England: Law and Jewishness in Marian Legends*. Cambridge: D. S. Brewer, 2010.

Boyle, Leonard E. "The Fourth Lateran Council and Manuals of Popular Theology." In *The Popular Literature of Medieval England*, ed. Thomas Heffernan. Knoxville: University of Tennessee Press, 1985. 30–43.

———. "Innocent III and Vernacular Versions of Scripture." In *The Bible in the Medieval World: Essays in Memory of Beryl Smalley*, ed. Katherine Walsh and Diana Wood. Oxford: Basil Blackwell for the Ecclesiastical History Society, 1985. 97–107.

———. "Robert Grosseteste and the Pastoral Care." In *Pastoral Care, Clerical Education and Canon Law, 1200–1400*. London: Variorum Reprints, 1981. Item I.

Bradbury, Nancy Mason. "Rival Wisdom in the Latin *Dialogue of Solomon and Marcolf*." *Speculum* 83.2 (2008): 331–65.

Bradley, Ritamary. "Backgrounds of the Title *Speculum* in Mediaeval Literature." *Speculum* 29.1 (1954): 100–115.

Breen, Katharine. *Imagining an English Reading Public, 1150–1400*. Cambridge: Cambridge University Press, 2010.

Briggs, Charles F. "Teaching Philosophy at School and Court: Vulgarization and Translation." In *The Vulgar Tongue: Medieval and Postmedieval Vernacularity*, ed. Fiona Somerset and Nicholas Watson. University Park: Pennsylvania State University Press, 2003. 99–111.

Brilliant, Virginia. "Envisaging the Particular Judgment in Late-Medieval Italy." *Speculum* 84.2 (April 2009): 314–46.

Broughton, Laurel. "The Rose, the Blessed Virgin Undefiled: Incarnational Piety in Gautier's *Miracles de Nostre Dame*." In *Gautier de Coinci*, ed. Krause and Stones. 281–99.

Brown, Catherine. *Contrary Things: Exegesis, Dialectic, and the Poetics of Didacticism*. Stanford, Calif.: Stanford University Press, 1998.

Brown, Peter. *The Cult of the Saints: Its Rise and Function in Latin Christianity*. Chicago: University of Chicago Press, 1981.

Brusegan, Rosanna. "Cocuce: La troisième voie de Rutebeuf dans *Le Pet au vilain*." In *Plaist vos oïr bone cançon vallant? Mélanges offerts à François Suard*, ed. Dominique Boutet, Marie-Madeleine Castellani, Françoise Ferrand, and Aimé Petit. Villeneuve d'Ascq: Université Charles-de-Gaulle–Lille 3, 1999. 133–40.

Bumke, Joachim. *Courtly Culture: Literature and Society in the High Middle Ages*. Woodstock, N.Y.: Overlook Press, 2000.

Busby, Keith. *Codex and Context: Reading Old French Verse Narrative in Manuscript*. 2 vols. Amsterdam: Rodopi, 2002.

Butterfield, Ardis. *The Familiar Enemy: Chaucer, Language, and Nation in the Hundred Years War*. Oxford: Oxford University Press, 2009.

Bynum, Caroline Walker. *"Docere verbo et exemplo": An Aspect of Twelfth-Century Spirituality*. Missoula, Mont.: Scholars Press, 1979.

———. *Jesus as Mother: Studies in the Spirituality of the High Middle Ages*. Berkeley and Los Angeles: University of California Press, 1984.

———. *The Resurrection of the Body in Western Christianity, 200–1366*. New York: Columbia University Press, 1995.

Cabaillot, Claire. "La Satire du *vilain* à travers quelques textes du Moyen-Age." *Chroniques italiennes* 15 (1988): 7–60.

Cabaniss, Allen. "The Harrowing of Hell, Psalm 24, and Pliny the Younger: A Note." *Vigiliae Christianae* 7.1 (1953): 65–74.

Campbell, Emma. "Clerks and Laity." In *The Cambridge Companion to Medieval French Literature*, ed. Simon Gaunt and Sarah Kay. Cambridge: Cambridge University Press, 2008. 210–24.

Cannon, Christopher. *The Grounds of English Literature*. Oxford: Oxford University Press, 2004.

Carruthers, Mary. *The Book of Memory: A Study of Memory in Medieval Culture*. Cambridge: Cambridge University Press, 1990.

———. *The Craft of Thought: Meditation, Rhetoric, and the Making of Images, 400–1200*. Cambridge: Cambridge University Press, 2000.

Cartlidge, Neil. "The Composition and Social Context of Oxford, Jesus College, MS 29 (II) and London, British Library, MS Cotton Caligula A.IX." *Medium Aevum* 66 (1997): 250–69.

———. "Sir Orfeo in the Otherworld: Courting Chaos?" *Studies in the Age of Chaucer* 26 (2004): 195–226.

Casagrande, Carla, and Silvana Vecchio. "Clercs et jongleurs dans la société médiévale (XIIe et XIIIe siècles)." *Annales* 34.5 (1979): 913–28.

Cavadini, John C. "Simplifying Augustine." In *Educating People of Faith: Exploring the History of Jewish and Christian Communities*, ed. John Van Engen. Grand Rapids, Mich.: William B. Eerdmans, 2004. 63–84.

de Certeau, Michel. *The Practice of Everyday Life*. Trans. Steven Rendall. Berkeley: University of California Press, 1984.

Chinnery, Ann. "Encountering the Philosopher as Teacher: The Pedagogical Postures of Emmanuel Levinas." *Teaching and Teacher Education* 26 (2010): 1704–9.

Clanchy, M. T. *Abelard: A Medieval Life*. Oxford: Blackwell, 1997.

———. *From Memory to Written Record: England, 1066–1307*. Oxford: Blackwell, 1993.

Coakley, John W. *Women, Men, and Spiritual Power: Female Saints and Their Male Collaborators*. New York: Columbia University Press, 2006.

Collet, Olivier. *Glossaire et index critiques des oeuvres d'attribution certaine de Gautier de Coinci (Vie de sainte Cristine et Miracles de Nostre Dame)*. Geneva: Librairie Droz, 2000.

———. "L'Œuvre en contexte: La place de Gautier de Coinci dans les recueils cycliques des *Miracles de Nostre Dame*." In *Gautier de Coinci*, ed. Krause and Stones. 21–36.

Combarieu du Grès, Micheline de. "Image et représentation du *vilain* dans les chansons de geste (et dans quelques autres textes médiévaux)." In *Exclus et systèmes d'exclusion dans la littérature et la civilisation médiévales*. Aix-en-Provence: Édition C.U.E.R.M.A., 1978. 7–26.

Constable, Giles. "The Structure of Medieval Society According to the Dictatores of the Twelfth Century." In *Law, Church and Society: Essays in Honor of Stephan Kuttner*, ed. K. Pennington and R. Somerville. Philadelphia: University of Pennsylvania Press, 1977. 252–67.

———. *Three Studies in Medieval Religious and Social Thought: The Interpretation of Mary and Martha, The Ideal of the Imitation of Christ, The Orders of Society*. Cambridge: Cambridge University Press, 1995.

Copeland, Rita. *Pedagogy, Intellectuals, and Dissent in the Later Middle Ages: Lollardy and Ideas of Learning*. Cambridge: Cambridge University Press, 2004.

Corbellari, Alain. *La Voix des clercs: Littérature et savoir universitaire autour des dits du XIIIe siècle*. Publications romanes et françaises 236. Geneva: Droz, 2005.

Corti, Maria. "Structures idéologiques et structures sémiotiques dans les *sermones ad status* du XIIIe siècle." In *Archéologie du signe*, ed. Lucie Brind'Amour and Eugene Vance. Toronto: Pontifical Institute of Mediaeval Studies, 1982. 145–63.

Crane, Susan. "Social Aspects of Bilingualism in the Thirteenth Century." In *Thirteenth Century England VI*, ed. Michael Prestwich, Richard Britnell, and Robin Frame. Woodbridge, Suffolk: Boydell Press, 1997. 103–15.

Cushing, Kathleen G. *Reform and the Papacy in the Eleventh Century: Spirituality and Social Change*. Manchester: Manchester University Press, 2005.

Dean, Ruth J., with the collaboration of Maureen B. M. Boulton. *Anglo-Norman Literature: A Guide to Texts and Manuscripts*. London: ANTS, 1999.

Deleuze, Gilles, and Félix Guattari. *A Thousand Plateaus: Capitalism and Schizophrenia*. Trans. Brian Massumi. Minneapolis: University of Minnesota Press, 1987.

Delumeau, Jean. *Sin and Fear: The Emergence of a Western Guilt Culture, 13th–18th Centuries*. Trans. Eric Nicholson. New York: Palgrave Macmillan, 1990.

Dinshaw, Carolyn, *Chaucer's Sexual Poetics*. Madison: University of Wisconsin Press, 1989.

Dixon, Rebecca. "Knowing Poetry, Knowing Communities." In *Poetry, Knowledge and Community in Late Medieval France*, ed. Rebecca Dixon and Finn E. Sinclair with Adrian Armstrong, Sylvia Huot, and Sarah Kay. Cambridge: D. S. Brewer, 2008. 215–24.

Donovan, Claire. "The Mise-en-Page of Early Books of Hours in England." In *Medieval Book Production: Assessing the Evidence*, ed. Linda L. Brownrigg. Los Altos, Calif.: Anderson-Lovelace, 1990. 147–61.

Dorn, Erhard. *Der sündige Heilige in der Legende des Mittelalters*. Munich: Wilhelm Fink, 1967.

Douglas, Mary. *Purity and Danger: An Analysis of the Concepts of Pollution and Taboo*. London: Routledge, 1966.

Doyle, Matthew A. *Bernard of Clairvaux and the Schools: The Formation of an Intellectual Milieu in the First Half of the Twelfth Century*. Spoleto: Fondazione Centro italiano di studi sull'alto medioevo, 2005.

Dronke, Peter. "Peter of Blois and Poetry at the Court of Henry II." *Mediaeval Studies* 28 (1976): 185–235.

Drzewicka, Anna. "La Vièle du coeur: Une métaphore musicale de Gautier de Coinci." In *"Contez me tout": Mélanges de langue et de littérature médiévales offerts à Herman Braet*, ed. Catherine Bel, Pascale Dumont, and Frank Willaert. Louvain: Peeters, 2006. 175–89.

Duby, Georges. *The Three Orders: Feudal Society Imagined*. Chicago: University of Chicago Press, 1980.

Duffy, Eamon. *The Stripping of the Altars: Traditional Religion in England, c. 1400–c. 1580*. New Haven, Conn.: Yale University Press, 1992.

Dunbabin, Jean. "From Clerk to Knight: Changing Orders." In *The Ideals and Practice of Medieval Knighthood II: Papers from the Third Strawberry Hill Conference*, ed. Christopher Harper-Bill and Ruth Harvey. Woodbridge, Suffolk: Boydell Press, 1988. 26–39.

———. "Jacques Le Goff and the Intellectuals." In *The Work of Jacques Le Goff and the Challenges of Medieval History*, ed. Miri Rubin. Woodbridge, Suffolk: Boydell Press, 1997. 157–67.

Duys, Kathryn A. "Minstrel's Mantle and Monk's Hood: The Authorial Persona of Gautier de Coinci in his Poetry and Illuminations." In *Gautier de Coinci*, ed. Krause and Stones. 37–63.

Duys, Kathryn A., assisted by Kathy M. Krause and Alison Stones. "Gautier de Coinci's *Miracles de Nostre Dame*: Manuscript List." In *Gautier de Coinci*, ed. Krause and Stones. 345–66.

Enders, Jody. "Rhetoric, Coercion, and the Memory of Violence." In *Criticism and Dissent in the Middle Ages*, ed. Rita Copeland. Cambridge: Cambridge University Press, 1996. 24–55.

Evans, G. R. *Bernard of Clairvaux*. New York: Oxford University Press, 2000.

Faral, Edmond. *Les Jongleurs en France au moyen âge*. Paris: Champion, 1910.

Felski, Rita. "After Suspicion." *Profession* (2009): 28–35.

Flint, Valerie I. J. "The Chronology of the Works of Honorius Augustodunensis." In *Ideas in the Medieval West: Texts and Their Contexts*. London: Variorum Reprints, 1988. Item VII. Reprinted from *Revue bénédictine* 82 (1972): 215–42.

———. "The 'Elucidarius' of Honorius Augustodunensis and the Reform in Late Eleventh-Century England." *Revue bénédictine* 85 (1975): 178–89.

Foehr-Janssens, Jasmina. "Histoire poétique du péché: De quelques figures littéraires de la faute dans les *Miracles de Nostre Dame* de Gautier de Coinci." In *Gautier de Coinci*, ed. Krause and Stones. 215–26.

Foucault, Michel. *Hermeneutics of the Subject: Lectures at the Collège de France, 1981–1982*. Ed. Frédéric Gros. Trans. Graham Burchell. New York: Palgrave Macmillan, 2004.

Frankis, John. "The Social Context of Vernacular Writing in Thirteenth Century England: The Evidence of the Manuscripts." In *Rethinking the South English Legendaries*, ed. Heather Blurton and Jocelyn Wogan-Browne. Manchester: Manchester University Press, 2011. 66–83.

Freedman, Paul. *Images of the Medieval Peasant*. Stanford, Calif.: Stanford University Press, 1999.

Fulton, Rachel. *From Judgment to Passion: Devotion to Christ and the Virgin Mary, 800–1200*. New York: Columbia University Press, 2002.

Fulton, Rachel, and Bruce W. Holsinger. "Afterword: History in the Comic Mode." In *History in the Comic Mode: Medieval Communities and the Matter of Person*, ed. Rachel Fulton and Bruce W. Holsinger. New York: Columbia University Press, 2007. 279–92.

Galderisi, Claudio, dir. *Translations médiévales: Cinq siècles de traductions en français au Moyen Âge (XIe–XVe siècles). Étude et Répertoire.* 3 vols. Turnhout: Brepols, 2011.

Gardiner, Eileen, ed. *Visions of Heaven and Hell Before Dante.* New York: Italica Press, 1989.

Gaunt, Simon. *Gender and Genre in Medieval French Literature.* Cambridge: Cambridge University Press, 1995.

Gehrke, Pamela. *Saints and Scribes: Medieval Hagiography in Its Manuscript Context.* Modern Philology vol. 126. Berkeley: University of California Press, 1993.

Georgianna, Linda. "Lords, Churls, and Friars: The Return to Social Order in the Summoner's Tale." In *Rebels and Rivals: The Contestive Spirit in "The Canterbury Tales,"* ed. Susanna Greer Fein, David Raybin, and Peter C. Braeger. Kalamazoo: Western Michigan University, Medieval Institute Publications, 1991. 149–72.

Gilbert, Jane. *Living Death in Medieval French and English Literature.* Cambridge: Cambridge University Press, 2011.

Gillespie, Vincent. "*Doctrina* and *Predicacio*: The Design and Function of Some Pastoral Manuals." *Leeds Studies in English* 9 (1980): 36–50.

Goering, Joseph. "The Internal Forum and the Literature of Penance and Confession." *Traditio* 59 (2004): 175–227.

———. "When and Where Did Grosseteste Study Theology?" In *Robert Grosseteste: New Perspectives on His Thought and Scholarship*, ed. James McEvoy. Turnhout: Brepols; Steenbrugis: In Abbatia S. Petri, 1995. 17–51.

Gouttebroze, Jean-Guy. "Entre les historiographes d'expression latine et les jongleurs, le clerc lisant." In *Le Clerc au moyen âge.* Senefiance 37. Aix-en-Provence: Centre Universitaire d'Études et de Recherches Médiévales d'Aix, 1995. 215–30.

Grabes, Herbert. *The Mutable Glass: Mirror-Imagery in Titles and Texts of the Middle Ages and English Renaissance.* Trans. Gordon Collier. Cambridge: Cambridge University Press, 1982.

Graef, Hilda. *Mary: A History of Doctrine and Devotion.* 2 vols. London: Sheed and Ward, 1963.

Grava, Yves. "Le Clerc marié." In *Le Clerc au moyen âge.* Senefiance 37. Aix-en-Provence: Centre Universitaire d'Études et de Recherches Médiévales d'Aix, 1995. 233–42.

Gravdal, Kathryn. *Vilain and Courtois: Transgressive Parody in French Literature of the Twelfth and Thirteenth Centuries.* Lincoln: University of Nebraska Press, 1989.

Gros, Gérard. "'Por ses myracles biau rimer . . .': Étude sur le projet hagiographique de Gautier de Coinci." *Revue des sciences humaines* 251 (July–September 1998): 73–87.

Gurevich, Aron. *Medieval Popular Culture: Problems of Belief and Perception.* Trans. János M. Bak and Paul A. Hollingsworth. Cambridge: Maison des Sciences de l'Homme and Cambridge University Press, 1990.

Haines, Roy M. "Education in English Ecclesiastical Legislation of the Later Middle Ages." In *Councils and Assemblies*, ed. G. J. Cuming and Derek Baker. Studies in Church History 7. Cambridge: Cambridge University Press, 1971. 161–75.

Hamilton, George L. "The Gilded Leaden Cloaks of the Hypocrites (Inferno XXIII, 58–66)." *Romanic Review* 12 (1921): 335–52.

Hanna, Ralph. "Augustinian Canons and Middle English Literature." In *The English Medieval Book: Studies in Memory of Jeremy Griffiths*, ed. A. S. G. Edwards, Vincent Gillespie, and Ralph Hanna. London: The British Library, 2000. 27–42.

Hanning, Robert. *The Individual in Twelfth-Century Romance.* New Haven, Conn.: Yale University Press, 1977.

Harkins, Franklin T. *Reading and the Work of Restoration: History and Scripture in the Work of Hugh of St. Victor.* Toronto: Pontifical Institute of Mediaeval Studies, 2009.

Harrison, Anna. "'If one member glories . . .': Community Between the Living and the Saintly Dead in Bernard of Clairvaux's Sermons for the Feast of All Saints." In *History in the Comic Mode: Essays in Honor of Caroline Walker Bynum*, ed. Rachel Fulton and Bruce Holsinger. New York: Columbia University Press, 2007. 25–35, 299–302.

Hasenohr, Geneviève. "Les Prologues des textes de dévotion en langue française (XIIIe–XVe siècles): Formes et fonctions." In *Les Prologues médiévaux*, ed. Jacqueline Hamesse. Turnhout: Brepols, 2000. 593–638.

Hessenauer, Matthias. "The Impact of Grosseteste's Pastoral Care on Vernacular Religious Literature: *La Lumière as Lais* by Pierre de Peckham." In *Robert Grosseteste: New Perspectives on His Thought and Scholarship*, ed. James McEvoy. Turnhout: Brepols; Steenbrugge, Belgium: Abbatia S. Petri, 1995. 377–91.

Holsinger, Bruce W. *Music, Body, and Desire in Medieval Culture: From Hildegard of Bingen to Chaucer*. Stanford, Calif.: Stanford University Press, 2001.

Hoogvliet, Margriet. "Encouraging Lay People to Read the Bible in the French Vernaculars: New Groups of Readers and Textual Communities." *Church History and Religious Culture* 93 (2013): 239–74.

———. "The Medieval Vernacular Bible in French as a Flexible Text: Selective and Discontinuous Reading Practices." In *Form and Function in the Late Medieval Bible*, ed. Eyal Poleg and Laura Light. Leiden: Brill, 2013. 283–306.

Hult, David F. "Poetry and the Translation of Knowledge in Jean de Meun." In *Poetry, Knowledge and Community in Late Medieval France*, ed. Rebecca Dixon and Finn E. Sinclair with Adrian Armstrong, Sylvia Huot, and Sarah Kay. Cambridge: D. S. Brewer, 2008. 19–41.

Hunt, Tony. *Miraculous Rhymes: The Writing of Gautier de Coinci*. Cambridge: D. S. Brewer, 2007.

Huot, Sylvia. "A Book Made for a Queen: The Shaping of a Late Medieval Anthology Manuscript (B.N. fr. 24429)." In *The Whole Book: Cultural Perspectives on the Medieval Miscellany*, ed. Stephen G. Nichols and Siegfried Wenzel. Ann Arbor: University of Michigan Press, 1996. 123–43.

———. "Polytextual Reading: The Meditative Reading of Real and Metaphorical Books." In *Orality and Literacy in the Middle Ages: Essays on a Conjunction and Its Consequences in Honour of D. H. Green*, ed. Mark Chinca and Christopher Young. Turnhout: Brepols, 2005. 201–22.

Imbach, Ruedi. *Laien in der Philosophie des Mittelalters: Hinweise und Anregungen zu einem vernachlässigten Thema*. Amsterdam: B. R. Grüner, 1989.

Izydorczyk, Zbigniew. "The *Evangelium Nicodemi* in the Latin Middle Ages." In *Medieval Gospel of Nicodemus*, ed. Izydorczyk. 43–101.

———. "Introduction." In *Medieval Gospel of Nicodemus*, ed. Izydorczyk. 1–19.

———, ed. *The Medieval Gospel of Nicodemus: Texts, Intertexts, and Contexts in Western Europe*. Tempe, Ariz.: Medieval and Renaissance Texts and Studies, 1997.

———. "The Unfamiliar *Evangelium Nicodemi*." *Manuscripta* 33.3 (1989): 169–91.

Jaeger, C. Stephen. *The Envy of Angels: Cathedral Schools and Social Ideals in Medieval Europe, 950–1200*. Philadelphia: University of Pennsylvania Press, 1994.

James, Sarah, and Huw Grange. "Spreading the Light: Mapping the Vernacular *Elucidarium* in Medieval England." Project website http://www.kent.ac.uk/mems/research/Elucidarium-1.html.

Jauss, Hans Robert. *Question and Answer: Forms of Dialogic Understanding*. Ed. and trans. Michael Hays. Minneapolis: University of Minnesota Press, 1989.

Justice, Steven. "Did the Middle Ages Believe in Their Miracles?" *Representations* 103.1 (Summer 2008): 1–29.

———. "Eucharistic Miracle and Eucharistic Doubt." *Journal of Medieval and Early Modern Studies* 42.2 (2012): 307–32.

Karl, L. "La Légende de l'ermite et le jongleur." *Revue des langues romanes* 63 (1925): 111–41.

Karras, Ruth Mazo. "Holy Harlots: Prostitute Saints in Medieval Legend." *Journal of the History of Sexuality* 1.1 (1990): 3–32.

Kay, Sarah. *The Place of Thought: The Complexity of One in Late Medieval Didactic Poetry.* Philadelphia: University of Pennsylvania Press, 2007.

Kieckhefer, Richard. "The Specific Rationality of Medieval Magic." *American Historical Review* 99 (1994): 813–36.

Kinne, Elizabeth. "Rhetorical Reasoning, Authority, and the Impossible Interlocutor in *Le Vilain qui conquist paradis par plait.*" In *The Old French Fabliaux: Essays on Comedy and Context*, ed. Kristin L. Burr, John F. Moran and Norris J. Lacy. Jefferson, N.C.: McFarland, 2007. 55–68.

Kittay, Jeffrey, and Wlad Godzich. *The Emergence of Prose: An Essay in Prosaics.* Minneapolis: University of Minnesota Press, 1987.

Kleinhans, Martha. "Zwischen Orthodoxie und Häresie: Die englischsprachige Rezeption des *Elucidarium.*" In *Elucidarium und Lucidaires: Zur Rezeption des Werks von Honorius Augustodunensis in der Romania und in England*, ed. Ernstpeter Ruhe. Wiesbaden: Ludwig Reichert Verlag, 1993.

Koch, Sr. Mary Pierre. *An Analysis of the Long Prayers in Old French Literature with Special Reference to the "Biblical-Creed-Narrative" Prayers.* Washington, D.C.: Catholic University of America Press, 1940.

Kolve, V. A. *The Play Called Corpus Christi.* Stanford, Calif.: Stanford University Press, 1966.

Krause, Kathy M., and Alison Stones, eds. *Gautier de Coinci: Miracles, Music, and Manuscripts.* Turnhout: Brepols, 2006.

Kristeva, Julia. *Powers of Horror: An Essay on Abjection.* Trans. Leon S. Rudiez. New York: Columbia University Press, 1982.

Kroll, Josef. *Gott und Hölle: Der Mythos vom Descensuskampfe.* Darmstadt: Wissenschaftliche Buchgesellschaft, 1963.

Kullmann, Dorothea, ed. *The Church and Vernacular Literature in Medieval France.* Toronto: Pontifical Institute of Mediaeval Studies, 2009.

Kumler, Aden. *Translating Truth: Ambitious Images and Religious Knowledge in Late Medieval England and France.* New Haven, Conn.: Yale University Press, 2011.

Kunstmann, Pierre. "Le Clerc de Notre-Dame: La littérature de miracle en langue vulgaire, traduction et création." In *The Church and Vernacular Literature in Medieval France*, ed. Dorothea Kullmann. Toronto: Pontifical Institute of Mediaeval Studies, 2009. 124–36.

Landes, Richard. "Economic Development and Demotic Religiosity." In *History in the Comic Mode: Medieval Communities and the Matter of Person*, ed. Rachel Fulton and Bruce W. Holsinger. New York: Columbia University Press, 2007. 101–16.

Latham, R. E., ed. *Revised Medieval Latin Word-List from British and Irish Sources, with Supplement.* London: Oxford University Press for the British Academy, 1980.

LaVere, Suzanne. "From Contemplation to Action: The Role of the Active Life in the *Glossa ordinaria* on the Song of Songs." *Speculum* 82.1 (January 2007): 54–69.

Leclercq, Jean. *The Love of Learning and the Desire for God: A Study of Monastic Culture.* Trans. Catharine Misrahi. New York: Fordham University Press, 1982.

Lefèvre, Yves. "*Elucidarium, Lucidaires.*" In *Dictionnaire des lettres françaises: Le moyen âge.* Rev. ed. Ed. Geneviève Hasenohr and Michel Zink. Paris: Fayard, 1994. 403–5.

———. *L'Elucidarium et les Lucidaires: Contribution, par l'histoire d'un texte, à l'histoire des croyances religieuses en France au moyen âge.* Paris: E. de Boccard, 1954.

Legge, M. Dominica. *Anglo-Norman in the Cloisters: The Influence of the Orders upon Anglo-Norman Literature.* Edinburgh: Edinburgh University Press, 1950.

———. *Anglo-Norman Literature and Its Background.* Oxford: Clarendon Press, 1971.

———. "The 'Lumiere as Lais': A Postscript." *Modern Language Review* 46 (1951): 191–95.

Le Goff, Jacques. *The Birth of Purgatory.* Trans. Arthur Goldhammer. Chicago: University of Chicago Press, 1984.

———. "Introduction: Medieval Man." In *Medieval Callings,* ed. Jacques Le Goff, trans. Lydia G. Cochrane. Chicago: University of Chicago Press, 1987. 1–35.

———. *Time, Work, and Culture in the Middle Ages.* Trans. Arthur Goldhammer. Chicago: University of Chicago Press, 1980.

Lerer, Seth. *Boethius and Dialogue: Literary Method in "The Consolation of Philosophy."* Princeton, N.J.: Princeton University Press, 1985.

Levinas, Emmanuel. *Of God Who Comes to Mind.* Trans. Bettina Bergo. Stanford, Calif.: Stanford University Press, 1998.

Levitan, Alan. "The Parody of Pentecost in Chaucer's Summoner's Tale." *University of Toronto Quarterly* 40 (1971): 236–46.

Levy, Brian J. "L'Ironie des métiers, ou le récit chiasmatique: À propos du conte pieux *De l'Ermite et du jongleur.*" *Reinardus* 5 (1992): 85–107.

———. "*Or escoutez une merveille!* Parallel Paths: Gautier de Coinci and the Fabliaux." In *Gautier de Coinci,* ed. Krause and Stones. 331–43.

Little, Katherine C. *Confession and Resistance: Defining the Self in Late Medieval England.* Notre Dame, Ind.: University of Notre Dame Press, 2006.

Lobrichon, Guy. "Un Nouveau genre pour un public novice: La paraphrase biblique dans l'espace romane du XIIe siècle." In *The Church and Vernacular Literature in Medieval France,* ed. Dorothea Kullmann. Toronto: Pontifical Institute of Mediaeval Studies, 2009. 87–108.

Lodge, R. A. "Language Attitudes and Linguistic Norms in France and England in the Thirteenth Century." In *Thirteenth Century England IV: Proceedings of the Newcastle-upon-Tyne Conference 1991,* ed. P. R. Coss and S. D. Lloyd. Woodbridge, Suffolk: Boydell Press, 1992. 73–83.

Lommatzsch, Erhard. *Gautier de Coincy als Satiriker.* Halle: Max Niemeyer, 1913.

Longère, Jean. "Enseignement du 'Credo.'" *Sacris erudiri* 32 (1991): 309–42.

Luscombe, D. E. "Conceptions of Hierarchy Before the Thirteenth Century." In *Soziale Ordnungen im Selbstverständnis des Mittelalters.* 2 vols. Ed. Albert Zimmerman. Berlin: Walter de Gruyter, 1979. 1:1–19.

———. *The School of Peter Abelard: The Influence of Abelard's Thought in the Early Scholastic Period.* Cambridge: Cambridge University Press, 1969.

Macy, Gary. "The 'Invention' of Clergy and Laity in the Twelfth Century." In *A Sacramental Life: A Festschrift Honoring Bernard Cooke,* ed. Michael Horace Barnes and William P. Roberts. Milwaukee, Wis.: Marquette University Press, 2003. 117–35.

Marx, C. W. *The Devil's Rights and the Redemption in the Literature of Medieval England.* Cambridge: D. S. Brewer, 1995.

Matsuda, Takami. *Death and Purgatory in Middle English Didactic Poetry.* Cambridge: D. S. Brewer, 1997.

McGinn, Bernard. *The Growth of Mysticism: Gregory the Great Through the Twelfth Century (The Presence of God: A History of Western Christian Mysticism, Vol. 2)*. New York: Crossroad, 1994.

McGrady, Deborah. "A Master, a *Vilain*, a Lady and a Scribe: Competing for Authority in a Late Medieval Translation of the *Ars amatoria*." In *Poetry, Knowledge and Community in Late Medieval France*, ed. Rebecca Dixon and Finn E. Sinclair with Adrian Armstrong, Sylvia Huot, and Sarah Kay. Cambridge: D. S. Brewer, 2008. 98–110.

McGrath, Alister E. *"Iustitia Dei": A History of the Christian Doctrine of Justification*. 3rd ed. Cambridge: Cambridge University Press, 2005.

Ménard, Philippe. "Une nouvelle version du dit *Des putains et des lecheors*." *Zeitschrift für romanische Philologie* 113 (1997): 30–38.

Menegaldo, Silvère. *Le Jongleur dans la littérature narrative des XIIe et XIIIe siècles: Du personnage au masque*. Paris: Champion, 2005.

Michaud-Quantin, Pierre. "Les Méthodes de la pastorale du XIIIe au XVe siècle." In *Methoden in Wissenschaft und Kunst des Mittelalters*, ed. Albert Zimmermann with the assistance of Rudolf Hoffmann. Berlin: Walter de Gruyter, 1970. 76–91.

———. "Le Vocabulaire des catégories sociales chez les canonistes et les moralistes du XIIIe siècle." In *Ordres et classes: Colloque d'histoire sociale Saint-Cloud 24–25 mai 1967*, ed. D. Roche and C. E. Labrousse. Paris: Mouton, 1973. 73–86.

Minnis, Alastair. *Fallible Authors: Chaucer's Pardoner and Wife of Bath*. Philadelphia: University of Pennsylvania Press, 2008.

Moore, R. I. *The First European Revolution, c. 970–1215*. Oxford: Blackwell, 2000.

———. *The Formation of a Persecuting Society: Power and Deviance in Western Europe, 950–1250*. Oxford: Blackwell, 1990.

Morawski, J. "Mélanges de littérature pieuse: Les miracles de Notre-Dame en vers français." *Romania* 61 (1935): 145–209.

Morenzoni, Franco. *Des Écoles aux paroisses: Thomas de Chobham et la promotion de la prédication au début du XIIIe siècle*. Paris: Institut d'Études Augustiniennes, 1995.

Morey, James H. "Peter Comestor, Biblical Paraphrase, and the Medieval Popular Bible." *Speculum* 68.1 (1993): 6–35.

Mulder-Bakker, Anneke. *Lives of the Anchoresses: The Rise of the Urban Recluse in Medieval Europe*. Philadelphia: University of Pennsylvania Press, 2005.

Murdoch, Brian. *The Apocryphal Adam and Eve in Medieval Europe: Vernacular Translations and Adaptations of the "Vita Adae et Evae."* Oxford: Oxford University Press, 2009.

Nash, Suzanne. "Rutebeuf's Contribution to the Saint Mary the Egyptian Legend." *French Review* 44.4 (1971): 695–705.

Newman, Barbara. *Medieval Crossover: Reading the Secular Against the Sacred*. Philadelphia: University of Pennsylvania Press, 2013.

Nims, Margaret F. "*Translatio*: 'Difficult Statement' in Medieval Poetic Theory." *University of Toronto Quarterly* 43 (1974): 215–30.

Novikoff, Alex J. *The Medieval Culture of Disputation: Pedagogy, Practice, and Performance*. Philadelphia: University of Pennsylvania Press, 2013.

Nykrog, Per. *Les Fabliaux*. New ed. Geneva: Droz, 1973.

O'Gorman, Richard. "The *Gospel of Nicodemus* in the Vernacular Literature of Medieval France." In *Medieval Gospel of Nicodemus*, ed. Izydorczyk. 103–31.

O'Sullivan, Daniel E. *Marian Devotion in Thirteenth-Century French Lyric*. Toronto: University of Toronto Press, 2005.

Olson, Glending. *Literature as Recreation in the Later Middle Ages*. Ithaca, N.Y.: Cornell University Press, 1982.

Orme, Nicholas. *From Childhood to Chivalry: The Education of the English Kings and Aristocracy, 1066–1530*. London: Methuen, 1984.

Otis, Leah Lydia. *Prostitution in Medieval Society: The History of an Urban Institution in Languedoc*. Chicago: University of Chicago Press, 1985.

Owen, D. D. R. *The Vision of Hell: Infernal Journeys in Medieval French Literature*. Edinburgh: Scottish Academic Press, 1970.

Owen, Dorothy L. *Piers Plowman: A Comparison with Some Earlier and Contemporary French Allegories*. London: University of London Press, 1912.

Pardue, Stephen. "Kenosis and Its Discontents: Towards an Augustinian Account of Divine Humility." *Scottish Journal of Theology* 65.3 (August 2012): 271–88.

Parker, John. *The Aesthetics of Antichrist: From Christian Drama to Christopher Marlowe*. Ithaca, N.Y.: Cornell University Press, 2007.

Parkes, M. B. "The Literacy of the Laity." In *The Medieval World*, ed. David Daiches and Anthony Thorlby. London: Aldus Books, 1973. 555–77.

Payen, Jean-Charles. *Le Motif du repentir dans la littérature française médiévale (des origines à 1230)*. Geneva: Droz, 1968.

Pelikan, Jaroslav. *Mary Through the Centuries: Her Place in the History of Culture*. New Haven, Conn.: Yale University Press, 1998.

Pelikan, Jaroslav, and Valerie A. Hotchkiss, eds. *Creeds and Confessions of Faith in the Christian Tradition, Vol. I: Early, Eastern, and Medieval*. New Haven, Conn.: Yale University Press, 2003.

Pilkington, Mark C. "The Raising of Lazarus: A Prefiguring Agent to the Harrowing of Hell." *Medium Aevum* 44 (1975): 51–53.

Pinvidic, Marie-Jane. "Apparition et disparition du clerc dans *Disciplina clericalis*." In *Le Clerc au moyen âge*. Senefiance 37. Aix-en-Provence: Centre Universitaire d'Études et de Recherches Médiévales d'Aix, 1995. 633–51.

Poleg, Eyal. "'A Ladder Set Up on Earth': The Bible in Medieval Sermons." In *The Practice of the Bible in the Middle Ages: Production, Reception, and Performance in Western Christianity*, ed. Susan Boynton and Diane J. Reilly. New York: Columbia University Press, 2011. 205–27.

Pontal, Odette. *Les Statuts synodales*. Typologie des sources du moyen âge occidental 11. Turnhout: Brepols, 1975.

Poor, Sara S. "Women Teaching Men in the Medieval Devotional Imagination." In *Women, Men, and Religious Life in Germany, 1100–1500*, ed. Fiona J. Griffiths and Julie Hotchin. Turnhout: Brepols, 2014. 339–65.

Pouzet, Jean-Pascal. "Augustinian Canons and Their Insular French Books in Medieval England: Towards an Assessment." In *Language and Culture in Medieval Britain*, ed. Wogan-Browne et al. 266–77.

Powell, Morgan. "Translating Scripture for *Ma dame de Champagne*: The Old French 'Paraphrase' of Psalm 44 *(Eructavit)*." In *The Vernacular Spirit: Essays on Medieval Religious Literature*, ed. Renate Blumenfeld-Kosinski, Duncan Robertson, and Nancy Bradley Warren. New York: Palgrave, 2002. 83–103.

Putter, Ad. "Knights and Clerics at the Court of Champagne: Chrétien de Troyes's Romances in Context." In *Medieval Knighthood V: Papers from the Sixth Strawberry Hill Conference, 1994*, ed. Stephen Church and Ruth Harvey. Woodbridge, Suffolk: Boydell Press, 1995. 243–66.

Reames, Sherry. "Mary, Sanctity, and Prayers to Saints: Chaucer and Late-Medieval Piety." In *Chaucer and Religion*, ed. Helen Phillips. Cambridge: D. S. Brewer, 2010. 81–96.

Rebillard, Éric. *"In hora mortis": Évolution de la pastoral chrétienne de la mort aux IVe et Ve siècles dans l'occident latin*. Rome: École française de Rome, 1994.

Rector, Geoff. "An Illustrious Vernacular: The Psalter *en romanz* in Twelfth-Century England." In *Language and Culture in Medieval Britain*, ed. Wogan-Browne et al. 198–206.

Reeves, Andrew. "Teaching the Creed and Articles of Faith in England: 1215–1281." In *A Companion to Pastoral Care in the Late Middle Ages (1200–1500)*, ed. Ronald J. Stansbury. Leiden: Brill, 2010. 41–72.

Regalado, Nancy Freeman. *Poetic Patterns in Rutebeuf: A Study in Noncourtly Poetic Modes of the Thirteenth Century*. New Haven, Conn.: Yale University Press, 1970.

Ribémont, Bernard. *"De natura rerum": Études des encyclopédies médiévales*. Orléans: Paradigme, 1995.

Rice, Nicole R. *Lay Piety and Religious Discipline in Middle English Literature*. Cambridge: Cambridge University Press, 2008.

Riché, Pierre. *Écoles et enseignement dans le Haut Moyen Âge, fin du Ve siècle–milieu du XIe siècle*. Paris: Picard, 1989.

Rider, Catherine. "Lay Religion and Pastoral Care in Thirteenth Century England: The Evidence of a Group of Short Confession Manuals." *Journal of Medieval History* 36 (2010): 327–40.

Roberts, Phyllis B. "Master Stephen Langton Preaches to the People and Clergy: Sermon Texts from Twelfth-Century Paris." *Traditio* 36 (1980): 237–68.

Robertson, Duncan. "The Experience of Reading: Bernard of Clairvaux, *Sermons on the Song of Songs*, I." *Religion and Literature* 19.1 (Spring 1987): 1–20.

———. *Lectio Divina: The Medieval Experience of Reading*. Collegeville, Minn.: Liturgical Press, 2011.

———. *The Medieval Saints' Lives: Spiritual Renewal and Old French Literature*. Lexington, Ky.: French Forum, 1995.

Robertson, Elizabeth. "*The Grounds of English Literature* by Christopher Cannon." *Journal of English and Germanic Philology* 106.4 (2007): 531–34.

Rossiaud, Jacques. *Medieval Prostitution*. Trans. Lydia G. Cochrane. New York: Blackwell, 1988.

Rothwell, William. "The Role of French in Thirteenth-Century England." *Bulletin of the John Rylands University Library of Manchester* 58 (1976): 445–66.

Rubin, Miri. *Emotion and Devotion: The Meaning of Mary in Medieval Religious Cultures*. Budapest: Central European University Press, 2009.

———. *Mother of God: A History of the Virgin Mary*. London: Allen Lane, 2009.

Ruhe, Ernstpeter. "Pour faire la lumière as lais?: Mittelalterliche Handbücher des Glaubenswissens und ihr Publikum." In *Wissensorganisierende und wissensvermittelnde Literatur im Mittelalter: Perspektiven ihrer Erforschung*, ed. Norbert Richard Wolf. Wiesbaden: Ludwig Reichert Verlag, 1987. 46–56.

———. "Praedicatio est translatio: Das *Elucidarium* in der altfranzösischen Predigt." In *Elucidarium und Lucidaires: Zur Rezeption des Werks von Honorius Augustodunensis in der Romania und in England*, ed. Ernstpeter Ruhe. Wissensliteratur im Mittelalter 7. Wiesbaden: Ludwig Reichert Verlag, 1993. 9–30.

Ruhe, Ernstpeter, ed. *Elucidarium und Lucidaires: Zur Rezeption des Werks von Honorius Augustodunensis in der Romania und in England*. Wiesbaden: Ludwig Reichert Verlag, 1993.

Russell, G. H. "Vernacular Instruction of the Laity in the Later Middle Ages in England." *Journal of Religious History* 2.2 (1962): 98–119.

Rychner, Jean. *Contribution à l'étude des fabliaux.* 2 vols. Geneva: Droz, 1960.

———. "Les Fabliaux: Genre, styles, publics." In *La Littérature narrative d'imagination: Des genres littéraires aux techniques d'expression.* Paris: Presses Universitaires de France, 1961. 41–52.

Salter, Elizabeth. "Culture and Literature in Earlier Thirteenth-Century England: National and International." In *England and International: Studies in the Literature, Art, and Patronage of Medieval England,* ed. Derek Pearsall and Nicolette Zeeman. Cambridge: Cambridge University Press, 1988. 29–74.

Sandler, Lucy Freeman. "The *Lumere as lais* and Its Readers: Pictorial Evidence from British Library MS Royal 15.D.II." In *Thresholds of Medieval Visual Culture,* ed. Elina Gertsman and Jill Stevenson. Woodbridge, Suffolk: Boydell Press, 2012. 73–94.

Sanok, Catherine. *Her Life Historical: Exemplarity and Female Saints' Lives in Late Medieval England.* Philadelphia: University of Pennsylvania Press, 2007.

Schmitt, Jean-Claude. "Au XIIIe siècle, une parole nouvelle." In *Histoire vécue du peuple chrétien.* 2 vols. Ed. Jean Delumeau. Toulouse: Privat, 1979. 1:257–79.

———. "Du Bon usage du 'Credo.'" In *Faire croire: Modalités de la diffusion et de la réception des messages religieux du XIIe au XVe siècle.* Collection de l'École française de Rome 51. Rome: École française de Rome, 1981. 337–61.

Schönbach, Anton E. "Studien zur Erzählungsliteratur des Mittelalters. Erster Theil: Der Reuner Relationen." In *Sitzungsberichte der Philosophisch-Historischen Classe der Kaiserlichen Akademie der Wissenschaften* 139. Vienna: Carl Gerold's Sohn, 1898.

Schulze-Busacker, Elisabeth. "Littérature didactique à l'usage des laics aux XIIe et XIIIe siècles." In *Le Petit peuple dans l'Occident médiéval: Terminologies, perceptions, réalités,* ed. Pierre Boglioni, Robert Delort, and Claude Gauvard. Paris: Publications de la Sorbonne, 2002. 633–45.

Schwob, Marcel. *La Légende de Serlon de Wilton.* Paris: Édition de la Vogue, 1899.

Short, Ian. *Manual of Anglo-Norman.* 2nd ed. Oxford: ANTS, 2013.

———. "Patrons and Polyglots: French Literature in Twelfth-Century England." In *Anglo-Norman Studies XIV,* ed. Marjorie Chibnall. Woodbridge, Suffolk: Boydell Press, 1992. 229–49.

Sinclair, K. V. "The Anglo-Norman Patrons of Robert the Chaplain and Robert of Greatham." *Forum for Modern Language Studies* 6 (1996): 193–208.

Smalley, Beryl. *The Study of the Bible in the Middle Ages.* Notre Dame, Ind.: University of Notre Dame Press, 1978.

Sneddon, Clive R. "The *Old French Bible*: The First Complete Vernacular Bible in Western Europe." In *The Practice of the Bible in the Middle Ages: Production, Reception, and Performance in Western Christianity,* ed. Susan Boynton and Diane J. Reilly. New York: Columbia University Press, 2011. 296–314.

Somerset, Fiona. "'As just as is a squyre': The Politics of 'Lewed Translacion' in Chaucer's Summoner's Tale." *Studies in the Age of Chaucer* 21 (1999): 187–207.

———. *Clerical Discourse and Lay Audience in Late Medieval England.* Cambridge: Cambridge University Press, 1998.

Sommerfeldt, John R. *Bernard of Clairvaux on the Life of the Mind.* New York and Mahwah, NJ: The Newman Press, 2004.

Southern, R. W. "The English Origins of 'Miracles of the Virgin.'" *Medieval and Renaissance Studies* 4 (1958): 176–216.

Stansbury, Ronald J. Introduction to *A Companion to Pastoral Care in the Late Middle Ages (1200–1500),* ed. Ronald J. Stansbury. Leiden: Brill, 2010. 1–6.

Stock, Brian. "History, Literature, and Medieval Textuality." *Yale French Studies* 70 (1986): 7–17.

———. *The Implications of Literacy: Written Language and Models of Interpretation in the Eleventh and Twelfth Centuries*. Princeton, N.J.: Princeton University Press, 1983.

Straub, Richard. "*Des Putains et des lecheors*: La version oubliée du manuscrit G." *Vox romanica* 52 (1993): 164–79.

Sullivan, Matthew. "A Brief Textual History of the *Manuel des Péchés*." *Neuphilologische Mitteilungen* 93 (1992): 337–46.

Swanson, R. N. "Angels Incarnate: Clergy and Masculinity from Gregorian Reform to Reformation." In *Masculinity in Medieval Europe*, ed. D. M. Hadley. London: Longman, 1999. 160–77.

Symes, Carol. *A Common Stage: Theater and Public Life in Medieval Arras*. Ithaca, N.Y.: Cornell University Press, 2007.

———. "The Confraternity of Jongleurs and the Cult of the Virgin: Vernacular Devotion and Documentation in Medieval Arras." In *The Church and Vernacular Literature in Medieval France*, ed. Dorothea Kullmann. Toronto: Pontifical Institute of Mediaeval Studies, 2009. 176–97.

———. "The Lordship of Jongleurs." In *The Experience of Power in Medieval Europe, 950–1350*, ed. Robert F. Berkhofer III, Alan Cooper, and Adam J. Kosto. Aldershot, Hamps.: Ashgate, 2005. 237–52.

Szittya, Penn R. "The Friar as False Apostle: Antifraternal Exegesis and the Summoner's Tale." *Studies in Philology* 71 (1974): 19–46.

Tanner, Norman, ed. *Decrees of the Ecumenical Councils*. 2 vols. London: Sheed and Ward; Washington, D.C.: Georgetown University Press, 1990.

Tanner, Norman, and Sethina Watson. "Least of the Laity: The Minimum Requirements for a Medieval Christian." *Journal of Medieval History* 32 (2006): 395–423.

Thompson, Victoria. "The Pastoral Contract in Late Anglo-Saxon England: Priest and Parishioner in Oxford, Bodleian Library, MS Laud Miscellaneous 482." In *Pastoral Care in Late Anglo-Saxon England*, ed. Francesca Tinti. Woodbridge, Suffolk: Boydell Press, 2005. 106–20.

Trachsler, Richard. "Uncourtly Texts in Courtly Books: Musings on MS Chantilly, Musée Condé 475." In *Courtly Arts and the Art of Courtliness*, ed. Keith Busby and Christopher Kleinhenz. Cambridge: D. S. Brewer, 2006. 679–92.

Tudor, Adrian P. *Tales of Vice and Virtue: The First Old French "Vie des Pères."* Amsterdam: Rodopi, 2005.

———. "Telling the Same Tale? Gautier de Coinci's *Miracles de Nostre Dame* and the First *Vie des Pères*." In *Gautier de Coinci*, ed. Krause and Stones. 301–30.

Uitti, Karl D. "The Clerkly Narrator Figure in Old French Hagiography and Romance." *Medioevo romanzo* 2.3 (1975): 394–408.

Van Engen, John. "Practice Beyond the Confines of the Medieval Parish." In *Educating People of Faith: Exploring the History of Jewish and Christian Communities*, ed. John Van Engen. Grand Rapids, Mich.: William B. Eerdmans, 2004. 150–77.

Van Liere, Frans. "Biblical Exegesis Through the Twelfth Century." In *The Practice of the Bible in the Middle Ages: Production, Reception, and Performance in Western Christianity*, ed. Susan Boynton and Diane J. Reilly. New York: Columbia University Press, 2011. 157–78.

Vaughan, Sally N., and Jay Rubenstein, eds. *Teaching and Learning in Northern Europe, 1000–1200*. Turnhout: Brepols, 2006.

Vitz, Evelyn Birge. *Orality and Performance in Early French Romance*. Cambridge: D. S. Brewer, 1999.

Warner, Marina. *Alone of All Her Sex: The Myth and Cult of the Virgin Mary*. New York: Vintage, 1983.

Waters, Claire M. *Angels and Earthly Creatures: Preaching, Performance, and Gender in the Later Middle Ages*. Philadelphia: University of Pennsylvania Press, 2004.

———. "The Labor of *Aedificatio* and the Business of Preaching." *Viator* 38 (2007): 167–89.

Watkins, C. S. "Sin, Penance and Purgatory in the Anglo-Norman Realm: The Evidence of Visions and Ghost Stories." *Past and Present* 175.1 (2002): 3–33.

Watson, Nicholas. "Conceptions of the Word: The Mother Tongue and the Incarnation of God." *New Medieval Literatures* 1 (1997): 85–124.

———. "Desire for the Past." *Studies in the Age of Chaucer* 21 (1999): 59–97.

———. "Lollardy: The Anglo-Norman Heresy?" In *Language and Culture in Medieval Britain*, ed. Wogan-Browne et al. 334–46.

———. "The Middle English Mystics." In *The Cambridge History of Medieval English Literature*, ed. David Wallace. Cambridge: Cambridge University Press, 1999. 539–65.

———. "Middle English Versions and Audiences of Edmund of Abingdon's *Speculum religiosorum*." In *Texts and Traditions of Medieval Pastoral Care: Essays in Honour of Bella Millett*, ed. Kate Gunn and Catherine Innes-Parker. York Medieval Publications. Cambridge: Boydell and Brewer, 2009. 115–31.

———. "Visions of Inclusion: Universal Salvation and Vernacular Theology in Pre-Reformation England." *Journal of Medieval and Early Modern Studies* 27 (1997): 145–87.

Watson, Nicholas, and Jocelyn Wogan-Browne. "The French of England: The *Compileison*, *Ancrene Wisse*, and the Idea of Anglo-Norman." *Cultural Traffic in the Medieval Romance World: Journal of Romance Studies* 4.3, special issue, ed. Simon Gaunt and Julian Weiss (Winter 2004): 35–58.

Wenzel, Siegfried. *Preachers, Poets, and the Early English Lyric*. Princeton, N.J.: Princeton University Press, 1986.

Westphal, Sarah. *Textual Poetics of German Manuscripts, 1300–1500*. Columbia, S.C.: Camden House, 1993.

Westra, Liuwe H. *The Apostles' Creed: Origins, History, and Some Early Commentaries*. Turnhout: Brepols, 2002.

Wilmart, André. *Auteurs spirituels et textes dévots du moyen âge latin*. Paris: Études Augustiniennes, 1971.

———. "Le Grand poème bonaventurien sur les sept paroles du Christ en Croix." *Revue bénédictine* 47 (1937): 235–78.

Wilson, Evelyn Faye. *The "Stella maris" of John of Garland, Edited, Together with a Study of Certain Collections of Mary Legends Made in Northern France in the Twelfth and Thirteenth Centuries*. Cambridge, Mass.: Wellesley College and the Mediaeval Academy of America, 1946.

Wogan-Browne, Jocelyn. "'Cest livre liseez . . . chescun jour': Women and Reading, c. 1230–c. 1430." In *Language and Culture in Medieval Britain*, ed. Wogan-Brown et al. 239–53.

———. "How to Marry Your Wife with Chastity, Honour, and *Fin' Amor* in Thirteenth-Century England." In *Thirteenth Century England IX: Proceedings of the Durham Conference 2001*, ed. Michael Prestwich, Richard Britnell, and Robin Frame. Woodbridge, Suffolk: Boydell Press, 2003. 131–50.

———. "Time to Read: Pastoral Care, Vernacular Access and the Case of Angier of St.

Frideswide." In *Texts and Traditions of Medieval Pastoral Care: Essays in Honour of Bella Millett*, ed. Cate Gunn and Catherine Innes-Parker. Woodbridge, Suffolk: York Medieval Press, 2009. 62–77.

———. "Women's Formal and Informal Traditions of Biblical Knowledge in Anglo-Norman England." In *Saints, Scholars, and Politicians: Gender as a Tool in Medieval Studies*, ed. Mathilde van Dijk and Renée Nip. Medieval Church Studies 15. Turnhout: Brepols, 2005. 85–109.

Wogan-Browne, Jocelyn, with Carolyn Collette, Maryanne Kowaleski, Linne Mooney, Ad Putter, and David Trotter, eds. *Language and Culture in Medieval Britain: The French of England, c. 1100–c. 1500*. York: York Medieval Press, 2009.

Woods, Marjorie Curry, and Rita Copeland. "Classroom and Confession." In *The Cambridge History of Medieval English Literature*, ed. David Wallace. Cambridge: Cambridge University Press, 1999. 376–406.

Young, Christopher. "At the End of the Tale: Didacticism, Ideology and the Medieval German *Maere*." In *Mittelhochdeutsche Novellistik im europäischen Kontext: Beiheft zur Zeitschrift für deutsche Philologie*, ed. Mark Chinca, Timo Reuvekamp-Felber, and Christopher Young. Berlin: Erich Schmidt Verlag, 2006. 24–47.

Zieman, Katherine. *Singing the New Song: Literacy and Liturgy in Late Medieval England*. Philadelphia: University of Pennsylvania Press, 2008.

Zink, Michel. *Medieval French Literature: An Introduction*. Trans. Jeff Rider. Binghamton, N.Y.: Medieval & Renaissance Texts & Studies, 1995.

———. *Poésie et conversion au moyen âge*. Paris: Presses Universitaires de France, 2003.

Ziolkowski, Jan M. "Juggling the Middle Ages: The Reception of *Our Lady's Tumbler* and *Le Jongleur de Notre Dame*." *Memory and Medievalism*, special issue of *Studies in Medievalism* 15 (2006): 157–97.

Index

Abelard, Peter, 4, 233 n.41; and Bernard of
   Clairvaux, 68–69, 71–72, 74; *Expositio
   Symboli quod dicitur Apostolorum*, 186,
   237 n.31, 238 n.55; influence of, 72, 231
   nn.23, 24; *Sic et non,* 69; *Soliloquium,* 69;
   as a teacher, 68–69, 71–72, 231 n.17
Abraham, 66, 91–92
Achan (Achor), 129
Ackerman, Robert W., 81, 233 n.46
Adam, father of humankind, 12, 113, 119,
   122–23, 239 n.72; and the Fall, 12,
   55–56, 106; afterlife of, 122–23, 156; *Jeu
   d'Adam,* 238 n.48. *See also* patriarchs and
   prophets
Adam de Perseigne, 35
Adam of Exeter, 52–53, 54, 60
Adgar, 167, 249 n.11
afterlife, 155; curiosity about, 61, 67, 106,
   107; visions/stories of, 8, 64, 78, 107, 147,
   234 n.66, 252 n.51
Alfonsi, Petrus, 20. See also *Chastoiement
   d'un père à son fils*
Aline de la Zouche, 27, 224 n.37; as collab-
   orator, 35–36; as patron, 27, 31, 35–36;
   as reader, 35–36, 42, 43, 227 n.61; as
   teacher, 43. *See also* patrons
Allen, Elizabeth, 75, 232 n.31
anchorites/anchoritism, 3, 215 n.9
Ancrene Riwle (Ancrene Wisse), xi, 127
André de Coutances, 116; *Évangile de
   Nicodème,* 116, 119, 122–24, 227 n.63,
   238 n.44, 246 n.64
Angier of St. Frideswide, 35
Anglo-Norman, x, 166, 213 n.2, 235 n.10
Anselm of Bec (or of Canterbury), St., 179,
   180, 207; *Cur Deus homo,* 116, 169; and
   the Virgin Mary, 169, 173, 251 n.43
apostles, 39, 102, 157, 160. *See also* Paul, St.;
   Peter, St.; Thomas, St.
Apostles' Creed. *See* Creed
Aquinas, Thomas, 48, 228 n.70

Ardent, Raoul, 61, 234 n.66
Arnold of Bonneval, *Tractatus de septem verbis
   Domini in cruce,* 103–5, 108, 121
Arnould, E. J., 216 n.14, 223 n.13
Aucassin and Nicolette, 140–41, 142, 188
Audigier, 154
Augustine, St., 1, 26, 92, 254 n.85; and categories of judgment, 143, 218 n.26, 234
   n.65; influence of, 226 n.50, 231 n.24;
   and kenosis, 226 n.50, 239 n.65; in medieval translation, 1, 2, 3, 14, 175, 202, 203,
   215 n.51; as teacher, 215 n.8, 220 n.46
Augustinian canons. *See* canons regular
Ave Maria: as basic instruction, 95, 167–68;
   biblical context of, 199–200, 249 n.14;
   and *clergie,* 191, 204; in Marian miracles,
   168, 183–85, 199–200, 254 n.77; salvific power of, 186, 192, 204; translated,
   184–85, 254 n.79. *See also* Mary, St.

bad thief (Gestas), 98–105, 236 n.16; as
   figure of those not saved, 107, 135–36; as
   foil for the good thief, 97, 98–102, 121,
   125, 129, 131
Baldwin, John W., 96, 235 n.7
baptism, 22–23, 129–30; and basic instruction, 21, 109, 110, 235 n.2, 237 n.41;
   and dialogue, 111; in the early church,
   110–11, 136, 236 n.30, 237 n.41
Barratt, Alexandra, 219 n.36, 227 n.63, 249
   n.13
Barthélemy, recluse of Molliens, 29, 31, 215
   n.9; *Miserere,* 41–42, 166, 173, 175, 249
   n.10; *Romans de carité,* 27, 29–30, 166,
   224 n.28, 227 n.60, 250 n.31
Baswell, Christopher, 222 n.2, 228 n.72
Bede, *In Lucae evangelium expositio,* 102,
   106, 126, 235 n.13
Bernard of Clairvaux, 27, 73, 74, 103, 128,
   233 n.41, 240 n.79; and Peter Abelard,
   68–69, 71–72, 74; on boundaries in

Bernard of Clairvaux (*cont.*)
teaching, 69–70, 72, 74; *In festo omnium sanctorum sermo I,* 70–71, 83, 84, 231 n.19; on levels of learning, 84, 91, 168, 231 n.26; on Mary, 174–75; on sinner-saints, 94, 173–74; as a teacher, 42, 80, 231 n.26
Bernstein, Alan, 129, 219 n.35
Bible, 121, 210; apocryphal, 94–95, 96; events of, 16, 113, 133, 199–201; exegesis of, 14, 35, 39, 43, 102, 130, 160; in French, xiv, 4, 43, 55, 95, 96, 214 n.19, 224 n.36, 247 n.78; in Latin, 95, 100, 113; lay access to, ix–x, 10, 53, 55, 95–96, 112, 113, 159, 218 n.26, 221 n.57, 235 nn. 2, 5. See also *Ci nous dit; Évangile de Nicodème;* Holkham Bible; *Miroir (Évangiles des domnées)*
Bible, specific citations of: Acts 4:13, 220 n.42; Ezekiel 33:12, 126, 203; Ezekiel 34:10, 6; Isaiah 9:2, 112–13; Isaiah 52:7, 232 n.38; Isaiah 53:12, 97, 102; John 10:28, 247 n.77; John 19:26–27, 98; Joshua 7:16–26, 129; Lamentations 4:4, 39–40, 41–42; Luke 1:46, 251 n.46; Luke 18:9–14, 116; Luke 23:27–43, 97, 102–3, 104, 106, 112, 125, 235 nn. 12, 13; Mark 4:3–20, 232 n.38; Mark 14:34, 114; Mark 15:27–32, 97, 235 n.13; Matthew 1:21, 254 n.87; Matthew 5:1–12, 70; Matthew 11:2–10, 44; Matthew 20:1–16, 123; Matthew 25:31–46, 86, 104, 160, 235 n.12; Matthew 26:38, 114; Matthew 27:38–44, 97; Revelation 3:12, 160. *See also* Descent into Hell, biblical bases for; Pauline epistles; Psalms
Bodel, Jehan, 147, 148, 244 n.38
Boethius, 20, 25, 229 n.87
Bolduc, Michelle, 166, 248 n.1
Boogard, Nico van den, 161, 246 n.67, 247 n.77
Books of Hours, 169, 248 n.2, 250 n.22
Boulton, Maureen B. M., 167, 249 n.12
Bovon, François, 103, 235 n.12
Boyarin, Adrienne Williams, 248 n.1, 250 n.21, 253 n.67, 254 n.88
Boyle, Leonard, 15, 214 n.19, 216 n.12, 221 n.51
Bradbury, Nancy Mason, 222 n.1, 247 n.81
Breen, Katharine, xi, 214 n.12, 221 n.53, 255 n.94

Brilliant, Virginia, 68, 232 n.36
Brusegan, Rosanna, 155, 245 n.57
Burrows, Daron, 145, 243 n.25
Busby, Keith, 146, 147, 148, 241 n.3, 243 n.33
Butterfield, Ardis, xii, 213 n.2, 214 n.11
Bynum, Caroline Walker, 3, 225 n.43, 231 n.12

Cannon, Christopher, x, 213 n.3
canons regular, 3–4, 28, 35, 45, 215 n.9, 225 n.43
Cartlidge, Neil, 65, 219 n.34
Casagrande, Carla, 140, 141, 143, 156, 241 n.6, 242 nn. 10, 16, 19, 245 n.63
catechism, 19, 23, 27, 131, 132, 239 n.72
Cavadini, John C., 215 n.8, 220 n.46
Certeau, Michel de, 18
Chasteau d'amour (Robert Grosseteste), 25–26, 168, 201, 204, 207, 254 n.81; manuscript contexts, 49, 62, 96, 167, 225 n.39, 249 n.13
Chastoiement d'un père à son fils (Petrus Alfonsi), 20, 21, 22
Chaucer, Geoffrey, xiii, 154
Chinnery, Ann, 39, 226 n.54
Chrestien, verse *Évangile de Nicodème,* 115, 117–19, 238 n.44
Chrétien de Troyes: *Chevalier de la charrette,* 241 n.1; *Yvain,* 142
Ci nous dit, 100, 156
Clanchy, M. T., 10, 11, 218 n. 29, 219 nn. 37, 38
clergie: etymology of, 10; as learning/learnedness, 25–26, 34, 55, 59, 191, 193, 226 n.53, 253 n.70; "lewed," 219 n.33; and social categories, 57–58, 151–52, 177, 189, 253 n.70
Cocuce, 154, 245 n.57
Collet, Olivier, 166, 251 n.41
Compileison, 126–27, 240 n.77. See also *Ancrene Riwle*
confession 1, 3, 7–8, 13, 15, 56, 71, 81, 129, 210, 221 n.55, 231 n.23; manuals, xiii, 129–30, 235 n.3; formula for, 29; of the good thief, 98, 126–27, 128–30; of Mary the Egyptian, 151; in Marian miracles, 197, 200; and teaching, 3, 7–8, 13, 23, 215 n.2, 217 n.22, 220 n.48, 235 n.3. *See also* penance
conversion, 10, 64, 66, 67–68, 77, 171, 197;

Foucauldian, 17, 179, 198; of sinner-
saints, 82, 100, 105, 149, 152
Creed, 108, 109, 119, 132–34, 238 n.55,
244 n.45; Abelard on, 186, 238 n.55; and
basic teaching, 10, 29, 95, 108, 110, 150,
167–68, 235 n.2; early development of,
107, 136, 236 nn. 29, 30; and the *Gospel
of Nicodemus*, 95, 106, 107, 111; of Innocent III, 237 n.31; Lateran, 237 n.31; in
prayers, 240 n.85; *Quicumque vult,* 17

David (biblical figure), 71, 113, 114; in the
Eructavit, 159, 166, 239 n.71, 246 n.74
Day of Judgment. *See* Last Judgment
Dean, Ruth J., 167, 249 n.12
debate of body and soul, 81–82, 233 nn.
46, 47
Delumeau, Jean, 8, 230 n.5
Descent into Hell (*Descensus ad inferos*),
72, 94, 105, 110, 111, 130, 138, 156,
200–201, 237 n.40, 244 n.45, 246 n.64;
biblical bases for, 102, 106, 112, 236 n.25;
and the Creed, 95, 106–9, 111, 132–36,
236 n.30, 237 n.31, 239 n.56; in drama,
238 nn. 46, 48; in the *Gospel of Nicodemus,*
111–15, 124, 238 n.44. 246 n.64; and
kenosis, 105, 108–9, 115; and temporality,
112, 115–16, 124, 136, 198; theological
aspects, 108–9, 115, 116, 130, 238 n.53,
239 n.65, 245 n.61
Devil (Satan), 3, 201, 245 n.61; claim on
humankind, 116, 237 n.40; as gatekeeper
of Hell, 113–15, 124, 155–56; and jongleurs, 140, 149; lack of understanding
of, 115, 116, 201, 239 n.72; in Marian
miracles, 178, 202; pride of, 37, 41; and
whores, 142, 149
Dialogue de saint Julien, 167
Dialogue du père et du fils, 6, 19, 20–23, 47,
95, 96, 222 n.8
Dinshaw, Carolyn, 38, 226 n.51
Disciplina clericalis (Petrus Alfonsi). See
Chastoiement d'un père à son fils
Dismas, St. *See* good thief
Dit des eles, 146
Dives and Lazarus (biblical figures), 66–67,
71, 82, 87, 91–92, 233 n.39, 238 n.46
Dorn, Erhard, 125, 240 n.73, 246 n.69
Douglas, Mary, 159, 246 n.71
drama: of biblical figures, 238 nn. 46, 48;
239 n.71; and *Gospel of Nicodemus,* 131,

237 n.43; liturgical, 113; of saints, 143,
148, 244 n.38
Duffy, Eamon, 9
Duys, Kathryn A., 205, 206

Edmund of Abingdon, 215 n.9; *Speculum
religiosorum,* 132, 133, 225 n.40. See also
Mirour de seinte eglyse
Elijah, 116–17, 124, 239 n.72
Elizabeth of Hungary, St., 148
Elucidarium. See Honorius Augustodunensis
Enoch, 116–17, 124, 239 n.72
Eructavit (?Adam de Perseigne), 35, 96, 159,
166, 227 n.60; role of King David in, 159,
166, 239 n.71, 246 n.74, 254 n.74
Esau, 189, 192, 253 n.67
Escommeniement au lecheor, L', 145, 245 n.63
Espurgatoire seint Patriz (Marie de France),
156–57
estates (of society), 11, 13, 65, 77, 79, 142,
143, 203, 243 n.26; satire on, 6, 29, 140–
41, 144–46, 203; in sermonic texts, 29,
74–78, 92, 134, 140; three orders of, 11,
142, 143, 145–46, 243 nn. 23, 26. See also
jongleurs; monks; peasants; priests; whores
Étienne de Bourbon, 72
Étienne de Fougères, 6
Eucharist, 13, 72, 105; miracles of, 105, 236
n.24
Eudes de Sully (bishop), 4, 249 n.15
Eutyches, 109, 238 n.51
*Evangelium Nicodemi. See Évangile de
Nicodème; Gospel of Nicodemus*
Évangile de Nicodème, 95–96, 102, 105,
107, 111–25, 235 n.10; and basic instruction, 95, 97, 125; and the Bible, 95, 96,
112–13, 115; manuscript contexts of, 96;
and (mis)recognition, 112–15, 116–19;
prose versions of, 96, 111, 113, 116, 119,
235 nn. 9, 10, 238 n.44. See also André de
Coutances; Bible; Chrestien; Creed; Descent into Hell; *Gospel of Nicodemus*
*Évangiles des domnées. See Miroir (Évangiles
des domnées)*
Evans, Gillian, 68, 72, 231 n.26
Everard of Gateley, Marian miracles of, 167
exempla, 75, 86, 148, 164, 168, 231 n.9,
233 n.51; on death and judgment, 66, 75,
78–79, 81, 84, 92, 246 n.68; in Honorius
Augustodunensis, 76–79, 81, 82, 198, 232
nn. 34, 35; manuscript contexts of, 24,

exempla (*cont.*)
167, 223 n.14, 246 n.71; in Pierre d'Abernon, 89–90; in Robert of Gretham, 33–34

fabliaux, 14, 82, 137, 152–63, 191, 209,
241 n.3, 243 n.34, 245 n.53; audience
of, x, 160, 220 n.49, 242 n.21, 247 n.79;
authors of, 146–48, 220 n.49, 244 n.38;
Continental origins of, 166; definition of,
139, 241 n.2; and hagiography, 146–48,
155–56, 157–59, 243 n.33; manuscript
context of, 146–48, 158, 161, 163; and
Marian miracles, 243 n.35; and Purgatory,
143; and reversal, 137, 139, 141, 144,
148, 155–61, 197, 202, 209; and teaching, 8, 138, 139, 160, 162–63, 209, 247
n.79. *See also titles of specific works*
Fall, the, 55–56, 106
felix culpa, 202
Flint, Valerie, 28, 223 n.20
Foehr-Janssens, Jasmina, 205, 253 n.65, 255
n.92
Foucault, Michel, 2, 15–16, 179, 198, 217
n.20, 220 n.50
Fourth Lateran Council, 4, 30, 126, 213 n.6,
215 n.2, 216 n.12; canons of, 1, 10, 13,
237 n.31
Frankis, John, 11, 219 n.35
Freedman, Paul, 12, 220 n.40, 242 n.11
French of England, x, 213 n.2. *See also*
Anglo-Norman
friars, 3, 154, 215 n.9
Fulton, Rachel, 171, 200, 254 n.78

Gabriel, St. (archangel), 199–200, 249 n.14
Gaunt, Simon, 147, 245 n.58
Gautier de Coinci, 165, 215 n.9, 248 n.1,
249 n.7, 250 n.30, 253 n.70; and Marian
theology, 171, 201–3; on peasants, 184,
189–92, 194–95, 253 nn.70, 71; self-
depiction, 176–77, 182–183, 185,
192–93, 205–6, 252 n.55, 253 nn.65, 71;
wordplay of, 177, 180, 181, 185, 191, 244
n.41, 252 n.61. *See also* Marian miracles
Gestas. *See* bad thief
Gilbert, Jane, 64, 68, 230 n.4, 231 n.11
Gillespie, Vincent, xi
Glossa ordinaria, 4, 102, 126, 216 n.10, 233
n.41, 236 n.18
Godric, St., 10
good thief (Dismas), 94, 95, 106, 130, 136,

153, 159, 176; in the Bible, 97–105,
109, 112, 125; entry into Heaven, 110,
122–23; in the *Évangile de Nicodème*,
111–25, 239 n.63; as example of rescue,
83, 93, 122, 130, 198; as figure of reversal,
116, 117–21, 127–30, 139; and penance,
125–30; as sinner-saint, xiii, 11, 70–71,
124, 125, 137, 160, 240 n.73; as teacher,
101–5, 119, 122, 124, 130, 131, 152,
159–60
Gospel of Nicodemus (Evangelium Nicodemi)
94–95, 98, 111–12, 113, 119, 125, 237
n.43; and basic instruction, 109, 110,
115; manuscripts of, 16, 138; origins of,
106–7, 111, 132, 136. *See also Évangile de
Nicodème*
Gower, John, xiii
Gravdal, Kathryn, 142, 154, 242 nn. 12, 19,
245 n.54
Gregorian Reform, 10, 28, 96, 209, 224 n.23
Gregory the Great, 59–60, 76, 252 n.51;
Dialogues, 6, 27, 35, 48, 89, 234 n.64; *Pastoralet (Cura pastoralis)*, 40, 227 n.58
Grosseteste, Robert, 10, 207, 215 n.9, 225
n.39, 229 n.85, 233 n.47; and basic teaching, 132, 168, 204; *Chasteau d'amour*,
25–26, 49, 62, 96, 167, 201, 204, 254 n.81
Guerric of Igny, 128, 240 nn. 79, 80

habitus, 206, 221 n.53, 255 n.94
hagiography, x, 8, 10, 82–84, 96, 142,
147–52, 219 n.32; and fabliaux, 146–48,
155–56, 157–62, 243 n.33. *See also names
of individual saints*; patriarchs and prophets; sinner-saints
Hail Mary. *See* Ave Maria
Haines, Roy M., 168, 250 nn. 16, 18
Hakamies, Reino, 189, 252 n.50
Handlyng Synne, xiii, 221 n.54, 234 n.58. See
also *Manuel des pechiez*
Harkins, Franklin T., 220 n.50, 221 n.58,
229 n.82
Harrowing of Hell. *See* Descent into Hell
Heaven (Paradise), 64, 68, 173, 203; and
Christ, 110, 198; entry into, 94, 95,
122–23, 140–41, 149, 153–60, 186–88,
201, 232 n.36, 239 n.71; gates of, 110,
120, 122, 157, 159, 198, 239 n.63; and
the good thief, 97, 116, 118, 120, 122–23,
125, 127, 130, 137; and jongleurs, 151,
155–56; and peasants, 153–55, 157–63,

184, 186–88, 191, 246 n.70; as place of
reward, 9, 57, 90, 108, 116, 119, 146,
191, 202; visible to the damned, 67; visions of, 107. *See also* Hell; Purgatory
Hélinand of Froidmont, 72–73
Hell, 8, 64; as a character (Enfer), 113–15,
116, 124; emptying of, 202, 204; gates of,
114, 198, 239 n.63; horrors of, 63, 73, 85,
129; and jongleurs, 155–56; knowledge
of, 62, 68; and the nobility, 140–41, 142,
184, 188, 203; and peasants, 154–55,
203; place of punishment, 75, 77, 81, 87,
90, 104, 113, 129, 181, 201, 202, 203;
visibility of Heaven from, 67; visits from/
to, 63, 64, 73, 78, 85, 107, 181–82, 245
n.56. *See also* Descent into Hell; Heaven;
Purgatory
heresy, x, xiii, 109, 215 n.3, 216 n.22, 247
n.78
Hesketh, Glynn, 57, 58, 221 n.56, 227 n.63,
228 n.73, 229 nn. 85, 87, 234 n.63, 254
n.85
Historia scholastica (Peter Comestor), 96,
121–22, 235 n.7, 236 n.14
Holkham Bible, 98–102, 104, 121, 236 n.14
holy simplicity, 9, 13, 85, 151, 163, 178–79,
192; in the Bible, 39, 108, 220 n.42; and
clerics, 175, 177–81, 183, 193–94; and
jongleurs, 168, 182–83; and learning, 12,
39, 68, 72, 141, 177, 180–81, 189; and
peasants, 12, 13, 183–88, 194; and status
reversal, 85, 108, 151, 164, 192. *See also*
kenosis
Honorius Augustodunensis, 27–28, 69, 80,
216 n.11, 231 n.24; audience of, 30, 47,
74, 79, 80, 155, 223 n.20; on clerical
status, 28–29, 30, 35, 75, 79, 92; and
dialogue, 46–47, 227 n.64; *Elucidarium
(Lucidaires),* 4, 6, 28, 45, 46–47, 96, 125,
140, 141–42, 155, 188, 222 n.8, 227
n.67; on the good thief, 83, 125–26, 203;
Imago mundi (Image du monde), 217 n.16;
on social classes, 74–79, 140, 141–42,
188; *Speculum ecclesiae (Sermo generalis),* 4,
27, 28–29, 74–79, 92, 220 n.4; theology
of, 223 n.20, 248 n.4; use of exempla by,
74–79, 81, 84, 198, 232 n.35
Hoogvliet, Margriet, 113, 214 n.19, 224
n.36, 235 n.5, 247 n.78
Hours of the Virgin, 164, 249 n.15. *See also*
Books of Hours

Hugh of Cluny, 195
Hugh of St. Victor, 79, 216 n.11, 220 n.50,
221 n.58; and the Victorines, 240 n.89
humility, xiv, 3, 13, 32, 36, 40–41, 85, 163,
210; of Christ, 37–38, 40–41, 46, 70–71,
108, 115, 120–21, 129, 170, 174, 227;
of the good thief, 127–28, 129, 136;
power of, 116, 120, 127–28, 136; and
sinner-saints, 71, 151, 159, 173–74; of the
teacher, 32, 36–42, 45, 46, 48, 70–71, 80,
193. *See also* holy simplicity; Incarnation;
kenosis
Hunt, Tony, 223 n.15, 228 n.78, 251 n.40,
252 n.49

Ignorantia sacerdotum (John Pecham), 132
In festo omnium sanctorum sermo I (St. Bernard), 70–71, 83, 84, 231 n.19
In Lucae evangelium expositio (Bede), 102,
106, 126, 235 n.13
individual judgment. *See* judgment,
individual/particular
Innocent III, Pope, 107, 214 n.19, 216 n.12,
237 n.31, 239 n.56. *See also* Fourth Lateran Council
Ioca monachorum, 239 n.72
Isidore of Seville, 54

Jacob, 173, 189, 192
Jacques de Vitry, 72, 148, 226 n.48
Jaeger, Stephen, 4, 216 n.11, 220 nn.40, 50
Jauss, H. R., 20
Jean de Journy, 216 n.14
Jenkins, T. Atkinson, 35, 225 n.44
Jesus Christ, 7, 44, 52, 54, 82, 88, 153,
207, 250 n.33, 254 n.81; in the Creed,
107, 110, 132–34; Crucifixion of, 82, 94,
97–103, 105, 110, 111, 121–22, 156,
201, 240 n.85; in the *Gospel of Nicodemus,*
111–25; Incarnation of, 2, 37–38, 46,
57, 105, 109–16, 120–21, 165, 169–71,
200, 202–3, 204, 236 n.24, 238 n.53, 239
n.72, 248 n.4; as judge, 86–87, 104, 204,
206; as king, 104, 112, 114–15, 118, 184,
199, 201, 204; and Mary, 82, 130–31,
153, 165, 166, 169, 171–72, 201, 203–6,
254 n.87; Passion of, 112, 122, 133, 135–
36, 174, 233 n.47, 243 n.23; Redemption
by, 12, 26, 57, 105, 116, 119, 132–34,
156, 201, 204, 237 n.40, 238 n.53, 245
n.61; Resurrection of, 106, 112, 117, 136,

Jesus Christ (*cont.*)
  158, 174, 243 n.23; as teacher, 45–46,
  70–71, 103; two natures of, 94, 97, 98,
  101, 103–4, 109–11, 112, 114–16, 122,
  129, 136, 238 n.51. *See also* Descent into
  Hell; humility; kenosis
John the Baptist, St., 44–45, 113
John the Evangelist, St., 82, 100
jongleurs, 242, 243, 247 n.76; and clerks,
  139, 142, 146, 147, 151, 153, 155, 182–
  83, 189, 220 n.49, 241 n.4; in fabliaux,
  144–47, 155–56; Gautier de Coinci as,
  183, 253 n.65; David as, 160, 239 n.71;
  in Marian miracles, 166, 168, 182–83,
  252 nn.53, 54; status of, 11, 13, 139–43;
  and peasants, 139, 142, 147; as teachers, 10,
  11, 139, 241 n.4; universality of, 141, 142,
  241 n.4; and whores, 144–46, 149, 151
Joseph, St., 112, 116, 254 n.87
Judgment, Day of. *See* Last Judgment
judgment, individual/particular, 8, 61–62,
  64, 81–82, 85, 92–93, 198, 210; exempla
  of, 75, 76–79, 81, 82–83, 89, 94, 109,
  138, 157, 161; and the good thief, 97,
  127; in Marian miracles, 181–82, 194–95,
  197, 205; of students, implications for
  teachers, 23, 81, 89; visual representations
  of, 232 n.36. *See also* Last Judgment
Justice, Steven, 105, 115, 171, 206, 236
  n.24, 239 n.58, 255 n. 94

Kalendar (Ralph of Lenham), 49
Karras, Ruth Mazo, 142, 242 nn. 15, 17
Kay, Sarah, 20
kenosis, 37, 103–4, 105, 108, 226 n.50, 237
  n.33. *See also* humility
Kieckhefer, Richard, 10–11, 219 n.34
Kristeva, Julia, 139, 241 n.5
Kumler, Aden, 4, 23, 31, 49, 215 n.2, 218
  n.28, 220 n.41, 222 nn.6, 11, 225 n.39,
  255 n.2

Langland, William, xiii, 210, 234 n.55
Langton, Stephen, 36, 80, 83–84
Last Judgment, 6–7, 85–87, 88–89, 150,
  231 n.12, 238 n.46. *See also* judgment,
  individual/particular
Laurent, Frère, 215 n.9; *Somme le roi,* 166,
  216 n.14
LaVere, Suzanne, 80, 233 n.41
Lazarus (biblical figure). *See* Dives and Lazarus

Le Goff, Jacques, 107, 143, 181, 231 n.9,
  233 n.52
Lefèvre, Yves, 216 n.12, 222 n.7, 223 n.13
Legge, Dominica, 226 n.47, 228 n.75
Leo I, Pope, 109–11, 238 n.51
Lerer, Seth, 20, 222 n.3
Levinas, Emmanuel, 217 n.20, 226 n.48;
  concept of *maître à penser* in, 39, 226 n.54
Levy, Brian J., 129
literacy, 9, 11–12, 31, 180; of the laity, xii, 5,
  20, 30–31, 49, 139, 219 n.38, 224 n.35,
  247 n.78, 253 n.69; in Latin, 30; and
  Mary, 164; in the vernacular, 9, 25
Little, Katherine C., xi, 7–8
liturgy, 121, 169, 200, 238 n.53, 254 n.79;
  liturgical drama, 113
Livre des manières (Étienne de Fougères), 6
Lobrichon, Guy, 96, 218 n.26, 221 n.57,
  235 nn. 6, 7
Lucidaires. See Honorius Augustodunensis
Lumere as lais, 17, 27, 45–60, 95, 162, 168,
  197; audience of, 26–27, 45–51, 57, 59,
  227 n.63, 229 nn. 84, 85, 89; on the
  Creed, 134–36; dialogue form of, 19, 21,
  47–48; exempla in, 90; manuscript contexts of, 24, 49, 82, 223 n.14, 233 n.47;
  on Mary, 202–3; orderliness of, 47, 54–55,
  88, 228 n.73, 229 nn. 80, 85, 234 n.62;
  on Purgatory, 89–91; and theology, 57–59,
  91–92; and translation, 59, 215 n.5, 229
  n.89

Manuel des pechiez (William of Waddington),
  1–3, 95, 176, 223 n.13, 224 n.33; on confession, 127–29; exempla from, 65–67, 72,
  91, 151, 232 n.37, 234 n.63; and the good
  thief, 128–29; and *Handlyng Synne,* xiii,
  221 n.54; on the Last Judgment, 86–87;
  manuscript contexts of, 24, 25, 82, 151,
  167, 223 n.14, 225 n.39, 233 n.47, 249
  n.13; orderliness of, 54; title of, 15–16,
  221 n.54; and temporality, 86–88; and
  translation, 2–3, 14, 15–16
manuscripts, xii, 4, 5, 24–25, 82, 96, 167,
  219 n.36, 223 n.16; fabliaux in, 146–48,
  158; illuminations in, 6, 20–22, 49,
  98–102, 192, 215 n.2, 220 n.47, 225
  n.39; large compilation, 161, 164, 203,
  217 n.16, 247 n.82; of Marian miracles,
  166–67; multilingual, 62, 113; ownership/
  readership of, 11, 27, 49, 95, 218 n.28

manuscripts, specific shelf-marks: Avignon, Bibliothèque municipal, MS 344, 227 n.67; Bern, Burgerbibliothek MS 354, 145, 148, 242 n.22; Cambridge: Emmanuel College, MS 106, 96; Fitzwilliam Museum, McClean MS 123, 96, 249 n.13; Pembroke College, MS 258, 223 n.14; St. John's College, MS F.30, 24; University Library, MS G.I.i, 24; Chantilly, Musée Condé, MS 475, 147; London, British Library: Additional MS 47682 (Holkham Bible), 98–102, 121, 236 n.14; Arundel MS 288, 233 n.47; Cotton MS Domitian A.xi., 53–54, 223 n.14; Harley MS 273, 234 n.60; Harley MS 1121, 249 n.13; Harley MS 3860, 249 n.13; Harley MS 4657, 234 n.60; Royal MS 15.D.II, 49, 228 n.74; Royal MS 16.E.IX, 49; Royal MS 19.C.XI, 227 n.67; Royal MS 20.B.XIV, 25, 151, 165, 167, 175, 192, 223 n.14, 226 n.53; London, Lambeth Palace Library: MS 209, 12; MS 522, 246 n.64, 249 n.13; New Haven, Yale, Beinecke Library MS 492, 24; Nottingham, University Library, MS Middleton L.M.6, 146, 147, 242 n.22; Oxford, Bodleian Library: MS Bodley 399, 49, 223 n.14; MS Digby 86, 247 n.81; MS Laud misc. 471, 62, 92, 223 n.17; MS Rawlinson poetry 241, 167; MS Selden supra 74, 233 n.47; Paris, Bibliothèque de l'Arsenal, MS 3516, 233 n.47; Paris, Bibliothèque nationale de France: fr. 187, 96; fr. 837, 146, 243 n.31; fr. 1136, 227 n.67; fr. 1807, 166; fr. 12581, 20–23, 222 n.5; fr. 13342, 222 n.6; fr. 19152, 146; lat. 12593, 175, 251 n.35; nouv. acq. fr. 4338, 227 n.67, nouv. acq. fr. 24541, 252 n.58; Princeton, University Library, Taylor MS 1, 65–67, 91, 92, 225 n.39, 249 n.13

Marian miracles, ix–x, 8, 82, 141, 147–48, 164–207; anonymous Anglo-French collection of, 25, 165, 167, 172, 175, 192–96; and basic instruction, 164, 168, 173, 175, 177–80, 183–84, 186, 193–94, 206, 210; by Gautier de Coinci, 165, 166, 170–71, 175–92, 199–202, 203–6; and jongleurs, 182–83; manuscript contexts of, 166–67; and peasants, 183–92, 195; temporality of, 198–201, 254 n.79; theological aspects, 165, 168–71, 201–7, 210;

universality of, 166, 175–76, 177, 203. *See also* Gautier de Coinci; holy simplicity; Marian miracles, specific narratives; Mary, St.

Marian miracles, specific narratives: drowned monk, 200–201, 203; Étienne and Perron (wicked judge), 181–82, 185; incestuous noblewoman, 173; jongleur at Rocamadour, 182–83; knight who wished to become a monk, 203–4, 205–6; lecherous sacristan, 196, 204; life of Mary the Egyptian, 173; monk of St. Peter, 202, 204–5; monk who made the prayer MARIA, 179–81, 185; nun who left her abbey, 196; nun who rushed her prayers, 199–200; peasant who rebuilt Mary's chapel, 195; peasant who said the Ave Maria, 183–92, 194–95, 204; pilgrim of St. James, 202; pregnant abbess, 196–97; priest of one mass, 169, 177–79, 180–81, 193–94; rich man saved from the Devil, 178–79, 180–81; Saracen devoted to an image of the Virgin, 170–71; Theophilus, 147–48, 173; thief rescued by Mary, 176; tumbler of our Lady, 166, 168, 183

Marie de Champagne, 35, 159, 227 n.60

Marie de France: *Espurgatoire seint Patriz*, 156–57

Martin, St., 83, 148

Marx, C. W., 115, 116, 237 n.40, 238 n.53

Mary, St., 112, 122, 142, 164, 171, 248 n.6, 250 n.30, 251 n.37; in the Creed, 132–34; in devotional/doctrinal literature, 25, 167, 169, 171–75, 223 n.14, 236 n.27; feasts of, 16, 169, 254 n.79. *See also* Ave Maria; Jesus Christ, Incarnation of; Jesus Christ, and Mary; Marian miracles

Mary Magdalene, St., 142, 143, 152; as sinner-saint, xiii, 70–71, 125, 173–74

Mary the Egyptian, St., 148–52; and Marian miracles, 173, 250 n.32; as sinner-saint, 11, 159, 173

Maurice de Sully, 10, 215 n.9, 249 n.15; sermons of, 4, 16, 17, 62, 96, 107, 224 n.36, 235 n.9

McGinn, Bernard, 54–55

McLuhan, Marshall, xiii

mediocriter boni/mali, 9, 90–91, 92, 143, 218 n.26, 234 n.65

Menegaldo, Silvère, 151, 241 n.6

Meyer, Paul, 223 n.13

Michael, St. (archangel), 113, 157
Middle English, x–xiv, 215 n.3, 234 n.61;
  texts in, 202, 210, 213 n.3, 238 n.46, 239
  n.72, 247 n.76; translations of French
  works, xiii, 113, 221 n.54, 227 n.57
miracles of the Virgin. *See* Marian miracles
Miroir ou Évangiles des domnées (Robert of
  Gretham), xiii, 19, 27, 31–45, 68, 197,
  252 n.51; audience of, 31–37, 42–45, 51,
  197; and humility, 36–41, 193; Middle
  English translation of, 113, 227 n.57; title
  of, 32–33, 225 n.40. *See also* Aline de la
  Zouche; Robert of Gretham
Mirour de seinte eglyse (St. Edmund of Abingdon), 207, 223 n.14, 225 n.40, 229 n.88;
  audience of, 19, 21, 132, 134, 223 n.15;
  and the Creed, 132–33; and dialogue, 19,
  21; images accompanying, 21, 222 n.6;
  manuscript contexts of, 24, 25, 82, 96,
  132, 151, 167, 233 n.47. *See also* Edmund
  of Abingdon, St.
Miserere. See Barthélemy, recluse of Molliens
monastic culture, ix, 5, 28, 169, 217 n.20,
  221 n.53, 222 n.10, 248 n.2
monks, 140, 145, 220 n.40; as audiences,
  28, 48, 74, 80, 189; as authors, 3, 27, 28,
  48, 72–73, 80, 165, 177; in exemplary
  narratives, 73, 77, 151. *See also* Marian
  miracles, specific narratives
Moore, R. I., 209, 255 n.1
moral theology. *See* tropology
Morenzoni, Franco, 216 n.12, 217 n.15, 224
  n.32
Morey, James, 95–96, 235 n.2
Murdoch, Brian, 106, 236 n.27

Nash, Suzanne, 150, 151, 244 nn. 42, 47, 50
native wit (*engin*), 157, 161–62, 163, 248
  n.84
Nims, Margaret, 111, 226 n.51
Noomen, Willem, 161, 246 n.67, 247 n.77
Novikoff, Alex J., 222 n.10, 227 n.64

O'Sullivan, Daniel, 171
otherworld. *See* afterlife
Owen, D. D. R., 106, 236 n.25
Owen, Dorothy, xiii

Parker, John, 95, 235 n.1, 237 n.43, 239
  n.66
Parkes, Malcolm, xi–xii

Pastoralet (Gregory the Great), 40, 227 n.58
Pater Noster, 10, 36, 95, 166; in didactic
  works, 29, 52, 96, 134, 150; in fabliaux,
  157; in Marian miracles, 168, 183, 184,
  186, 223; parodic, 148
patriarchs and prophets: in the *Évangile de
  Nicodème,* 112–13, 116–21, 123–25, 131,
  136, 152, 159. *See also* Adam
patrons, 8, 31, 215 n.2; relationship to clerical authors, 36, 42, 45, 224 n.36, 226
  n.47, 241 n.4; women, 27, 31, 224 n.37,
  225 n.39, 227 n.60. *See also* Aline de la
  Zouche
Paul, St., 125, 158–59, 173, 174, 246 n.69.
  See also Pauline epistles
Pauline epistles, 3, 30, 51, 53–54, 69, 96,
  139, 182; 1 Corinthians 2:1, 224 n.34; 1
  Corinthians 4:13, 139; 1 Corinthians 13,
  51, 61, 69, 102; 1 Corinthians 14:16, 220
  n.42; Ephesians, 108; Philippians 2:5–11,
  108–9, 110, 115, 171; Romans 1:14, 42;
  Romans 10:15, 232 n.38. *See also* Descent
  into Hell, biblical bases for
Pearl, 210, 239
peasants, 11–13, 75, 77, 145; and clerks,
  153–54, 155, 186, 189–92, 195, 244
  n.52, 235 n.13; in fabliaux, 146–47, 152–
  55, 156–63, 247 n.82; and jongleurs, 139,
  142, 147; and learning, 11, 139, 160–63,
  183–92, 211, 219 n.37, 247 n.81; in Marian miracles, 175, 183–92, 194–95, 211,
  252 n.60; social role of, 12–13, 142–43,
  203, 220 n.39, 242 n.11; universality of,
  12, 75, 142, 160, 253 n.64
Pecham, John, 132
Pelikan, Jaroslav, 168–69, 236 n.30, 237
  n.41, 248 n.6
penance/penitence, 4, 126, 129, 154, 174,
  202; at point of death, 77, 87, 184, 203.
  See also confession; good thief
Pet au vilain, Le (Rutebeuf), 146–47, 152–
  55, 156–57, 184, 190, 246 n.71
Peter, St., 144, 158, 191, 202, 204; in fabliaux, 144–46, 147, 155–56, 157–59; as
  sinner-saint, 83, 125, 127, 158, 173–74
Peter Comestor, 96, 121–22, 235 n.7, 236
  n.14
Peter Lombard, 108–9
Peter the Chanter, 80, 96, 224 n.32
Petit sermon, 24, 25, 54–55, 60, 223 n.14,
  228 n. 79, 233 n.47

Pierre d'Abernon of Fetcham, 3, 45, 69, 176, 193, 215 n.9, 227 n.63. See also *Lumere as lais*
Piers Plowman (William Langland), xiii, 85, 210, 234 n.55
Pilate, 107, 112, 239 n.70
Poor, Sara S., 226 n.50, 244 n.49, 246 n.74
Poore, Richard, 167–68
Powell, Morgan, 35, 159, 227 n.60, 239 n.71, 246, nn. 73, 74, 254 n.74
preacher(s): Christ as, 70–71, 103; good thief as, 104–5; at judgment, 75–76, 80–81, 89, 92; relationship to audience of, 3, 5, 10, 27–45, 48, 77, 79, 173, 191, 192
priests, 28–30, 140–41, 229 n.89; in exempla, 72–73, 76, 151; and flock, 6–7, 13, 42, 75–79, 81, 83; in Marian miracles, 163, 177–78, 181, 193–94, 195; parish, 3, 4, 11, 24, 167–68, 219 n.37, 220 n.48; and peasants, 153, 184, 186, 189–92. See also preachers
prostitutes. See whores
proverbs, 44, 161–62, 230 n.2, 247 n.81
Psalms, 47, 96, 169, 179–80, 186, 221 n.57; in *Eructavit* (Psalm 44), 35, 159, 166; in prayer to Mary, 251 nn. 46, 47; Psalm 24:7 [23:7], 237 n.43, 239 n.63; Psalm 48:14, 75; in the psalter, 180, 190, 248 n.2
Purgatory, 8, 63, 65, 75, 107, 143, 233; intermediate nature of, 9, 90–91, 143, 144; in narrative, 89–90, 65, 181, 231 n.9, 234 n.63. See also *mediocriter boni/mali*
Putains et des lecheors, Des, 144–46, 148, 153, 155

Quicumque vult, 17

Ralph of Lenham, *Kalendar,* 49
Raoul de Houdenc, *Dit des eles,* 146
Reames, Sherry, 164, 248 n.3
Reeves, Andrew, 95, 132, 235 n.3
Regalado, Nancy Freeman, 161
Renclus de Molliens. See Barthélemy, recluse of Molliens
Rice, Nicole, 24, 210, 215 n.4, 222 n.12, 255 n.2
Rider, Catherine, xiii, 129, 218 n.28, 235 n.3
Robert of Gretham, 27, 31, 176, 193, 215 n.9, 224 n.37. See also *Miroir (Évangiles des domnées)*

Robert of Sorbon, 72, 73–74
Roberts, Phyllis B., 36, 226 n.49
Robertson, Duncan, 42, 221 n.58, 227 n.59, 242 n.14, 254 n.79
Robson, C. A., 72, 231 n.24, 235 n.9
Roman de Philosophie (Simond de Freine), 25
Roman des romans, 25, 226 n.53
Romans de carité. See Barthélemy, recluse of Molliens
Rubin, Miri, 170, 236 n.27
Ruhe, Ernstpeter, 23, 223 n.13
Rutebeuf, 146–48, 155, 215 n.9, 220 n.49, 244 n.41; *Le Pet au vilain,* 146–47, 152–55, 156–57, 184, 190, 246 n.71; *Vie de sainte Marie l'Egypcienne,* 148–51, 152

S. Pierre et le jongleur, 146–47, 155–56, 161
sacraments, 95, 132, 216 n.13. See also baptism; confession; Eucharist; penance
saints. See hagiography; *names of specific saints*
salvation, universal, 125, 202, 245 n.61
Sanok, Catherine, 124
Satan. See Devil
Schmitt, Jean-Claude, 59–60, 119 n.223
scholasticism, ix, 5, 46, 57, 90, 169, 229 n.85
Seneca, 15, 220 n.50
Serlo of Wilton, 73–74, 230 n.2
sermones ad status. See estates (of society), in sermonic texts
Seth, 113, 238 n.50
Short, Ian, 50, 213 n.2, 214 n.13
Simeon (biblical figure), 112, 113
Simond de Freine, *Roman de Philosophie,* 25
sinner-saints, xiii, 11, 70–71, 82, 94, 122, 125, 137, 144, 159, 166, 173–75, 246 n.69
Somerset, Fiona, xi, 14, 213 nn.5, 6, 219 n.33, 253 n.64
Somme le roi (Frère Laurent), 166, 216 n.14
Souhaiz que saint Martins dona, Les (Jehan Bodel), 148
Stephen, St., 159
Stock, Brian, 12, 216 n.10, 218 n.29, 220 n.42, 224 n.35
Sullivan, Matthew, 223 nn. 13, 14
sündige Heilige. See sinner-saints
Symes, Carol, 131, 240 n.87, 244 n.38, 252 n.53

synodal statutes: English, 4, 132, 167–68, 216 n.13, 250 n.16; French, 4, 71, 167, 249 n.15

Tanner, Norman, 206, 218 n.28
temporality: and death, 64, 76, 79, 85–89, 94, 98; in the Descent into Hell, 112, 115–16, 124, 136, 198, 238 n.46; and the good thief, 98, 121–22, 127; in Marian miracles, 198–206, 254 n.79; in teaching, 11, 69–70, 74
Theophilus, 148, 173
Thomas, St., 157–59, 246 n.69
Thomas of Chobham, 27, 30, 80, 224 n.32; *Summa de arte praedicandi,* 30–31, 35, 44, 80–85, 92, 94, 234 n.57
three orders. *See* estates (of society)
Trachsler, Richard, 147
Tractatus de septem verbis Domini in cruce (Arnold of Bonneval), 103–5, 108, 121
translation, ix, 5, 13–14, 167, 207, 215 n.3, 217 n.16, 235 n.8; authorial discussions of, 6, 18, 58–59; and authorial role, 31–45, 176, 189, 193, 195, 227 n.63; of the Bible, 53, 55, 95–96, 112, 224 n.36; formal effects of, 2, 202, 215 n.5, 224 n.36; Incarnation as, 38, 111, 205; into Middle English, x–xiii, 113, 233 n.46, 253 n.64; in preaching, 15, 28; salvation as, 127; as *translatio,* 5, 138
Trethewey, W. H., 127, 240 n.77
Trois commandemens, Des. See *Putains et des lecheors, Des*
tropology, 16, 79; and exegesis, 14, 34; in relation to teaching, 71–72, 91, 95, 215 n. 2
Tudor, Adrian P., 166, 249 n.9

Usurer's Paternoster and *Creed,* 148

Valdes, Peter, 10
Vecchio, Silvana, 140, 141, 143, 156, 241 n.6, 242 nn. 10, 16, 245 n.63
Vie des pères, 166
Vilain de Bailluel, Le, 147
Vilain qui conquist paradis par plait, Le, 156–63, 173, 211, 246 nn. 67, 75; manuscript contexts of, 146–47
vilains. See peasants
Virgin Mary. *See* Mary, St.
Vitae patrum, 151

Waldensians, 4, 247 n.78
Watkins, C. S., 73, 232 n.29
Watson, Nicholas, xi, xii, 11, 37, 53, 132, 214 n.8, 215 n.3, 221 n.59, 223 n.13, 245 n.61
Watson, Sethina, 206, 218 n.28
Westra, Liuwe, 110, 236 n.29
whores, 11, 13, 138, 139, 142–43, 148–52, 153
William of Malmesbury, 72, 253 n.69
William of Waddington, 215 n.9. See also *Manuel des pechiez*
Wilshere, A. D., 132, 134, 223 n.15, 229 n.88
Wilson, Evelyn, 175
Wogan-Browne, Jocelyn, xi, 12, 13, 35, 213 n.2, 219 n.36, 224 n.37, 226 n.47
Woods, Marjorie Curry, 215 n.4, 220 n.48
Wycliffism, x, xiii, 215 n.3

.xxiij. manieres de vilains, Les, 189, 244 n.52

Zink, Michel, 18, 221 n.61, 226 n.46, 244 n.43, 246 n.71
Zozimas, 150–52, 153, 244 n.45, 253 n.63

Acknowledgments

This is, as sometimes happens, not quite the book I expected to write. It emerged in its current form thanks to the chance to spend an extended time in manuscript libraries, and I am deeply grateful for the University of California President's Research Fellowship in the Humanities that allowed me that opportunity. The Bibliothèque nationale de France, the British Library, Lambeth Palace Library, Cambridge University Library, and the Bodleian Library all hosted and helped shape the project's emergence, and I appreciate the assistance given me by their staffs; at a later stage, the Morgan Library and Princeton University Library were similarly welcoming. The support of a National Endowment for the Humanities summer stipend and an American Council of Learned Societies fellowship, as well as the hospitality of research libraries at Columbia and the University of Virginia, was as important to the book's completion as these others to its beginnings and progress, and it is a pleasure to acknowledge that support here.

I have lived in five cities while writing this book and have thus accumulated even more than the usual number of debts. Its beginnings in Paris and London were enlivened by the presence of old friends—Gerry and Veronica della Paolera, Pierre and Elisabeth Sicsic, Philippe and Veronique Manière, Helen, Rebecca, and Chloe Lianos and David and Laura Shorto, Rachel Bartlett, Peter and Carole Armstrong, and Terry Roopnaraine and Silke Seco. A long middle period benefited from the patience, wise suggestions, and friendship of Becky Krug, Susie Phillips, Elizabeth Allen, Cathy Sanok, Jessica Brantley, Emily Steiner, Katy Breen, Andrea Denny-Brown, Kellie Robertson, and Bobby Meyer-Lee; and I am grateful to George Shuffelton for one of the most useful questions anyone has ever asked me, without which Chapter 3 would have been something else entirely. The company of colleagues in California—especially Seeta Chaganti, Emily Albu, Gina Bloom, Catherine Chin, Joshua Clover, Fran Dolan, Margie Ferguson, Noah Guynn, Desirée Martín, Liz Miller, Catherine Robson, Parama Roy, Matthew Stratton, and most recently Anna Uhlig and Matthew Vernon—has also sustained me in many different ways. I am indebted to John Marx for beginning a fascinating Foucauldian conversation (among many others) and to Ian Cornelius for continuing it across the country. Christopher Young and Joyce Coleman kindly shared their work on related topics. In New York, Chris Baswell, Tricia Dailey and Eleanor Johnson provided intellectual companionship, and Tricia gave me a home away from home at Columbia.

Along the way, I benefited greatly from the chance to present parts of this work at Northwestern, the University of California–Irvine, the University of Minnesota, Columbia, the Ohio State University, and Harvard, and at conferences in Kalamazoo and London; all of these audiences influenced my thinking in ways that they may not immediately recognize but for which I am *très reconnaissante*. I am especially grateful to James Simpson and Ethan Knapp for their illuminating responses. Two reading groups, at Columbia and the University of Virginia, were kind enough to comment on chapters; I am grateful to Susan Boynton, Consuelo Dutschke, Fiona Griffiths, Lauren Mancia, and Neslihan Senocak at Columbia and to Bruce Holsinger, Deborah McGrady, Ahmed al-Rahim, Erin Rowe, Karl Shuve, and Tony Spearing at the University of Virginia. I was extremely lucky to be part of the wonderful medieval community at Virginia, where Bruce, Deborah, Tony, John Parker, Amy Ogden, and Elizabeth Fowler in particular made it an extraordinarily fruitful two years. Their warm welcome, lively company, and intellectual engagement meant a great deal to me and continue to do so.

A number of people—including some already mentioned, who have clearly gone beyond the call of duty—generously read and responded to parts of the manuscript: Elizabeth Allen, Adrienne Williams Boyarin, Catherine Chin, Tricia Dailey, Noah Guynn, Eleanor Johnson, Amy Ogden, and John Parker improved things immensely. I was also very fortunate in having the best press readers I could have wished for: Sarah Kay and Jocelyn Wogan-Browne provided generous and thorough readings and valuable suggestions, as did an anonymous reader for *Medium Aevum* at an earlier point. Material that is now part of the Introduction and Chapter 1 appeared there and I thank the editor for permission to re-present it in modified form. Jerry Singerman's flexibility and good suggestions, finally, and the careful attention of Erica Ginsburg and the editorial team at Penn Press, helped me bring the project to a conclusion. I alone am responsible for any remaining shortcomings.

Writing a book about teaching has made me think often of my own many teachers and students, too numerous to mention but fondly recalled; the new light in which I have understood my time with them has been one of the pleasures of reading these instructive accounts from the past. A few people who have taught and helped me more than can be adequately acknowledged here deserve final mention. Barbara Newman, Nicholas Watson, and Sally Poor have enriched my working life for many years now through their thinking, writing, and conversation, and I am grateful for my good fortune in knowing and learning from them. And my family, extended, immediate, and feline, continues to provide the most important context for what I do, including some valuable distractions. I am grateful to Bandersnatch, Butterfly, and Bamboo for understanding the importance of keyboards and thus the need to walk on them; to Alan for grasping the idea of this book well enough to propose its true title, "No Peasant Left Behind"; and to Livy and Seb for finding out so many new things and teaching me some of them. It is to the last two that this book is dedicated, in hopes that they will always love to learn.